GUIDE TO BETTER ACOL BRIDGE

For thos needing to grasp the fundamentals of sound bidding and play, *Basic Bridge: he Guide to Good Acol Bidding and Play* is the answer. *Guide to Better A l Bridge* is addressed to the vast majority who are ready and keen to rise abc the basics.

There a higher plane to which players should aspire after they have managed to dle the early part of the auction. To reach the best contract time and time ag to understand and cooperate with partner, to get the most out of your car … these are the objectives which *Guide to Better Acol Bridge* will help yo achieve. If you are able to master even 50 per cent of the material in this b k, your results will reflect your enhanced expertise.

Whil *uide to Better Acol Bridge* emphasises better bidding, each chapter contains examples of play. These incorporate the bidding principles of the chapter d also highlight many areas of winning declarer technique and defen he book can be used by teachers conducting intermediate courses or as a self-teacher. Each chapter contains plentiful exercises and partnership bidding practice. At the end of each section, a revision test enables the reader to meas re the rate of progress.

Th l System is still the most popular system by far in Great Britain and many uer places. Its essential structure has changed very little, but with the passing of time a number of methods have become outmoded and have been discarded from this new edition. Some important modern practices have been included while a number of play hands have been altered, as have some exercises. *uide to Better Acol Bridge* continues to be as described by *Bridge Magazir* This is a book which is absolutely packed with good material – and when v y packed, we mean packed for not a scrap of space is wasted.'

****

also by Fon Klinger

SIC BRIDGE: *the Guide to Better Acol Bidding and Pl y*
GUIDE TO BETTER CARD PLAY
GUIDE TO BETTER DUPLICA E BRIDGE

Ron Klinger, an international player, Australian Grand Master and World Bridge Federation International Master, is one of the world's leading bridge teachers. He is also the author of over fifty very successful bridge books, a number of which have been translated into other languages.

GUIDE TO BETTER ACOL BRIDGE

Ron Klinger

WEIDENFELD & NICOLSON
IN ASSOCIATION WITH
PETER CRAWLEY

First published in Great Britain 1988
in association with Peter Crawley by Victor Gollancz Ltd
Sixth impression 1994
Second edition 1996
published in association with Peter Crawley by Cassell
Fifth impression 2004
Third edition 2007
Second impression 2009
published in association with Peter Crawley
by Weidenfeld & Nicolson, an imprint of the Orion Publishing Group
5 Upper Saint Martin's Lane, London WC2H 9EA

3 5 7 9 10 8 6 4 2

A catalogue record for this book is available
from the British Library.

ISBN 978 0 297 85352 7

Printed and bound in Finland by WS Bookwell

www.orionbooks.co.uk

GUIDE TO BETTER ACOL BRIDGE

THE BASICS

The following material is assumed to be known before you start on the Guide.

Hand Valuation : High card points (HCP): A = 4   K = 3   Q = 2   J = 1
Distributional points after a trump fit has been found: Void = 5   Singleton = 3   Doubleton = 1
Hand Shapes: Balanced patterns: 4-3-3-3   4-4-3-2   5-3-3-2 – No void, no singleton, not two doubletons
Semi-balanced patterns: 5-4-2-2   6-3-2-2   7-2-2-2 – No void, no singleton, two or three doubletons
Unbalanced patterns: All other patterns. Unbalanced patterns all contain at least one void or one singleton.
Points needed for games: 3NT *or* 4♡ *or* 4♠: 26 points   For 5♣ *or* 5◇: 29 points
Points for slams: Small slam (any 6-contract): 33 points   Grand slam (any 7-contract): 37 points
Trumps needed for games and slams: At least an 8-card trump fit is required.
Opening the bidding: 0-12 points: Pass   12-21 points: Open with a 1-bid.   21-up: Open with a 2-bid.
Which suit to open : **1.** Start with your longest suit.
Exception : With 11-13 HCP and five good spades and six poor hearts, prefer to open 1♠.
2. With a 5-5 or 6-6 pattern, bid the higher-ranking suit first. This also applies to five clubs and five spades.
3. (a) 4-3-3-3: Open 1NT or 2NT with the right point count. If not, open the 4-card suit (or 2♣ with 23+).
(b) 4-4-3-2 pattern: Open 1NT or 2NT with the correct point count. Open 2♣ with 23+ HCP. In the 15-19 zone, open the cheaper 4-card suit.
(c) 4-4-4-1 pattern : Black singleton, open the middle suit. Red singleton, open the suit below the singleton.

1NT opening: 12-14 points, balanced shape

2NT opening: 20-22 points, balanced shape

With 15-19 balanced: Open with 1-in-a-suit and rebid no-trumps later according to the strength held.

With 23-up balanced: Open 2♣ and rebid no-trumps next (unless you can support responder).

Responding to a suit opening: Single raise = 6-9, 1NT response = 6-9 1-level suit = 6+ points. 2-level new suit reply = 10+ points. Jump-shift = 16+ points and a powerful one-suiter or a strong suit and support for opener's suit. Jump-raise = 10-12 points, 4-card support. 2NT response = 11-12, balanced. 3NT response = 13-15 points, 4-3-3-3 pattern. Responder's change of suit is forcing (unless responder is a passed hand or there has been a 1NT bid in the auction).

Responding to 1NT: With a balanced hand, pass with 0-10, bid 2NT with 11-12, 3NT with 13-18 and explore slam with 19+. With an unbalanced hand, bid a suit at the 2-level with 0-10 points, jump to the 3-level or to game with a long suit and 11+ HCP. Any suit bid over 1NT shows a 5-card suit at least.

Responding to 2NT: With a balanced hand, pass with 0-3 points, bid 3NT with 4-10 points and explore slam with 11+ points. The 2NT opening is not forcing, but any reply commits the partnership to game. A suit bid at the 3-level shows a 5-card suit and is forcing.

4NT Blackwood Convention asking for aces: 5♣ = 0 or 4 aces, 5◇ = one ace, 5♡ = two aces, 5♠ = three aces. After the reply to 4NT, a bid of 5NT indicates all the aces are held and asks for kings: 6♣ = no kings, 6◇ = one king, 6♡ = two kings, 6♠ = three kings and 6NT = four kings.

Overcalls: A suit overcall at the 1-level shows a strong 5+ suit and 8-16 HCP. A suit overcall at the 2-level (not a jump-overcall) shows a strong 5+ suit and 10-16 HCP. The 1NT overcall shows 16-18 points, balanced shape and at least one stopper in their suit. Doubling a suit at the 1-level or 2-level is for takeout if partner has not bid. A double of no-trumps is normally for penalties.

Leads: Top from a sequence of three or more cards as long as the sequence contains at least one honour. Fourth-highest from a long suit with no sequence. Top from a doubleton. Middle-up-down from three rags.

Signals: High-low is encouraging on partner's lead or as a discard. Lowest card is discouraging.

INTRODUCTION

Most players do not aspire to be world champions at bridge, but that does not mean there is a lack of ambition. We all would like to play better. We do not like to make a hash of our good hands and it pains us when we miss an easy opportunity or land in a woeful contract. We know that we are not as bad as that – we know that we are capable of doing better.

The *Guide To Better Acol Bridge* is designed to remedy any shortcomings you may feel. Assuming you know the basics, the *Guide* aims to make you into an accomplished player, one who knows what to do and how to do it. It covers areas beyond the basics, but which are still part and parcel of sound, competent bridge.

It helps if you have regular partners with whom you can practise and play the topics you cover. This way you will gain confidence in each other and be able to trust partner when any new material crops up. Each chapter contains specific exercises for partnership bidding practice. If you do these with one of your partners, do not look at each other's cards as you do the bidding. Best of all is to have a book each and cover your partner's cards as you bid each hand. It is a sound idea to write the bidding down so that you can discuss the sequence and each bid later, if need be. There are more than 350 hands for partnership bidding and the recommended auction for each set is found in the answers at the back of the book. Before comparing hands and before consulting the recommended bidding, each partner should state what they know about their partner's hand: shape, strength and any special features. If there is any significant discrepancy, the partners should determine how the misunderstanding arose and how to eliminate similar misunderstandings in future. Needless to say, such practice sessions should be conducted in a spirit of keenness to learn, with a willingness to admit fallibility and a complete absence of acrimony or hostility. The aim should be to fix any mistakes, not to fix the blame.

You do not need to wait for any partner, of course, in order to make the most of the exercises in this book. You should glance through the subject headings within each chapter, then read through the chapter carefully. After your first reading, start on the exercises. With the standard exercises, do a line of five questions before looking at the answers. Tick the questions that you answered correctly and place a cross next to the ones where the answer was wrong. In a few months time you might do the exercises again and you will be able to check your improvement. If you find that you are answering fewer than 80% correctly, this is an indication that it may pay you to read the relevant portions of the text again.

There is no reason why you cannot do the partnership bidding practice exercises on your own. Even if you do them on your own. you can still bid them again at a later date with a partner. There are so many hands that there is little risk that you will recall a significant number of them. To do the partnership bidding on your own, start on the West hands and cover the East cards. West is the dealer unless stated otherwise. Write down the West action on all the hands in the set. Then uncover the East cards and cover the West cards. Now write down the East reply to the West action you have chosen on each of the hands in the set. Then uncover the West cards, cover the East cards and write down West's rebid on each hand. Continue this process until each auction is complete. Do not look at the East and West hands at the same time until you have completed the whole set. Then decide whether you feel you have reached the best contract and finally check the recommended auction in the answers. If the recommended auction does not agree with yours, sort out any discrepancy and re-read the text if necessary. If you feel indignantly that your auction is correct and the recommended auction is inferior, check it again. If you are still adamant that your sequence is better, you are welcome to drop a line to me c/- Cassell / Peter Crawley.

Do not cheat on any of the exercises by looking at the answers first or by looking at both the West and East hands when you are doing the bidding exercises. You are only cheating yourself and fooling nobody else. Your aim should be to improve your standard, not to fake an achievement.

You should also practise on the four play hands in each chapter. If you can arrange a group of four players, you can play the hands at home by having each player sort out the appropriate hand from the lists of hands on pages 176-183. This way the hands can be arranged without anyone yet knowing the point of the hand. Bid the hand through – it is helpful to use written bidding or bidding boxes – and when the auction is over, whoever is dummy should consult the relevant hand number in the text. The dummy should read out the recommended bidding and the contract to be played is the one in the text. (If this is not the same as the one reached, you may care to replay the hand later in the contract you reached, but initially, play the recommended contract.) The opening lead is made and dummy checks that it is the recommended lead. If not, replace it and make the lead suggested. The play is conducted without further reference to the text until the hand is over. Dummy then indicates how the play should have gone if the play in the text differs from the actual play. It makes it easier if the cards are played duplicate style, keeping the cards in front of each player, so that the hand can be replayed conveniently.

Even if you cannot arrange a group of players, you can work on the four play hands by yourself. If you wish to practise the bidding, expose only one hand at a time, starting with the dealer, and write down how the bidding should go. If you wish to treat the hands as declarer play exercises, read the auction and cover the defenders' hands. Note the suggested opening lead and then decide on your plan of play before reading the 'correct play' section in the text. Almost all the hands contain significant points of declarer play.

Each part consists of eight chapters and at the end of each part, there is a revision test of 50 questions. Do all 50 questions before checking the answers at the back and if you score below 40, you should read the relevant chapters again. The good news is that it matters not a whit if you make any mistakes here. The object is to eliminate the mistakes when you are actually playing. That is when mistakes cost.

If some of the areas in this book are new to you, it will reward you to read through the book again in about 3-6 months time and then again in a year's time. That way you may pick up something that slipped under your guard originally and refresh your memory as well. The more often you cover a topic, the easier it will become to reproduce the required performance at the table, when it counts. There are some useful books which deal with particular subjects in greater depth than is possible in this book. You will hardly go wrong if you read any of these: *The Modern Losing Trick Count, 100 Winning Bridge Tips* and *Improve Your Bridge Memory*.

Above all. remember that bridge is a game and is meant to be enjoyed. It can and should be a lot of fun and that is how you should approach it. Who wants a grim, dour, humourless time? Play the game with a smile and a chuckle. I hope that you will derive as much pleasure and satisfaction from it as I have.

TO THE BRIDGE TEACHER

The *Guide To Better Acol Bridge* is ideal for classroom use. It is set out as four courses of eight lessons each. Parts 1 and 2 are suitable for Improver-Intermediate classes and Parts 3 and 4 are better for Intermediate-Advanced groups. Parts 1 and 3 cover constructive bidding with virtually no interference while Parts 2 and 4 deal with defensive and competitive bidding. The play hands in each chapter are progressively more difficult. The hands in Parts 3 and 4 are significantly tougher than those in Parts 1 and 2.

The bidding throughout follows the Acol System and the answers and the play hands are compatible with almost all local differences. Perhaps a hand here or there might have a different opening bid or a slightly different sequence because of local teaching practice. You will be aware of that and can attend to it, should the problem arise.

Each chapter contains more material than you will need in the normal 2-3 hour lesson. The subject matter can be covered in less than an hour but the exercises and the partnership bidding practice in each chapter are often more than required. You should pick and choose the exercises to be done in class and leave the rest for the students to do at home. The partnership bidding hands make ideal classroom practice. The students should be encouraged to use written bidding and allowed to bid the hand completely before you discuss it. You should discuss the bidding hand by hand rather than wait for the students to bid all the hands. That way the problems are still fresh in their minds when you provide the solutions.

Most important of all are the four play hands, which are prepared so that each player is declarer once. The hands incorporate the bidding area of the lesson and feature some significant declarer play technique. It is urged that these hands be included in each lesson for playing makes much greater impact than listening. Students learn more quickly and will enjoy your classes more with these practical examples. There are many who can grasp the essence of what you are trying to convey only by actually seeing it happen in play.

It is recommended that the students bid the hand through without help but do not let them start play until the recommended auction has been given. The students should play the given contract, not the one reached at the table if this differs. After you have stated and explained the correct auction, the opening lead should be chosen by the students without help. This should then be checked and explained before the play continues. If a different lead has been chosen, that card should be replaced and the stated lead made. The declarers should then be allowed to play the hand without assistance. Cards are kept in front of each student in duplicate style. At the end of play, explain the correct line of play and have the students replay the hand if necessary.

It is worth spending more time on this play part in class than on any other because the students will derive more benefit from it than from simply listening to a lecture, no matter how skilful and entertaining you might be. Some declarers will succeed, some will fail. Whatever happens, encourage those who fail and compliment those who make it. You can achieve more by encouragement than by denigration. Avoid outright criticism and tend to be constructive at all times. Make sure that you never embarrass a student for failing to do the right thing. If a student does not bid or play correctly, it means that you, the teacher, have failed so far in your task to implant the student with the required knowledge and technique. Criticism of a student is really a self-criticism of the teacher.

It is hoped that the *Guide* will provide a useful tool for your students and make the teaching and learning of bridge an easier, pleasant and rewarding pastime.

A word about notation: Standard abbreviations, HCP for high card points, LHO for left-hand opponent, RHO for right-hand opponent, and so on, are used. When bidding is written in a straight line, bids that occur on the same round of bidding are separated by a colon (:). The end of a round of bidding is indicated by a comma (,). Bids by the opponents are in brackets. Bids by your side appear without brackets. For example, 1 ♡ : 2 ♣ means you opened one heart, partner responded two clubs and there was no opposition bidding. 1 ♡ : (1 ♠) : 2 ♣ : (2 ♠) indicates that you opened one heart, second player bid one spade, partner responded two clubs and fourth player bid two spades. 1 ♡ : 2 ♣, 2 ◇ : 2 ♡ means that you opened one heart, partner responded two clubs, you rebid two diamonds and partner rebid two hearts, all without any interference by the opponents. The same sequence, but with an overcall of 1 ♠ by your LHO, looks like this 1 ♡ : (1 ♠) : 2 ♣ : (No), 2 ◇ : (No) : 2 ♡ : (No).

The '+' symbol is used to signify 'or more'. Thus '5+ points' means '5 points or more', 4+ spades = 4 spades or more, a 5+ suit = a 5-card or longer suit, and so on.

Ron Klinger, January, 2007

CONTENTS

PART 1

CONSOLIDATE YOUR CONSTRUCTIVE BIDDING

Constructive bidding refers to auctions where your side has opened the bidding. This part examines auctions between you and partner without significant interference by the opposition, about 25% of your bidding problems. Some of the areas should be familiar to you, but do not skip over the chapters on that account. You will find more detail on the later bidding than is found in the average basic textbook. Even if you have been there before, it will not harm you to refresh your memory and note some new angles.

Chapter 1 deals with valuing your cards as opener or as responder; what adjustments are to be made; 'opening points': how to judge when to open light in first and second seat; when to open light in third or fourth seat; when you should use length points and when to count shortages; using length points for superior valuation at no-trumps.

Chapter 2 covers responder's problems when holding a weak hand, up to a poor 10 points; responder's strategy; resolving a choice of options depending on whether partner opened with a major suit or with a minor suit; opener's rebids and responder's rebids after an initial weak response; how often responder may bid; the skip-over principle; the barrier principle.

Chapter 3 pursues responder's strategy when holding a strong responding hand of 10+ points; responder's options and priorities; how to develop a strong responding hand; opener's rebids and responder's rebids after a strong response initially.

Chapter 4 tackles the problems associated with raising partner's suit, whether you are opener or responder, how the bidding proceeds after a raise; raising partner's second suit; giving a preference; simple preference, jump-preference and false preference; when and how to give delayed support; handling the 1♠ : 2♡ auction; bidding fake suits to elicit delayed support; bidding by a passed hand.

Chapter 5 deals with suit responses to 1NT and 2NT other than Stayman; when to give support and when to deny support; how to distinguish weak support and strong support; how to indicate weak support or strong support to partner to assist in slam exploration.

Chapter 6 covers the use of Stayman in response to a 1NT or 2NT opening; the requirements for Stayman; when to use Stayman and when not to; subsequent bidding after the reply to Stayman; how to make sure that the no-trump opener remains declarer.

Chapter 7 details the subsequent bidding after opener rebids 1NT or 2NT; responder's actions with a weak hand or with a strong hand; forcing bids and sign-off bids; opener's 2NT rebid after a 1-level response, after a 2-level response or after a jump-shift.

Chapter 8 is concerned with demand opening bids and slam bidding; when is your hand worth a demand opening; the Acol 2◇, 2♡ and 2♠ openings; the 2♣ Demand; how the bidding proceeds in each case; weak responses and strong responses; recognising slam potential; the use of Blackwood; when Blackwood is not necessary; when 4NT is not Blackwood; when to use the 5NT ask for kings and when not to; the use of 5NT as a trump ask; and cue bidding to slams.

CHAPTER 1

HAND VALUATION FOR OPENER AND RESPONDER

THE HIGH CARD POINT COUNT

Standard systems start hand valuation by counting the high card content of the hand on this scale:

$$A = 4 \qquad K = 3 \qquad Q = 2 \qquad J = 1$$

POINTS TO BE ADDED BY OPENER OR RESPONDER

Add 1 point when holding all four aces.

POINTS TO BE SUBTRACTED BY OPENER OR RESPONDER

Deduct 1 point for a singleton king, singleton queen or singleton jack.
Deduct 1 point for a hand with a queen-doubleton (Q-x), jack doubleton (J-x) or Q-J doubleton.
Deduct 1 point for a hand of 13+ HCP which contains no aces.
Deduct 1 point for a 4-3-3-3 pattern.

POINTS USED WHEN OPENING THE BIDDING

To assess your hand for opening the bidding, three factors are important: strength, shape and defensive potential. With 13+ High Card Points (HCP), always open. For hands with 9-12 HCP in first or second seat, high card values are not enough for a 1-opening. Add your HCP (strength) to the number of cards in your two longest suits (shape) and the number of quick tricks (defensive values).

Quick tricks are tricks likely to be won in the first two rounds of a suit whether you are the declarer side or defending. The quick trick scale: A-K = 2, A-Q = 1½ , A = 1, K-Q = 1, K = ½ (not if the king is singleton).

If the total of HCP + 2 longest suits + quick tricks comes to 22 or more, you have a sound 1-opening. If you are an aggressive bidder, you might make 21½ your standard for a 1-opening in first or second seat. At favourable vulnerability, be prepared to open if the total is 21+. Here are two examples:

♠ A J 8 6 5	10 (HCP) plus 10 (two longest	♠ A J 8 6 5	10 (HCP) plus 9 (two longest
♡ 7 3	suits) plus 2 quick tricks = 22 and	♡ K 8 3	suits) plus 1½ quick tricks = 20½
◇ K Q 6 4 2	so you have a respectable one-	◇ Q 6 4 2	and so this is not enough for one-
♣ 9	opening.	♣ 9	opening.

If below 10 HCP with a 7+ suit, open with a pre-empt, not a 1-opening, if the opening points total is not reached.

OPENING IN THIRD SEAT

In third seat, still open with 13+ HCP. With less, open only if you are bidding a strong suit, a suit that you are happy for partner to lead. A suit such as K-Q-J-x, A-Q-J-x, A-K-J-x or better is fine.

OPENING IN FOURTH SEAT

In fourth seat there are different considerations. Since you can simply pass the hand in, it is unfortunate to open and finish with a minus score. With fewer than 13 HCP you generally expect no more than a part-score. The side that owns the spade suit is likely to go plus, either by making 2♠ or by forcing the other side to the three-level, where they are likely to fail. In fourth seat add your HCP to the number of spades in your hand. If the total is 15+, open the bidding, but with less, pass the hand in.

LENGTH POINTS

After your side has opened, hand valuation for later bidding is based on HCP plus Length Points (LP) when no trump fit has been located and HCP plus Ruffing Points (RP) when an 8-card or better trump fit exists. The difference arises because of the manner in which tricks are won.

If partner has shown a balanced hand, count an extra point for the fifth card in a suit, two extra for the sixth card and three extra for the seventh card. As partner has a balanced hand, a long suit is likely to bring in several extra tricks beyond the high card values. With the 12-14 1NT opening, a 5-3-3-2 pattern with 14 HCP is too strong to open 1NT (because of the extra length point for the 5-card suit). Similarly, 5-3-3-2 patterns with 16 HCP and 18 HCP should be treated as 17-point and 19-point hands, respectively, and a 5-3-3-2 hand of 22 HCP is too strong for the 20-22 2NT and should be opened 2♣.

In suit bidding count one point for each card beyond four in a suit until a good trump fit has been found. Once a trump fit has come to light, switch to HCP + Ruffing Points (Void = 5, Singleton = 3, Doubleton = 1). The point count assesses trick-taking potential. In no-trumps or when there is no trump fit, tricks are usually taken by high cards or long suits. When there is a trump fit, tricks are normally won with high cards and by ruffing.

Counting Length Points as responder is important after opener has shown a balanced hand. Since opener does not hold a void or a singleton, responder's long suit is more likely to be useful in producing additional tricks. Thus, opposite a 12-14 1NT, a 5-3-3-2 hand with 10 HCP is worth 2NT, showing 11-12 points, while a 5-3-3-2 with 12 HCP should be treated as 13 points and raise to 3NT. Likewise, a 6-3-2-2 with 11 HCP is worth a bid of game opposite a weak 1NT, because of the three extra points allowed for the long suit (see above).

Where the responder to a no-trump opening has enough for a borderline game (combined total 25-27 points) and holds length in the minor suits, respond in no-trumps rather than in the long minor. It is much easier to score 3NT (9 tricks) than 5♣ or 5♦ (11 tricks).

Honour cards in long suits are more valuable than honour cards in short suits. Combined honours in one suit (A-K-Q) are superior to honours split among suits (A-x-x, K-x-x, Q-x-x).

PARTNERSHIP BIDDING PRACTICE: How should the following hands be bid? West is the dealer on all hands. Assume you are using a 12-14 1NT opening and a 20-22 2NT opening.

SET 1 – WEST	SET 1 – EAST	SET 2 – WEST	SET 2 – EAST
1. ♠ 9 8 2 ♡ A 5 4 ◊ A 8 4 ♣ A 9 7 5	1. ♠ A Q 3 ♡ 7 6 ◊ K Q 9 7 5 2 ♣ 6 4	1. ♠ A K 7 3 ♡ K 9 8 ◊ A Q J 3 ♣ A 9	1. ♠ 5 4 2 ♡ 7 6 ◊ 9 8 6 2 ♣ 8 5 4 3
2. ♠ 7 5 3 ♡ A Q 3 ◊ A 10 8 6 ♣ K 7 3	2. ♠ A K 4 ♡ 8 6 ◊ 9 2 ♣ A 10 9 6 4 2	2. ♠ 8 7 6 ♡ 8 4 ◊ K J 7 6 2 ♣ 9 5 4	2. ♠ 9 5 2 ♡ A K 3 ◊ A Q 9 4 ♣ A K J
3. ♠ K 2 ♡ 4 3 ◊ A 9 8 6 4 ♣ Q J 4 3	3. ♠ A J 3 ♡ A J 10 ◊ 7 5 3 ♣ A 8 7 2	3. ♠ A K 4 ♡ A 8 7 ◊ A Q 5 ♣ K 9 8 3	3. ♠ 8 6 3 ♡ 5 4 ◊ K 9 6 4 3 2 ♣ 5 4
4. ♠ A 4 ♡ A 6 5 4 ◊ A J 8 6 ♣ 9 7 2	4. ♠ 5 ♡ 7 3 2 ◊ Q 2 ♣ A K 8 6 5 4 3	4. ♠ 5 4 ♡ 7 2 ◊ 7 5 3 ♣ K 7 6 5 3 2	4. ♠ A J ♡ A K 6 3 ◊ A 9 4 2 ♣ A 9 4
5. ♠ 7 5 2 ♡ A 8 6 ◊ 10 9 7 6 ♣ A Q 7	5. ♠ A Q ♡ K Q 3 ◊ 4 3 2 ♣ K 9 6 4 2	5. ♠ K 8 ♡ A Q 3 ◊ A K 8 ♣ A 7 6 4 2	5. ♠ A 9 2 ♡ K 7 4 ◊ Q J 5 2 ♣ Q J 10

PLAY HANDS ON HAND VALUATION FOR OPENER AND RESPONDER

Hand 1: Length points for no-trumps – Taking care not to block your long suit

Dealer North : Love all

WEST	NORTH	EAST	SOUTH
	1NT	No	2NT
No	3NT (1)	All pass	

```
            NORTH
            ♠ A 6
            ♡ 8 4 3
            ◇ 10 4 2
            ♣ A K Q 5 2
WEST                      EAST
♠ K 7 4 2                 ♠ Q 10 9 8 5
♡ J 9 5 2                 ♡ 10 7 6
◇ A K                     ◇ J 9 6 5
♣ J 10 8                  ♣ 4
            SOUTH
            ♠ J 3
            ♡ A K Q
            ◇ Q 8 7 3
            ♣ 9 7 6 3
```

Bidding: (1) Worth 14 points because of the fifth club. Without that fifth club, 3NT could be defeated.

Lead: ♠ 10. When holding K-10-9-x-x or Q-10-9-x-x, lead the 10 (but lead the jack, of course, from J-10-9-x-x). Q-10-9-x-x is an interior sequence and you lead top of the touching cards.

Correct play: After winning the ♠ A, play the ace, king and queen of clubs, *unblocking the 9-7-6 from dummy* and retaining dummy's 3 of clubs. Continue with the ♣ 5, keeping the lead in your own hand, as dummy has the ♣ 3 left, and then the ♣ 2. This allows you to make five club tricks, three hearts and one spade.

Wrong Play: Playing the ♣ 3 from dummy on any of the first three rounds of clubs. This means the fourth round of clubs will be won in dummy and declarer's fifth club will be stranded. A few bitter experiences of blocking suits will lead to the recognition that to make five club tricks here the lead must stay in your hand. Thus, the ♣ 5 must win a trick and to achieve that, dummy must not be left with a higher club.

Hand 2: Staying with no-trumps when holding length in a minor – Avoiding a blockage

Dealer East : North-South vulnerable

WEST	NORTH	EAST	SOUTH
		2NT	No
3NT (1)	No	No	No

```
            NORTH
            ♠ K J 5 4
            ♡ 10 8 3
            ◇ Q 8
            ♣ Q J 10 5
WEST                      EAST
♠ 9 2                     ♠ A 7
♡ J 4 2                   ♡ A K Q
◇ K 7 6 4 3 2             ◇ A 9 5
♣ 7 3                     ♣ A 8 6 4 2
            SOUTH
            ♠ Q 10 8 6 3
            ♡ 9 7 6 5
            ◇ J 10
            ♣ K 9
```

Bidding: (1) With barely enough values for game, do not explore a minor suit game. Stick with no-trumps.

Lead: ♠ 6. It is normal to lead your long suit against no-trumps and fourth-highest is standard if no sequence is held.

Correct play: With only seven top tricks and the spades wide open, you need a 2-2 break in diamonds to succeed. After winning North's ♠ K with the ♠ A, cash the ◇ A and then carefully play the *9 of diamonds* (unblocking) when leading to dummy's ◇ K. After the 2-2 split, dummy's diamonds are high: again be careful to continue with the ◇ 7 or ◇ 6 from dummy (not a lower card) to ensure that the lead stays in dummy. If the diamonds happened to be 3-1, the contract was destined to fail on the spade lead.

Wrong play: It would be all right to lead the ◇ 9 to the king on the first round, back to your ◇ A and overtake the ◇ 5 on the third round. However, the contract will fail if you do not unblock the ◇ 9 on the first or second round of diamonds. The third round of diamonds would be won in hand and three diamond winners would be stranded in dummy, leaving declarer with only eight tricks.

Hand 3: Creating an entry to a blocked suit – Not playing mechanically and carelessly

Dealer South : East-West vulnerable

NORTH
- ♠ 6 3
- ♡ J 4
- ◇ Q J 10
- ♣ J 10 8 6 4 3

WEST
- ♠ K 9 8
- ♡ Q 7 6
- ◇ K 8 6 3 2
- ♣ 7 2

EAST
- ♠ Q 7 5 4 2
- ♡ A 10 9 2
- ◇ 5 4
- ♣ 9 5

SOUTH
- ♠ A J 10
- ♡ K 8 5 3
- ◇ A 9 7
- ♣ A K Q

WEST	NORTH	EAST	SOUTH
			2NT
No	3NT (1)	All pass	

Bidding: (1) As in Hand #2, with length in a minor but only 25-27 points in the combined hands, stick with no-trumps and do not look for the minor suit game.

Lead: ◇ 3. Fourth-highest from your long suit is normal.

Correct play: When dummy's diamond holds the trick, there is a natural instinct to play low from hand. When dummy appears, count your tricks and, if you have the tricks needed, check whether there is any problem in taking those tricks. Here South has one spade, two diamonds and six clubs, enough tricks, but the club suit is blocked. Dummy needs an outside entry, and the only possible entry is in diamonds.

The solution is simple, though contrary to instinct: Win the diamond lead with your *ace,* cash ♣ A-K-Q and then lead a diamond. North's diamonds ensure an entry to dummy later to cash the clubs. Winning the first diamond 'cheaply' turns out to be expensive. If you win the first diamond in dummy, you make two diamond tricks, but winning the first diamond with the ace also makes two diamond tricks! Keep a constant lookout for blocked suits and the entry needed to reach the winners after unblocking.

Hand 4: Length points for no-trumps – Overtaking in order to set up a long suit

Dealer West : Game all

NORTH
- ♠ Q J 9 7 3
- ♡ J 8
- ◇ J 8 7 6 5
- ♣ 3

WEST
- ♠ 10 8 5
- ♡ A 7 5 3
- ◇ A 9 4 3
- ♣ K Q

EAST
- ♠ A K
- ♡ 10 6 2
- ◇ 10 2
- ♣ A 10 9 8 7 6

SOUTH
- ♠ 6 4 2
- ♡ K Q 9 4
- ◇ K Q
- ♣ J 5 4 2

WEST	NORTH	EAST	SOUTH
1NT	No	3NT (1)	All pass

Bidding: (1) East is worth 14 points, counting one for the fifth club and two for the sixth. With enough for game but not a slam, prefer to stay with no-trumps rather than introduce a minor suit

Lead: ♠ Q. Top of a near-sequence is the standard lead.

Correct play: There are seven top tricks and the clubs are needed to provide the additional tricks. Most of the time the clubs will divide 3-2 and if so, it would be adequate to play ♣ K, ♣ Q, cross to the ♣ A and run the club winners. When North shows out on the second club, declarer can cope with the bad split by overtaking with dummy's ace and continuing dummy's clubs, forcing South to take the jack sooner or later.

When North shows out, it is clear that a club has to be lost anyway and the ♣ A is vital as an entry to dummy later. Declarer thus makes two spades, one heart, one diamond and five clubs. At teams or rubber bridge, it would be correct to overtake the second club even if North follows, just in case *North* has ♣ J-x-x-x. At pairs duplicate, as overtricks are vital, it is better to play low from dummy if North follows to the second club. At match-points, it is more important to make an overtrick most of the time than to play safe for your contract.

CHAPTER 2

WEAK RESPONDING HANDS AFTER A SUIT OPENING

VALUING YOUR HAND AS RESPONDER

No trump fit yet found: Count just your HCP (but add 1-2 points for a good, long suit)

An 8-card or better trump fit has been found: Count HCP and add the 5-3-1 Count

Ruffing Points (5-for-a-void, 3-for-a-singleton, 1-for-each-doubleton) are used by both responder and opener after a trump fit has come to light. The shortage itself has no value. It is the ability to ruff and score tricks with low trumps that is valuable. All point count methods measure trick-taking potential and counting for shortages should not be used when opening, as you may not finish in a trump contract.

WHAT IS A WEAK RESPONDING HAND?

Hands in the 0-9 point range are considered weak. Hands with 10+ HCP are strong responding hands (see Chapter 3). Responding hands with nine HCP and a good 5-card suit should be upgraded to ten points. Likewise, a hand with eight HCP and a strong 6-card suit should be upgraded to ten points. This is very important when considering whether to make a 2-over-1 response. For a 1-level response, six points will do, but since a 2-over-1 response requires 10+ points, upgrading your hand for a good, long suit can overcome the necessity to respond 1NT with an unsuitable hand.

RESPONDER'S STRATEGY

0-5 Points: Usually pass. It is riskier to bid than to pass with a rotten hand, even with a misfit.

Pass is best, because the chance for game is so remote. If you do respond, partner will assume you hold some values and may make a jump-rebid on the next round. Even if you do not hold support for partner's suit, it is better to pass with nothing than to reply and find the partnership much higher on the next round. Rather pass 1 ◊ than reply and hear 3 ◊ next time. If opener is weak, fourth player will usually bid after you pass, while if opener is strong, the likely jump-rebid after you respond can put you overboard.

6-9 Points: BID. Bid something, anything. Do not pass. Now it is more dangerous to pass than to bid.

You should respond with 6+ points ('to keep the bidding alive') just in case opener has a huge hand and a game might be made. It is better to bid and risk failing in a part-score than to pass and risk missing a game. Responder is worth action even with 5 HCP and a 5+ suit or 4 HCP and a 6+ suit.

CHOICE OF RESPONSES WITH 6-9 POINTS

• **Raise opener's suit** = 6-9 points plus support for opener's suit. Support is the number of trumps needed to make at least eight trumps between you and partner. Three trumps are support for a 5-card suit, while four trumps qualify as support for a possible 4-card suit. A jump-raise, whether as opener or responder, requires four trumps. In general it is not attractive to give a 3-card raise for a 4-card suit, but a single raise is acceptable with a minimum hand (as opener or as responder) if you have a singleton elsewhere.

• **Bid your own suit at the 1-level** = 6+ points and at least a 4-card suit. The change of suit is forcing and the strength for a new suit bid at the 1-level includes hands with 10+ points. This extra strength will be revealed later (see Chapter 3).

• **Bid 1NT as a last resort** = 6-9 points and denies support for opener and denies a 4-card suit that could have been bid at the 1-level. 1 ♣ : 1NT, for example, denies four spades, four hearts and four diamonds. It is easy to deduce that the 1NT response to 1 ♣ must therefore include at least four clubs.

• **Do not bid a new suit at the 2-level if you have only 6-9 points** — *the 2-over-1 response promises 10+ points.* This restriction is very important. A consequence is that the 1NT response need not be a balanced hand. With 6-9 points, you must not pass, but if your suit is lower-ranking than opener's, do not bid it at the 2-level with such a weak hand. Bid 1NT as the least of evils.

WHERE RESPONDER HAS A CHOICE OF ACTIONS

Where responder's hand fits more than one possible action, the order of priorities will depend on whether partner opened with a major suit or with a minor suit.

If the opening bid was in a major suit:
1. **Raise opener's major.***
2. **Over a 1♡ opening, bid 1♠ with 4+ spades if unable to support hearts.**
3. **Bid 1NT as a last resort.**

If the opening bid was in a minor suit:
1. **Bid a major suit at the 1-level.**
2. **Raise opener's minor suit.****
3. **Bid 1NT as a last resort.**

Basically, with a weak hand, major suit action comes first and 1NT is the last choice.

*The normal raise would be to the 2-level, but a pre-emptive raise (the 'weak-freak') to the 4-level is also available. The 1♡ : 4♡ and 1♠ : 4♠ raises show less than 10 HCP, excellent trump support (at least nine trumps together) and an unbalanced hand. The function of these shut-out raises is to keep fourth hand out of the bidding, to bid game and win the contract without promising a strong hand. If you have support for opener and a stronger hand, bid 1♡ : 3♡ or 1♠ : 3♠ (10-12 points each) or change suit first, support later.

**Shut-out raises in the minors (1♣ : 4♣ or 1♣ : 5♣ or 1♢ : 4♢ or 1♢ : 5♢) are also available, but these are very rarely used, since they bypass a possible 3NT contract. These raises do show the same sort of hand as the shut-out raise in the major suits, namely weak in high cards (usually 6-9 HCP, perhaps even weaker), 5-card or longer trump support and an unbalanced hand (must have a void or a singleton).

Where responder's action is to change suit and responder has a choice of new suits to bid, the order is:
- **Bid your longest suit first.**
- **With any 5-5 or 6-6 pattern, bid the higher-ranking suit first (bid 'down-the-line').**
- **With two or three 4-card suits, bid the cheapest suit first (bid 'up-the-line').**

It is important to bid your longer suit first, since the aim is to reach the partnership's best combined trump suit. If responder bids two suits, opener's choice with no clear-cut preference will be to support the suit responder bid first. For example, after a 1♣ opening, if you hold five diamonds and four spades, respond 1♢ and not 1♠. Since the 1♢ bid is forcing, opener is obliged to bid again and you will have a chance to show the spades later if you think that is desirable. If you bid the spades first and the diamonds later, you suggest the spades are longer than the diamonds, or at least that the suits might be equal in length.

Even with four diamonds and a 4-card major, it is preferable to respond 1♢ to 1♣. Partner can introduce a major over 1♢ and if partner does not do so, the inference is that partner does not have that major.

One of the few occasions when the above order of showing new suits is *not* followed is when responder has a 4-card major and a longer minor with 6-9 points and to bid the longer suit would take you to the 2-level. For example, partner opens 1♢ and you have four hearts, five clubs and, say, 7 points. Because a 2-over-1 response requires 10+ points, you are too weak to bid 2♣. Bid 1♡, even though that is not your longer suit. The 2-over-1 rule requiring 10+ points takes precedence over the rule to bid your longer suit first.

EXERCISE

A. Partner opened 1♣. What is your response with each of these hands?

1. ♠ K 7 4 3 2	2. ♠ A J 4 2	3. ♠ 3	4. ♠ 8 7	5. ♠ A 8 7 2
♡ 2	♡ J 8 6 3	♡ K J 6 5	♡ K 9 4 3	♡ 6 3
◇ A 9 6 4 2	◇ 6 4	◇ K 8 7 3 2	◇ K J 6 2	◇ 9 4
♣ 7 3 1♡	♣ 7 3 2 1♡	♣ 5 4 3 1♢	♣ 9 7 5 1♢	♣ Q 6 4 3 2 1♠

B. What would your response be on the above hands if the opening had been 1◇?

C. What would your response be on the above hands if the opening had been 1♡?

D. What would your response be on the above hands if the opening had been 1♠?

OPENER'S REBIDS AFTER A WEAK RESPONSE

Opener's hand is generally divided into three ranges: 12-15 minimum, 16-18 strong, 19+ maximum.

Strategy: If the partnership might hold 26 points, keep on bidding since game is feasible. If the combined total is 25 points *at least* and there might be more, bid for a game. If the combined total is 25 points *at most* and there might be less, do not bid for a game.

Opener's action after a raise to the 2-level (e.g., 1♡ : 2♡ ...)

Apply the 5-3-1 count (void 5, singleton 3, doubleton 1). With 12-15 points, pass (as responder has 6-9, the partnership does not have 26 points); with 16-18, bid again (raise a major suit to the 3-level or change suit; if your suit is a minor, raise to the 3-level, change suit or try 2NT); with 19+, bid game (if your suit is a major, raise it to the 4-level; if it is a minor, consider 3NT if your hand is balanced or semi-balanced).

After a 1NT response (e.g., 1♡ : 1NT ...)

If satisfied with no-trumps, pass with 12-16 points, raise to 2NT with 17-18 and 3NT with 19. If not keen on no-trumps: *with 12-15 points,* bid a new suit lower than your first suit *or* repeat your first suit with extra length; *with 16-18 points,* bid any new suit or with no second suit, jump to 3-in-your-first-suit with at least six cards in it; with 19+ points, jump to the 3-level in a new suit (jump-shift) or jump to game in your suit with a powerful 6+ suit.

After a suit response at the 1-level (e.g., 1♣ : 1♡ ...)

THE SKIP-OVER PRINCIPLE

Where opener's rebid skips over a suit, opener does not hold that suit. After 1♢ : 1♡, opener's 1NT or 2♢ rebid denies four spades. Similarly, after 1♣ : 1♢, opener's 2♣ denies four spades or four hearts, since the 1♡ and 1♠ rebids were bypassed. After 1♣ : 1♠, 2♣, however, opener may still hold four hearts or four diamonds, since the 1♢ and 1♡ rebids were not available. Similarly, if a 1NT rebid is available and opener bypasses 1NT (e.g., 1♢ : 1♠, 2♣), assume that opener does not hold a balanced hand. With a 5-3-3-2 pattern, opener should usually choose a rebid in no-trumps rather than rebid the 5-card suit.

THE BARRIER PRINCIPLE

Whichever suit is opened, the opener creates a barrier of 2-of-that-suit when making a rebid; any bid beyond that barrier (except raising partner) shows a strong hand, normally 16 points at least.

Suppose you have opened 1♣. Your barrier is 2♣ and all these rebids show a strong hand as the rebid is beyond the barrier: 1♣ : 1♡, 2♢   1♣ : 1♠, 2♢   1♣ : 1♠, 2♡   1♣ : 1♠, 3♣

These sequences do not promise a strong hand: 1♣ : 1♢, 1♡   1♣ : 1♡, 1♠   1♣ : 1♡, 2♣

Suppose you have opened 1♢. Your barrier is 2♢ and all these rebids show a strong hand, as the rebid is beyond the barrier: 1♢ : 1♠, 2♡   1♢ : 2♣, 2♡   1♢ : 2♣, 2♠   1♢ : 1NT, 2♡

These sequences do not promise extra strength: 1♢ : 1♡, 1♠   1♢ : 1♠, 2♣   1♢ : 2♣, 3♣

Suppose you have opened 1♡. Your barrier is 2♡ and all these rebids show a strong hand as the rebid is beyond the barrier: 1♡ : 2♢, 2♠   1♡ : 2♢, 3♣   1♡ : 2♣, 2NT   1♡ : 2♢, 3♡

These sequences do not promise extra strength: 1♡ : 1♠, 2♣   1♡ : 2♣, 2♢   1♡ : 2♣, 3♣

The crux of making a natural rebid is this: **Opener should make a natural rebid unless that rebid goes beyond opener's barrier and opener has only a minimum opening.** A new suit rebid at the two-level beyond the barrier is called a 'reverse'. After a 1-over-1 response, a reverse is forcing for one round.

Within the framework of the above rules, opener chooses a rebid over a new suit response as follows:

(a) Opener has 12-15 points

With a minimum opening, make a minimum rebid. You must not make a jump-rebid unless you have a strong opening. In order of preference, opener's possible rebids are:

● **Raise responder's suit.** This requires four trumps as responder's suit need not have more than four cards. *Exception:* With 3-card support, a singleton and a minimum opening, raise responder's major to two. With a 4-card major as well as support for responder's minor, bid the major first rather than support partner's minor.

● **Bid a new suit at the 1-level.** The new suit must have four cards in it, but any suit quality will do for a rebid. Prefer to bid a new suit at the 1-level to a rebid of 1NT or repeating your first suit.

● **Rebid 1NT with 15-16 points and a balanced hand.** Choose the 1NT rebid also with 15-16 points and a 5-4-2-2 pattern if most of your strength is in the short suits. Rebid 1NT with 15-16 points even with a 5-4-3-1 pattern and a singleton in responder's suit, if your 5-card and 4-card suits are weak. If your strength is in the short suits, choose a 1NT rebid with 15-16 points; if most of the strength is in the long suits, bid your second suit.

● **Bid a new suit at the 2-level lower-ranking than your first suit.** With a minimum opening, you should not rebid higher than 2-of-your-first-suit (your barrier) unless you are supporting responder's suit.

● **Rebid your first suit as a last resort.** To rebid your first suit after a 1-level response, the suit must be at least five cards long, that is, it must have more length than the opening bid promised.

(b) Opener has 16-18 points: In order of preference, opener should:

● **Jump-raise responder's suit to the 3-level.** Opener must have 4-card support for this action. If opener has support for responder, opener would decline to raise responder only if opener had an unbid major as well as support for responder's minor suit. In that case, show the major first.

● **Bid a new suit at the 1-level or 2-level.**

● **Rebid 2NT if your hand is balanced and you have 17-18 points.**

● **As a last resort, jump to the 3-level in the suit opened with at least six cards in that suit.**

None of the above rebids is forcing after a 1-over-1 response except for opener's reverse.

(c) Opener has 19+ points: In order of preference, opener should:

● **Jump to game in responder's major.** This requires 4-card support. After 1♣ : 1♦, opener would decline to support diamonds with four trumps only if opener has an unbid 4-card major as well. In that case, opener would jump-shift in the unbid major rather than support the minor yet. Majors come first.

● **Jump to 3NT, provided that your hand is balanced.**

● **Jump-shift.** The jump-shift denies a balanced hand, but it is forcing to game as it shows 19+ points.

● **As a last resort, if none of the above is available, jump to game in your first suit as long as you have a very powerful 6-card suit (at least four honours) or a very strong 7-card suit (3+ honours).**

RESPONDER'S REBID WITH A WEAK RESPONDING HAND

If opener has made a minimum rebid, confirming a hand in the 12-15 point range, responder is allowed to pass. However, responder is not obliged to pass if opener's rebid is unsuitable, but responder with a weak hand must not make a strong rebid. Even if opener changes suit, which is a wide-range rebid, responder *is* entitled to bid again with a weak hand, provided that responder's rebid is:

● **A raise of opener's second suit to the 2-level** (e.g., 1♣ : 1♥, 1♠ : 2♣). This shows 6-9 points just as an immediate raise shows 6-9 points. *Four trumps are needed to raise opener's second suit.*

● **A preference to opener's first suit** (e.g., 1♦ : 1♥, 1♠ : 2♦). This also shows just 6-9 points in the same way that an immediate raise of opener's first suit (1♦ : 2♦) shows only 6-9 points.

● **A rebid of 1NT shows 6-9 points just as an initial response of 1NT shows 6-9 points.**

● **As a last resort, rebid your own suit if it contains at least 6 cards or is a powerful 5-card suit.**

If opener's rebid is a jump, showing 16-18 points, responder is permitted to pass with just 6-7, but is expected to bid on with 8+ points since the partnership could then have 26 or more. With enough to bid, support opener's major suit as first priority; repeat your own 5-card suit as last choice.

If opener's rebid is a change of suit, opener may have up to 18 points (opener's range for a change of suit is 12-18 since 19+ points are needed for a jump-shift rebid). Accordingly, responder strives to find a rebid with 8 points or better, since the partnership could have 26 points.

If opener's rebid is a jump showing 19+ points (a jump-shift or a jump to 3NT or a jump to some other game), responder is obliged to bid again if game has not yet been reached, but is permitted to pass, of course, if opener's rebid is already a game (e.g., 1♥ : 1♠, 4♥).

EXERCISES

A. Partner opened 1 ♣. What is your response with each of these hands?

1. ♠ K 8 7 4 2	2. ♠ 8	3. ♠ J 8 7 5	4. ♠ Q 9 8 3	5. ♠ 7
♡ Q 8 7 3	♡ K 7 5 4	♡ 5 2	♡ 6	♡ J 8 7 4 3
◇ J 2	◇ Q 7 6 3	◇ K 4 3 2	◇ Q 9 7 6 3	◇ K Q 8 5 4
♣ 7 2	♣ 8 6 3 2	♣ Q 5 4	♣ K 7 2	♣ 5 3

B. What would your response be on the hands in A. if partner had opened 1 ♡?

C. You opened 1 ♣ and partner responded 1 ◇. What is your rebid with each of these hands?

1. ♠ K 7 6 4	2. ♠ A K 9 8	3. ♠ A 8	4. ♠ A Q 7 2	5. ♠ A 8 5
♡ Q 7 3 2	♡ A J 6 4	♡ K 6 3	♡ - - -	♡ 6 3
◇ J	◇ - - -	◇ A 7 6	◇ K 8 6 2	◇ K Q
♣ A K 9 7	♣ K 9 7 3 2	♣ Q J 8 5 4	♣ A Q 9 7 3	♣ A K J 9 5 2

D. What would your rebid be on the hands in C. if partner's response had been 1 ♡?

E. You opened 1 ◇ and partner responded 1 ♡. What is your next action with each of these hands?

1. ♠ K 7 4 2	2. ♠ J 7 6 4	3. ♠ J 6 4	4. ♠ A	5. ♠ A 8 7
♡ 3	♡ K Q	♡ 5	♡ A 8 6 3	♡ K 3 2
◇ K Q 9 8 7 3	◇ A K Q 3	◇ A K 4 3 2	◇ A Q 9 7 5	◇ A J 7 4
♣ A 2	♣ 6 3 2	♣ K Q 5 4	♣ 8 7 2	♣ K 5 3

F. What would your next action be on the hands in E. if partner's response had been 1NT?

PARTNERSHIP BIDDING: How should the following hands be bid? West is the dealer on all hands.

SET 3 – WEST	SET 3 – EAST	SET 4 – WEST	SET 4 – EAST
1. ♠ A Q 5 2	1. ♠ 9 6 3	1. ♠ A Q J 2	1. ♠ K 7 6
♡ A 7	♡ K 5 4	♡ A 8	♡ K 5 4
◇ Q 6 4	◇ 8 2	◇ K J 6 4	◇ 9 5 2
♣ K 9 5 4	♣ Q J 7 6 2	♣ 9 4 3	♣ Q J 7 6
2. ♠ K 2	2. ♠ A J 10 3	2. ♠ Q 7 2	2. ♠ K 5 3
♡ 8 7 5	♡ K 6 2	♡ 8 6	♡ A K 7 4 3
◇ Q 6 3 2	◇ A K 9 4	◇ K 9 5	◇ A J 4
♣ K 8 5 3	♣ A 10	♣ Q 10 9 3 2	♣ K J
3. ♠ A Q 9 4	3. ♠ J 8	3. ♠ A J 8 6 5	3. ♠ 4 2
♡ K 8 7 6 2	♡ A 9 4 3	♡ K 4 3 2	♡ Q 8 6 5
◇ J 9	◇ K 7 5 2	◇ 7	◇ A 8 4 3
♣ K 4	♣ 8 7 2	♣ K Q 3	♣ 7 6 5
4. ♠ 9 6 4 3	4. ♠ A J 10 7 2	4. ♠ K 6 3	4. ♠ A J 8
♡ K 7	♡ A Q 10 4 3	♡ Q 7	♡ A J 10 5 4 2
◇ 7 6 2	◇ A Q	◇ A 8 4 2	◇ 3
♣ K 8 4 3	♣ 6	♣ 7 6 5 2	♣ K Q J
5. ♠ J 9 8 7 2	5. ♠ Q 10 6 5 4	5. ♠ A Q J 7 6 2	5. ♠ 4 3
♡ A K 3	♡ 8 6	♡ A K 3	♡ 8 7 5
◇ A J 4	◇ 3	◇ Q 4	◇ 9 6 5 2
♣ 8 2	♣ A 7 6 4 3	♣ 3 2	♣ A Q 6 4
6. ♠ K 5 4 3	6. ♠ A J 8 7 6 2	6. ♠ 3	6. ♠ A K 7 6 2
♡ Q 6 4 2	♡ J 7	♡ K 5 4 3	♡ A Q 9 8
◇ J 9 7	◇ 6 5	◇ K 7 5 3	◇ A Q 4
♣ 6 5	♣ A K Q	♣ 8 7 6 2	♣ 3

G. You opened 1♠ and partner responded 2♠. What is your next action with each of these hands?

1. ♠ A 8 7 5 3	2. ♠ A Q 7 6 4	3. ♠ K Q 8 6 4 3	4. ♠ Q J 7 5 3 2	5. ♠ A J 7 6 4
♡ K Q	♡ A K	♡ A K 4	♡ A 2	♡ J 9
◊ A 7 4	◊ A J 9 3	◊ K J 3	◊ A 4 3	◊ 8 2
♣ 6 4 2	♣ J 3	♣ 5	♣ J 6	♣ A K 6 4

H. What would your next action be on the hands in G. if partner's response had been 1NT?

I. Partner opened 1♣, you responded 1♡ and opener rebid 1♠. What do you do next with these hands?

1. ♠ K 8 4 3	2. ♠ K 9 8	3. ♠ 8 7	4. ♠ A 7	5. ♠ 10 6 3
♡ K 7 6 2	♡ A 7 6 4	♡ A 10 6 4	♡ J 10 9 4 3 2	♡ Q 9 7 4 2
◊ Q 3	◊ Q 9 8	◊ 8 3	◊ J 8	◊ K Q 3
♣ 8 7 6	♣ 7 3 2	♣ K 10 7 5 4	♣ 6 4 2	♣ 8 6

J. What would your next action be on the hands in I. if partner's rebid had been 2♣?

K. Partner opened 1♡, you responded 1♠ and opener rebid 2♣. What is your next action with these hands?

1. ♠ Q J 6 4	2. ♠ A J 7 6 4 2	3. ♠ Q 9 8 7 2	4. ♠ J 9 7 5 4	5. ♠ Q J 8 7 6 2
♡ 10 5	♡ J	♡ 9 7	♡ 8	♡ 7 2
◊ K 9 7	◊ J 4 3	◊ Q 5 4 2	◊ K Q 4 2	◊ 9 8 4
♣ J 7 3 2	♣ 7 6 4	♣ A 6	♣ J 5 2	♣ K 7

L. What would your next action be on the hands in K. if opener's rebid had been 3♠?

PARTNERSHIP BIDDING: How should the following hands be bid? West is the dealer on all hands.

SET 5 – WEST	SET 5 – EAST	SET 6 – WEST	SET 6 – EAST
1. ♠ A J 3	1. ♠ K 6 5	1. ♠ A 7 6 4	1. ♠ K 9 5 3 2
♡ A 7	♡ Q 9 6 5 3 2	♡ A 7 2	♡ K 6
◊ K 8 4	◊ J 7 2	◊ 4	◊ J 8 5 2
♣ K 9 7 3 2	♣ 5	♣ A K Q 7 6	♣ 4 3
2. ♠ A 8	2. ♠ K Q 6 2	2. ♠ K 7 3	2. ♠ A Q 8
♡ Q 7 4 3 2	♡ 9 8	♡ A 10 3 2	♡ 9 5 4
◊ Q 9 2	◊ A J 10	◊ 9 8	◊ A Q 7 3
♣ 8 5 3	♣ A J 9 4	♣ J 10 7 6	♣ A Q 4
3. ♠ A 8	3. ♠ K J 9 7	3. ♠ K Q 4	3. ♠ A J 8 7 3 2
♡ 7 2	♡ A 9 5 3	♡ A Q 8 6 4	♡ 5
◊ Q J 9	◊ 6 5	◊ A K 9 8	◊ J 6
♣ K Q J 6 4 3	♣ 8 5 2	♣ Q	♣ 8 6 3 2
4. ♠ Q 6 5 2	4. ♠ A 7 4 3	4. ♠ 8 6	4. ♠ A Q 7 3
♡ Q 9 5 3	♡ K 4	♡ K 7 3 2	♡ A J 8 4
◊ 7 4	◊ A Q 9 3 2	◊ K 9 8 4 3	◊ - - -
♣ K 8 4	♣ 7 6	♣ 7 5	♣ K Q 6 3 2
5. ♠ 8 7	5. ♠ J 10 9 5 3 2	5. ♠ A 9 6 2	5. ♠ K Q
♡ K Q	♡ J 8 6	♡ K 6 2	♡ J 10 9 7 5 3
◊ A J 7 6 4 3	◊ - - -	◊ - - -	◊ 5 3 2
♣ K 3 2	♣ A 7 5 4	♣ A K J 8 6 4	♣ 7 3
6. ♠ K Q 8 7	6. ♠ 5 3	6. ♠ K 9 5 3	6. ♠ Q 2
♡ K 5 4 3	♡ A 2	♡ 7	♡ A Q J 10 6 4 3
◊ 7 5 3	◊ K Q 9 6 2	◊ 8 7 4 3	◊ K Q
♣ 6 4	♣ A J 7 2	♣ K 7 6 2	♣ A 8

PLAY HANDS BASED ON WEAK RESPONDING HANDS

Hand 5: Weak rebid by opener – Taking a discard before tackling trumps

Dealer North : North-South vulnerable

	NORTH		
	♠ 10 7 6 4 2		
	♡ A 10		
	◊ 10 9 5		
	♣ A 9 8		
WEST		**EAST**	
♠ A K 8 3		♠ Q	
♡ J 5		♡ K Q 9 8 6 2	
◊ 8 3 2		◊ A 7 4	
♣ 7 5 4 2		♣ Q 10 6	
	SOUTH		
	♠ J 9 5		
	♡ 7 4 3		
	◊ K Q J 6		
	♣ K J 3		

WEST	NORTH	EAST	SOUTH
	No	1♡	No
1♠	No	2♡	All pass

Bidding: East's 2♡ rebid shows a long heart suit and a minimum opening. There is no reason for West to bid any further since the partnership cannot have 25+ points.

Lead: ◊ K. An unbid suit is normal and a sequence is the most attractive of leads against a contract.

Correct play: On most trump play hands, it can be best to draw trumps as soon as possible. There are also many cases where drawing trumps must be delayed. Counting losers, East can see that there are two diamond losers, possibly three club losers, one heart loser (on normal breaks) and no spade losers. This comes to six losers and if declarer tackles trumps at trick 2, the opponents can take the ♡ A, two diamonds and three clubs to defeat the contract.

Suppose declarer takes the ◊ A and leads hearts. North wins and returns a diamond. After two diamond tricks, it is natural for South to switch to clubs. The ♣ 3 to North's ace and a club back gives the defence three club tricks. A greedy declarer might win the ◊ A, cash the ♠ Q and lead a heart, hoping the jack would be an entry. This fails when North has the ♡ A or when South has the ♡ A and rises with the ace on the first trump lead. It can be vital to delay trumps when an urgent discard is needed. Take the ◊ A, play the ♠ Q and overtake it in dummy, cash the other spade winner and discard a diamond. Then, and only then, lead a trump. Declarer loses one heart, one diamond and three clubs. The right play would be easier if East had a low spade. The fact that the ♠ Q is a winner is a red herring.

Hand 6: Strong opening hand – Delaying trumps until vital discards are taken

Dealer East : East-West vulnerable

	NORTH		
	♠ 7 4 3		
	♡ 8 5 4 2		
	◊ A K Q		
	♣ 4 3 2		
WEST		**EAST**	
♠ K Q J 10 5		♠ 8 6	
♡ A 9		♡ 7	
◊ J 10 2		◊ 9 8 7 6 5 4	
♣ 10 9 6		♣ A 8 7 5	
	SOUTH		
	♠ A 9 2		
	♡ K Q J 10 6 3		
	◊ 3		
	♣ K Q J		

WEST	NORTH	EAST	SOUTH
		No	1♡
1♠ (1)	2♡	No	4♡ (2)
No	No	No	

Bidding: (1) A 1-level overcall is clearcut with a strong 5-card suit and 8-15 HCP. To pass is timid and poor strategy.
(2) After the raise, opener's hand is worth 19 points, counting three for the singleton. That means the partnership has at least 25 points, and maybe more, so that game should be bid.

Lead: ♠ K. Top of the sequence is normal.

Correct play: It is clear what would happen if declarer won the ace of spades and immediately set about trumps. West would take the ♡ A and cash two more spades. The unavoidable club loser later would defeat the game.

The folly of such a plan will be obvious to declarer upon counting the losers: two spades, one heart and one club. All of these would be lost if trumps are led, since that gives the opponents the lead. Declarer's solution is to delay trumps and utilize dummy's diamond winners first: win the ♠ A, lead the ◊ 3 to dummy, discard both spade losers on the next two diamonds from dummy, and then start trumps. This way declarer makes an overtrick instead of going down. Playing trumps first would be correct if South's trumps were winners, so that playing trumps did not entail losing the lead.

Hand 7: Strong opening hand – Setting up an extra winner in dummy to discard a loser

Dealer South : Game all

NORTH
♠ A 5
♡ Q J 10
♢ 7 6 5 4
♣ A 10 3 2

WEST
♠ K Q J 10 6
♡ A 9 6
♢ K 2
♣ K Q 7

EAST
♠ 9 8 4 3 2
♡ K 4 3
♢ Q J 8
♣ 6 4

SOUTH
♠ 7
♡ 8 7 5 2
♢ A 10 9 3
♣ J 9 8 5

WEST	NORTH	EAST	SOUTH
			No
1♠	No	2♠	No
4♠	No	No	No

Bidding: East is worth only 2♠, because of the balanced nature of the hand. To jump to 4♠ would be fine with five trumps and a singleton or a void. After the raise, West is worth 19 points and should bid to game.

Lead: ♡Q. Top of sequence is the most attractive lead against trump contracts. You need a very powerful reason to choose something else when a 3-card or longer sequence is available.

Correct play: It is instinctive to start on the trumps, but a check on the losers will prevent your playing too hastily. You have a loser in each suit. As nothing can be done about the three missing aces, can you do anything about the heart loser?

Losers can be eliminated by ruffing (not applicable to hearts here) or by discarding. There are no extra winners in dummy yet, but you can set up an extra diamond winner by knocking out the ♢A. This must be done at once, before starting trumps, else the opponents come to their heart trick before the extra diamond winner is set up. If you lead trumps at trick 2, North can win and play a second heart. Now you cannot escape the heart loser. Win the opening lead with the ♡A (not the king) and lead the ♢K (if they duck this, play a second diamond). After they take the ♢A and play another heart, win with the ♡K (your entry to dummy) and cash the diamonds, discarding the losing heart. Then, and only then, start on the trumps.

Hand 8: Weak freak raise to game – Setting up a winner in dummy for a discard

Dealer West : Love all

NORTH
♠ Q 7 6
♡ K 8 7 6 5
♢ A Q
♣ A 6 4

WEST
♠ K J 5 4 3
♡ A
♢ 9 8 6 4
♣ Q 8 2

EAST
♠ A 10 8 2
♡ 10
♢ K 10 5 3
♣ J 10 9 3

SOUTH
♠ 9
♡ Q J 9 4 3 2
♢ J 7 2
♣ K 7 5

WEST	NORTH	EAST	SOUTH
No	1♡	No	4♡ (1)
No	No	No	

Bidding: (1) South's jump to 4♡ is known as a 'weak freak' raise because it is a hand weak in high cards and freakish in shape. It is also known as a pre-emptive or shut-out raise because one aim is to shut the fourth player out of the bidding.

Lead: ♣J. Top of a sequence is usually best.

Correct play: There are four possible losers, one in each suit. If you start trumps at once, West wins and a second club lead leaves declarer with a club loser in addition to the inevitable losers in each major. Then if the diamond finesse fails, you will go one off. It also does not help to win the ♣K and take the diamond finesse at once. When that loses, the next club lead knocks out your ace and there is no quick entry to dummy's ♢J after the ♢A has been unblocked. Again, one off.

The diamond finesse looks appealing but is an illusion. How many diamond tricks do you win if the diamond finesse works? Two. And how many if it loses? Also two. Therefore the finesse does not gain.

You can eliminate the club loser by setting up the ♢J as an extra winner in dummy. Forget the finesse in diamonds. The finesse is only a 50% chance – the right play is much better: Win the first trick with the ♣A (not with the ♣K which you need as an entry to dummy later), play the ♢A and then the ♢Q. Now the ♢J is high and the ♣K is the entry to reach it. If they refuse to take the ♢Q with the ♢K, you have no diamond loser. If they take the ♢K and return a club, you win with the ♣K, discard your club loser on the established ♢J and then, but no earlier, start trumps. Delay trumps if an early discard has to be found and a winner in dummy needs to be set up first.

CHAPTER 3

STRONG RESPONDING HANDS AFTER A SUIT OPENING

VALUING YOUR HAND AS RESPONDER

No trump fit yet found: Count just your HCP (but add 1-2 points for a good long suit).

An 8-card or better trump fit has been found: Count HCP and add the 5-3-1 count for shortages.

WHAT IS A STRONG RESPONDING HAND?

Any responding hand with 11+ HCP is automatically considered strong, even with poor features. Hands with support for opener and 11+ points, counting shortages, are too good for a single raise and are treated as strong. Unbalanced hands of 10+ HCP are also in the strong category. Treat balanced hands with 10 points and no poor feature as strong, but with any poor feature, downgrade the hand to 9 points. Treat 9 HCP plus a 5-card suit or 8 HCP plus a 6-card suit as a strong hand, too, if it contains no poor feature. Poor features include singleton king, queen or jack, Q-x, J-x or Q-J doubleton.

Strong hands should reach game (13+ points) or at least invite game (10-12 points). A strong responding hand *must* avoid clearly weak responses or weak rebids (such as a 1NT response or rebid, or raising opener to the 2-level, or rebidding your own suit at the 2-level).

RESPONDER'S STRATEGY FOR THE INITIAL RESPONSE

A strong hand chooses one of these actions for the initial response:

CHANGE OF SUIT   *or*   A JUMP-RESPONSE

A change of suit at the l-level (e.g., 1♣ : 1♠) is ambiguous: it could be 6-9 or it could be 10+. It is a wide-ranging bid and responder will clarify the strength on the next round, taking minimum action with the 6-9 range and strong action with 10+ points. A change of suit to the 2-level (e.g., 1♡ : 2♣) is always strong and a jump-response is always strong, except for a pre-emptive jump to game, such as 1♠ : 4♠. A change-of-suit by responder forces opener to bid again, but if responder's action is not a change of suit or a jump, opener is permitted to pass. Bidding 1NT is not a change of suit.

Responder's most common action with a strong hand is to change suit, await further information from opener and then either make a decision as to the best contract or make a further descriptive bid to help partner decide the contract. When responder changes suit, the standard order of priorities applies:

- **Bid your longest suit first.**

- **With 5-5 or 6-6 patterns, bid the higher-ranking suit first.**

- **4-card suits are bid up-the-line, that is, bidding the cheaper suit first.** You can decide later, on the basis of opener's rebid, whether to show the other suit or not. With four diamonds and a 4-card major, it is normal to respond 1♢, but this is not written in stone. If you know that you will have a convenient rebid and slam is not a consideration, it is acceptable to bid the major and bypass the diamonds.

A weak responder may bid suits in abnormal order or respond 1NT on an unsuitable hand if it is not strong enough for a natural 2-level response (see Chapter 2), but a strong responder has no need to make an unnatural response. When choosing a new suit response, bid it at the cheapest level. A new suit response at the 1-level does not deny a strong hand. If responder combines both strong actions, jump-bid *and* change-of-suit, this very strong response is a 'jump-shift'. It shows 16+ points, is forcing to game and suggests slam if opener is not minimum. The jump-shift to 2♡ or 2♠ should be a strong 5+ suit, but the jump-shift to 3♣ or 3♢ can be a strong 4+ suit. Where responder holds support for opener's major, a jump-shift in a 3-card minor is permissible, with the intention of supporting opener's major on the next round.

A new suit response is taken as a 4-card suit and opener needs 4-card support to raise. This is true for any 1-level response and for a 2-level response in a minor suit. A response of 2-of-a-major, such as 1♠ : 2♡, is taken as a 5+ suit and opener should raise with 3+ trumps in normal circumstances.

You should particularly note that in the sequence 1♠ : 2♡ (discussed fully in Chapter 4), responder guarantees 5+ hearts and so opener should raise hearts with 3+ support.

Aside from changing suit, responder has three specific strong jump-responses, but the hand must fit the requirements before these bids are chosen:

- 2NT response* – 11-12 points, balanced shape and stoppers in unbid suits. With precisely 10 points, change suit first and decide on your rebid after opener's next action. A later 2NT rebid may be suitable.

- 3NT response – 13-15 points, 4-3-3-3 pattern and stoppers in the unbid suits. The 3NT response should not contain a 4-card major.

- Jump-raise, e.g., 1♠ : 3♠ – 10-12 points and good support (any 4+ trumps will do).

The 2NT and 3NT responses are not all that common, but if the hand fits, prefer that response to a change of suit. The minimum holdings which qualify as stoppers are A-x, K-x, Q-x-x or J-x-x-x.

*A popular modern treatment of the 2NT response is to show 12+ HCP and support for opener's suit. This is known as the Jacoby 2NT and it is forcing to game. For further information about Jacoby 2NT, see *Guide to Better Duplicate* or *Bridge Conventions, Defences and Countermeasures*. If using the Jacoby 2NT, show the balanced 11-12 point hand by changing suit and rebidding 2NT.

RESPONDER'S GENERAL STRATEGY OF DEVELOPING A STRONG HAND

With 10-12 points: Respond with a change of suit initially and then bid again, inviting game. For example, 1♠ : 2♣, 2◇ : 3◇ ... *or* 1♠ : 2♣, 2◇ : 3♣ ... *or* 1♡ : 2♣, 2◇ : 2♡ ... *or* 1♡ : 1♠, 2♠ : 3♠ ... With 10-12 points, counting distribution, and support for opener's suit, give a jump-raise. The 2NT response showing a balanced 11-12 should not contain a 4-card major that could have been bid at the 1-level.

With 13-15 points: This is enough for game. If the hand fits a 3NT response, choose that. If not, change suit and bid game next round if you know the best spot *or* change suit again which forces opener to bid once more, e.g., 1◇ : 1♠, 2♠ : 4♠ ... *or* 1♡ : 2♣, 2♡ : 4♡ ... *or* 1♡ : 2♣, 2♡ : 2♠ (the new suit is forcing).

With 16+ points: You can jump-shift to insist on game. If opener promises better than minimum, look for a slam. If you have made a jump-shift and you have just 16-18 points, be satisfied to bid game later. Opener has heard the jump-shift and can bid on to slam with suitable values. However, with 19+ points slam is likely even opposite a minimum opening if a fit is found and responder should not be satisfied with game.

If for some reason an immediate jump-shift is not suitable, change suit and decide on your next move after opener's rebid. Make sure you do not make a bid that can be dropped below game.

An opening hand facing an opening hand should produce a game.

An opening hand facing an opener who jumps should produce a slam if a good trump fit is located.

A 19+ hand opposite an opening will usually produce a slam if a good trump fit is located.

WHERE RESPONDER HAS A CHOICE OF ACTIONS

Where responder's hand is strong and fits more than one possible action, the order of priorities will depend on whether partner opened with a major suit or with a minor suit.

After a 1♡ or a 1♠ opening:
1. Jump-raise opener's major with 4+ support and 10-12 points (e.g., 1♡ : 3♡).
2. Use the 2NT or 3NT response if the hand fits the requirements.
3. Bid a new suit.

With a short suit, you may raise a major with 3-card support, but it is desirable to have 4-card or better trump support for the jump-raise, so that a good trump fit is assured if opener wishes to explore slam possibilities.

Note that a response of 1NT, 2NT or 3NT to any 1-level opening should deny holding a 4-card major. Always prefer a major suit response to a no-trump response. Where the opening was 1♠ and responder has a hand suitable for 2NT and also has 4 hearts, respond 2♣ or 2◇. With 5 spades and 4 hearts, opener will rebid 2♡ over 2♣ or 2◇ and the heart fit will be located.

After a 1♣ or a 1◇ opening:

1. Bid a major suit (rather than 2NT or 3NT).

2. Use the 2NT or 3NT response if the hand fits the requirements.

3. Jump-raise opener's minor with 4+ support and 10-12 points.

4. Change suit by bidding the other minor suit if none of the above actions is suitable.

Basically, where responder has a strong hand, major suit action is first priority, no-trumps is next priority and minor suit action is the least attractive action (in contrast to a weak responding hand where the 1NT response is the last choice). This reflects the chance of success of game contracts: major suit games have the best chance of success, followed by 3NT, with minor suit games as the least likely to succeed, all things being equal. The assumption here is that there is a genuine choice and that responder's hand does fit each of the possible actions. Often, of course, responder will not have a choice of actions. For example, after a 1♣ or a 1◇ opening, if responder has 11-15 points with no 4-card major, less than adequate support for opener and some suit unguarded, the only choice might be to bid the other minor. 2NT or 3NT is unattractive with one or more unbid suits unprotected.

OPENER'S REBIDS AFTER A STRONG RESPONSE

After a suit response at the 1-level

A suit response at the 1-level can be weak or strong. See Chapter 2 for opener's rebids.

After a jump-raise response

A minimum opener should pass. With better than minimum (14+ points), bid game. With exceptional strength and freakish distribution, opener may explore slam possibilities.

After a response of 2NT

If minimum opener may pass or rebid the suit opened (e.g., 1♡ : 2NT, 3♡), not forcing. With extra values, bid game (not forcing) if the right contract is clear, or change suit (forcing) to explore the best contract.

After a response of 3NT

A minimum opener will pass or bid another game. With a powerful opening and good shape, explore slam.

After a jump-shift response

Opener should support responder's suit if possible. Without support, make a natural rebid, bidding a second suit if possible, or no-trumps if balanced, or rebidding the first suit as a last resort.

After a suit response at the 2-level (e.g., 1♡ : 2♣)

With a minimum opening, your order of priorities is:

● Support responder to the 3-level (e.g., 1♡ : 2♣, 3♣), but after 1♠ : 2♣ or 1♠ : 2◇, with support for the minor and also four hearts, bid 2♡ to show the other major rather than support responder's minor.

● Bid a new suit, lower-ranking than the first suit (e.g., 1♠ : 2♣, 2◇).

● Repeat the first suit with at least five cards in the suit (e.g., 1♠ : 2◇, 2♠). The suit need not be more than five cards long. After a 2-over-1 response, the rebid of opener's first suit is used to confirm a minimum opening with no cheaper suit to bid (see The Barrier Principle, Chapter 2, page 8).

With a strong opening, your order of priorities is:

● Jump-support responder's suit to the 4-level. If it is a minor suit, the sequence is forcing to game and inviting responder to explore slam possibilities.

● Rebid 2NT, forcing, with 15+ points and a balanced hand.

● Rebid 3NT with 18-19 points and a 4-3-3-3 pattern.

● Bid a new suit. With 19+ points, you can jump-shift.

● Jump-rebid the suit opened (e.g., 1♠ : 2◇, 3♠) which promises a good 6-card suit, 16+ points and denies holding a second suit (change of suit would receive priority).

Where opener's rebid is clearly a strong action (a jump-rebid or a new suit higher than the barrier), the auction is logically forcing to game, since opener's strong action shows 16+ points and responder's 2-level reply has promised 10+ points. Opener's change of suit to a lower suit (e.g., 1♠ : 2◊, 2♡) is wide-ranging, about 12-18 points, since a jump-shift needs 19+ points. Thus it may be a minimum opening or a strong opening and change-of-suit after a 2-level response is forcing.

A new suit by opener above 2-in-the-suit-opened (e.g., 1◊ : 2♣, 2♡) will promise better than a minimum opening (see The Barrier Principle, page 8). Strong rebids by opener include 1♡ : 2♣, 2♠ (above 2♡) *or* 1♠ : 2♡, 3♣ (beyond 2♠) and any jump-rebid by opener. Opener's 2NT rebid after a 2-level response should be played as forcing, since opener has 15-17 points and responder has 10+ points (or a long suit if weaker than 10 HCP). With the former, responder would change suit (forcing) or bid game, and with the latter, responder would rebid the long suit (not forcing). Either way, 2NT would not be dropped.

RESPONDER'S REBIDS WITH A STRONG HAND

Responder can rebid to show a strong hand in one of three ways:

CHANGING SUIT   *or*   A JUMP-REBID   *or*   REBIDDING 2NT

Responder's change-of-suit rebid is forcing for one round in normal circumstances and a jump-rebid shows 10-12 points, not forcing opposite a minimum opener. A bid of the fourth suit is played as strong and forcing – the details are in Chapter 17. Responder's 2NT rebid is played as 10-12 points. It is not forcing after a minimum rebid by opener, but with 14+ points, opener is expected to proceed to game. *With a strong hand, do not rebid 1NT or rebid your suit at the 2-level or raise opener to the 2-level (these are all weak rebids).*

Responder's general strategy for rebidding:

10-12 points: Raise opener's 1NT rebid to 3NT *or* raise opener's suit to three to invite game. For example, 1◊ : 1♠, 1NT : 3NT . . . *or* 1♠ : 2♣, 2◊ : 3◊ . . . *or* 1♡ : 1♠, 2♣ : 3♡ . . .*or* 1◊ : 1♡, 1♠ : 3♠ . . . Responder also shows 10-12 points by a jump-rebid of responder's suit to three, e.g. 1♣ : 1♡, 1♠ : 3♡ . . . If the initial response was already at the 2-level, thus already promising at least 10+ points, responder shows just 10-12 points by giving preference to opener's first suit at the 2-level (e.g., 1♡ : 2♣, 2◊ : 2♡ . . .) or by rebidding responder's suit (e.g., 1♡ : 2♣, 2◊ : 3♣ . . .). Repeating your own suit as responder after a 2-level response is taken as showing 9-11 HCP and a 6+ suit with no support for opener's suit(s).

13-15 points: Above all, make sure that you do not make a rebid that could be dropped. If the correct game is obvious, bid it. With 13-15 points and support for opener's original major, the standard approach is to change suit first and jump to game in opener's major with your rebid (the *delayed game raise*). If you are not sure of the right game, change suit (in particular, fourth-suit-forcing is useful here – see Chapter 17). Make sure you avoid the *encouraging but droppable* sequences, which show 10-12 points (see the paragraph above). With 13+ points as responder, do not simply raise opener's 1-level rebid in a suit to the 2- or 3-level or opener's 2-level suit rebid to the 3-level, all of which are droppable. You must not give a simple preference to opener's first suit *or* rebid your own suit at the cheapest level (both droppable except after a jump-shift rebid by opener). If opener's rebid was 1NT, you will need to jump to force opener *or* bid a new suit higher than your initial response. After opener's 1NT rebid, a new suit at the 2-level is not forcing if it is lower-ranking than responder's first suit (e.g. 1◊ : 1♠, 1NT : 2♡ is *not* forcing). See Chapter 7 for details.

16-18 points: Opposite a minimum opener, slam is not likely to succeed if responder holds only 16-18 points, unless an exceptionally good trump fit comes to light. Where the trump fit is only 4-4 or 5-3, slam is usually not a good bet with 30 HCP or less together. Often a finesse to capture a critical card will be necessary and there is about a 1-in-3 chance of a bad trump break as well. Be satisfied to find the best game. With 16-18 points and a suitable hand, jump-shift and rebid in game, allowing opener to move on to slam. However, with a particularly strong trump fit (9+ trumps together), slam has good chances of success if responder is in this point range, even opposite a minimum opening.

If opener has made a strong rebid, showing 15+ points (e.g., 1◊ : 2♠, 2NT . . .), head for a slam if a good fit is found. If opener's rebid is not clearcut, such as a change of suit (e.g., 1♡ : 2♠, 3♣), make a suitable natural rebid and allow opener to take control. You have already shown your values with the jump-shift.

19+ points: Slam is likely even opposite a minimum opener if a trump fit is found. If the best fit is not yet known after opener's reply to your jump-shift, make a rebid below game and consider slam later.

EXERCISES

A. Partner opened 1♣. What is your response with each of these hands?

1. ♠ K 8 7 4 2	2. ♠ A K Q 8	3. ♠ A 8 7 5	4. ♠ A Q 9 8	5. ♠ A Q 7 3
♡ 3	♡ A Q 5 4	♡ A 2	♡ 6 2	♡ K 9
◊ A K J 5 2	◊ 7 6	◊ K Q 3 2	◊ Q 9	◊ Q J 7 6 2
♣ 7 2	♣ 8 6 3	♣ J 5 4	♣ K Q 7 4 2	♣ 5 3

B. Partner opened 1♡. What is your response with each of these hands?

1. ♠ 8 7	2. ♠ A K 9 8	3. ♠ K 8 2	4. ♠ Q J 7 2	5. ♠ 8 5
♡ Q	♡ 6 4	♡ 6 3	♡ 4	♡ Q 8 6 3
◊ K Q 7 6 3	◊ Q 2	◊ A J 6 3	◊ A J 6 2	◊ 9 4 2
♣ A J 7 3 2	♣ K 9 7 3 2	♣ Q J 8 5	♣ A Q 9 7	♣ A K J 5

C. Partner opened 1♠. What is your response with each of these hands?

1. ♠ 4 2	2. ♠ J 7	3. ♠ K 6	4. ♠ A J 2	5. ♠ A 8 7 4
♡ A J 6 4 3	♡ K Q 4 2	♡ A Q 5 3	♡ 9 2	♡ K 5 3
◊ Q 9 8	◊ A J 8 3	◊ K 4 3	◊ A K 9 7	◊ 9 8 7
♣ A 6 2	♣ 6 3 2	♣ Q 9 5 4	♣ Q 9 7 2	♣ A 5 3

D. You opened 1♣ and partner responded 1◊. What is your next action with each of these hands?

1. ♠ K J 7 2	2. ♠ A J 4 3	3. ♠ A J	4. ♠ 8 4	5. ♠ 5 3 2
♡ Q J 4 3	♡ A 7 3 2	♡ 4 3	♡ K Q J	♡ A 6
◊ - - -	◊ 6	◊ A 8 3 2	◊ 4 3	◊ A J
♣ A K 9 6 2	♣ K 9 4 2	♣ A K 7 5 2	♣ A K 9 6 4 2	♣ A K J 7 5 3

PARTNERSHIP BIDDING: How should the following hands be bid? West is the dealer on all hands.

SET 7 – WEST	SET 7 – EAST	SET 8 – WEST	SET 8 – EAST
1. ♠ K 7 4 3	1. ♠ Q J 9 2	1. ♠ A J	1. ♠ K Q 9 7 6 3
♡ A Q	♡ K 8 4 3	♡ 7 6 2	♡ 4 3
◊ 6 4 2	◊ Q 3	◊ A Q 8 6 4	◊ J 3
♣ A K 7 3	♣ Q J 8	♣ K J 9	♣ A Q 3
2. ♠ A Q	2. ♠ K 9 8 2	2. ♠ A Q	2. ♠ 5 3 2
♡ 7 4 3	♡ A K 5 2	♡ 6	♡ K Q 8 7 5 2
◊ A Q 8	◊ 7 4 3	◊ A 10 7 4 2	◊ K Q
♣ K 9 7 5 2	♣ Q 3	♣ K Q 10 6 3	♣ J 2
3. ♠ J 8	3. ♠ K Q 6 2	3. ♠ A 6 3	3. ♠ K Q 8 4 2
♡ K 9 7 2	♡ Q J 4 3	♡ 7 2	♡ K Q J 8
◊ J 5	◊ A 4	◊ A Q 10 7 6 2	◊ 5 3
♣ A K 5 4 2	♣ J 7 3	♣ K 3	♣ Q 4
4. ♠ Q J 6 2	4. ♠ 10 7 5 4	4. ♠ 10 4 3	4. ♠ A J
♡ 2	♡ A Q 8 6 3	♡ A 9 8 6	♡ 7 2
◊ A 3	◊ K 9	◊ K 7	◊ A Q 9 6 4
♣ A Q 9 8 6 4	♣ 5 2	♣ A 9 8 3	♣ K J 5 2
5. ♠ Q J 6	5. ♠ K 7 5 4	5. ♠ A 2	5. ♠ K Q 7 4
♡ 4 3	♡ A Q 8 6	♡ 7	♡ K Q J 2
◊ A 3	◊ K J 8	◊ A K 8 7 4	◊ 9 5 3
♣ A Q 7 5 4 2	♣ 8 3	♣ A Q J 5 3	♣ 8 6
6. ♠ 8 2	6. ♠ K 7 3	6. ♠ A J 7	6. ♠ K 5
♡ J 4	♡ K Q 8 2	♡ K 4 3	♡ J 2
◊ A Q 8	◊ K 4 3	◊ A 9 8 4 3	◊ K Q 6 5 2
♣ A K Q 7 4 3	♣ 6 5 2	♣ A 6	♣ J 9 8 3

EXERCISES

E. You opened 1 ♡ and partner responded 2 ♣. What is your next action with these hands?

1. ♠ A Q 7 3	2. ♠ A Q 7 3	3. ♠ 4	4. ♠ A 7 3	5. ♠ 7
♡ K Q 10 5 3	♡ A Q 8 5 4	♡ K 8 7 4 2	♡ A Q 7 6 4	♡ A Q J 7 4 2
◇ A J 2	◇ 7 4	◇ A 5 2	◇ 8	◇ A K 8
♣ 4	♣ 3 2	♣ A J 4 3	♣ A K 4 3	♣ Q 9 3

F. You opened 1 ♠ and partner responded 2 ◇. What is your next action with these hands?

1. ♠ A K 7 6 2	2. ♠ A K 7 6 3	3. ♠ A J 6 4 3	4. ♠ K Q J 7 4	5. ♠ A Q J 8 6 4 3
♡ K Q 4 3	♡ 7 3 2	♡ 7 2	♡ A Q	♡ K J 2
◇ 6	◇ 6	◇ A K 9 5	◇ A 8 3	◇ A J
♣ 7 3 2	♣ K Q 4 3	♣ 8 3	♣ K 5 2	♣ 2

G. Partner opened 1 ♣, you responded 1 ◇ and opener rebid 1 ♡. What is your next action with these hands?

1. ♠ K Q 4 2	2. ♠ 8 7	3. ♠ 7 6	4. ♠ A J 7	5. ♠ A Q J
♡ A J	♡ 6 3	♡ 5 2	♡ 6 5 3	♡ 9 3
◇ Q 9 8 6 4 3	◇ A J 8 3 2	◇ A K Q 7 4 3	◇ A Q 8 7	◇ A K 9 7
♣ 2	♣ K Q 9 2	♣ J 5 4	♣ 5 3 2	♣ 9 6 4 3

H. Partner opened 1 ♡, you responded 2 ♣ and opener rebid 2 ♡. What is your next action with these hands?

1. ♠ K J 7 2	2. ♠ A 4 3	3. ♠ A J	4. ♠ J 8 4	5. ♠ 5 3
♡ 3	♡ A 7 3	♡ 4 3 2	♡ 5	♡ 6
◇ 8 6 2	◇ 6 2	◇ 8 3 2	◇ 4 3 2	◇ A J 10 2
♣ A K J 6 2	♣ K Q 9 4 2	♣ K Q 7 5 2	♣ A K J 9 4 2	♣ A K J 7 5 3

PARTNERSHIP BIDDING: How should the following hands be bid? West is the dealer on all hands.

SET 9 – WEST	SET 9 – EAST	SET 10 – WEST	SET 10 – EAST
1. ♠ A J 8 7 2	1. ♠ 5 3	1. ♠ A 7 6	1. ♠ Q 3
♡ K 8 3	♡ A 6 4 2	♡ K 8 5 3	♡ A 6 4 2
◇ K Q	◇ J 10 4 2	◇ A Q 8 7 2	◇ 9 3
♣ 7 4 2	♣ A K Q	♣ 3	♣ K Q J 5 4
2. ♠ A 8 7 4 3	2. ♠ K 6	2. ♠ K Q	2. ♠ 4 3
♡ K Q 9 3	♡ A 10 4 2	♡ A J 8 6 4 2	♡ K 7 5
◇ K 7	◇ Q J 10 3	◇ K 4 3	◇ A 7 5 2
♣ 8 3	♣ Q J 7	♣ 6 2	♣ A 9 8 4
3. ♠ A J 10 9 2	3. ♠ 4 3	3. ♠ A 10 8 6 5 2	3. ♠ 3
♡ A Q J 2	♡ 8 5	♡ A	♡ K Q 5 2
◇ 7 4 3	◇ A K 6 2	◇ K J 3	◇ Q 10 7 4
♣ 8	♣ Q J 9 7 6	♣ 6 3 2	♣ K Q J 10
4. ♠ A 9 7 4 2	4. ♠ 8 5 3	4. ♠ K Q 8 5 4	4. ♠ 6 3 2
♡ 8 3	♡ Q J 10	♡ A 6 3	♡ 7 2
◇ K J 6	◇ A Q 4	◇ 7	◇ A J 8 4
♣ A 9 4	♣ K Q J 2	♣ A 6 4 3	♣ K Q J 7
5. ♠ A Q 7 5 4	5. ♠ K 10 6 2	5. ♠ Q	5. ♠ K 3 2
♡ K 8 6 4	♡ A 5 2	♡ A K J 6 4 3	♡ 5 2
◇ A 6 2	◇ J 9	◇ A Q 3	◇ K 7 5 2
♣ 7	♣ K Q 6 2	♣ 10 9 6	♣ K Q 5 3
6. ♠ A 8 7 4 3	6. ♠ K 6 2	6. ♠ 7	6. ♠ A Q 6
♡ K Q	♡ A 9 8 2	♡ K Q 5 3 2	♡ 8
◇ K 7 6	◇ A Q 4 3	◇ J 4 3	◇ A 10 7 2
♣ J 5 3	♣ 9 2	♣ A Q 7 2	♣ K J 6 4 3

PLAY HANDS BASED ON STRONG RESPONDING HANDS

Hand 9: Discarding a loser – Ruffing a loser in dummy

Dealer North : East-West vulnerable

WEST	NORTH	EAST	SOUTH
	1♠	No	2◇
No	2♡	No	2♠
No	4♠	All pass	

NORTH
♠ A 10 5 4 3
♡ A K 7 6
◇ Q 6
♣ Q 4

WEST
♠ J 6
♡ J 8
◇ J 10 7 4 3
♣ A K 5 2

EAST
♠ Q 9 8
♡ Q 10 9 5 4
◇ 9
♣ J 10 9 6

SOUTH
♠ K 7 2
♡ 3 2
◇ A K 8 5 2
♣ 8 7 3

Bidding: South has too many points for a raise to 2♠ and too few spades to raise to 3♠. *Lead:* ♣J. Prefer a sequence lead to a singleton lead, especially when you have a certain or probable trump trick anyway. Singleton leads are best from weak hands when you can ruff with a worthless trump.

Correct play: West takes the ♣K (it would be a serious error to duck) – a defender wins with the cheapest possible card – cashes the ♣A and North wins trick 3. North should play ♠A, ♠K and leave the last trump out. Next comes the ◇Q and another diamond – play the winner from the short hand first.

If East discards, take the ◇A and discard a heart on the ◇K. Later play ♡A, ♡K and ruff a heart. You lose just one spade and two clubs.

Wrong play: (1) Playing a third round of trumps. Now dummy cannot ruff a heart.
(2) Trying to ruff a heart before starting trumps. West can over-ruff dummy and the contract would fail.
(3) Ruffing a heart before starting the diamonds. This would be an unlucky way to fail, but taking the discard before going for the ruff is sound technique. If you ruff the third club, play ♠A, ♠K, ♡A, ♡K, ruff a heart and then play a diamond to the queen and another diamond, East can ruff the second diamond and cash a heart before North obtains the discard. By playing on diamonds first, North's deep heart losers are not yet exposed.

Hand 10: Setting up a winner for a discard before going for a ruff

Dealer East : Game all

WEST	NORTH	EAST	SOUTH
		1♡	No
2♣ (1)	No	2♡ (2)	No
4♡	No	No	No

NORTH
♠ A 10 6 4 2
♡ Q 10 9
◇ 9 4 3
♣ A 10

WEST
♠ 8
♡ K J 7 6 4
◇ A 5 2
♣ K J 8 6

EAST
♠ Q J 3
♡ A 8 5 3 2
◇ K 8 6
♣ Q 3

SOUTH
♠ K 9 7 5
♡ - - -
◇ Q J 10 7
♣ 9 7 5 4 2

Bidding: South (1) West is too good for 1♡ : 3♡ (10-12 points) or 1♡ : 4♡, (see Chapter 2). For a raise with 13-15 points, change suit first, bid game in opener's major with your rebid.
(2) East's 2♡ rebid shows a minimum opening with 5+ hearts. East is too weak to rebid 2NT.

Lead: ◇Q. Top of the sequence is normal.

Correct play: Win the ◇K, cash the ♡A and play a heart to the king. Leave the top trump out. Continue with a low club to your queen. If North ducks this, win with the ♣Q and play a second club to dummy's jack, forcing out the ace. Win the ◇A next and discard a diamond loser on the ♣K.

If North takes the ♣A on the first round of clubs and continues diamonds, win the ◇A, play the ♣K to keep the lead in dummy (even though you have to play the ♣Q under your king), and then the ♣J, discarding a diamond and losing just one spade, one heart and one club.

Wrong play: (1) Giving up the lead in trumps too early. If you concede a trump to North on the second or third round of hearts, the ◇A would be knocked out before the clubs are set up to discard the diamond loser.
(2) Playing either spades or diamonds after cashing the ace and king of hearts instead of knocking out the ace of clubs. If the defenders take a diamond trick, the contract can be defeated.

Hand 11: Setting up your second suit by ruffing losers in dummy

Dealer South : Love all

NORTH
- ♠ 3
- ♡ 9 8 6 4
- ◊ A J 4 3
- ♣ A Q 6 4

WEST
- ♠ K 10 7 5
- ♡ K Q J
- ◊ 8 5 2
- ♣ 10 8 7

EAST
- ♠ Q 9 8
- ♡ 10
- ◊ Q 10 9 6
- ♣ K J 9 5 3

SOUTH
- ♠ A J 6 4 2
- ♡ A 7 5 3 2
- ◊ K 7
- ♣ 2

WEST	NORTH	EAST	SOUTH
			1 ♠
No	2 ♣ (1)	No	2 ♡
No	4 ♡ (2)	All pass	

Bidding: (1) 4-card suits are bid up-the-line, cheapest first.
(2) Worth 14 points now, counting 3 points for the singleton after the heart fit is known.

Lead: ♡ K. The heart lead is safe. With strength in declarer's other suit (spades), trump leads may reduce dummy's capacity to ruff declarer's spade losers.

Correct play: Win the ♡ A. Do not lead another trump – you need dummy's trumps for ruffing. Play the ♠ A, ruff a spade, play a diamond to the king, ruff a spade, cash the ♣ A, ruff a club and ruff another spade, setting up your fifth spade as a winner. Ruff a club and play the fifth spade. You lose only two heart tricks.

Wrong play: (1) Winning the ace of hearts and leading a heart back. This allows West to draw three rounds of trumps, preventing three spade ruffs in dummy and leading to two more losers later.
(2) Ducking the first heart. In other circumstances this manoeuvre can be correct, but it is inappropriate here. If West continues hearts, it costs you one spade ruff in dummy.
(3) Ruffing clubs or diamonds in your own hand, except as necessary entries. As your spades are longer than dummy's suits, you should play to set up your second suit by ruffing spade losers in dummy.

Hand 12: Ruffing losers in dummy – Setting up a ruff before drawing trumps

Dealer West : North-South vulnerable

NORTH
- ♠ K J 8 7
- ♡ Q 10 6
- ◊ J 10 9 8
- ♣ Q 9

WEST
- ♠ Q 10 6
- ♡ A K 9 7 4 2
- ◊ A 7 6
- ♣ 8

EAST
- ♠ 3
- ♡ J 5 3
- ◊ K Q 4 2
- ♣ A J 7 5 2

SOUTH
- ♠ A 9 5 4 2
- ♡ 8
- ◊ 5 3
- ♣ K 10 6 4 3

WEST	NORTH	EAST	SOUTH
1 ♡	No	2 ♣ (1)	No
2 ♡ (2)	No	4 ♡ (3)	All pass

Bidding: (1) Unsuitable for any immediate raise in hearts.
(2) Only worth a minimum rebid. 3 ♡ would confirm six hearts, but it would also promise more than minimum opening.
(3) Worth 14 points, counting 3 points for the singleton.

Lead: ◊ J. Top of sequence.

Correct Play: Win the ◊ K and lead dummy's singleton spade at once. If South wins and leads a second diamond, win the ace, ruff a spade, play a heart to your ace and ruff a spade. Then cash the ace of clubs, ruff a club and cash the king of hearts. When the trumps are not 2-2, declarer loses just one spade and one heart.

If South wins the ♣ A at trick 2 and leads a heart, win the ace, ruff a spade, cash the ♣ A, ruff a club, ruff a spade, cross to the ◊ A and play the ♡ K, producing the same result. You should ruff two spades in dummy.

Wrong play: If West were to win the opening lead and play ♡ A, ♡ K first, the contract could be defeated. When West leads a spade, North could win and cash the ♡ Q. It is good defensive strategy when possible to play your top trump and thereby remove a trump from dummy and a trump from declarer – you take out two of their trumps for one of yours and cut down declarer's ruffing potential. The ♡ Q would draw dummy's last trump and then the defence could take two more spade tricks. Even if this defence is not found, cashing the ♡ A, ♡ K first is an error. As you want to ruff two spades in dummy, playing off the ♡ A, ♡ K leaves dummy with only one trump. When dummy is short in trumps and you need ruffs in dummy, take those ruffs before drawing trumps. When dummy has plenty of trumps, you can afford to draw trumps first.

CHAPTER 4

RAISING PARTNER'S SUIT AND GIVING A PREFERENCE

AFTER RESPONDER HAS GIVEN OPENER A SINGLE RAISE

After 1♡ : 2♡ or 1♠ : 2♠ – Pass if minimum, while with 19+ points, counting short suits, bid game. Hands in the 16-18 zone should invite game and this can be via a re-raise (e.g., 1♡ : 2♡, 3♡) or via a change of suit (e.g., 1♡ : 2♡, 3♣), known as a trial bid. With a strong holding in the trial suit, responder should bid game in opener's major, but with a poor holding, sign off in 3-of-opener's-major. Trial bids are detailed in Chapter 24. Opener can also try 2NT with a balanced 15-18, offering partner a choice of games: if minimum, responder should pass or sign off in 3-major, but if maximum, bid 3NT or jump to 4-major.

After 1♣ : 2♣ or 1◇ : 2◇ – Pass with a minimum, but with 19+ points, bid game (3NT if balanced or 5-minor if unbalanced) or change suit. After a raise, change of suit is forcing, whether the raise is in a minor or a major. With 16-18 points, invite game, either by a re-raise (e.g., 1♣ : 2♣, 3♣) or by changing suit or by a 2NT rebid. A new suit shows a strong holding in that suit, indicating a stopper in the suit for no-trumps.

AFTER RESPONDER HAS GIVEN OPENER A JUMP-RAISE

After 1♡ : 3♡ or 1♠ : 3♠ – The sequence strongly invites game, but with just 12-13 points opener should pass. With more, bid game, and with great strength and excellent shape, you have slam prospects.

After 1♡ : 4♡ or 1♠ : 4♠ – Responder's immediate raise to game is a weak, pre-emptive raise and responder should not hold more than 9 HCP. Accordingly, slam prospects are remote and opener will pass except with a powerful, freakish hand. Opener's 4NT is Blackwood while a new suit would be a cue-bid.

After 1♣ : 3♣ or 1◇ : 3◇ – The jump-raise is a strong invitation to game. Pass if minimum (12-13 points), but with better, it is not compulsory to continue in the minor. Prefer to try for the easier 3NT. With a balanced hand, bid 3NT or bid a new suit at the 3-level to show a stopper in that suit and aiming for 3NT. For stopper-showing, see Chapter 21. With an unbalanced hand, jump to 5-minor or, with hopes for slam, use 4NT Blackwood or raise the minor to the 4-level (forcing and asking partner to start cue-bidding).

After 1♣ : 4♣ or 1♣ : 5♣ or 1◇ : 4◇ or 1◇ : 5◇ – Normally pass, but with significant extra values, opener may bid on after the jump to the 4-level. After the weak-freak raise, a good slam will be very rare.

OPENER RAISES RESPONDER AFTER A 1♡ OR 1♠ RESPONSE

- Raise to the 2-level (e.g., 1♣ : 1♡, 2♡) = Minimum opening, 12-15 points
- Jump-raise to the 3-level (e.g., 1♣ : 1♡, 3♡) = Strong opening, 16-18 points
- Jump-raise to game (e.g., 1♣ : 1♡, 4♡) = Maximum opening, 19+ points

Do not mix up opener's game raise (e.g., 1◇ : 1♠, 4♠) with responder's game raise (e.g., 1♠ : 4♠). *Responder's jump to game is weak and aims to keep fourth hand out of the auction. Opener's jump-to-game rebid is never weak and is not a shut-out bid. There are no shut-out bids on the second round of bidding.* If the bidding has been 1◇ : (No): 1♠ : (No), whom would you want to shut-out? Two opponents who could not bid on the first round? Opener's rebids show the value of the hand and opener's jump to game in opener's suit or in responder's suit is stronger than a jump-rebid in these suits below game.

Opener should jump-raise responder's suit only with four trumps since responder has promised no more than a 4-card suit. However, a single raise of responder's *first* bid suit (e.g., 1◇ : 1♠, 2♠) is permitted with just three trumps, provided that opener holds a shortage and has no better descriptive bid available.

After opener's raise to the 2-level: Responder passes with 6-9 points, invites game with 10-12 points, bids game with 13+ points and should consider slam with 18+ points.

After opener's jump-raise to the 3-level: Responder passes with just 6-7 points, bids game with 8+ points and should consider slam with 15+ points.

After opener's jump-raise to game: Responder passes unless slam is possible opposite opener's 19+ points.

OPENER RAISES RESPONDER AFTER A 2♣ OR A 2◇ RESPONSE

● Raise to the 3-level (e.g., 1♡ : 2♣, 3♣)   = Minimum opening, 12-15 points

● Jump-raise to the 4-level (e.g., 1♡ : 2♣, 4♣) = Strong opening, 16+ points, forcing to game

After opener's raise to the 3-level: Pass with a minimum, but look for game with 12+ points. A new suit at the 3-level (e.g., 1♡ : 2♣, 3♣ : 3◇) would show a stopper in the quest to reach 3NT.

After opener's jump-raise to the 4-level: This is forcing to game. It is up to responder to explore for slam. Unless the bidding indicates there is no chance for slam, do not jump-raise a minor to game. 1♡ : 2♣, 5♣ eliminates responder's slam investigation and the 4NT ask for aces, so be satisfied with the jump-raise to the 4-level as a game-force. Raising a minor to the 4-level is usually strong, game-forcing and suggesting slam.

If responder used a 2♣ or 2◇ response with support for opener's major and opener has raised the minor, responder now supports the major (e.g., 1♡ : 2♣, 3♣ : 3♡ or 1♡ : 2♣, 3♣ : 4♡ or 1♡ : 2♣, 4♣ : 4♡).

RAISING PARTNER'S SECOND SUIT

Since a new suit bid by opener or responder might be only four cards long, it is *vital to* have 4-card support to raise a second suit. It is standard to treat responder's raise of opener's second suit at the 1-level to mean the same as responder's raise of opener's first suit. For example, 1◇ : 1♡, 1♠ : 2♠ has the same strength as 1♠ : 2♠. Likewise, treat 1◇ : 1♡, 1♠ : 3♠ to have the same values as 1♠ : 3♠.

GIVING PARTNER A PREFERENCE

When partner bids two suits, you are asked to give preference to the suit for which you have better support.
1. Prefer the suit in which you hold more cards.
2. With the same number of cards in each suit, prefer partner's first bid suit, irrespective of the quality of the cards involved (e.g., with 6-4-2 in the first suit and A-K-5 in the second, give preference to the first suit).

With the same number of cards in each of partner's suits, it is immaterial to you which suit is trumps. If partner also has equal length, it will not matter, but if the suits have unequal length, the first bid suit will be longer. As it pays to end up in the partnership suit which has greater length, show preference for the first suit.

Where partner's last bid does not force you to bid again and you have no significant extra values, you may indicate your preference for the last bid suit by passing.

Simple preference means that you give support to partner's first bid suit at the cheapest possible level (e.g., 1♡ : 1♠, 2◇ : 2♡ or 1◇ : 1♡, 1♠ : 2◇ or 1♠ : 1NT, 2♡ : 2♠). Simple preference shows that you prefer partner's first suit *but you have no extra values* (i.e., no more than already promised). In the examples given above, responder would have 6-9 points.

Jump-preference means that you still revert to the first suit bid by partner, but skip one level in doing so (e.g., 1♡ : 1♠, 2◇ : 3♡ or 1♠ : 2♣, 2♡ : 3♠). Jump-preference shows that you prefer partner's first suit and you have more strength than previously promised. After an initial 1-level response, jump-preference to the 3-level implies 10-12 points. After a 2-level response, 10+ points, simple preference indicates 10-11 points with 2-3 card support and jump-preference promises 3-card support and 11-12 points.

False preference means that you give support for partner's first bid suit even though you have more cards in partner's second suit. False preference is used in situations such as these:

1. Partner bids a major first and a minor next. With three cards in the major and four cards in the minor, give preference to the major if game is the limit of your aims. If a slam is feasible, prefer to give the 4-card support to the minor.

2. Partner's rebid is forcing and you do not have genuine support for either suit and no stopper in the missing suit for no-trumps. The following hands are examples:

♠ A K 4 3	Partner opens 1♡, you respond 1♠ and partner rebids with a 3◇ jump-shift. What next?
♡ 9 3	The jump shift is forcing to game, but you cannot rebid your spades with only four and you
◇ 8 4 3	have no club stopper for 3NT. Best is to give false preference to 3♡. There is no perfect
♣ 5 4 3 2	solution and 3♡ false preference is the least of evils.

♠ K 7 ♡ K 8 3 ◊ 7 4 2 ♣ A 9 7 4 2	Partner opens 1 ♠, you respond 2 ♣ and partner rebids 2 ♡. What next? Change of suit after a 2-over-1 response is forcing, but you should not rebid your clubs (3 ♣ would imply six clubs or a superb 5-card suit) and you have no diamond stopper for no-trumps. It is better to give false preference to 2 ♠ than to raise the hearts with just three trumps.

3. Partner's rebid is not forcing, but you are at the upper end of your minimum range and do not wish to pass in case game is still available.

♠ K 7 ♡ K 4 3 ◊ 8 7 6 2 ♣ K 9 4 3	Partner opens 1 ♠ and rebids 2 ♡ over your 1NT response. What next? With a minimum (take one of the kings away) you should pass, but with a maximum, you should bid again, in case opener has 16-18 points, just short of a jump-shift. False preference to 2 ♠ is better than either passing or bidding 3 ♡. If partner is minimum, you will play in a 5-2 fit rather than a 4-3, perhaps, but with extra strength, partner has another chance to bid. Your failure to raise spades at once will make partner wary of the degree of your support.
♠ Q 7 6 4 2 ♡ 8 4 3 ◊ A 9 ♣ K 7 2	Partner opens 1 ◊, you respond 1 ♠ and partner rebids 2 ♣. This is not forcing, but as opener's range is 12-18, it is not appealing to pass, since there could be enough for game. You need four clubs to raise to 3 ♣, but 2 ◊, false preference, is superior to rebidding 2 ♠ with such a flimsy suit.

DELAYED SUPPORT

'Delayed support' is intrinsic to all systems. It is vital to grasp the concept and be able to apply its principles.

As opener is expected to raise responder's suit only with four trumps and responder is expected not to rebid a 5-card suit except as a last resort, the partnership has to be careful not to miss 5-3 trump fits where responder holds the 5-card suit. Since responder bids 4-card suits up-the-line, if responder bids higher suit, then lower new suit (e.g., 1 ◊ : 1 ♠, 2 ◊ : 2 ♡) responder will hold at least five cards in the first suit (failure to bid up-the-line). With 4-4, you would have bid up-the-line, bidding hearts first; your actual sequence of bids was 'down-the-line', and therefore your suits cannot be 4-4; they must be at least 5-4. In such a case, it is easy for opener to give 3-card support for the first bid suit, as it is known to contain at least five cards.

In many auctions, opener cannot tell whether responder's first suit has five cards, for example, if responder rebids in no-trumps, (e.g., 1 ◊ : 1 ♡, 1 ♠ : 2NT), raises opener's second suit (1 ◊ : 1 ♠, 2 ♣ : 3 ♣) or gives preference to opener's first suit (1 ◊ : 1 ♠, 2 ♣ : 2 ◊). To cater for the *possibility* that responder might have a 5-card suit, opener should give 'delayed support', i.e., support responder's first suit on a later round of bidding. Immediate support = four trumps normally. Delayed support = three trumps normally.

♠ K 7 ♡ Q 8 4 ◊ A K 8 7 6 4 ♣ J 3	You open 1 ◊, partner responds 1 ♡, you rebid 2 ◊ and partner rebids 2 ♠. What now? As 2 ♠ is forcing, you must find some bid. Delayed support with 3 ♡ is best. You do not know that partner has five hearts, but partner knows that you do not hold four (else you would raise 1 ♡ to 2 ♡). Your 3 ♡ shows three hearts and partner can choose what to do next.
♠ K 8 2 ♡ Q 7 4 2 ◊ A 3 ♣ A K 6 2	After 1 ♣ : 1 ♠, 1NT partner raises to 2NT. What next? With better than a minimum 1NT rebid, you should accept the game invitation, but bid 3 ♠, delayed support, not 3NT. Partner knows you do not have four spades (you would have raised spades) and over 3 ♠ by you, partner can choose 4 ♠ if holding five spades or 3NT with only four spades.
♠ A Q 8 6 ♡ Q 3 2 ◊ A K 9 8 2 ♣ 4	After 1 ◊ : 1 ♡, 1 ♠, partner invites game with a jump to 2NT (10-12 points). What next? Partner might or might not have five hearts. You are strong enough for game, but give delayed support with 3 ♡. That leaves it up to partner whether to bid 4 ♡ or 3NT. Your failure to raise hearts at once means partner knows you have only three hearts.
♠ K 8 2 ♡ A K 6 5 3 ◊ A Q J 4 ♣ 5	After 1 ♡ : 1 ♠, 2 ◊, partner gives preference to 2 ♡. What now? Partner has about 6-9 points, but you are worth one more try for game. Give delayed support to 2 ♠. Not only does this show three spades, but it also implies a strong opening hand, about 15-18 HCP. If weaker, pass 2 ♡ and with a 3-5-4-1 pattern in the 12-14 point range, you should have raised 1 ♠ to 2 ♠ at once, having 3-card support and a singleton outside (see page 8).

THE 1♠ : 2♡ AUCTION

The 2♡ response to 1♠ promises five hearts. This enables you to find 3-card support quickly and also eliminates problems at the 3-level (such as whether to try for 3NT or whether to repeat the heart suit). Since *five* hearts are promised, opener should raise the hearts with 3+ support on all normal hands. In standard style, 1♠ : 2♡, 3♡ shows support and a minimum hand, while 1♠ : 2♡, 4♡ shows extras values, enough for game opposite responder's 10-count. It follows that 1♠ : 2♡, 2♠ denies three hearts, as does 1♠ : 2♡, 2NT or 3NT. If opener changes suit (e.g., 1♠ : 2♡, 3♣) assume opener does not hold three hearts. Responder's 3♡ rebid shows six hearts. Opener supports with a doubleton or with singleton queen, king or ace.

MORE ON DELAYED SUPPORT

Where partner has had a chance to show 3-card support for a known 5-card suit, but denied such a holding, then later delayed support will show a doubleton.

Delayed support for a possible 4-card suit   = 3-card support

Delayed support for a known 5-card suit   = 2-card support

♠ A Q 8 6 4 3 ♡ A 2 ◊ K 7 ♣ 4 3 2	You open 1♠, partner replies 2♡, you rebid 2♠ (denying three hearts) and partner now rebids 3◊. What next? Best is 3♡, delayed support. Since you previously denied three hearts, this delayed support can be no better than a doubleton and partner will recognise that you cannot hold three hearts because of your failure to raise hearts at once.
♠ K 2 ♡ 7 2 ◊ A 8 3 ♣ A Q 8 6 4 2	After 1♣ : 1♠, 2♣, partner rebids 2♡, showing at least five spades – four hearts. You rebid 2NT, showing the diamond stopper, denying three spades and denying four hearts. Partner rebids 3♡, showing at least 5-5 in the majors. What now? Best is 3♠, delayed support, showing only a doubleton since 2NT had denied three spades.
♠ K 2 ♡ 4 3 ◊ A 10 9 4 2 ♣ A 7 3 2	After 1♠ : 2◊, 2♡, you rebid 2NT, denying three spades. Partner now bids 3◊. What next? Partner probably has a 5-4-3-1 pattern with a singleton club. This makes 3NT unappealing with only one club stopper and the marked club lead. You could stay with the diamonds but 3♠, delayed doubleton support (as 2NT denied three spades), may locate a cheaper and higher-scoring game. Partner knows you have only *two* spades and if partner does not wish to play in spades, partner can revert to diamonds or no-trumps. With a singleton spade and K-x-x in hearts, you could have produced delayed heart support with 3♡.

BIDDING FALSE SUITS TO OBTAIN PREFERENCE OR DELAYED SUPPORT

The Skip-Over Principle was mentioned in Chapter 2 (see page 8), so that where opener bypasses a suit that could have been bid conveniently, opener denies holding that suit. For example, 1♣ : 1◊, 1♠ denies four hearts and 1♣ : 1◊, 1NT denies four spades. Also, a jump-rebid in the suit opened will deny any second suit (e.g., 1◊ : 1♠, 3◊ denies four hearts). Responder can use this principle to solve many bidding problems.

It is safe for responder to bid a suit that opener has denied, *even with only 2 or 3 cards in that suit*, since opener needs four cards to raise responder's second suit and opener has denied holding four cards in that suit.

♠ A K ♡ A Q 8 3 2 ◊ J 9 2 ♣ 6 4 3	Partner opens 1◊, you respond 1♡ and partner rebids 2◊. You have enough for game, but 3◊ is not forcing, 3♡ would show *six* hearts and the lack of a club stopper makes a no-trumps bid unpalatable. What to do? A rebid of 2♠ is best *and is safe*. Partner's 2◊ denied four spades so that 2♠ will not beget 3♠ or 4♠. (If it does, you will bid 5◊.) If partner bids 3♡, delayed support, bid 4♡, while if partner bids 2NT, showing a club stopper, raise to 3NT. If partner bids 3◊, make one more effort with 4◊.
♠ A Q 8 7 3 ♡ K Q 4 ◊ 7 3 2 ♣ 6 4	After 1◊ : 1♠, partner rebids 3◊. What next? The 3◊ rebid denied four hearts and so 3♡ is now safe. Partner would have rebid 2♡, introducing a major, rather than jump to 3◊. If you can afford 3◊, you can afford 2♡. If partner bids 3♠, go to 4♠, and if partner has the clubs stopped, partner will rebid 3NT. Bidding a suit which partner has denied is more in the nature of a stopper bid than a real suit, although it might be a real suit, of course.

BIDDING BY A PASSED HAND

Once you have passed initially, the meaning of some of your bids will be affected, since it is no longer possible for you to hold 13 points, else you would have opened. Your weak responses are not affected: a raise of opener's suit to the 2-level is still 6-9 points and the 1NT response is also still 6-9 points. A change of suit at the 1-level has a range of 6-12 points as opposed to the wide-ranging 6+ points attached to the response of a new suit at the 1-level normally.

The bids with changed meanings are the jump-responses and the change of suit to the 2-level. Since a passed hand cannot hold 13 points, and rarely 12 points, a jump-response now shows 10-11 points. The specific meanings:

● Jump to 2NT by a passed hand (e.g., No: 1♡, 2NT) shows 10-11 points, balanced shape and denies support for opener's suit. A poor 12-count, too weak to open 1NT, is also possible.

● Jump-raise by a passed hand (e.g., No : 1♠, 3♠) still shows 10-12 points and support for opener's suit. The shape need not be balanced.

● Jump-shift by a passed hand (e.g. No : 1♢, 2♠) shows 10-12 points and a strong 5-card suit. If the suit is only four cards long or if the suit is not strong, bid the suit at the cheapest level without a jump. A popular treatment is to play 'fit-showing jumps': a jump-shift by a passed hand not only shows a good 5-card suit, but also promises a fit (4-card support) for opener's suit.

The most important rule for a passed hand is this: **A BID BY A PASSED HAND IS NOT FORCING.**

This applies whether it is a jump-bid or a change of suit, so that change-of-suit forcing or jump-shifts forcing to game by a passed-hand responder do not apply. As any bid by a passed hand is not forcing, it is vital to give partner the most important message in one bid – there might be no second chance. Therefore, raise a major suit as first priority. Do not bid a new suit if you have a major suit raise available.

The change of suit to the 2-level still requires 10 points, but the range is 10-12 points rather than the normal 10+ points. A very significant difference is that a 5-card or longer suit is promised (since it may be passed by opener). With only 4-card suits, bid a suit at the 1-level (a new suit at the 1-level does not promise more than four cards) or respond 1NT or 2NT.

EXERCISES

A. Partner opened 1♢, you responded 1♡ and partner rebid 1♠. What is your next action with these hands?

1. ♠ K 8 2	2. ♠ A 9 8 3	3. ♠ A 7 3	4. ♠ Q 7	5. ♠ 8 7 4 2
♡ Q 9 8 2	♡ K 7 6 4	♡ K 9 8 6	♡ K J 8 4	♡ A K 7 6
♢ 7 6 4	♢ 7	♢ A 6 4 3	♢ Q 7 5 2	♢ K 9 6
♣ K 7 6	♣ A 7 4 3	♣ 4 3	♣ 8 4 3	♣ 6 3

B. The bidding has started 1♢ : 1♡, 2♣ : ? What is your next action as responder with each of these hands?

1. ♠ K 7	2. ♠ 8 6	3. ♠ A J 8 3	4. ♠ 8 7 3	5. ♠ 6 4
♡ Q 7 5 3	♡ A 9 3 2	♡ K J 9 2	♡ A Q J 6	♡ A K 7 6 2
♢ 9 6 4	♢ 9 7 6 2	♢ A J 7	♢ J 8	♢ Q J 10 4
♣ Q 8 7 2	♣ K 7 3	♣ 5 2	♣ K 9 7 4	♣ 8 7

C. The bidding has started 1♡ : 1♠, 2♢ : ? What is your next action as responder with each of these hands?

1. ♠ K J 7 4 3	2. ♠ A Q J 5	3. ♠ K 8 7 5	4. ♠ J 7 4 3 2	5. ♠ K Q 3 2
♡ 7 4 2	♡ K 7 4	♡ 2	♡ Q 8	♡ K J
♢ 8 6 2	♢ 3 2	♢ K 8 4 3	♢ K 6	♢ J 4 2
♣ A 3	♣ J 8 3 2	♣ 9 8 5 3	♣ 8 6 5 2	♣ 9 7 3 2

D. The bidding has been 1♣ : 1♠, 2♣ : 2♡. What is your next action as opener with each of these hands?

1. ♠ Q 7 2	2. ♠ Q 7	3. ♠ K	4. ♠ J 2	5. ♠ 7 3 2
♡ 8 3	♡ 8 3 2	♡ 7 4 2	♡ K 3	♡ 8
♢ A 7	♢ A 7	♢ A J 9	♢ 7 4 2	♢ A Q 8
♣ A K 8 6 3 2	♣ A K 8 6 3 2	♣ A Q 8 5 4 2	♣ A K J 9 7 4	♣ A Q 8 7 4 3

E. You opened 1 ♠ and partner responded 2 ♡. What is your next action with each of these hands?

1. ♠ A K 9 8 2	2. ♠ A Q 8 3 2	3. ♠ A K 8 7 5 3	4. ♠ A Q 7 4 3	5. ♠ Q J 8 7 2
♡ Q 9 8	♡ K 7 6	♡ K J 6	♡ 4	♡ A 7
◇ Q J 4	◇ A 4 3 2	◇ A 6	◇ K Q 7 5 2	◇ A K Q 7
♣ 7 6	♣ 2	♣ 4 3	♣ J 3	♣ 3 2

F. The bidding has been 1 ♠ : 2 ♡, 3 ◇ : ? What is your next action as responder with each of these hands?

1. ♠ K J	2. ♠ Q 7	3. ♠ K J	4. ♠ 7	5. ♠ 4 2
♡ A Q 9 7 4 3	♡ K 9 5 4 2	♡ A J 9 5 2	♡ A Q 8 5 4	♡ K Q J 8 6 5 3
◇ 8 6	◇ J 2	◇ Q 8	◇ K Q 7 2	◇ 9 8
♣ 6 3 2	♣ A Q 3 2	♣ 6 4 3 2	♣ Q J 2	♣ A 3

G. You passed as dealer and partner opened 1 ♡. What action do you take with each of these hands?

1. ♠ K 7 2	2. ♠ Q 7 5 2	3. ♠ K Q 2	4. ♠ A 2	5. ♠ K 2
♡ A 3	♡ 3 2	♡ 7 4 2	♡ K 9 5 3	♡ A J 6 5 2
◇ Q 7 5 2	◇ A K 9	◇ J 9 6 4	◇ K 4 2	◇ 9 8 6 4 3
♣ 7 6 5 3	♣ J 6 3 2	♣ A J 7	♣ 8 7 3 2	♣ 2

H. Partner passed as dealer, you opened 1 ♡ and partner responded 2 ◇. What is your next action as opener?

1. ♠ K Q 6	2. ♠ Q 9 7 2	3. ♠ A Q 8 5	4. ♠ K Q	5. ♠ 3
♡ Q 9 7 3 2	♡ A J 8 5 2	♡ A J 8 6 2	♡ A J 6 5 2	♡ A 9 7 6 2
◇ J 9 6	◇ 9 7	◇ A J	◇ 2	◇ A Q 6 4
♣ A 8	♣ K Q	♣ 6 3	♣ A Q 7 3 2	♣ A 8 4

PARTNERSHIP BIDDING: How should the following hands be bid? West is the dealer on all hands.

SET 11 – WEST	SET 11 – EAST	SET 12 – WEST	SET 12 – EAST
1. ♠ A 9 7 3	1. ♠ K 6 5 4 2	1. ♠ A Q 7 5 4	1. ♠ 2
♡ K Q	♡ A 9 3	♡ K 3 2	♡ A 9 8 6 5
◇ Q 7 6 4	◇ K 3	◇ K 6 2	◇ A Q 5 4
♣ 8 3 2	♣ A 7 4	♣ 4 3	♣ Q 7 2
2. ♠ K 7 3	2. ♠ Q J 5 4 2	2. ♠ K Q 8 6 4 3	2. ♠ 2
♡ A 9	♡ K Q 6 2	♡ K 2	♡ A Q J 6 5
◇ 6 4	◇ A 3 2	◇ K Q	◇ A J 8 4 3
♣ A Q 7 6 4 2	♣ 3	♣ 7 6 4	♣ 3 2
3. ♠ 8 3	3. ♠ A K 7 4 2	3. ♠ A Q 8 7 6	3. ♠ K
♡ Q 6	♡ A K 9 3	♡ K 2	♡ A J 8 7 4 3
◇ A Q 8	◇ 4 3	◇ 4	◇ Q 7 3
♣ A J 9 7 6 4	♣ 5 2	♣ A K 7 3 2	♣ 8 6 4
4. ♠ A Q 9 4	4. ♠ 6 3	4. ♠ A J 8 6 4 2	4. ♠ 3
♡ 7 2	♡ K Q 8 6 5	♡ 7	♡ A K 9 4 2
◇ A K 7 6 2	◇ 9 8 5 3	◇ K 7 6	◇ A Q 5
♣ Q 8	♣ J 6	♣ K J 8	♣ Q 10 7 2
5. ♠ A Q 3	5. ♠ K 9 6 5 4	5. ♠ 7	5. ♠ K 9 6 5 4
♡ A Q 7 6 4	♡ J 2	♡ J 8 2	♡ Q 7 6 3
◇ 7	◇ 9 6 4	◇ A Q 7 6 4	◇ J 5
♣ A 8 5 3	♣ K Q 2	♣ A K 4 3	♣ Q 2
6. ♠ A 2	6. ♠ K Q 8 4	6. ♠ K 4 3	6. ♠ A 8 7 5 2
♡ K 3 2	♡ Q J 8 6 5	♡ 7	♡ 9 8 3
◇ A K 8 6 4 2	◇ Q 3	◇ A K 8 6 2	◇ Q 5 4
♣ 8 4	♣ 7 2	♣ A Q 9 8	♣ K 4

PLAY HANDS BASED ON PREFERENCES & DELAYED SUPPORT

Hand 13: Jump-preference – Discarding a loser to take a ruff in dummy

Dealer North : North-South vulnerable

NORTH
- ♠ A 9 6
- ♡ 10 4 3
- ◊ K J 8 7 5
- ♣ J 8

WEST
- ♠ K J 5 4 2
- ♡ K Q 6 2
- ◊ A 3 2
- ♣ 3

EAST
- ♠ Q 7 3
- ♡ A 9
- ◊ 6 4
- ♣ A K 7 6 4 2

SOUTH
- ♠ 10 8
- ♡ J 8 7 5
- ◊ Q 10 9
- ♣ Q 10 9 5

WEST	NORTH	EAST	SOUTH
	No	1♣	No
1♠	No	2♣	No
2♡(1)	No	3♠(2)	No
4♠(3)	No	No	No

Bidding: (1) New suit is forcing here. 1♠ followed by 2♡, bidding down-the-line, promises 5+ spades and 4+ hearts.
(2) Delayed support = three trumps. The jump to 3♠ shows a 'good' minimum opening with 3-card support.
(3) Note how badly 3NT would fare on a diamond lead.

Lead: ◊ 7. The unbid suit is the normal lead.

Correct play: Best is to win the ◊ A, play a heart to the ace and back to the ♡ K, followed by the ♡ Q on which you discard a diamond from dummy. Continue with a diamond ruff, cash the ♣ A, ruff a club, ruff a diamond and play the ♣ K to discard the heart loser. When this is ruffed by North you finish with eleven tricks.

As the cards lie, it would work to lead trumps at trick 2, but this could fail, for if trumps were 4-1, declarer might lose two spades and two tricks in the red suits. When you can discard a loser and you hold six cards or fewer in the suit which provides the discard (the hearts in the above hand), it is unlikely that the opposition will be able to ruff that suit on the first three rounds.

Hand 14: Delayed support – Ruffing losers in dummy

Dealer East : East-West vulnerable

NORTH
- ♠ K Q 5 2
- ♡ Q 10 8 4 2
- ◊ 5
- ♣ A J 3

WEST
- ♠ J 9 8 6
- ♡ A J 9
- ◊ J 8
- ♣ Q 9 5 2

EAST
- ♠ 10 7
- ♡ 5 3
- ◊ K 10 9 7
- ♣ K 10 8 7 6

SOUTH
- ♠ A 4 3
- ♡ K 7 6
- ◊ A Q 6 4 3 2
- ♣ 4

WEST	NORTH	EAST	SOUTH
		No	1◊
No	1♡	No	2◊(1)
No	2♠(2)	No	3♡(3)
No	4♡	All pass	

Bidding: (1) Do not raise responder's possible 4-card suit with only three trumps unless there is no better choice.
(2) Although South has denied spades, North uses 2♠ (new suit forcing) to gain more information to locate the best game contract. North's plan is to play in 4♡ if partner can show 3-card heart support and to end in 3NT if South cannot support the hearts.
Delayed support = three trumps. North cannot be misled since South did not raise the hearts on the previous round. Note that 3NT would be easily defeated on a club lead.

Lead: ♣ 7. Leading the unbid suit is best unless you have a strong reason for a different choice.

Play: Win the ♣ A, ruff a club, play a spade to the king, ruff the third club, then lead the ♡ K. With normal breaks, you lose only two hearts and perhaps a spade. If West wins the ♡ A and plays a fourth club, you ruff, cash the ♡ Q and take the diamond finesse while dummy still has the ♠ A as an entry. Whether the finesse wins or loses, you can discard a spade on the ◊ A later. As it happens, the diamond finesse works and you make eleven tricks.

Wrong play: It would be an error to lead trumps at trick 2. When dummy is able to ruff and has few trumps, it is best to start ruffing early and delay drawing trumps till the ruffs have been taken.

Hand 15: The 1♠ : 2♡ auction – Unblocking and discarding losers from hand

Dealer South : Game all

NORTH
- ♠ 10 5 3
- ♡ 8
- ◊ K Q 8 7 5
- ♣ Q 10 5 4

WEST
- ♠ A K 8 6 2
- ♡ Q 6
- ◊ 6 4
- ♣ A K J 2

EAST
- ♠ Q
- ♡ K J 9 7 5 3
- ◊ A 9 3
- ♣ 9 7 3

SOUTH
- ♠ J 9 7 4
- ♡ A 10 4 2
- ◊ J 10 2
- ♣ 8 6

WEST	NORTH	EAST	SOUTH
			No
1♠	No (1)	2♡ (2)	No
3♣ (3)	No	3♡ (4)	No
4♡ (5)	No	No	No

Bidding: (1) Too weak to overcall 2 ◊ .
(2) Shows 5+ hearts, 10+ points.
(3) Strong rebid as it bypasses the 2♠ barrier.
(4) Shows six hearts since 2♡ already showed five. The auction is forcing since West has shown 16+ points (with the 3♣ rebid) and East has shown 10+ points (with the 2♡ response).
(5) Note how badly 3NT fares on the diamond lead, marked by the bidding.

Lead: ◊ J. From J-10-x, the jack is standard (top of touching honours from a 3-card suit).

Correct play: Win the ◊ A, cash the ♠ Q (unblocking), lead a club to the ace and discard your diamond losers on the ♠ A and ♠ K. There is only one spade now missing and quite a good plan is to continue with another spade. If North ruffs, over-ruff. You have now set up dummy's last spade as a winner. Lead a trump now, but later when you win dummy's ♣ K, you can discard your club loser on the fifth spade. This is better than taking the club finesse. You lose just two trumps and make eleven tricks.

Hand 16: The 1♠ : 2♡ auction – Delayed support – Unblocking a second suit before drawing trumps

Dealer West : Love all

NORTH
- ♠ K Q 8 6 4 3
- ♡ K 2
- ◊ K Q
- ♣ 7 6 4

WEST
- ♠ 10 7 5
- ♡ 10 9 4 3
- ◊ 10 7
- ♣ A K 10 8

EAST
- ♠ A J 9
- ♡ 8 7
- ◊ 9 6 5 2
- ♣ Q J 9 5

SOUTH
- ♠ 2
- ♡ A Q J 6 5
- ◊ A J 8 4 3
- ♣ 3 2

WEST	NORTH	EAST	SOUTH
No	1♠	No	2♡ (1)
No	2♠ (2)	No	3 ◊ (3)
No	3♡ (4)	No	4♡ (5)
No	No	No	

Bidding: (1) With a 5-5 pattern, bid the higher suit first.
(2) The 2♡ response showed 5+ hearts and 10+ points. Failure to support hearts denies 3-card support.
(3) New suit by responder is forcing.
(4) Delayed support here = only two trumps since 2♠ denied 3-card support. With no club stopper, 3NT is out and 3♡ is superior to repeating the spades again.
(5) South knows 4♡ is a 5-2 fit, but cannot bid 3NT with no cover in clubs. Note how poor the 3NT and 4♠ contracts are.

Lead: ♣A. Ace from A-K suits is standard, although some pairs lead the king. It matters little as long as you are consistent and partner knows which you do.

Correct Play: East should encourage the club lead and South ruffs the third round. Lead a heart to king, cash the king and queen of diamonds, and then continue with a heart to the ace, followed by the queen and jack of hearts, drawing trumps. Finally, cash the ace of diamonds, the jack of diamonds and the fifth diamond. You thus make five hearts and five diamond tricks.

Wrong Play: (1) Drawing trumps before unblocking the ◊ K, ◊ Q. As long as East does not discard a diamond, declarer would fail, as South is out of trumps and has no entry after playing ◊ K and ◊ Q, while if South plays ◊ K and overtakes the ◊ Q, East's ◊ 9 becomes high on the fourth round of diamonds. East should retain all four diamonds, following the principle 'Keep length in declarer's known second suit'.
(2) Failing to draw all the trumps before cashing your other winners or losing count in trumps.

CHAPTER 5

SUIT RESPONSES TO 1NT AND 2NT

After a balanced 1NT or 2NT opening, bidding is considered easiest of all, since opener's point range is narrow and the possible hand patterns are also known within closely defined limits. As opener has no singleton or void and a major suit game is the #1 priority, responder with a 6+ major and sufficient values for game can simply bid 4 ♡ * or 4 ♠ *, knowing that the partnership has at least eight trumps.

A suit response to a 1NT or 2NT opening promises a 5+ suit.

Exception: 1NT : 2 ♣ Stayman and 2NT : 3 ♣ Stayman – see Chapter 6.

The standard approach to suit responses to 1NT and 2NT is:

1NT : 2 ◇ *	Weakness takeout, 5+ suit, no interest in reaching game. Opener must pass (but there is
1NT : 2 ♡ *	one exception – see below). 1NT : 2 ♣ is not used to show a real suit, but is the Stayman
1NT : 2 ♠ *	Convention (see Chapter 6).

1NT : 3 ♣	Game-force, 5+ suit, no 4-card major, suggests slam possibilities. Prefer to bid 1NT : 3NT
1NT : 3 ◇	or 2NT : 3NT with most hands with a 5+ minor, no 4-card major and no prospects beyond
2NT : 3 ◇ *	game rather than introduce the minor suit, even if the hand has some singleton.

1NT : 3 ♡	Game-force, 5+ suit, denies four cards in the other major. Opener shows support for
2NT : 3 ♡ *	responder's major with 3+ trumps, else bids 3NT. Weak support or strong support can be
1NT : 3 ♠	shown (see opposite page). The 2NT opening is not forcing, but if responder does reply,
2NT : 3 ♠	then in standard methods it is forcing to game: there is no weakness takeout over 2NT.

1NT : 4 ♡ *	6+ suit, no prospects for slam and opener is obliged to pass. Responder's bid of game after
2NT : 4 ♡ *	1NT or 2NT is an absolute sign-off, no ifs, no buts, even if the opening was 2NT. With any
1NT : 4 ♠ *	chance for slam responder would bid 3 ♡ / 3 ♠, not 4 ♡ / 4 ♠. Responder knows opener's
2NT : 4 ♠ *	range and after 1NT or 2NT, it is responder's duty to explore slams, not opener's.

A 1NT or 2NT bidder (whether opener or responder) has no right to bid beyond game.

After 1NT : 2 ◇ *or* 1NT : 2 ♡ *or* 1NT : 2 ♠* – the weakness takeout: Although the rule is that opener *must* pass and novices should be trained early to pass regularly and to pass quickly, opener is permitted *one* further action: you may raise responder's suit with excellent support, a maximum 1NT and a doubleton outside (ruffing value). You may raise only to the 3-level and if you choose not to raise, you MUST pass.

After 1NT : 3 ♣ *or* 1NT : 3 ◇ *or* 2NT : 3 ◇ * – Responder should not hold a 4-card major in addition to the long minor, since it is better to use the Stayman Convention when holding 4-major – 5-minor hands.

With a doubleton or three rags in responder's suit opener should rebid 3NT over 3 ♣ or 3 ◇. With better support for the minor, opener should cue-bid (bid your cheapest ace, e.g., 1NT : 3 ♣, 3 ♠) as responder usually has at least mild slam interest for the 3 ♣ or 3 ◇ response. Since responder must be prepared to play in 5-of-the-minor opposite moderate support and a minimum no-trump, there must be slam chances if opener has excellent support and a maximum no-trump. If opener holds support but no ace, raise the minor suit to the 4-level (e.g., 1NT : 3 ◇, 4 ◇). Responder can sign off in game with no further slam interest or, with hopes for slam, cue-bid an ace or use 4NT.

After 1NT : 3 ♡ * *or* 2NT : 3 ♡ * *or* 1NT : 3 ♠ *or* 2NT : 3 ♠ * – Responder is showing a 5-card suit and opener should support with any three trumps. Opener has two basic choices:

DENY SUPPORT with any doubleton: Bid 3NT (e.g., 2NT : 3 ♡, 3NT *or* 1NT : 3 ♠, 3NT), *or*

SHOW SUPPORT with any 3 trumps. Opener may give weak support or strong support (see next page):

---

*After 1NT and 2NT most tournament players prefer artificial bids, known as transfers, especially to show major suits. A transfer bid is the suit below the actual suit, thus 1NT : 2 ◇ or 2NT : 3 ◇ shows 5+ hearts, 1NT : 2 ♡ or 2NT : 3 ♡ shows 5+ spades. For more on transfers, see the *Guide To Better Duplicate Bridge*.

WEAK SUPPORT: Raise responder's major (e.g., 2NT: 3♡, 4♡ *or* 1NT: 3♠, 4♠)

STRONG SUPPORT: Cue-bid your cheapest ace (e.g., 2NT: 3♡, 3♠ *or* 1NT: 3♠, 4◇)

The no-trump bidder is not permitted to bid beyond game, but when holding support for partner's suit, you can indicate how suitable the hand is for slam. With the weaker type of supporting hand, raise the major to the 4-level. The features which make up the weak type of raise are: three trumps rather than four, minimum HCP and any 4-3-3-3 pattern. The features which indicate strong support are: four trumps rather than three, maximum HCP and an outside doubleton (ruffing value). Two out of the three strong features justify making a cue-bid to indicate the strong raise, e.g. 1NT: 3♠, 4◇ = spade support, maximum values, ◇A (cue), but no ♣A (4♣ was bypassed). With no ace to cue, raise the major. Absence of outside aces is itself a poor feature.

The above approach also applies in comparable NT auctions. For example, it would apply when you have made a no-trump rebid, e.g., after 1♣ : 1♠, 1NT : 3♡ – raising to 4♡ is weak support, while a 4♣ or 4◇ cue-bid is strong support for hearts, the last bid suit. 3♠ would be strong preference, 4♠ weaker preference.

Responder uses the 1NT : 3♡ and 1NT : 3♠ responses on two types of hands:

(a) Game-going hands without slam prospects with *exactly* five cards in the major suit bid.

(b) Hands which have slam possibilities with five *or more* cards in the major suit bid.

If opener rebids 3NT (no support), responder will pass with type (a). If responder rebids the major over 3NT (e.g., 1NT : 3♡, 3NT : 4♡), responder is showing type (b), a mild slam invitation with 6+ trumps.

If opener raises responder's major, responder passes with type (a) and may also pass with type (b) if opener's weak supporting raise has dampened responder's hopes for slam. If responder is still interested in slam despite opener's weak supporting raise, responder may use 4NT or make a cue-bid.

If opener shows strong support via a cue-bid, type (a) responder simply bids game (e.g., 1NT : 3♠, 4♣ : 4♠), but with slam interest, type (b) responder can continue with a cue-bid or with 4NT, asking for aces.

PARTNERSHIP BIDDING: How should the following hands be bid? West is the dealer on all hands.

SET 13 – WEST	SET 13 – EAST	SET 14 – WEST	SET 14 – EAST
1. ♠ A Q ♡ 10 6 3 ◇ A K 8 7 ♣ 7 6 5 4	1. ♠ K 4 2 ♡ A K 8 7 2 ◇ Q J 9 ♣ 9 3	1. ♠ Q J 7 6 3 2 ♡ J 3 ◇ 7 5 2 ♣ 7 4	1. ♠ A K ♡ K Q 2 ◇ K Q 8 3 ♣ A 8 6 2
2. ♠ J 3 ♡ K 6 5 2 ◇ K 9 5 2 ♣ A Q 9	2. ♠ K 7 6 4 2 ♡ A 3 ◇ A 7 4 3 ♣ K 8	2. ♠ A K 6 ♡ A 7 ◇ A 9 4 3 ♣ K Q J 9	2. ♠ - - - ♡ J 8 6 5 4 3 2 ◇ 6 5 2 ♣ 8 6 3
3. ♠ K 7 ♡ A 4 2 ◇ A K 7 2 ♣ 9 8 6 4	3. ♠ A 8 6 5 3 2 ♡ 7 6 ◇ 6 5 ♣ A Q J	3. ♠ K 8 7 5 4 ♡ 7 ◇ Q 9 3 ♣ 6 5 4 2	3. ♠ Q J 2 ♡ A 6 3 ◇ K J 8 ♣ A K Q J
4. ♠ J 8 6 5 4 2 ♡ K 6 ◇ J 4 3 ♣ 6 2	4. ♠ A 9 ♡ A 9 8 2 ◇ 9 8 5 ♣ A Q 4 3	4. ♠ K Q J 2 ♡ K 5 ◇ A 9 7 ♣ A K J 9	4. ♠ A 3 ♡ Q 7 6 4 3 ◇ 6 4 2 ♣ 8 7 6
5. ♠ A 9 4 ♡ 8 7 5 ◇ Q J 4 ♣ K Q J 4	5. ♠ 6 ♡ A J 9 6 4 3 2 ◇ A 7 ♣ 8 3 2	5. ♠ A 5 3 ♡ Q 8 6 4 3 ◇ 8 6 4 ♣ 5 4	5. ♠ K Q 2 ♡ K 5 2 ◇ A K Q ♣ A 9 8 3
6. ♠ J 8 7 2 ♡ A 8 ◇ A K Q 2 ♣ 8 7 3	6. ♠ 5 4 ♡ Q J 10 7 2 ◇ 6 4 ♣ Q 6 5 2	6. ♠ A J 8 ♡ K 3 ◇ K 9 5 4 2 ♣ A K Q	6. ♠ 4 ♡ J 5 2 ◇ A 8 6 ♣ 9 8 7 5 3 2

PLAY HANDS BASED ON STRONG RESPONDING HANDS

Hand 17: Weakness takeout – Drawing trumps – Discarding losers

Dealer North : Love all

NORTH
- ♠ K 2
- ♡ 7 6 5 4
- ◊ A 8 3
- ♣ A K 9 4

WEST
- ♠ Q J 8
- ♡ K
- ◊ K Q J
- ♣ 10 8 7 6 3 2

EAST
- ♠ 10 9
- ♡ A Q J 9 2
- ◊ 9 7 6 2
- ♣ J 5

SOUTH
- ♠ A 7 6 5 4 3
- ♡ 10 8 3
- ◊ 10 5 4
- ♣ Q

WEST	NORTH	EAST	SOUTH
	1NT	No (1)	2♠ (2)
No	No (3)	No	

Bidding: (1) Too weak to call over the 1NT opening, but with one more heart and a singleton, 2♡ would be reasonable.
(2) The weakness takeout, a rescue from 1NT. With a weak hand, a long suit and no entries in the other suits, it is much safer to play in your long trump suit. It is clearly better to end in 2♠, making eight or nine tricks, than to play 1NT, one off.
(3) Opener must pass (except with support and a maximum, when opener can raise responder's suit to the 3-level).

Lead: ◊ K. Top of sequence.

Correct play: Win ◊ A, cross to the ♣ Q (unblocking) and cash the ♠ A and ♠ K. Then play ♣ A-K, discarding either diamond or heart losers on the clubs. Making nine tricks.

On the ◊ K, East should play the ◊ 2, the lowest card, a discouraging signal.

Wrong play: (1) Failing to unblock the ♣ Q before playing the ♠ A and ♠ K. This costs one trick.
(2) Failing to draw two rounds of trumps. If you play ◊ A, ♣ Q, spade to the king and then ♣ A-K, East ruffs the third club. If you discard, you make only eight tricks, while if you over-ruff, you go down.
(3) Playing ♠ A, ♠ K and a third spade after taking the ◊ A. When West wins the third round of trumps, the defence can cash five tricks to defeat 2♠ by one trick. On most hands, it is best to leave the top trump out.

If North plays 1NT, East leads the ♡ Q (interior sequence) and West wins the ♡ K. If West switches to a club, knocking out an entry to dummy, declarer has no more than six tricks available.

Hand 18: Suit bidding after a 2NT opening – Ruffing finesse to discard losers

Dealer East : North-South vulnerable

NORTH
- ♠ J 10
- ♡ 9 8
- ◊ A 9 7 4 3 2
- ♣ K Q 5

WEST
- ♠ A K 7 3
- ♡ K Q
- ◊ K Q J 6
- ♣ A 8 6

EAST
- ♠ 8 6 5
- ♡ J 10 7 6 5 4 3
- ◊ - - -
- ♣ 9 3 2

SOUTH
- ♠ Q 9 4 2
- ♡ A 2
- ◊ 10 8 5
- ♣ J 10 7 4

WEST	NORTH	EAST	SOUTH
		No	No
2NT	No	4♡ (1)	All pass (2)

Bidding: (1) East knows that the partnership holds at least nine hearts and can thus count shortage points. Five for the void makes the East hand worth 6 points, easily enough for game opposite 2NT. Note how poor it would be to pass 2NT (or try 3NT!): West would find it almost impossible to make more than six tricks in no-trumps, yet ten tricks in hearts are relatively comfortable. Again, with a long trump suit and no outside entries, it is clearly superior to play with the long suit as trumps.
(2) A no-trump bidder is not permitted to bid beyond game. 2NT already revealed a powerful hand and any slam bidding is up to responder.

Lead: ♣ 4. It is better to lead from a suit with two honours than from a suit with only one honour.

Correct play: Win the ♣ A and lead the ◊ K. If North plays low, discard a club, but when North plays the ace, ruff and cross to the ♠ A in order to play the ◊ Q and ◊ J on which you discard two club losers. Then start the trumps. Making eleven tricks, losing one spade and one heart. You could start on the trumps at once and play the ruffing finesse in diamonds later, but then you would make only ten tricks, as the defence could cash two clubs upon winning the ♡ A. Playing on diamonds first cannot harm you.

Hand 19: Ducking the opening lead in dummy – Deceptive technique in drawing trumps

Dealer South : East-West vulnerable

NORTH
♠ K Q J 10 9 8
♡ 9 6 4
♢ A
♣ 9 6 5

WEST
♠ A 7 6
♡ A 7
♢ 10 9 6 5 2
♣ 10 7 2

EAST
♠ 3
♡ Q J 10 3 2
♢ K J 8
♣ J 8 4 3

SOUTH
♠ 5 4 2
♡ K 8 5
♢ Q 7 4 3
♣ A K Q

WEST	NORTH	EAST	SOUTH
			1NT
No	4♠(1)	All pass	

Bidding: (1) North knows that the partnership has at least eight spades and, counting the singleton, North is worth 13 points, enough for game. North's 4♠ is an absolute sign-off – opener must pass. Note that 3NT could be defeated on a diamond lead and repeated diamond leads later if West ducks the ♠A until the third round of spades.

Lead: ♡Q. Top of sequence.

Correct play: Play low in dummy – do not play the king. On the next heart, play low from dummy again – playing the king will lose to the ace. West wins the ♡A and should lead a diamond. Win the ◊A and play the ♠8. Later draw trumps, losing two hearts and one spade.

Wrong play: (1) Playing the ♡K on the opening lead: West is marked with the ace and you will just lose your king. Playing low is not certain to win, but playing the king is sure to lose. West would win the ♡A and return a heart and you would lose three hearts and one spade.
(2) Playing the ♠K when in with the ◊A. To you it is irrelevant which trump you use to dislodge the ace, but it is possible that East has A-x in trumps and West has x-x. If you lead the king, East wins and plays a third heart, allowing West to ruff your ♡K. By leading the ♠8, East may play low although holding the ace and then your second round of trumps will draw the missing trumps. If you wish to sneak a round of trumps through an opponent, lead the lowest of equal trumps, not the highest.

Hand 20: Suit bidding over 2NT – The double finesse

Dealer West : Game all

NORTH
♠ 8 6 5
♡ Q 9 5
♢ K Q 10 9
♣ 10 7 5

WEST
♠ A 2
♡ 8 7 6 4 2
♢ 7 5
♣ 8 6 4 3

EAST
♠ K Q J 4
♡ A J 10
♢ J 4 2
♣ A K Q

SOUTH
♠ 10 9 7 3
♡ K 3
♢ A 8 6 3
♣ J 9 2

WEST	NORTH	EAST	SOUTH
No	No	2NT (1)	No
3♡ (2)	No	4♡ (3)	All pass

Bidding: (1) The diamond holding is a drawback, but 2NT is still the sensible opening. To open with a 1-bid risks being left there (West would pass 1♠) and a 2-opening does not solve the diamond problem. It is reasonable to take a risk and open 2NT with one unguarded suit, as long as the hand is balanced.
(2) Promises five hearts (need not be strong hearts) and is forcing to game. Explore for the major rather than bid 3NT. Not only might you lose the first five or six diamond tricks in 3NT, but West also does not have a second entry for the double finesse in hearts. In no-trumps, East has only eight tricks even though the defence can take only four diamonds.
(3) Shows support for hearts, but a relatively weak hand. The weak features are minimum HCP and the 4-3-3-3 pattern. Even if East had cue-bid, West would sign off in 4♡.

Lead: ◊K. Top from K-Q holdings is standard in suit contracts.

Correct Play: South encourages the diamond lead and West ruffs the third round. Lead a heart to the ten and king (first finesse). Regain the lead (ruff a diamond continuation *in your* hand or come to hand via the ♠A) and lead another heart: nine – jack – the second finesse wins. Cash the ♡A and the rest of the tricks are yours. The double finesse is the best chance for success with low cards opposite A-J-10. If dummy had only two diamonds, you could come to hand twice for the double heart finesse via the ♠A and by ruffing a spade winner.

CHAPTER 6

STAYMAN OVER 1NT AND 2NT

After a 1NT or a 2NT opening, the partnership may have a 4-4 fit in a major suit, which is likely to be a superior game to 3NT. A suit bid after a 1NT or a 2NT opening shows a 5+ suit (Chapter 5), so that this route is not suitable to find a 4-4 fit. Partner would be misled about the length of your suit and may support you with only three trumps, landing you in an inferior 4-3 trump fit.

The solution is the Stayman Convention, a 2♣ response to 1NT and a 3♣ response to 2NT, each of which is a question to opener: 'Do you hold a 4-card major?' If so, opener bids the major (e.g., 1NT : 2♣, 2♡ *or* 2NT : 3♣, 3♠) or bids diamonds to deny holding either major (e.g., 1NT : 2♣, 2◊ *or* 2NT : 3♣, 3◊). With 4-4 in the majors, show the hearts first, following the normal rule that 4-card suits are bid up-the-line. In other words, 1NT : 2♣, 2♡ *or* 2NT : 3♣, 3♡ does not deny holding four spades, but 1NT : 2♣, 2♠ and 2NT : 3♣, 3♠ does deny holding four hearts.

BASIC REQUIREMENTS FOR THE USE OF STAYMAN

You need at least one 4-card major and enough points to be able to invite game or to insist on game.

These apply when you are looking to find the best game contract. The use of Stayman for weakness rescue is covered in Chapter 22. For now, the use of Stayman is confined to hands with game potential or better.

WHEN SHOULD YOU USE STAYMAN?

With enough points to make game a possibility, you should use Stayman in each of these situations:

1. Your hand pattern is 4-4-4-1, 4-4-3-2 including at least one 4-card major or 4-3-3-3 with a 4-card major.

2. You hold both majors in a 4-4, 5-4, 6-4, 5-5 or 6-5 pattern. Any hand with both majors is suitable. If you bid 1NT : 3♠ with a 5-5 pattern, you may end in a 5-3 spade fit with a 5-4 fit available in hearts.

3. You hold a 5-card or longer minor and a 4-card major as well. Use Stayman to search for the major fit.

♠ A Q 8 6 ♡ A J 7 4 ◊ Q 8 6 5 ♣ 7	If partner opens 1NT, bid 2♣. If partner rebids 2♡ or 2♠, raise to 4♡ / 4♠. If partner bids 2◊ (no 4-card major), rebid 3NT. While the singleton club poses a risk, 3NT is now your best chance for game. With no 4-card major, partner has length in the minor suits and is likely to have the clubs under control.
♠ A 7 ♡ K J 7 3 ◊ A J 6 3 ♣ 7 5 2	If partner opens 1NT, bid 2♣. Many players would wrongly jump to 3NT at once. You have the values for game, but should explore the possibility of 4♡. If partner replies 2♡ to 2♣, raise to 4♡. If partner replies 2◊ or 2♠, each of which denies four hearts, rebid 3NT. You have found there is no 4-4 heart fit, so that 3NT figures to be best.
♠ K Q 4 3 ♡ 9 5 2 ◊ A J 7 ♣ A 8 3	If partner opens 1NT, bid 2♣. Although a hand pattern of 4-3-3-3 suggests no-trumps, a 4-4 fit in spades might exist and opener might have a doubleton, allowing an extra trick via a ruff. Bid 1NT : 2♣. If partner bids 2♠, raise to 4♠. Otherwise, rebid 3NT. With four spades, opener is much more likely to have a 4-4-3-2 pattern than a 4-3-3-3.*

SUBSEQUENT BIDDING AFTER STAYMAN HAS BEEN USED

A 2NT rebid by responder or raising opener's major to three shows the values to invite game.

♠ Q J 3 ♡ A J 8 4 ◊ K 9 7 2 ♣ 9 4	If partner opens 1NT, bid 2♣. Then if opener rebids 2♡, raise to 3♡ – opener will pass if minimum or bid 4♡ if maximum. If opener's reply to 2♣ is 2◊ or 2♠, rebid 2NT, inviting game. Opener will pass if minimum or bid 3NT if maximum. The 2NT rebid after Stayman shows the same values as the 1NT : 2NT response without Stayman.

*Popular modern style among top players is to open 1NT or 2NT with a 5-3-3-2 pattern, even if the 5-card suit is a major. This has led to bidding methods after 1NT and 2NT which are different to the standard methods described above. See *Five-Card Major Stayman* and *Bid Better, Much Better After Opening 1NT*.

A change of suit by the Stayman bidder promises a 5-card suit.

♠ Q 8 6 4 2   If partner opens 1NT, bid 2♣. You have the values for game, but it is not clear yet
♡ A K 8 3   whether to play 3NT, 4♡ or 4♠. Whenever you hold both majors, investigation via 2♣
◇ 7   Stayman is best. After 2♣, if opener bids 2♡ or 2♠, raise the major to game. If, however,
♣ A 7 5   opener replies 2◇ – no major – there is no 4-4 heart fit, but a 5-3 spade fit might exist.

Jump to 3♠, showing a strong hand (you jumped) and *five* spades (change of suit). Opener will raise to 4♠
with three spades and will rebid 3NT with a doubleton spade. The jump to 3-major after using Stayman
shows the same values as the jump to 3-major without Stayman, i.e., a force to game with a 5+ suit.

If opener bids hearts in reply to 2♣, a no-trump rebid by the Stayman bidder promises four spades.

Thus, 1NT : 2♣, 2♡ : 2NT or 1NT : 2♣, 2♡ : 3NT shows that responder has four spades. Similarly,
responder promises four spades if the auction goes 2NT : 3♣, 3♡ : 3NT.

♠ K Q 4 2   If partner opens 2NT, bid 3♣. If opener replies 3♠, bid 4♠. If opener bids 3◇, no
♡ J 8   major, you should rebid 3NT. If opener's reply is 3♡, opener might have four spades,
◇ 7 4 2   but responder should still rebid 3NT, not 3♠. It would be inferior to reach 4♠ with the
♣ 9 6 5 2   weaker hand as declarer.

Bidding 3NT over 3♡ promises four spades. If opener does not hold four spades, opener will pass 3NT. If
opener does have four spades as well as four hearts, opener will rebid 4♠ over 3NT. Thus the strong hand
will be declarer whether the contract is 3NT or 4♠.

After 1NT : 2♣, 2♡ or 2NT : 3♣, 3♡ it is perfectly logical that 3NT by responder shows four spades.
The 2♣ response said, 'I am interested in a major suit.' Opener's heart bid said, 'I have four hearts,' and
responder's 3NT then said, 'That is not the major I was seeking.'

PARTNERSHIP BIDDING: How should the following hands be bid? West is the dealer on all hands.

SET 15 – WEST	SET 15 – EAST	SET 16 – WEST	SET 16 – EAST
1. ♠ Q 6 3 ♡ K 9 7 3 ◇ A 3 ♣ A 7 6 4	1. ♠ A K ♡ Q J 10 2 ◇ 8 4 ♣ K 8 5 3 2	1. ♠ K 6 ♡ A K 5 2 ◇ A Q 6 2 ♣ A J 10	1. ♠ 8 5 2 ♡ 8 7 6 3 ◇ K J 7 4 3 ♣ 6
2. ♠ 9 8 4 2 ♡ A Q 2 ◇ K Q 9 4 ♣ 8 4	2. ♠ A K 6 3 ♡ K 5 3 ◇ A 6 3 ♣ 6 3 2	2. ♠ A Q 6 5 ♡ K J 9 7 ◇ K 8 ♣ A K J	2. ♠ K 7 3 2 ♡ A 4 ◇ 6 4 2 ♣ 9 8 5 3
3. ♠ Q 6 2 ♡ A J 10 4 ◇ A J 8 ♣ Q 10 2	3. ♠ K J 10 3 ♡ K 6 ◇ K 10 3 ♣ J 8 7 6	3. ♠ J 8 7 3 ♡ K 6 5 2 ◇ J 8 ♣ 9 8 3	3. ♠ A K 2 ♡ A Q 3 ◇ K Q 6 ♣ A 7 5 4
4. ♠ A 6 5 2 ♡ A 7 ◇ 9 6 5 4 ♣ K 8 2	4. ♠ 8 7 4 ♡ K 9 ◇ A K 3 ♣ Q J 10 7 6	4. ♠ K 8 7 6 3 ♡ K 7 6 4 ◇ 5 4 ♣ 6 2	4. ♠ A 2 ♡ A 9 3 2 ◇ A K 3 ♣ K Q J 4
5. ♠ K 6 5 4 ♡ K Q 6 4 ◇ A 6 4 ♣ Q 6	5. ♠ A 8 7 3 ♡ A 2 ◇ K Q 7 ♣ 8 7 3 2	5. ♠ Q 7 5 4 ♡ A 9 4 3 2 ◇ 7 ♣ 4 3 2	5. ♠ A K 2 ♡ Q J 6 ◇ A 9 3 ♣ K Q J 6
6. ♠ K Q 8 6 2 ♡ A 7 4 2 ◇ 6 3 ♣ J 6	6. ♠ A 3 ♡ K 9 8 3 ◇ A K 4 ♣ 8 7 3 2	6. ♠ K J 3 ♡ K J 5 4 ◇ A K ♣ A Q 7 6	6. ♠ Q 8 7 6 2 ♡ Q 7 6 3 2 ◇ 8 ♣ 4 2

PLAY HANDS ON STAYMAN

Hand 21: Stayman over 1NT – Technique in drawing trumps – Marked finesse

Dealer North : North-South vulnerable

```
                NORTH
                ♠ Q 10 5
                ♡ A J 9 7
                ◇ K 4
                ♣ K J 7 3
WEST                        EAST
♠ K 7 6                     ♠ A J 8 4 2
♡ 10 8 6 3                  ♡ Q
◇ 9 7 5 2                   ◇ J 10 8 6
♣ 10 8                      ♣ 9 6 2
                SOUTH
                ♠ 9 3
                ♡ K 5 4 2
                ◇ A Q 3
                ♣ A Q 5 4
```

WEST	NORTH	EAST	SOUTH
	1NT	No	2♣ (1)
No	2♡	No	4♡
No	No	No	

Bidding: (1) A common error would be to raise to 3NT, which fails on East's ♠4 lead. West takes the ♠K and returns the ♠7 (top from a remaining doubleton). East-West have the first five tricks, despite North's respectable stopper in spades. After a 1NT or 2NT opening, make sure you explore the possibility of a major suit game. (The same strategy requires you to choose a major after partner's suit opening bid rather than a response in no-trumps.) South's approach is to find out whether North holds four hearts and 2♣ enables South to discover the relevant information. If North shows hearts, South intends to play in 4♡. Over any other reply, South would rebid 3NT.

Lead: ◇ J. Top of a near-sequence.

Correct play: With eight trumps including A, K and J, it is correct to finesse for the queen, but this finesse is normally taken on the second round of the suit. Cash a top honour first in case the queen is singleton. So, win the ◇ K and lead a low heart to the king. When East plays the queen it is clearly a singleton. After a heart to the jack, cross to the ♣A and lead a heart, finessing the nine if West plays low. Draw the remaining trump, cash the clubs and the diamonds, discarding a spade loser on the third diamond. Making 11 tricks.

Wrong play: Taking a first round finesse in trumps, losing a trick unnecessarily to the singleton queen.

Hand 22: Stayman with 4-major – 5-minor – Establishing winners before cashing long suit

Dealer East : East-West vulnerable

```
                NORTH
                ♠ 9 5 4 2
                ♡ K Q 10 6
                ◇ J 8 4
                ♣ J 10
WEST                        EAST
♠ J 10 7 6                  ♠ K Q
♡ 4 2                       ♡ A J 7 3
◇ K 7                       ◇ Q 10 3
♣ A K 8 4 3                 ♣ Q 9 5 2
                SOUTH
                ♠ A 8 3
                ♡ 9 8 5
                ◇ A 9 6 5 2
                ♣ 7 6
```

WEST	NORTH	EAST	SOUTH
		1NT	No
2♣ (1)	No	2♡ (2)	No
2NT (3)	No	3NT (4)	All pass

Bidding: (1) With a 4-card major and a 5-card minor, explore the major suit game possibility as first priority.
(2) Shows four hearts, but does not deny four spades.
(3) Stayman followed by a no-trump rebid after opener shows hearts promises four spades, otherwise why did you bother to use Stayman? Prefer 2NT (11-12 points, invitational) to 3♣, which would be a weakness sign-off.
(2) With 14 points, a maximum, East accepts the invitation. The ♣K-Q should be useful opposite West's spades.

Lead: ◇ 5. Fourth-highest of the long suit is normal.

Correct play: Play low from dummy and let the lead come to your Q-10-x. This guarantees two tricks in diamonds. Play the ♠ K and if they duck, continue with the ♠ Q before starting on clubs. You need to set up dummy's spade winners while you still have an entry to dummy and the only entries are in clubs. If they take the first spade and knock out your diamond stopper, unblock the ♠ Q before crossing to dummy. If they duck the first two spades, cross to dummy and lead the ♠ J. Take care when playing the clubs: queen first, then the nine, unblocking, so that you cannot be stuck in your own hand later.

Hand 23: Stayman when holding both majors – Setting up an extra winner

Dealer South : Game all

NORTH
- ♠ 3 2
- ♡ 10 9 4
- ◊ Q 9 6 2
- ♣ K Q 6 5

WEST
- ♠ 9 5
- ♡ K Q 5 2
- ◊ A K 10 3
- ♣ 8 7 4

EAST
- ♠ K Q 8 6 4
- ♡ A 8 7 3
- ◊ J 7
- ♣ A 2

SOUTH
- ♠ A J 10 7
- ♡ J 6
- ◊ 8 5 4
- ♣ J 10 9 3

WEST	NORTH	EAST	SOUTH
			No
1NT (1)	No	2♣ (2)	No
2♡	No	4♡	All pass

Bidding: (1) Do not worry about unguarded suits if the rest of the hand fits the no-trump opening. Partner will be anxious to explore a major suit contract if possible, and partner usually has length and strength where you are weak and short.

(2) With both majors, Stayman is best. 3NT, a poor choice, could be defeated on a club lead. 2♣ allows you to discover whether a heart fit exists; if not, you can then rebid 3♠ to find out whether a 5-3 spade fit exists.

(3) Having found the 4-4 fit, stick with hearts. It is possible to rebid 3♠ over 2♡, showing five spades, but if opener has three spades and raises the spades, you would be in a 5-3 fit instead of the superior 4-4 fit.

Lead: A spade, a trump or the ♣K is possible. A diamond from just one honour is the least attractive.

Correct play: On, say, the ♣K lead, declarer should take the ace, draw trumps ending in dummy and lead the ◊J. When South plays low, let the jack go. North wins the ◊Q, but your ◊10 is now high. Thus you lose one spade, one diamond and one club, the other club loser being ruffed in dummy. It would be an error to draw three rounds of trumps and then play ◊A, ◊K and ruff a diamond, as dummy has only one trump left, which is not enough to ruff two diamond losers and one club loser.

Hand 24: Stayman over 2NT – Marked finesse – Discarding losers and ruffing in dummy

Dealer West : Nil vulnerable

NORTH
- ♠ A 5 4 3
- ♡ J 2
- ◊ 8 7 2
- ♣ 8 7 6 2

WEST
- ♠ K
- ♡ 8 7 4 3
- ◊ Q 9 6 4
- ♣ K 9 4 3

EAST
- ♠ J 9 7 2
- ♡ A 9 5
- ◊ 10 5 3
- ♣ J 10 5

SOUTH
- ♠ Q 10 8 6
- ♡ K Q 10 6
- ◊ A K J
- ♣ A Q

WEST	NORTH	EAST	SOUTH
No	No	No	2NT
No	3♣ (1)	No	3♡
No	3NT (3)	No	4♠ (4)
No	No	No	

Bidding: (1) North has enough for a game, but as South might have four spades, North checks via Stayman 3♣.

(2) With both majors, the hearts are shown first in reply to the Stayman inquiry.

(3) North could bid 3♠, but then North would be declarer in 4♠. Where possible, let the strong hand be declarer, since the opening lead into strength is an advantage. Here, if South is declarer, a club or a diamond lead gives South a trick, while the same lead if North is declarer is no help at all.

(4) Stayman followed by a NT rebid over opener's heart reply always promises spades: why else would responder ask for a major? Therefore, where opener has both majors, opener will bid spades over partner's rebid in no-trumps.

Lead: ♡7. It is very risky to lead a suit with just one honour (or two split honours) into a 2NT opener.

Correct Play: On gaining the lead, South should play a low spade to the ace. When West plays the king, lead a spade back and finesse the eight if East plays the seven. Next play hearts and discard a diamond on the third heart, followed by the ◊A, ◊K and a diamond ruff. Next comes another spade, finessing the ten when East plays the nine (it does not help East to play a higher card at any stage). Draw East's last trump. Making eleven tricks. (An initial club lead gives declarer twelve tricks: win the club, play the ♣6 to the ace, take a spade finesse, a heart to the jack, discard a diamond later on the third round of hearts and ruff a diamond to reach dummy for the second spade finesse).

CHAPTER 7

BIDDING AFTER 1NT AND 2NT REBIDS BY OPENER

AFTER OPENER'S 1NT REBID (e.g., 1♣ : 1♡ , 1NT . . .)

Opener's 1NT rebid shows a balanced 15-16 HCP.* A 5-3-3-2 pattern with 14 HCP also qualifies. The 1NT rebid denies a 4-card major that could have been bid at the 1-level (e.g., 1♣ : 1♡, 1NT denies four spades). On the odd occasion, opener may hold a singleton in responder's suit. Do not rebid 1NT with a singleton anywhere else. With a 5-4 pattern, a change of suit is preferable if unable to raise responder. Use the 1NT rebid with 15-16 points and a singleton in responder's suit only when opener's long suit is weak.

With two exceptions, bidding over the 1NT rebid is exactly the same as bidding over a 1NT opening (see Chapter 5). Bids at the 2-level are weak, looking for the best part-score, the raise to 2NT is invitational, jumps to game are sign-offs, while jumps to the 3-level force to game. If responder jumps to the 3-level in the suit first bid (e.g., 1♣ : 1♠, 1NT : 3♣), this is exactly the same as a jump to the 3-level over a 1NT opening (e.g., 1NT : 3♣) and shows a 5-card suit, asking for 3-card support. If responder has a 6-card major and no ambitions beyond game, responder can jump straight to game over 1NT (e.g., 1♣ : 1♠, 1NT : 4♠).

Exception 1: **There is no Stayman after a 1NT rebid.** Stayman does not apply after suits have been bid genuinely. Thus, 1◇ : 1♡, 1NT : 2♣ really shows clubs and is a weak rebid, because it is at the 2-level). *(Note:* After opener's 1NT rebid, some pairs do use a 2♣ rebid as an artificial bid with enough to invite game.)

Exception 2: A new suit by responder at the 2-level higher-ranking than responder's first suit is forcing. For example, 1◇ : 1♠, 1NT : 2♡ is not forcing, but 1◇ : 1♡, 1NT : 2♠ is forcing for one round.

AFTER OPENER'S 2NT REBID TO A 1-LEVEL RESPONSE (e.g., 1◇ : 1♠, 2NT . . .)

With 17-18 points balanced and a 4-card major, should opener rebid to show the major or jump to 2NT to show the points? If opener's major can be shown at the 1-level (e.g., 1◇ : 1♡, 1♠), always show the major. If responder bid 1♠ and opener holds four hearts, jump to 2NT with a balanced hand rather than rebid 2♡. The hearts are useful only if responder holds four hearts. If so, responder has five spades, since with four spades and four hearts, the initial response would have been 1♡ (bid 4-card suits up-the-line). With five spades and four hearts, responder will rebid 3♡ over 2NT and the heart fit will not be missed.

As opener is showing a balanced 17-18 points and responder need have only 6 points for a 1-level response (or even a good 5 points), the 2NT jump-rebid is encouraging, but not forcing. Responder may pass with just 5-7 points, but with 8+ points, responder should bid for game at least, as the combined total will be 25+. Responder has three weak actions, Pass (best with a balanced 5-7, including a 5-3-3-2 pattern), a rebid of responder's suit (e.g., 1◇ : 1♠, 2NT : 3♠) or a preference to opener's suit (e.g., 1♣ : 1♡, 2NT : 3♣), all not forcing. A game bid is a sign-off and a new suit rebid (e.g., 1◇ : 1♠, 2NT : 3♡) or a jump below game (e.g., 1♣ : 1♡ , 2NT : 4♣) is forcing. A rebid of 3♣ is not Stayman, but shows at least four clubs.

The rebid of responder's suit (e.g., 1◇ : 1♡ , 2NT : 3♡) is a sign-off, showing a 6-card suit in a very poor hand. With a better hand, responder can bid game (e.g., 1◇ : 1♡ , 2NT : 4♡). With a weak 5-3-3-2, pass 2NT rather than rebid your suit, but what if you have a good 5-3-3-2? How can you explore the possibility of 4-Major vs. 3NT? Rebid in the unbid minor (e.g., 1◇ : 1♡ , 2NT : 3♣). This is forcing and opener gives delayed support for the major, with 3NT as second choice with only a doubleton in responder's major.

After 1-minor : 1♠, 2NT : 3♡, opener would support hearts only with 4-card support, but should give delayed 3-card support for spades, as responder will be at least 5-4 in spades-hearts (did not bid up-the-line). With support for both spades and hearts, prefer the 4-card heart support. If responder has a weak 5-5 hand in say, spades and hearts, it is better to rebid 3♡, even though that is forcing, than to pass 2NT or rebid 3♠. With such good distribution, taking a shot at game is not an unreasonable gamble (you could even rebid 4♡ over 2NT to insist that opener chooses a major by passing 4♡ or giving preference to 4♠).

---

*A popular treatment, especially among tournament players, and recommended, is to rebid 1NT with 15-17 points and jump to 2NT with 18-19 points (forcing). This allows more exploration for the best game contract over 2NT. This is superior to opener's jump-rebid to 3NT to show 19 points.

PROBLEMS WITH THE 1NT REBID

The 1♡ : 1♠, 1NT rebid will show 15-16 points, so that if opener has a 5-3-3-2 pattern with five hearts and 12-14 points, opener must choose the opening bid carefully. If the heart suit is strong, you can open 1♡ and rebid 2♡. If you have a decent 3-card spade holding, you can try 1♡ : 1♠, 2♠. With neither of these rebids attractive, choose a 1NT opening and forego the chance of showing that you have *five* hearts.

With 12-14 points and four diamonds, five clubs and 2-2 in the majors, opener again must open carefully. If the clubs are strong, open 1♣ and a 2♣ rebid will be all right. If the clubs are too weak to rebid, either open 1NT with strong doubletons or open 1♢, planning to rebid 2♣ (which does not show a strong hand, as it is below your barrier). With four diamonds, five clubs, 3-1 or 1-3 in the majors and 12-14 points, open 1♣ if able to rebid 2♣. If the clubs are too weak to rebid, open 1♢ and then rebid 2♣ or give partner a 3-card raise, depending on partner's response. Do not rebid 1NT with only 12-14 points in total.

THE 1♡ : 1♠, 2NT AUCTION

Opener should choose the 2NT rebid with a 5-3-3-2 and 17-18 points rather than repeat the 5-card suit. Responder may now show 3-card heart support with 3♡ (forcing). If opener has only four hearts, opener can bid 3♠ with 3-card support or 3NT with a doubleton spade. With other hands not ideal for 3NT, responder can bid 3♣ or 3♢. Opener can then bid 3♡ with a powerful 5-card suit with four honours, which can thus stand doubleton support, bid 3♠ with 3-card support or rebid 3NT.

OPENER'S 2NT REBID AFTER A 2-LEVEL RESPONSE

If the 2-level response was a jump-shift, opener's 2NT rebid still shows 15+ points. With fewer points, choose a different rebid. With 17+ points, opener may still rebid 2NT, but will push on to slam if the jump-shift responder attempts to subside in game, since responder has shown 16+ points.

Where opener is 5-3-3-2 and 15+ points, prefer the 2NT rebid (e.g., 1♡ : 2♣, 2NT) to a rebid of the 5-card suit. Responder can show delayed support for the major if appropriate (e.g., 1♡ : 2♣, 2NT : 3♡, forcing). Responder's change-of-suit over opener's 2NT rebid is forcing and natural. If responder rebids the minor suit (e.g., 1♡ : 2♣, 2NT : 3♣), this is not forcing or encouraging, but opener is entitled to bid on.

PARTNERSHIP BIDDING: How should the following hands be bid? West is the dealer on all hands.

SET 17 – WEST	SET 17 – EAST	SET 18 – WEST	SET 18 – EAST
1. ♠ 8 3	1. ♠ A J 6	1. ♠ A J 6	1. ♠ K 8 5 4 2
♡ Q 9 8 5 2	♡ J 4	♡ A Q 8	♡ K 9 7 3
◇ K 9 6 4	◇ A Q 7 3 2	◇ K 8 4 3 2	◇ 7
♣ J 3	♣ K 8 7	♣ K 4	♣ Q J 3
2. ♠ K J 4	2. ♠ A Q 8	2. ♠ K 8 6 3	2. ♠ A J 5 2
♡ Q 9	♡ K J 10 8 6 3	♡ A 9 5 2	♡ A 6
◇ K Q 7 3	◇ 9 8 2	◇ 7 2	◇ K 8 3
♣ A 8 4 2	♣ 5	♣ Q 8 3	♣ A J 10 4
3. ♠ A J 3	3. ♠ K 9 6 4 2	3. ♠ Q 7	3. ♠ J 10 8 6 5 4
♡ K 9 5 2	♡ A 4 3	♡ A 8 4 2	♡ - - -
◇ A 2	◇ 9 8	◇ Q 8 5	◇ K J 6 2
♣ A 8 4 3	♣ K Q 2	♣ A K Q 2	♣ J 4 3
4. ♠ K 8 7	4. ♠ A Q 5 3	4. ♠ K J 5 4 2	4. ♠ Q 7 6
♡ A 8 6	♡ K 9 5 4 3	♡ J 4	♡ A 3 2
◇ K Q 3	◇ 6 2	◇ K 9 7	◇ A 8 4 2
♣ A 6 4 2	♣ 9 5	♣ Q 8 4	♣ A K 7
5. ♠ K 9 7	5. ♠ Q J 6 5 2	5. ♠ K 7 4	5. ♠ Q J 10 3 2
♡ A 7 2	♡ K Q 4 3	♡ Q 8 5	♡ K 10 9 6 4
◇ Q 9 4	◇ 7	◇ A K 6	◇ 8 3
♣ A K 6 2	♣ Q 9 8	♣ A J 6 2	♣ 5

PLAY HANDS ON OPENER'S 1NT AND 2NT REBIDS

Hand 25: Unblocking a long suit – Card-reading – Marked finesse

Dealer North : East-West vulnerable

NORTH
- ♠ K Q
- ♡ Q 9 3
- ◊ A Q 9 6 4
- ♣ Q 10 7

WEST
- ♠ A
- ♡ K J 5 4
- ◊ 10 8 7 5
- ♣ J 6 4 3

EAST
- ♠ 9 8 5 3 2
- ♡ 10 7
- ◊ J
- ♣ A 9 8 5 2

SOUTH
- ♠ J 10 7 6 4
- ♡ A 8 6 2
- ◊ K 3 2
- ♣ K

WEST	NORTH	EAST	SOUTH
	1◊	No	1♠
No	1NT (1)	No	3♡ (2)
No	3NT (3)	All pass	

Bidding: (1) It would be very poor to rebid 2◊.
(2) The jump is forcing to game and 3♡ shows 4+ hearts and therefore at least five spades, as spades were bid first.
(3) No support for hearts, no delayed support for spades.

Lead: ♣5. The unbid suit is the normal lead.

Correct play: The ♣K wins, West encouraging with the six. Declarer should tackle spades next, as some spade tricks are needed to make 3NT. West wins and leads a low club. As the ♣A is marked with East from trick 1, finesse the ♣10, which luckily forces out the ace. Later, unblock your spade winner, cash the ◊A, play a diamond to the king (noting East's ◊J and subsequent discard); cash the ♠J and ♠10, discarding two hearts, and then take the marked finesse of the ◊9. Making eleven tricks.

Hand 26: Locating the 5-3 fit – Correct technique with an 8-card suit missing the queen

Dealer East : Game all

NORTH
- ♠ 9 7 5 4 3 2
- ♡ 3
- ◊ A 8 5 3
- ♣ 9 4

WEST
- ♠ Q J 6
- ♡ K 10 8 4 2
- ◊ J 10 6
- ♣ A 5

EAST
- ♠ A K
- ♡ A J 6
- ◊ K 9 4
- ♣ 8 7 6 3 2

SOUTH
- ♠ 10 8
- ♡ Q 9 7 5
- ◊ Q 7 2
- ♣ K Q J 10

WEST	NORTH	EAST	SOUTH
		1♣	No
1♡	No	1NT	No
3♡ (1)	No	4♡ (2)	All pass

Bidding: (1) The jump to 3♡ is forcing to game, promises five hearts and asks for 3-card support. Without support, opener would rebid 3NT.
(2) East is not quite worth a cue-bid of 3♠, showing heart support, maximum values and the ♣A. It is a close decision and 3♠ would appeal if East's long suit were particularly strong.

Lead: ♣4. A singleton trump is a poor choice, as is a suit headed by the ace (diamonds). A doubleton club is unlikely to gain a ruff when only one trump is held. By elimination, lead a spade.

Correct play: Win the ♠A and start on the trumps. Cash the ♡A (in case the queen is singleton) and then lead the ♡J. If South plays low, let the jack run and repeat the finesse on the next round. If South covers with the queen, North shows out, so that South is known to have 9-x left: cross to the ♠K and lead another heart from dummy, finessing the eight. With eight trumps missing the queen, it is normal to finesse for the queen on the second round. When the trump length includes the eight, you can pick up Q-9-x-x under the trump length. That is why the ♡J is led from dummy on the second round of trumps.

After trumps are drawn, lead the ◊J and let it run. This finesse loses to South's queen but declarer makes ten tricks, losing two diamonds and one club.

Hand 27: Rebidding after opener's 2NT rebid – Not leading an honour card for a finesse

Dealer South : Love all

NORTH
- ♠ A 9 3
- ♡ K Q 3
- ◇ A 8 3
- ♣ K Q 8 6

WEST
- ♠ Q
- ♡ 10 7 6 4
- ◇ Q J 9 6
- ♣ 9 5 4 3

EAST
- ♠ K 8 7 6
- ♡ J 8
- ◇ 10 7 5 2
- ♣ A J 10

SOUTH
- ♠ J 10 5 4 2
- ♡ A 9 5 2
- ◇ K 4
- ♣ 7 2

WEST	NORTH	EAST	SOUTH
			No
No	1♣	No	1♠
No	2NT (1)	No	3♡ (2)
No	3♠ (3)	No	4♠
No	No	No	

Bidding: (1) Shows 17-18 points and a balanced hand. The 2NT rebid is encouraging but not forcing.
(2) Showing 5+ spades and 4+ hearts. Forcing.
(3) With the same number of cards in each suit, prefer partner's first suit.

Lead: ◇ Q. Top of a near sequence.

Correct play: Win the lead with the ◇ K and lead a *low* spade, planning to finesse the nine if West plays low, and later to lead the jack for a second finesse.

As it happens, the ♠ Q is singleton with West, so take it with the ace and continue spades, making sure to draw all of East's trumps after forcing out the king. Later lead a club to dummy's king. As East has the ♣ A, South has only one club trick and should lose one spade, one heart and one club.

Trap to avoid: Do not lead the ♠ J or ♠ 10 on the first round of spades. If you do, East will score two spade tricks and 4♠ can then be defeated.

Hand 28: Rebidding after opener's 2NT rebid – Play at trick 1 – Double finesse

Dealer West : North-South vulnerable

NORTH
- ♠ K Q J 10
- ♡ 9 4
- ◇ A 7 6 5
- ♣ 8 5 3

WEST
- ♠ 9 5 3
- ♡ A Q 10 6
- ◇ K 3
- ♣ A K Q 6

EAST
- ♠ A 8 7 4 2
- ♡ 8 7 3 2
- ◇ Q 2
- ♣ J 2

SOUTH
- ♠ 6
- ♡ K J 5
- ◇ J 10 9 8 4
- ♣ 10 9 7 4

WEST	NORTH	EAST	SOUTH
1♣	No (1)	1♠	No
2NT	No	3♡ (2)	No
4♡ (3)	No	No	No

Bidding: (1) Not quite good enough for a vulnerable overcall, although the spades are very strong. A powerful 4-card suit may justify a 1-level overcall to indicate a good lead.
(2) Show the other major, even though it is very weak, rather than rebid the first suit There is no suit quality requirement for responder. 3♡ promises four hearts – any four will do – and implies five spades, as spades were bid first.
(3) West can support spades and hearts. Prefer the 4-4 fit.

Lead: ◇ J, top of sequence.

Correct play: Play low in dummy – if North also plays low, you win the ◇ Q and can discard the other diamond on the third round of clubs. North should also realize the danger: the ◇ J lead denies the queen and with five spades and four hearts on the bidding, East cannot hold more than four minor suit cards. North can deduce that East would win the ◇ Q and could discard the other diamond(s) if North plays low. Therefore, North should take the ace at trick 1, followed by a switch to the ♠ K.

One trick has been lost and two spade losers are unavoidable. Declarer must avoid losing a trump trick and the only chance with this holding is a double finesse: win the ♠ A and lead a heart, playing the ten if South plays low. When the ten wins, play a club to your jack and lead another heart. South plays the jack and dummy's queen, wins. Cash the ♡ A and ten tricks are there.

CHAPTER 8

DEMAND OPENINGS AND SLAM BIDDING

THE 2♠, 2♡ and 2◇ OPENINGS*

These are forcing for one round and promise 5+ cards in the suit bid in a hand just short of game. Opener needs more than eight playing tricks and the potential is generally in the 8½-9½ trick range. These are hands where if partner has one trick, game has a reasonable chance, yet responder might pass a 1-opening with only an ace or a king. With exactly eight playing tricks, there is less urgency to open with a 2-bid. Responder needs about two tricks for game and with such potential responder will reply to a 1-opening. Accordingly, if two tricks are needed for game, a 1-opening is safe enough. The 2♣ opening is used to force to game.

How to count your playing tricks: *In 3-card or longer suits:* count the ace and king as winners, count the queen as a winner if the suit has another honour and count every card after the third card as a winner. If the suit has the queen but no other honour, count the queen as a ½-winner. *In a doubleton:* count A = 1, K = 1, K-Q = 1, A-K = 2 and A-Q = 1½, but weaker holdings are losers. *In a singleton:* count the ace as a winner and all others as losers. A void is counted as no losers.

There is no set point count for these two-openings since it is the trick-taking power that is critical. Commonly, the point count will be around the 19-22 mark, but a 2-opening on a bit less is feasible, even as low as about 16 HCP when a powerful 7-card or 8-card suit is held. Count your tricks, not your points, for these actions. If you are accustomed to counting losers, hands in the 3½-4½ loser zone are suitable.

The 2♠, 2♡ or 2◇ opening might be a 1-suiter or a 2-suiter, but the long suit is always strong. There is no equivalent action where the long suit is clubs: up to nine tricks, open 1♣; with better than that, open 2♣.

RESPONDING TO THE 2♠, 2♡ AND 2◇ OPENINGS

The negative reply with any poor hand is 2NT. With 1½ quick tricks or more or with 8+ HCP, give some other response. The quick trick count is A-K = 2, A-Q = 1½, A = 1, K-Q = 1, K-x = ½. With 3+ support, raise opener's major to three if your hand contains an ace (e.g., 2♡ : 3♡), but raise to game (e.g., 2♡ : 4♡) with no aces, but with second-round controls (two kings or a king plus a singleton). Without support, bid your own suit in the normal order (longest first, higher first with a 5-5 pattern and up-the-line with 4-card suits). A jump-shift response (e.g., 2◇ : 3♠) is very rare and shows a solid suit (A-K-Q-J-x-x or A-K-Q-x-x-x-x or better). A response of 3NT shows 10-12 points balanced without decent support for opener's suit.

If right-hand opponent (RHO) interferes over partner's 2♠ / 2♡ / 2◇ opening, pass shows the negative response, bids are based on a positive response and double is for penalties. Because the opening 2-bid is usually very strong, it is not common to encounter an intervening bid.

After the negative 2NT response, responder is not obliged to bid again if opener repeats the suit opened (e.g., 2♠ : 2NT, 3♠) or bids game (e.g., 2♠ : 2NT, 4♡). However, responder is also not forced to pass. Responder could raise opener's suit or, without tolerance for opener's suit, introduce a good new suit.

After the 2NT response, a new suit by opener is forcing. The first priority is to support one of opener's suits. Responder may give preference to opener's first suit without promising any values (e.g., 2♠ : 2NT, 3♡ : 3♠). With anything worthwhile, responder would bid 4♠ over 3♡. Likewise, a raise to 4♡ in the above auction shows heart support, but little strength. As responder is forced to bid, no strength is promised by support at the cheapest level. Without support for opener, responder can introduce a new suit (5+ cards) or try 3NT.

Any response other than 2NT is forcing to game. In these auctions, support below game is more encouraging than bidding game, since it allows scope for cue-bidding. For example, 2◇ : 2♡, 2♠ : 3♠ is stronger than 4♠, and 2♡ : 2♠, 3♠ is more encouraging than 4♠. In general, it is responder's duty to explore slam after a 2♠, 2♡ or 2◇ opening, since opener has shown the playing strength within one trick. However, with a freakish hand, opener may take control and push to slam if a good trump fit has been found.

---

*A popular treatment, especially among tournament players, is to use these 2-opening as a weak pre-empt, but with only a 6-card suit. Strength: 6-10 HCP. For more information, see the *Guide To Better Duplicate*.

THE 2♣ GAME-DEMAND

The 2♣ opening shows 23+ HCP, or with less it will have three losers or fewer. Hands with three losers are worth ten playing tricks and that is sufficient to insist on game. The negative response to 2♣ is 2◇ and all other responses are positive, either 8+ HCP or a hand with 1½ quick tricks. Balanced hands of 23-24 points are opened 2♣, followed by a 2NT rebid. The 2♣ : 2◇, 2NT sequence (23-24 points balanced) is the only sequence that can be passed after a 2♣ opening (but with 2+ points, responder would bid on to game anyway). All other sequences are game-forcing. Balanced hands with 25+ HCP are opened 2♣, but over 2◇, opener will rebid 3NT (25-28 points) or higher.

Positive responses to 2♣: A suit bid other than 2◇ is taken as a 5+ suit and 2NT is used for a positive reply with no 5+ suit. If your long suit is clubs or diamonds, the response will be 3♣ / 3◇. A positive and a 4-4-4-1 pattern is awkward. Recommended is to respond 2◇ and bid a lot more later.

After a positive reply, a suit bid by opener is a 5+ suit and further bidding is natural. A positive reply to 2♣ frequently leads to a slam (23 HCP facing 8+ HCP, or 10+ tricks opposite 1½ tricks or better). After 2♣: 2NT, opener's 3♣ is Stayman; other suit bids show a 5+ suit and seek 3+ support. After 2♣ : 2NT, opener with 23-24 points balanced should not bid beyond game. The 2♣ opening already promised at least 23 HCP. With 25+HCP, opener has enough to push on to a small slam.

After 2♣ : 2◇ negative: A suit bid by opener is expected to be a 5+ suit and responder should support a major suit at once with 3+ support. Where responder raises opener's suit, a jump to game is weaker than a raise below game (e.g., 2♣ : 2◇, 2♠ : 4♠ is weaker than 2♣ : 2◇, 2♠ : 3♠). The jump-rebid to game says, 'I can support your suit, but have no ace, king, singleton or void,' while the raise below game says, 'I can support your suit and I have some additional values as well. My hand is not utterly hopeless for a slam.'

If responder changes suit after opener's suit bid, this also shows a 5+ suit (e.g., 2♣ : 2◇, 2♠ : 3◇ promises 5+ diamonds). If you cannot support opener's suit and do not have a 5-card suit, bid no-trumps at the cheapest level (e.g., 2♣ : 2◇, 2♠ : 2NT or 2♣ : 2◇, 3◇ : 3NT). After 2♣ : 2◇, 2NT responder can bid 3♣ Stayman, while other suits at the 3-level also have the same meaning as after a 2NT opening. Although 2♣ : 2◇, 2NT is not forcing, if responder does rebid, that creates a game-force.

If right-hand opponent intervenes over the 2♣ opening, the standard approach applies: Pass confirms a negative response, bids show a positive response and double is for penalties.

SLAM BIDDING

With balanced hands, either partner can bid 6NT at once if the partnership holds 33+ HCP and 7NT if the partnership has 37+ HCP. A slam can also be bid at once (e.g. 1♠ : 3♠, 6♠) with sufficient values for a slam and adequate trumps if the bidder can see that the opponents cannot cash the first two tricks. The slam bidder would need first-round control in all suits or first-round control in three suits and second-round control in the other suit. A first-round control is an ace or a void; a second-round control is a king or a singleton.

Most slams, however, cannot be bid directly. After it is apparent that the values for slam are present and a trump suit has been agreed (or you hold a self-sufficient trump suit, one which needs no support from partner), it is normal to ask for aces using 4NT Blackwood. A small slam needs about 33+ points and a grand slam about 37+ points. As these points need not all be high card points, you may hold 33+ points, but have two aces missing or 37+ points and an ace, a key king or a key queen missing. If you are in any doubt, settle for a good small slam rather than take a risk for a grand slam. Some good guides for slams include:

An opening hand opposite an opening hand is worth a game – an opening hand opposite an opener who can make a jump-rebid has prospects for slam if a decent trump fit can be found.

A positive reply to a 2♣ opening indicates slam values are present.

A small slam is a good bet if you have a strong trump fit, a secondary solid suit and cannot lose the first two tricks in any suit. A 5+ side suit which is headed by the A-K-Q is so valuable because it provides discards for losers in partner's hand

A grand slam is a good bet it you have a strong trump fit and are not missing any aces or the K-Q of trumps and there are no losers in the first three rounds of any suit. With 13 sure winners, play in 7NT.

Before using Blackwood, be sure of two things: firstly, adequate strength – enough aces cannot cure a deficiency in points – all four aces produce only four tricks and four aces and four kings add up to only eight tricks – secondly, the final destination. Perhaps there is a strong trump fit, or you have a powerful trump suit, or you are confident that no-trumps will be all right. If you are not sure of the correct denomination for the slam, keep making forcing bids until you learn enough about partner's hand. Then and only then should you embark on Blackwood 4NT.

BLACKWOOD 4NT AND 5NT – ASKING FOR ACES AND KINGS

A JUMP TO 4NT AFTER A SUIT BID ASKS PARTNER: 'HOW MANY ACES DO YOU HAVE?' THE REPLIES ARE:	AFTER THE ANSWER TO 4NT, A 5NT BID ASKS PARTNER: 'HOW MANY KINGS DO YOU HAVE?' THE REPLIES ARE:
5♣ = 0 or 4	6♣ = 0
5♢ = 1	6♢ = 1
5♡ = 2	6♡ = 2
5♠ = 3	6♠ = 3
	6NT = 4

A 4NT bid is usually Blackwood, asking for aces. The exception is if 4NT is a response to an opening bid in no-trumps (e.g., 1NT : 4NT *or* 2NT : 4NT). This is not Blackwood, but an invitation to 6NT. Opener is asked to pass with a minimum opening and to bid on with more than minimum points. Pass with the absolute minimum, bid 5NT with one extra point and 6NT if absolutely maximum. To check on aces after a no-trump opening, bid a suit first (e.g., 1NT : 3♡ *or* 2NT : 3♢) and rebid 4NT later. It is an ask for aces if a suit has been bid in the auction.

The answer to 4NT includes only aces, not voids. To deal with voids, use cue-bidding (see below). A bid of 5NT without using 4NT first is a Trump Ask for the A-K-Q of trumps. This is one possible set of replies to the 5NT Trump Ask: 6 of trump suit = 0 or 1 top honour, 7 of trump suit = 2-3 top honours. A simple and superior set of answers is: 6♣ = no trump honour, 6♢ = one, 6♡ = two and 7-of-the-trump-suit = all three.

In order to use the 5NT ask for kings after the answer to 4NT, you should have prospects for all thirteen tricks. The partnership should have the values for a grand slam, a strong trump suit and no aces should be missing. In other words, the use of 5NT asking for kings promises that the partnership holds all the aces.

The Blackwood 4NT bidder is in control of the final decision whether to stop at the 5-level if two aces are missing, whether to bid six, whether to try for seven, whether to play in a suit or in no-trumps and partner should accept that decision in normal circumstances. If you have the values for a slam and find one ace is missing, bid the small slam – do not give up at the 5-level.

CUE-BIDDING TO SLAMS: This is a more precise method than simply asking for aces and kings. In cue-bidding, partners are able to show each other specific aces, kings, voids and singletons. Aces and voids are first-round controls, kings and singletons are second-round controls. After a trump suit has been agreed and a game-force exists, the bid of a new suit is a cue-bid. For example, in 1♡ : 1♠, 3♠ : 4♢, the 4♢ bid is a cue-bid. The cue-bid states that you have interest in slam and have first-round control in the suit bid.

When making a cue-bid, first-round controls are shown before second-round controls. With two or more first-round controls, bid the cheapest first. The 4♢ cue-bid above not only shows the ace (or void) in diamonds, it also denies first-round control in clubs. With club control and diamond control, the cheaper 4♣ cue-bid would have been chosen. After a cue-bid, partner replies with another cue-bid or signs off in the trump suit. The bid of the trump suit does not show any specific control: it denies the ability or the willingness to make a further cue-bid. For example, after 2♠ : 3♠, 4♣ : 4♢, a 4♠ rebid by opener would deny first-round control in hearts.

A second-round control is shown by a bid in a suit where first-round control has already been shown by either partner, or by a bid in a suit where the bidder has previously denied first round control. With two or three second-round controls, bid the cheapest. To locate trump honours use 4NT or the 5NT Trump Ask (see above). Cue-bidding is best when you hold a void or an unguarded suit or you need to know about specific kings in partner's hand. Cue-bidding continues until one partner or the other has enough information to place the contract.

EXERCISES

A. How many playing tricks are each of these suits worth?

1. A K Q x x x
2. K Q J x x x x x
3. A K x x x x x
4. A K Q x x x x x
5. A Q J x x x x
6. A x x x x x
7. Q J 10 x x x x
8. A K x x x x x x
9. A J x x x x x
10. K x x x x x
11. K Q J x x x x
12. K J x x x x
13. Q J x x x x x x
14. A Q J x x x x x
15. J x x x x x x x

B. What is your response with these hands if partner opened (a) 2♣? (b) 2♢? (c) 2♡? (d) 2♠?

1.	972	2. ♠	K 8 5 4 2	3. ♠	8 6	4. ♠	K 7 2	5. ♠	K J 7 2
	♡ 7 3	♡	Q 6 4	♡	Q 7 6 3 2	♡	9 2	♡	6
	♢ 9 7 4 3 2	♢	9	♢	A Q 8 7 6	♢	K 8 6 2	♢	J 10 5 2
	876	♣	8 7 3 2	♣	4	♣	A J 4 3	♣	A Q 9 5

C. You opened 2♣ and partner bid 2♢, the negative response. What is your rebid with these hands?

1.	K Q	2. ♠	7	3. ♠	A J 5 2	4. ♠	A Q J 2	5. ♠	A K J 2
	♡ A K J 10 6 2	♡	A K Q	♡	A K J	♡	A	♡	A Q J 10
	♢ A K	♢	A K Q J 4	♢	K Q 6 4	♢	A 8	♢	A K Q 4
	Q J 3	♣	Q J 3 2	♣	A Q	♣	A K J 8 4 3	♣	6

D. The bidding has been 2♣ : 2♢, 2♠ : ? to you. What is your next action as responder with these hands?

1.	9 7	2. ♠	A 7 2	3. ♠	5	4. ♠	Q 7 6 2	5. ♠	- - -
	♡ 8 7 3	♡	6	♡	Q 8 7 6 3 2	♡	J 2	♡	6 2
	♢ 10 6 5 2	♢	9 7 6 4	♢	8 7 6	♢	9 6 2	♢	J 9 8 6 3 2
	♣ 9 7 5 3	♣	8 7 5 3 2	♣	J 8 5	♣	Q 9 7 2	♣	8 7 5 3 2

PARTNERSHIP BIDDING: How should these hands be bid? West is the dealer on all hands.

SET 19 – WEST	SET 19 – EAST	SET 20 – WEST	SET 20 – EAST
1. J 10 7 6	1. ♠ A K	1. ♠ K 9 5 2	1. ♠ A Q J 8 6 3
♡ 8 5 4 2	♡ A K 6	♡ Q 8 3	♡ 9 2
♢ A Q 3	♢ K J 6 4	♢ 6 4	♢ A K Q J
♣ A 4	♣ K Q 5 3	♣ K 7 4 3	♣ J
2. J 7 5 4 3 2	2. ♠ A 9	2. ♠ Q 8 7	2. ♠ A K J 9 5 2
♡ 7	♡ A K 5 4	♡ A J 8 6 3	♡ Q
♢ 7 4 2	♢ A K Q	♢ K 7 4	♢ A Q J
♣ 8 6 2	♣ A 9 4 3	♣ 3 2	♣ K Q J
3. K Q 10 3	3. ♠ J 7 6 4	3. ♠ K Q 9 7 4 2	3. ♠ 8
♡ A J 10	♡ Q 8 3 2	♡ A 8 6	♡ Q 9 5 4 3 2
♢ K 4	♢ 8 7	♢ A K	♢ 7 6 3
♣ A K Q J	♣ 9 5 3	♣ A K	♣ 8 5 4
4. 9 6 5 3 2	4. ♠ K 8	4. ♠ A K Q J	4. ♠ 8
♡ Q J 3 2	♡ A K 5 4	♡ 3	♡ A K 4
♢ 8	♢ K Q 6 3	♢ K Q 4 3 2	♢ A 9 7 6 5
♣ 7 3 2	♣ A K J	♣ A K J	♣ 9 7 4 3
5. ♠ K 6 5	5. ♠ A Q 2	5. ♠ - - -	5. ♠ A K Q 7 3 2
♡ A K 5 2	♡ 4 3	♡ A 9 8 4 2	♡ K Q 7 6 5
♢ A K Q 4	♢ 10 2	♢ 7 4 3 2	♢ A
♣ A 7	♣ K Q J 10 4 2	♣ 9 6 4 2	♣ A
6. ♠ A 9	6. ♠ K Q 7 4 3 2	6. ♠ A 6	6. ♠ J 8 3
♡ K Q J 10 8 6	♡ A 9 5	♡ 8 7 2	♡ 9 6 5 4
♢ A Q J	♢ K 5 3	♢ A K Q J 6 4 3	♢ 7 2
♣ K 9	♣ 8	♣ A	♣ 8 6 5 3

PLAY HANDS BASED ON DEMAND OPENINGS AND SLAM BIDDING

Hand 29: Slam bidding – Unblocking your winners – Protecting an entry to dummy

Dealer North : Game all

NORTH
♠ A K J 4 2
♡ J 4
◇ A K
♣ A K Q 2

WEST
♠ 8 7 5
♡ A 10 9 8
◇ 10 7 2
♣ 5 4 3

EAST
♠ Q 9 3
♡ 7 6
◇ 9 8 6 5
♣ 10 9 8 7

SOUTH
♠ 10 6
♡ K Q 5 3 2
◇ Q J 4 3
♣ J 6

WEST	NORTH	EAST	SOUTH
	2♣ (1)	No	2♡ (2)
No	2♠	No	3◇
No	4NT (3)	No	5♣ (4)
No	6NT (5)	All pass	

Bidding: (1) Artificial, forcing to game.
(2) Positive response, 8+ points and a 5+ suit.
(3) As no trump fit exists, but the values are there for a slam, North heads for 6NT. North plans to ask for aces and if South has the ♡ A, North intends to continue with 5NT, confirming that all the aces are held and looking for a grand slam if South happens to have significantly extra values.
(4) Shows 0 or 4 aces, clearly zero.
(5) If the values for a small slam are there, do not sign off just because an ace is missing. Take the plunge, bid the small slam.

Lead: ♣ 10. Top of sequence in the unbid suit is best.

Correct play: There are ten instant winners (two spades, four diamonds, four clubs) and two extra tricks can be set up in hearts. The ◇ A-K must be unblocked and dummy needs an entry to the diamonds. In addition, the heart tricks need to be established and if the defence ducks the first heart, dummy needs an entry to the second heart trick. It would be wrong to win the ♣ J, cash the ◇ A-K and then lead a heart: if West ducks this, declarer cannot enjoy two heart tricks and have an entry to dummy. Leave the ♣ J in dummy as an entry: win the ♣ A, cash ◇ A-K and then lead the ♡ J. If this is ducked, play another heart. Later, lead the ♣ 2 to dummy's jack to score your red suit winners and use the spade entries to hand for your black suit winners.

Hand 30: 2NT response to 2♣ – Use of Stayman – Finessing and safety plays

Dealer East : Love all

NORTH
♠ Q 10 6 5
♡ 10 9 8 4
◇ 7 6
♣ K 8 7

WEST
♠ A J 7 2
♡ J 6 2
◇ 9 4 3
♣ Q J 10

EAST
♠ K 9 4 3
♡ A K Q 5
◇ A K Q
♣ A 6

SOUTH
♠ 8
♡ 7 3
◇ J 10 8 5 2
♣ 9 5 4 3 2

WEST	NORTH	EAST	SOUTH
		2♣	No
2NT (1)	No	3♣ (2)	No
3♠ (3)	No	4NT	No
5◇ (4)	No	5NT (5)	No
6♣	No	6♠ (6)	All pass (7)

Bidding: (1) Positive reply with a balanced hand, no 5+ suit.
(2) Stayman, asking for a 4-card major.
(3) Shows four spades, denies four hearts.
(4) One ace.
(5) Confirms all aces are held and is looking for a grand slam.
(6) With a king missing, and perhaps the ♠ Q, too, a grand slam is too risky. 6NT is reasonable, but it may be necessary to ruff a heart or a club for the twelfth trick. On the actual cards, the play in 6♠ or 6NT would be the same.
(7) North should not tip off the bad break by doubling.

Lead: ♡ 10. Top of sequence is normal.

Correct play: The play of the spades varies according to whether you need three or four tricks. West should take the club finesse first: win the ♡ J, lead the ♣ Q. North should play low and the ♣ Q wins. Now you need only three spade tricks. To guard against a bad break, cash the ♠ A and lead low towards ♠ K-9-4. Play the nine if North plays low: if South wins, the ♠ K will draw the last spade. As the cards lie, the nine wins. If North plays the ♠ 10, win the ♠ K and force out the ♠ Q. Had the club finesse lost, play ♠ K and finesse the ♠ J.

Hand 31: Assessing grand slam prospects – Ruffing a loser – Coping with a bad trump break

Dealer South : North-South vulnerable

NORTH
- ♠ A K Q 4
- ♡ K Q J 9
- ◇ A K Q
- ♣ A 8

WEST
- ♠ 9 2
- ♡ 10 8 7 6
- ◇ 7 5 3 2
- ♣ J 10 9

EAST
- ♠ J 10 7 5 3
- ♡ 4
- ◇ 10 9 8
- ♣ Q 6 4 3

SOUTH
- ♠ 8 6
- ♡ A 5 3 2
- ◇ J 6 4
- ♣ K 7 5 2

WEST	NORTH	EAST	SOUTH
			No
No	2♣	No	2NT
No	3♣ (1)	No	3♡
No	4NT	No	5◇
No	5NT (2)	No	6◇
No	7♡ (3)	All pass	

Bidding: (1) Stayman. If a 4-4 major fit exists, this may produce one trick more than if the deal is played in no-trumps. If no major fit is found, you can still bid at least 6NT later.
(2) If partner has the ♣K, North has enough to bid seven.
(3) North can count twelve top winners and so there is no guarantee of a thirteenth trick for 7NT, a very poor contract which should be defeated easily, as long as East retains four spades, following the discarding rule, 'Keep length with dummy'. Played in hearts, the 13th trick can come from a ruff.

Lead: ♣J. Top of sequence.

Correct play: Win the lead and start on the trumps, ♡K, then ♡Q. If trumps were 3-2, it would be correct to draw the last trump. When trumps are 4-1, you must take one ruff before drawing all the trumps. Best is to switch to ♠A, ♠K and ruff the ♠4 with the *ace* of hearts: if you can afford it, ruff high. Lead your last heart to finesse dummy's ♡9 and then draw West's last trump. It would be an error to ruff a club in dummy because the South hand has no convenient entry to draw West's trumps.

Hand 32: Slam prospects after a negative response – Finding the best fit – Marked finesse

Dealer West : East-West vulnerable

NORTH
- ♠ - - -
- ♡ J 10 7
- ◇ K Q 8 6
- ♣ Q 9 6 5 4 3

WEST
- ♠ A K Q 10
- ♡ A K Q 8 6 4 2
- ◇ 4
- ♣ A

EAST
- ♠ 8 6 5 4 3
- ♡ 5
- ◇ A 7 3 2
- ♣ J 7 2

SOUTH
- ♠ J 9 7 2
- ♡ 9 3
- ◇ J 10 9 5
- ♣ K 10 8

WEST	NORTH	EAST	SOUTH
2♣ (1)	No	2◇	No
2♡ (2)	No	2♠ (3)	No
4NT (4)	No	5◇	No
7♠ (5)	No	No	No

Bidding: (1) There is a temptation on freak hands like this to open 6♡, but not only does this risk missing a grand slam, but you may also be in the wrong trump suit. With only one loser, you are worth 6♡, but you can still bid 6♡ later if nothing better turns up.
(2) It is quite enough to bid 2♡ as this is forcing to game. A jump to 3♡ would be suitable with a solid 1-suiter, but not when a second suit is held.
(3) Shows 5+ spades and denies heart support. Without support and with only four spades, East would rebid 2NT.

(4) West knows that a 9-card fit exists in spades and checks whether East has the missing ace. If not, West would rebid 6♠.
(5) West should not rebid 7♡ or 7NT, both of which could be defeated on a diamond lead, which removes the only entry to East before the bad spade break is revealed.

Lead: ◇ J, top of sequence.

Correct play: Win the ◇ A and lead a spade to the ace. If both opponents had followed, you would draw the remaining trumps and then run the heart suit. When North shows out, you need to return to hand to finesse the ♠ 10. The only entry is via a heart ruff, so cash the ♡A, ruff a low heart next and then lead a spade, finessing the ♠ 10 when South plays low. Draw South's last two trumps with the ♠ K-Q and claim the rest.

REVISION TEST ON PART 1

The answers to all these questions can be found in Chapters 1-8. Give yourself 1 mark for each correct answer. If you score less than 40, it will profit you to revise the relevant sections.

A. You opened 1 ◇ and partner responded 1 ♠. What is your rebid with each of these hands?

1. ♠ K Q 2	2. ♠ A 7	3. ♠ - - -	4. ♠ A 7	5. ♠ A 8 7 2
♡ A 2	♡ K 8 6 3	♡ A K 8 2	♡ A J 3 2	♡ - - -
◇ A Q 9 6 4	◇ J 9 7 6 4	◇ K 7 6 4 3	◇ A K 9 8 6 2	◇ A K 10 9 4 3
♣ 7 6 2	♣ A Q	♣ K 8 5 4	♣ 7	♣ K J 6

6. ♠ K 7 2	7. ♠ 7	8. ♠ 7	9. ♠ J 7	10. ♠ A 8 7 2
♡ K 9 7 3	♡ K J 3 2	♡ A K J	♡ 2	♡ J 2
◇ A Q 9 6 4	◇ Q 9 7 6 4	◇ K Q J 8 7 6 4	◇ A K 8 6 2	◇ A Q 9 4 3
♣ 3	♣ A K Q	♣ J 8	♣ A K Q J 7	♣ K Q

B. Partner opened 1 ♣ and rebid 1 ♠ over your 1 ♡ response. What is your rebid with each of these hands?

1. ♠ K 7 3	2. ♠ A 7	3. ♠ A	4. ♠ J 3 2	5. ♠ A 8 7 2
♡ Q 8 7 3 2	♡ Q 8 6 3 2	♡ K J 10 9 8 6 4	♡ A Q 7 6	♡ A K 9 6 2
◇ J 7 3	◇ 7 6	◇ 8 7	◇ 2	◇ 4 3
♣ Q 9	♣ J 9 7 3	♣ K 8 5	♣ K 9 8 4 2	♣ Q 2

6. ♠ 8 7 3 2	7. ♠ Q 7 6	8. ♠ K Q 9 5 2	9. ♠ A 7 2	10. ♠ A 6 2
♡ K Q 8 6 5	♡ A Q 8 6	♡ A K Q 6 3 2	♡ J 10 7 6 3 2	♡ Q J 7 5
◇ 6 4	◇ K 9 7	◇ 3	◇ 2	◇ K Q 6
♣ Q 7	♣ 8 3 2	♣ 6	♣ J 9 7	♣ K 8 5

C. Partner opened 1NT. What is your response with each of these hands?

1. ♠ A J 8 7	2. ♠ J	3. ♠ A J 5 3 2	4. ♠ J 8 2	5. ♠ J 8 7 5 4 2
♡ 7 3	♡ A Q 6 5 4 3	♡ K J 6 2	♡ A J 7 3	♡ 6
◇ A Q 9 2	◇ 7 6 4	◇ J 7 6	◇ K 6 5 2	◇ Q 9 4 3
♣ 10 5 2	♣ K Q 3	♣ 4	♣ 9 7	♣ 7 3

D. What would your answer be on the hands in C. if partner had opened 2NT?

E. Partner opened 1NT and replied 2 ◇ to your 2 ♣ Stayman. What is your rebid on each of these hands?

1. ♠ K 7 4 2	2. ♠ A 7	3. ♠ A 5 3	4. ♠ A 7 3 2	5. ♠ A 9 8 7 2
♡ A Q 7 3	♡ A Q 3 2	♡ Q J 7	♡ A J 5 4 3	♡ K J 8 4 2
◇ A J 9	◇ J 10 4	◇ A J 3	◇ 2	◇ K Q
♣ A 2	♣ 9 7 3 2	♣ A K Q 4	♣ A 9 7	♣ 5

F. If partner opened 2NT, what would your response be on the hands in E. above?

G. Partner opened 1 ♣, you responded 1 ♠ and partner rebid 1NT. What is your rebid on these hands?

1. ♠ K 7 6 4 3	2. ♠ A J 7 5 2	3. ♠ A 8 6 3 2	4. ♠ K J 9 7 2	5. ♠ Q J 10 9 3 2
♡ Q J 7 3	♡ A Q 3 2	♡ J 2	♡ A J	♡ - - -
◇ J 6 4	◇ Q 9 7	◇ 4 3	◇ 8 6 2	◇ A 9 4 3
♣ 3	♣ 3	♣ J 8 5 4	♣ A 9 7	♣ K 8 2

H. Partner opened 1 ♣, you responded 1 ♡ and partner rebid 2NT. What is your rebid on these hands?

1. ♠ K 7	2. ♠ K 7 5 2	3. ♠ A 9 7 2	4. ♠ A 7 2	5. ♠ A 8 7
♡ J 10 8 6 3	♡ A 9 6 4	♡ K J 6 4 3	♡ A J 3 2	♡ Q 10 9 4 3 2
◇ 9 6 4	◇ Q 9	◇ 8	◇ A J 8	◇ 3
♣ A 3 2	♣ 7 3 2	♣ 9 5 4	♣ 8 4 2	♣ 8 5 2

PART 2

DEFENSIVE AND DESTRUCTIVE BIDDING

This part covers your side's actions after the opponents have opened the bidding and how you can try to shut the opposition out of the bidding.

Chapter 9 deals with overcalls: when to overcall and when to pass, when to overcall with a suit and when to overcall 1NT, and what action to take in response to an overcall.

Chapter 10 deals with jump-overcalls: the standard strong jump-overcall and also the weak and the intermediate jump-overcalls and partner's responding strategy in each case.

Chapter 11 deals with the 'unusual 2NT' for the minor suits: when to use it, partner's actions after you use it, when to sacrifice and when to defend, and defence against the unusual 2NT. It also deals with other 2-suited overcalls.

Chapter 12 covers pre-emptive openings and pre-emptive overcalls: when to pre-empt and when to overcall, how high to pre-empt, when to pre-empt with a good hand and how to use the gambling 3NT overcall.

Chapters 13, 14, 15 and 16 deal with takeout doubles: when to make a takeout double and when to prefer an overcall, how to respond to partner's takeout double with hopelessly weak hands (Chapter 13), with moderate hands (Chapter 14), with strong hands (Chapter 15) and how to reply to the double when third player takes action over the double (Chapter 16).

CHAPTER 9

STANDARD OVERCALLS AND RESPONSES

THE SIMPLE SUIT OVERCALL

The functions of a simple suit overcall ('simple' means 'at the cheapest level') are:

- To indicate a sound lead to partner
- To rob the opponents of bidding space
- To compete for the part-score
- To lay a basis for reaching a game

Note: An overcall does not require as many points as an opening bid. An opener needs about 12+ points, but you may overcall at the 1-level with 8+ HCP or at the 2-level with 10+ HCP. The emphasis *when opening* is on strength, the number of points held, and length of suit, but the quality of the suit opened is immaterial. *For overcalling,* the quality of the suit is the paramount consideration; the length of the suit is also important, but the points held are not the deciding factor. You may overcall on a weak hand if your long suit is strong, but you should not overcall even with a strong hand if the suit is weak. Where your long suit is weak, you may be able to enter the auction with a double or with a 1NT overcall, but if these are also unsuitable, you should pass at first and perhaps enter the auction later. With length and strength in the opposition's suit(s), it is usually best to pass initially and plan to defend unless the hand is worth a 1NT overcall (see later) or you hold 19+ points (strong enough to double first and bid no-trumps later).

Normally an overcall suit should have 5+ cards with at least two honours, including the ace, king or queen.

Strength expected: at the 1-level, 8-16 HCP; at the 2-level, 10-16 HCP; at the 3-level, about 12-16 HCP.

Some players feel that they must double whenever they hold 13+ HCP. This approach is not sound since if you double with a 1-suited hand, partner will almost never bid your long suit and the bidding may climb too high to show your long suit later. It is quite safe to overcall on hands up to 16 HCP, since partner should reply to the overcall when holding 9+ HCP, and may reply with even less if holding support for your suit or with something useful to bid. Thus, you cannot miss a game if you overcall and it is not necessary to double with the 1-suited hand in the 12-15 HCP range. Takeout doubles are suitable for 2-suited or 3-suited hands and are also used for 1-suited hands with 17+ HCP, those too strong for the simple overcall.

OVERCALLING WITH A 4-CARD SUIT: This is permitted only at the 1-level and the suit must contain three of the top four honours. Suits such as A-K-Q-x, A-K-J-x, A-Q-J-x and K-Q-J-x have such a strong lead-directing element that they justify misleading partner as to length of the suit held. At worst, partner may raise you with just three trumps. If so, your suit is so powerful that you should be able to handle it. The main benefits of these 4-card overcalls are that partner makes the best lead and the opponents may forego 3NT.

THE SUIT QUALITY TEST: How strong a suit must you have to justify an overcall? A sound guide is the Suit Quality Test, which measures your suit strength. The hand may be strong enough for an overcall, but if the suit quality is below par, you should be very wary of overcalling in that suit.

COUNT THE CARDS IN THE SUIT YOU WISH TO BID.

ADD THE HONOUR CARDS IN THE SUIT YOU WISH TO BID.

IF THE TOTAL EQUALS OR EXCEEDS THE NUMBER OF TRICKS TO BE BID, OVERCALL.

IF THE TOTAL IS LESS THAN THAT, DO NOT OVERCALL IN THAT SUIT.

Thus, Length + Honours should equal or exceed tricks to be bid. When counting honours for this test, count the J or 10 only if the suit also has a higher honour. Thus, the suit quality of K-10-x-x-x is 7, and the suit quality of Q-J-x-x-x-x is 8, but J-x-x-x-x measures only 5 – do not count the jack if no higher honour is held in that suit.

If you intend to overcall at the 1-level, your suit's quality should be 7+. For an overcall at the 2-level, your suit's quality should be 8+, and if you wish to overcall at the 3-level, your suit's quality should be 9+. Of course, if the suit quality total is more than the tricks for which you intend to bid, that is quite all right. Do not jump-overcall just because your suit is especially good. Jump-overcalls are covered in Chapter 10.

RESPONDING TO THE SUIT OVERCALL

The modern style is to reply to an overcall with about the same strength as replying to a suit opening, even though the overcall might be quite a bit below opening bid strength. This applies particularly when giving a single raise to partner's overcall. A change of suit at the 1-level or a 1NT reply is a touch stronger than the same action in reply to an opening 1-bid. It is safe to raise the overcall with a weak hand. If you have 6-9 points and partner has only 8 points, the opponents will not let your side play at the 2-level.

0-4 HCP: Pass, even with good support for partner.

5-6 HCP: Normally pass unless you can raise partner's suit. Do not support with such a poor hand if balanced or with a weak 3-card holding as your support.

7-8 HCP: Bid with support for partner's suit, or bid 1NT or bid a new suit at the 1-level with something worthwhile, otherwise pass. Chances for game are not good. You are too weak for a new suit at the 2-level.

9+HCP: Find some bid or other. Support partner, bid no-trumps or bid your own 5-card or longer suit.

A single raise = 6-9 HCP with three or four trumps, balanced shape, and a jump raise = 6-9 HCP with 4+ trumps and a singleton, whether partner's overcall was at the 1-level or 2-level. Raising a 1-level major suit overcall to game is based on excellent shape, normally 5+ trumps and an unbalanced hand. To show a strong raise, 10+ HCP, of partner's overcall, bid the opponents' suit with three trumps for partner and jump-bid their suit with 4+ support for partner.

If you do not have a hand suitable for a raise, you can respond to a 1-level overcall with 1NT with 8-11 points, 2NT with 12-14 and 3NT with 15+. In each case, you must have at least one stopper in the enemy suit. If their suit is known to be at least a 5-card suit, it is desirable to hold a second stopper or at least a potential second stopper. Single stoppers are A-x, K-x, Q-x-x, J-x-x-x or better. Double stoppers include A-Q, A-J-10, K-Q-10, Q-J-9-x or better. Potential double stoppers include A-J-x, K-Q-x, K-J-x, Q-10-x-x or better, and these become full double stoppers if an extra card is held, e.g., K-J-x-x can be considered a double stopper. A 2NT response to a 2-level overcall is about 11-13 HCP and a jump to 3NT is justified with about 14+ HCP or better. In each case, you must again hold at least one stopper in the enemy suit.

If you respond with a new suit at the 1-level, this can be a 4+ suit with 7+ HCP. A new suit at the 2-level would be a good 5-card suit and 10+ HCP. Should a change-of-suit response to an overcall be forcing? Either approach is playable, but recommended is to play a new suit reply as forcing for one round.

A 2NT jump-response to an overcall is not forcing, even though it shows opening values. The jump-shift reply to an overcall is 16+ HCP and this is forcing to game.

After partner's non-forcing reply to your overcall, pass if your overcall was minimum and you are reasonably satisfied with partner's bid. Keep on bidding if:

● Partner's reply was forcing,   *or*

● You have more than a minimum overcall (e.g., you are in the 12-16 HCP zone),   *or*

● You are minimum, but you have something extra worth showing or you dislike partner's bid.

EXERCISE: Your right open-hand opponent opened 1 ◇ . What action should you take with these hands?

1. ♠ 7 2	2. ♠ A 9	3. ♠ A K Q J	4. ♠ 8 4	5. ♠ J 7 2
♡ K Q 9 4 2	♡ Q 7 3 2	♡ 7 3	♡ K Q 9	♡ 6
◇ A J 5	◇ A J 9	◇ 8 2	◇ 4 3	◇ A K 9 4 3
♣ 9 8 3	♣ J 7 3 2	♣ 8 7 5 4 3	♣ A Q J 6 4 2	♣ K Q J 2

TREATMENT OF BALANCED HANDS AFTER THEY OPEN

0-11 HCP: Always pass unless you have a powerful suit to overcall.

12-15 HCP: Pass, unless your hand is suitable for a takeout double or you have a strong suit to overcall.

16-18 HCP: Overcall 1NT with a stopper in their suit; without a stopper in their suit, double for takeout. Takeout doubles are covered in Chapters 13-15.

19+ HCP: Make a takeout double initially and bid again later.

The above strategy applies only if your hand is balanced and may not apply for unbalanced hands. If you hold a balanced hand after they open the bidding, it is risky to enter the bidding, because it is very easy for them to double your side for penalties. If you do not have a strong suit or a good trump fit, the penalties can be very severe. Even with opening values in the 13-15 range, it is better to pass than to intervene with a balanced hand unless the hand qualifies for a takeout double (see Chapter 13) or you have a suit strong enough for an overcall. In general, if your main strength is in the enemy suit, prefer to pass unless your hand qualifies for a 1NT overcall or if you hold 19+ HCP. With that you can double and rebid no-trumps with a suitable hand as long as you have one or more stoppers in their suit.

THE 1NT OVERCALL

This shows 16-18 HCP, balanced shape and at least one stopper in their suit. With a double stopper, you may overcall 1NT with just 15 HCP, as your points are well placed over the opening bidder. If suitable for no-trumps, it is better to overcall 1NT with 15 points than to pass.

If your hand fits a 1NT overcall, nevertheless prefer to double if they opened with 1♣ or 1◇ *and* your pattern is 4-4-3-2 *and* you hold two 4-card majors. As always, a major suit trump fit is more attractive than no-trumps and if you have 4-4 in the majors, the chance of finding a major suit fit is very high if you make a takeout double. If you overcall 1NT, partner will normally pass with 0-7 points, but if you double, partner is forced to reply and any major suit fit will come to light.

BIDDING AFTER THE 1NT OVERCALL

Use the same structure after a 1NT overcall as after a 1NT opening. Thus, 2NT invites game (but only 8-9 points here), a 2♣ response is Stayman and other suit bids have their normal meaning. This means you do not have to remember two sets of bids, one when your side opens 1NT and another when your side overcalls 1NT. However, you must remember the different point range for the 1NT overcall.

After a 1NT overcall, some pairs prefer to use a bid of the enemy suit as Stayman and 2♣ as a natural, weak bid, showing a long club suit (unless the opening bid was 1♣). The logic of this approach is that if the opponents have opened and partner has overcalled 1NT, there is a greater need than usual to make a weak takeout bid, so that 2♣ is often more useful for the weak hand with long clubs. Each partnership needs to settle which approach is to be used, preferably *before* a disaster occurs.

EXERCISE A: Your right open-hand opponent opened 1◇. What action should you take with these hands?

1. ♠ K J 4 2	2. ♠ A K Q 9	3. ♠ A 9	4. ♠ A Q 6	5. ♠ K 7 4 2
♡ A 3	♡ Q 2	♡ K Q 9 2	♡ K Q 9 3	♡ Q 4
◇ Q 9 6	◇ 7 6 4	◇ A J 6	◇ 6 5	◇ A K 8
♣ J 8 4 3	♣ 9 7 3 2	♣ K 8 4 3	♣ A J 5 3	♣ Q 6 3 2

6. ♠ K 7 2	7. ♠ A 7 3 2	8. ♠ A 9 8	9. ♠ K Q	10. ♠ A 4
♡ A K 2	♡ A Q 4 3	♡ K 9 2	♡ A J 2	♡ A Q J 7 3
◇ 9 6 4	◇ K 6	◇ A Q 4	◇ A K 8 6	◇ A 7 2
♣ A Q 7 3	♣ K 8 2	♣ Q 10 5 4	♣ K 9 7 5	♣ K 8 2

B: Your right open-hand opponent opened 1♠. What action should you take with these hands?

1. ♠ Q J 3	2. ♠ 9 7	3. ♠ A Q 2	4. ♠ A J 2	5. ♠ A J 10 8 7 2
♡ 7	♡ A 2	♡ J	♡ K J	♡ - - -
◇ A K 9 6	◇ A Q J 9 7 6	◇ 8 7 6 4 3	◇ A K 8 6	◇ A K 9 4
♣ Q 8 5 4 2	♣ 7 5 2	♣ A K 5 4	♣ Q J 7 2	♣ J 4 2

C. Left-hand opponent opened 1♣, partner overcalled 1♡ and right-hand opponent passed. What action would you take with each of these hands?

1. ♠ K 8 4 3	2. ♠ 8 7 5	3. ♠ 6 4	4. ♠ A 7 2	5. ♠ A K 7
♡ 7 6	♡ Q 9 6 3 2	♡ K 9 3 2	♡ 8 3 2	♡ K 6 3
◇ K 7 6 3	◇ 6 4	◇ A 7 6 4	◇ Q J 2	◇ Q J 6 5 3
♣ 9 4 3	♣ Q 7 5	♣ 9 3 2	♣ 9 8 5 2	♣ 8 2

6. ♠ A K 7 5 2	7. ♠ A K 7 5 2	8. ♠ A 9 6	9. ♠ A J 2	10. ♠ A Q 7
♡ 7 3	♡ A J 8 6 4	♡ J 2	♡ Q 4 2	♡ 6
◇ A J 8 6 4	◇ 7 3	◇ J 9 6 2	◇ J 10 7 3	◇ K Q 8 4 3
♣ 3	♣ 2	♣ K 8 5 4	♣ K Q 10	♣ J 8 3 2

11. ♠ A Q 2	12. ♠ A 7 4	13. ♠ A J 10 6 2	14. ♠ Q 7 2	15. ♠ A K J
♡ K 3	♡ 8 3 2	♡ K 2	♡ A J	♡ 6 3 2
◇ Q J 10 4	◇ J 9 7 6	◇ A K Q 4	◇ A K Q J 2	◇ A K Q 3
♣ K Q 9 3	♣ K 7 3	♣ 5 4	♣ 9 7 3	♣ 8 6 2

D. Right-hand opponent opened 1♣, you overcalled 1♠, left-hand opponent passed and your partner responded 1NT. Right-hand opponent has passed. What action would you take now with these hands?

1. ♠ K Q 10 4 2	2. ♠ A J 9 6 3 2	3. ♠ A Q J 9 2	4. ♠ A J 8 7 2	5. ♠ A K Q 2
♡ A 3	♡ 4 2	♡ J 9 8	♡ J	♡ 6 2
◇ J 7 3 2	◇ K Q J	◇ A 4	◇ A Q 8 6 2	◇ K 9 4 3
♣ 6 2	♣ 3 2	♣ K 8 5	♣ 9 7	♣ 8 7 3

PARTNERSHIP BIDDING: How should the following hands be bid? South is the dealer and there is no North-South bidding other than that indicated for each hand.

SET 21 – WEST	SET 21 – EAST	SET 22 – WEST	SET 22 – EAST
1. South opens 1♡.	1. South opens 1♡.	1. South opens 1♠.	1. South opens 1♠.
♠ A Q 10 5 4	♠ K 9 8 7 6	♠ 6 2	♠ 9 5 3
♡ 5 3 2	♡ 7	♡ K 7 3	♡ A Q 9 6 5
◇ 7 5	◇ A K 8 3 2	◇ A 4	◇ K Q 8
♣ K J 8	♣ 9 5	♣ A Q 8 6 4 2	♣ 7 3
2. South opens 1◇.	2. South opens 1◇.	2. South opens 1◇.	2. South opens 1◇.
♠ A J 10 8 6	♠ K 7 5 2	♠ A J 10 7 2	♠ K 9 8 3
♡ Q J 2	♡ K 8 6	♡ K Q 9	♡ A 7
◇ 7 3	◇ J 9	◇ 7	◇ 9 8 5 3
♣ K J 9	♣ A Q 3 2	♣ A 8 4 3	♣ Q 5 2
3. South opens 1♣.	3. South opens 1♣.	3. South opens 1♠.	3. South opens 1♠.
♠ 7 2	♠ K Q J	♠ A K 8	♠ 6 4 2
♡ A K Q 8 2	♡ J 9 5 4	♡ J 10 3	♡ A Q 2
◇ 7 6 4	◇ A J 10 3	◇ K 4	◇ A 8 5
♣ 8 3 2	♣ Q 6	♣ A J 10 7 2	♣ 9 6 4 3
4. South opens 1♡.	4. South opens 1♡.	4. South opens 1♡.	4. South opens 1♡.
♠ 4 3	♠ K 9 7	♠ A Q J	♠ 8 6 5 4 2
♡ 6 3 2	♡ A Q 7	♡ A 9 8	♡ 7
◇ A 8	◇ K 6 3	◇ K Q 3	◇ A J 8
♣ A K Q 7 4 3	♣ 8 6 5 2	♣ Q 7 5 4	♣ K J 6 2
5. South opens 1♣.	5. South opens 1♣.	5. South opens 1◇.	5. South opens 1◇.
♠ K Q J 8 6	♠ A 7 4	♠ A Q J 7 2	♠ K 4 3
♡ A 8 7	♡ 9 6	♡ 8 6 2	♡ K Q 5
◇ 4 3	◇ J 8 7 6 2	◇ 7 2	◇ A Q 8 3
♣ 9 8 5	♣ K Q 7	♣ Q J 3	♣ K 9 8

PLAY HANDS ON STANDARD OVERCALLS AND RESPONSES

Hand 33: 1NT overcall – Stayman – Card combination and compulsory duck – Card-reading

Dealer North : Love all

          NORTH
          ♠ Q 7 6 2
          ♡ 7
          ◊ A 8 4 3 2
          ♣ Q 9 7

WEST   **EAST**
♠ J 9 4   ♠ A 10
♡ 6 5 3 2   ♡ K J 10 9 4
◊ 10 7   ◊ K Q J
♣ 8 4 3 2   ♣ 10 6 5

          SOUTH
          ♠ K 8 5 3
          ♡ A Q 8
          ◊ 9 6 5
          ♣ A K J

WEST	NORTH	EAST	SOUTH
	No	1♡	1NT (1)
No	2♣ (2)	No	2♠
No	4♠	All pass	

Bidding: (1) 16-18 balanced, stopper in their suit.
(2) Stayman, as though partner had opened 1NT. (If the partnership is using 2♣ over a 1NT overcall as a weak hand with long clubs, North would bid 2♡, the enemy suit, as Stayman, and the rest of the auction would be the same.)

Lead: ♡ 5. It is normal to lead partner's suit unless you have a very strong reason to choose another lead. From three or four rags, lead second top (middle-up-down).

Correct play: Declarer is bound to lose two diamonds, so that it is vital to hold the trump losers to just the trump ace.

With Q-x-x-x opposite K-x-x-x, to lose just one trick, you must lead towards one of your honours and hope second player holds ace-doubleton: *no other holding allows you just one loser.* If second player plays the ace, your king and queen are high; if second player plays low, play your honour, which will win, and then duck the next round of the suit, praying that the ace will fall. If it does, your remaining honour is high and can capture the last card in that suit. To succeed, you must make the player with the ace play second on the first round of the suit. As there are 25 HCP between declarer and dummy, and only 15 HCP are missing, the ♠ A should be with East for the opening bid. As you intend to play East for the ♠ A, win the heart, ruff a heart and lead a low spade to your king. When it wins, duck the next spade – do not play dummy's queen! Once the ace has dropped, you will be able to play the ♠ Q later to draw West's last trump.

Hand 34: 1NT overcall – Suit response – Card-reading – Avoiding a futile finesse

Dealer East : North-South vulnerable

          NORTH
          ♠ 9 7
          ♡ 8 7 6
          ◊ 9 8 6 4 3
          ♣ 10 9 6

WEST   **EAST**
♠ A Q J   ♠ K 5 4 3 2
♡ A K   ♡ J 10
◊ Q J 10   ◊ 7 5 2
♣ 8 7 5 4 2   ♣ A Q 3

          SOUTH
          ♠ 10 8 6
          ♡ Q 9 5 4 3 2
          ◊ A K
          ♣ K J

WEST	NORTH	EAST	SOUTH
		No	1♡
1NT (1)	No	3♠ (2)	No
4♠ (3)	No	No	No

Bidding: (1) 16-18 points, balanced, stopper in hearts.
(2) Promises five spades and is forcing to game.
(3) Shows 3+ spade support.

Lead: ◊ K. From A-K-x or A-K-x-x or longer, the standard lead is the ace. When the king is led, followed by the ace, this indicates A-K doubleton and a desire to ruff. Partner should give a suit-preference signal on the second round to indicate where an entry is held. If a partnership systemically leads the king from A-K-x, A-K-x-x or longer, then the A-K doubleton is shown by leading the ace, followed by the king.

Correct play: After cashing ◊ A, ◊ K, South switches to a heart. The club shift is too risky. As South plus dummy hold 30 HCP, East should hold virtually all of the missing points for the jump to 3♠.

When East gains the lead, East should draw trumps and then tackle the clubs. With two diamond losers, declarer cannot afford two club losers. The normal club play is to finesse the queen, but here that play is bound to fail. Declarer and dummy hold 27 HCP. With 13 HCP missing, the ♣ K will be with South because of the opening bid. *When the finesse cannot win, play for the drop.* After trumps have been drawn, play a club to the ace and then a low club. When the king falls doubleton, the ♣ Q is high.

Hand 35: Raising partner's overcall – Card combination – Card-reading

	WEST	NORTH	EAST	SOUTH
				1 ◇
	1 ♠	No	3 ♠ (1)	No
	4 ♠ (2)	No	No	No

Dealer South : East-West vulnerable

NORTH
♠ 5
♡ 10 8 6 5
◇ 10 9 2
♣ 8 7 6 5 3

WEST
♠ A J 10 6 2
♡ K 7 2
◇ J 7
♣ A J 4

EAST
♠ K 9 7 3
♡ Q J 4 3
◇ K 3
♣ K Q 9

SOUTH
♠ Q 8 4
♡ A 9
◇ A Q 8 6 5 4
♣ 10 2

Bidding: (1) Shows support and the equivalent of a minimum opening hand. It is not forcing, but highly encouraging. Some pairs prefer to use the jump-raise as pre-emptive and would bid 3 ◇ to show 4-card support and a strong raise.
(2) With 12+ HCP, accept the invitation.

Lead: ◇ 10. It is normal to lead partner's suit and from K-Q-x, Q-J-x, J-10-x and 10-9-x, the top card is led. From 3-card suits headed by an honour *plus a touching card,* lead top.

Correct play: Play low from dummy, but South wins the ◇ Q and cashes the ◇ A. South's best switch then is to the ♡ A and another heart, hoping that North might hold the ♡ K.

Having lost the first three tricks, declarer must avoid a trump loser. The normal play with nine trumps missing the queen is to play the ace and king, hoping that the queen drops singleton or doubleton. However, if you can deduce the location of the queen, you may be able to capture the queen via a finesse. The best guide is to count dummy's HCP, add your own and deduct the total from 40. Here dummy has 14 HCP and declarer has 14, so that 12 are missing. As South opened the bidding, it is a virtual certainty that the ♠ Q is with South. Therefore, do not play for the drop but play South to hold the ♠ Q. When you gain the lead, play a spade to dummy's king and a spade back, finessing when South plays low. Draw South's trump and claim.

Hand 36: Bidding over a suit overcall – Card combination – Card-reading for a passed hand

	WEST	NORTH	EAST	SOUTH
	No	No	No	1 ♣
	1 ♠ (1)	2 ♡ (2)	No	4 ♡ (3)
	No	No	No	

Dealer West : Game all

NORTH
♠ 6 5 4 3 2
♡ A J 10 9 5
◇ 9
♣ A 2

WEST
♠ A K Q 9 8
♡ 6 4
◇ 10 8 6 3 2
♣ 5

EAST
♠ 7
♡ K 2
◇ Q J 7 5 4
♣ 9 7 6 4 3

SOUTH
♠ J 10
♡ Q 8 7 3
◇ A K
♣ K Q J 10 8

Bidding: (1) Even though neither West nor East could open, West should overcall, as spades is the only lead West wants.
(2) Shows at least five hearts and 10-12 points, not more since North passed initially.
(3) South is worth 18 points in support of hearts. It would be a serious error to rebid clubs when support for partner's major is present, and 3 ♡ would not do the South hand justice.

Lead: ♠ 7. A singleton in partner's suit is a very attractive lead.

Correct play: West wins with the ♠ Q (a defender should win with the cheapest card possible) and cashes another spade.

The best chance to defeat the contract is for West to switch to a club, hoping for a club ruff if East has the ♣ A or can win the lead before trumps have been drawn.

The normal way to play the heart suit is to finesse for the king, but if declarer does that here East would win and the club return ruffed by West would defeat the game. *When a finesse is sure to fail play for the drop.* When East shows out on the second round of spades, it is not hard to work out that West began with A-K-Q-x-x in spades, a total of 9 HCP. As West passed as dealer, can West hold the ♡ K? That would give West 12 HCP and a strong 5-card suit. With as much as that, West would have opened. Thus, East has the ♡ K, the heart finesse is futile and so you should play the ♡ A first. It is not the losing finesse that defeats you. It is the club ruff that follows. Even if the location of the ♡ K is not known, playing the ♡ A is a sound precaution against a possible club ruff.

CHAPTER 10

SINGLE JUMP-OVERCALLS AND RESPONSES

A jump-overcall skips at least one level over a bid by an opponent, who has opened or responded to an opening bid. When writing the order of bidding, a common approach is to write bids by the opponents in brackets. Thus, (1♠) : 2♣ indicates that an opponent opened 1♠ and our side overcalled 2♣. A single jump-overcall is an overcall one above the minimum possible. For example, (1♢) : 1♠ is a simple overcall and (1♢) : 2♠ is a single jump-overcall. Likewise, (1♠) : 2♡ is a simple overcall and (1♠) : 3♡ is a single jump-overcall. Double and triple jump-overcalls are pre-emptive (see Chapter 12 on Pre-empts).

Regardless of the system you play for your opening bids, the partnership may stipulate which kind of single jump-overcalls shall be played. A bidding system (Acol, Standard American, Precision and so on) refers to the rules and agreements governing the bidding when your side opens the bidding. It need not restrict the approach you adopt when the opponents open the bidding. There are three basic types of single jump-overcalls: Weak, Intermediate or Strong.

WEAK JUMP-OVERCALLS

These basically show 6-10 HCP and a good 6+ suit. Where the jump is to the 3-level, such as (1♡) : 3♣, the suit is often a 7-card suit. Weak jump-overcalls are popular at duplicate because they occur more frequently than the other kinds of jump-overcalls. They aim to shut the opponents out of the auction or at least impede their bidding. Partner needs a strong hand to take the bidding further. With no fit for the overcalled suit, partner should have 16+ points to bid (since the maximum opposite is 10), but with a trump fit, a hand with more than three winners warrants a raise. Change of suit is forcing.

If playing weak jump-overcalls, a simple overcall is made, up to 16 HCP, when the hand is too strong for a weak jump. With 17+ HCP and a strong suit, double first and bid the long suit on the next round.

INTERMEDIATE JUMP-OVERCALLS

These show 11-15 HCP and a good 6+ suit, typically a minimum opening bid with at least a 6-card suit, the sort of hand which opens 1♠ and rebids 2♠ after a 1NT response, for example. These are constructive and allow the overcaller to show a goodish hand and a good suit with one bid. Players not using intermediate jumps will often just overcall and rebid the long suit, as long as the bidding has not climbed too high.

Partner is expected to respond to an intermediate jump-overcall with 9+ HCP and may bid with less when holding support for the overcaller's suit. Support and 3+ winners would be enough to raise an intermediate jump in a major suit to game. Players using intermediate jump-overcalls will make a simple overcall when holding a long, strong suit and about 7-10 HCP. With a long, strong suit and 17+ HCP, double first and bid the long suit later.

STRONG JUMP-OVERCALLS

The strength is 15-18 HCP, like a 1NT overcall but with a 6+ suit. Most learn the strong jump-overcall initially and it is most commonly used in rubber bridge games. It is not popular at duplicate, because it crops up rarely, and this kind of hand can be shown by doubling first and bidding the long suit later. Pairs using strong jump-overcalls will make simple overcalls with a long, strong suit and weaker values.

The strong jump-overcall is not forcing, but partner is expected to reply with 6+ HCP. Raising a major suit would be first priority. Support and two winners would be enough to raise a strong jump in a major suit to game. If the strong jump is in a minor suit, 3NT takes precedence over a minor suit raise, but any no-trump bid promises at least one stopper in the enemy suit. Change of suit is forcing after a strong jump and promises at least a 5-card suit.

In response to a single jump-overcall in a major, a bid of the enemy suit is artificial and shows a strong hand with support for partner's suit. After a jump-overcall in a major, bidding the enemy suit is looking for game and usually asks partner for a stopper in the enemy suit This action is covered in detail in Chapter 25.

EXERCISES

A. Right-hand opponent opened 1 ♣. What action would you take on these hands using weak jump-overcalls?

1. ♠ K Q 8 4 3 2	**2.** ♠ 7 5	**3.** ♠ 6 4	**4.** ♠ A K 2	**5.** ♠ J 7
♡ A K	♡ A Q J 3 2	♡ A Q J 8 5 2	♡ K Q J 9 3 2	♡ K 6
◇ 7 6 3	◇ 6 4	◇ 9 7 6 4	◇ A J 2	◇ A J 10 9 7 2
♣ 9 4	♣ Q 7 5 2	♣ 2	♣ 2	♣ 8 4 2

B. What would answers be for the hands in Question A if the partnership is using:
(1) Intermediate jump-overcalls?   (2) Strong jump-overcalls?

C. Left-hand opponent opened 1 ◇, partner overcalled 2 ♠, a weak jump-overcall, and your right-hand opponent bid 3 ◇. What action would you take now with these hands?

1. ♠ K Q 10 4 2	**2.** ♠ 6 2	**3.** ♠ 2	**4.** ♠ A J 8	**5.** ♠ 9
♡ A 6 3	♡ K Q J 2	♡ A J 9 8 4	♡ A Q 10 2	♡ K Q J 9 7 5 2
◇ J 7 3	◇ J 4	◇ A 4	◇ 8 6 2	◇ A Q
♣ A 4	♣ A 8 5 3 2	♣ J 8 5 3 2	♣ Q J 7	♣ K Q J

PARTNERSHIP BIDDING: South is the dealer and there is no North-South bidding other than indicated. You and partner are playing weak jump-overcalls on Set 23 and intermediate jump overcalls on Set 24.

SET 23 – WEST	SET 23 – EAST	SET 24 – WEST	SET 24 – EAST
1. South opens 1 ♣.	**1.** South opens 1 ♣.	**1.** South opens 1 ◇.	**1.** South opens 1 ◇.
♠ K Q J 8 6 2	♠ 3	♠ A Q J 8 7 4	♠ K 9 5
♡ K 8 7	♡ 9 6 2	♡ K Q 3	♡ A 7
◇ 4	◇ K J 8 6 3 2	◇ 7 6	◇ 9 8 4 2
♣ 9 8 5	♣ A K 6	♣ 4 2	♣ Q J 10 3
2. South opens 1 ♣.	**2.** South opens 1 ♣.	**2.** South opens 1 ♣.	**2.** South opens 1 ♣.
♠ 7	♠ A Q 6 2	♠ K 4 3	♠ A Q 9 8 5
♡ A Q J 8 6 4 3	♡ 10 7 2	♡ A J 9 8 7 2	♡ 6
◇ J 10 3	◇ A 2	◇ K Q J	◇ 9 6 2
♣ 6 2	♣ K Q 5 4	♣ 4	♣ A 8 7 3
3. South opens 1 ♡.	**3.** South opens 1 ♡.	**3.** South opens 1 ◇.	**3.** South opens 1 ◇.
♠ 10 6	♠ A 9 5	♠ A K 7 5 4 2	♠ - - -
♡ 4 3	♡ A 7 6 2	♡ 9 8	♡ J 7 6 3 2
◇ 8 2	◇ A 9 4 3	◇ A J	◇ 9 8 7 4
♣ A K 9 8 7 4 2	♣ Q 3	♣ 6 3 2	♣ K Q J 5
4. South opens 1 ♠.	**4.** South opens 1 ♠.	**4.** South opens 1 ♡.	**4.** South opens 1 ♡.
♠ 4	♠ 9 7 3 2	♠ 8 6	♠ K 9 4
♡ K Q J 8 7 5	♡ A 9 3	♡ 4 3	♡ A J 5
◇ A K 3	◇ Q J 5 4	◇ A K 2	◇ J 10 4 3
♣ 8 4 2	♣ A 7	♣ A Q 9 8 6 4	♣ K 3 2
5. South opens 1 ♡.	**5.** South opens 1 ♡.	**5.** South opens 1 ♡.	**5.** South opens 1 ♡.
♠ 8 6 3	♠ A 9 2	♠ 5	♠ A Q 7 3 2
♡ 7	♡ Q J 8 6 5 2	♡ J 8 2	♡ Q 9 5 3
◇ K Q 10 8 6 4	◇ 7 2	◇ K 9 4	◇ 8 3 2
♣ A 9 3	♣ 8 6	♣ A K Q 8 7 2	♣ 6
6. South opens 1 ♡.	**6.** South opens 1 ♡.	**6.** South opens 1 ♣.	**6.** South opens 1 ♣.
♠ 8 6 2	♠ K 9 4 3	♠ A K Q	♠ 9 6
♡ 7	♡ K Q 10	♡ Q J 9 6 4 2	♡ A K 7
◇ K Q J 8 6 4	◇ A 9 3	◇ 7 2	◇ A Q 10 9 3
♣ K 9 3	♣ A 5 2	♣ 9 3	♣ 8 6 4

PLAY HANDS ON WEAK JUMP-OVERCALLS
Note the dealer on hands 39 and 40 in particular.

Hand 37: Weak jump-overcall – Coping with a bad break

Dealer North : North-South vulnerable

	NORTH		
	♠ A K 4		
	♡ K J 10 9 4		
	◇ J		
	♣ J 10 9 8		
WEST		EAST	
♠ Q 8 5 3		♠ J 6	
♡ A Q 8		♡ 7 3	
◇ A K Q		◇ 10 8 3	
♣ 5 3 2		♣ A K Q 7 6 4	
	SOUTH		
	♠ 10 9 7 2		
	♡ 6 5 2		
	◇ 9 7 6 5 4 2		
	♣ - - -		

WEST	NORTH	EAST	SOUTH
	1♡	3♣ (1)	No (2)
3NT (3)	No	No	No

Bidding: (1) Weak jump-overcall, 6-10 HCP, good 6-card suit. If not using weak jump-overcalls, East could make a simple overcall of 2♣ and West would still reply 3NT.
(2) Much too weak to compete.
(3) All suits covered and a powerful hand. Partner's clubs should produce the tricks and West provides the stoppers. It is permissible to have one suit unguarded, provided that you do have any suit bid by the opposition stopped and that you do not have a shortage (singleton or void) in an unbid suit.

Lead: ♡ J. Lead top of the touching honours from an interior sequence. You hope to set up the hearts before declarer can use the clubs. A top spade first is also a sound choice.

Correct play: On most days, declarer would have an easy road to eleven tricks with six clubs, three diamonds and two hearts. Here, declarer wins the heart lead and leads a club to the ace, but receives a nasty shock when South shows out. It would be an error to continue with the K-Q of clubs and a fourth club. This sets up two club winners in dummy but with no entry to reach them. *If you must give up a trick to set up winners, give up the necessary loser early.* After the ♣A reveals the break, duck one round of clubs (in other words, play a low club from both hands). When you regain the lead, the K-Q of clubs will draw the remaining clubs and allow you to cash the other two club winners.

Hand 38: Weak jump-overcall – Ducking to set up a long suit in dummy

Dealer East : East-West vulnerable

	NORTH		
	♠ A 9 8 3		
	♡ A J 3 2		
	◇ 5 4		
	♣ A Q J		
WEST		EAST	
♠ 10 7 5 4		♠ K Q 2	
♡ 9 8 6 5		♡ K Q 7	
◇ J 10 9		◇ Q 3	
♣ 9 8		♣ K 10 5 4 3	
	SOUTH		
	♠ J 6		
	♡ 10 4		
	◇ A K 8 7 6 2		
	♣ 7 6 2		

WEST	NORTH	EAST	SOUTH
		1♣	2◇ (1)
No	3NT (2)	All pass	

Bidding: (1) This is worth a weak jump-overcall only if not vulnerable. If vulnerable, the South hand does not have sufficient playing tricks to justify a weak jump-overcall and would either make a simple overcall or pass. If not using weak jump-overcalls, South is worth 1 ◇ and again North-South should reach 3NT.
(2) 16 HCP is worth a shot at game opposite a simple overcall or a weak jump-overcall. Here North has the stoppers and hopes to use South's diamond suit for most of the tricks.

Lead: ♣4. The long suit is normal, but as North clearly has clubs covered, it would be reasonable to lead the king from one of the major suits, hoping to hit a long suit with partner.

Correct play: North should win the first club with the *queen.* It is sound technique for declarer to *win with the higher of equal winners.* Declarer needs to set up diamond winners, but it would be an error to play ace, king and a third diamond as dummy has no entry to the established winners. As a trick has to be lost anyway to set up the diamonds, give up the inevitable loser early. Duck a round of diamonds at once and when you regain the lead, continue with the ◇ A, ◇ K, which draw the remaining diamonds. Cash the other diamond winners. Had the diamonds been 4-1, the contract would have failed. Just grin and bear it.

Hand 39: Raising partner's weak jump-overcall – Ducking to keep control

Dealer North : North-South vulnerable

NORTH
- ♠ 10 9
- ♡ K J 10 9 7
- ◇ 10 5
- ♣ A K Q J

WEST
- ♠ 7 2
- ♡ A Q 3
- ◇ A K Q J 4 3
- ♣ 8 6

EAST
- ♠ A K 8 6 4 3
- ♡ 6
- ◇ 7 6 2
- ♣ 10 5 2

SOUTH
- ♠ Q J 5
- ♡ 8 5 4 2
- ◇ 9 8
- ♣ 9 7 4 3

WEST	NORTH	EAST	SOUTH
	1♡	2♠ (1)	No (2)
4♠ (3)	No	No	No

Bidding: (1) Worth a weak jump-overcall only if you are not vulnerable. When vulnerable, a weak jump-overcall should have potential for six tricks at the 2-level and seven tricks at the 3-level. If not playing weak jump-overcalls, East is worth a simple overcall of 1♠ and would rebid 3♠ over West's 3◇, enabling West to raise to 4♠.
(2) Much too weak to warrant a raise to 3♡.
(3) Partner should have a decent 6-card spade suit and around 5-6 playing tricks. As West has at least five winners a raise to game is reasonable. As the cards lie, 3NT would succeed but with the weakness in clubs, this is not sure and it is better to stick with the known 8-card major fit.

Lead: ♡5. It is normal to lead partner's suit and from three or four rags, prefer second highest (middle-up-down). Leading the 4th-highest from a 4-card suit implies at least one honour card in the suit.

Correct play: Take the ♡A and lead a spade, ducking in hand. On regaining the lead, cash the ♠A-K, drawing the missing trumps and then run the diamonds. This way the opponents can score only one spade and two clubs. The danger is to play ♠A-K first. Then if a third spade is played, the opponents can cash three clubs, or if you start on the diamonds, an opponent will ruff and again three clubs can be cashed. By ducking a round of spades at once, dummy is left with a spade to cater for the third round of clubs. You could win the lead and play a club, hoping to ruff a club in dummy, but the opponents can counter that by switching to a trump.

Hand 40 : Raising partner's weak jump-overcall – Ducking to set up an extra trick – Timing

Dealer East : Love all

NORTH
- ♠ A K 4 2
- ♡ A 5
- ◇ Q 3
- ♣ 8 7 6 4 2

WEST
- ♠ 10 8 6
- ♡ J 8 3
- ◇ 10 7 5
- ♣ Q 10 9 3

EAST
- ♠ Q J 9
- ♡ 7 4
- ◇ A K J 9 4
- ♣ K J 5

SOUTH
- ♠ 7 5 3
- ♡ K Q 10 9 6 2
- ◇ 8 6 2
- ♣ A

WEST	NORTH	EAST	SOUTH
		1◇	2♡ (1)
No	3♡ (2)	No	4♡ (3)
No	No	No	

Bidding: (1) This hand has potential for six tricks and would be worth a weak jump-overcall if vulnerable.
(2) Just enough to scrape up a raise opposite a weak jump. With support and more than 3 winners, an invitation to game is justified. Here, the potential for a diamond ruff provides the extra chance needed to warrant the invitation to game.
(3) 9-10 HCP is a maximum for a weak jump-overcall and so South accepts the invitation.

Lead: ◇5. Partner's suit is the normal lead and with three cards including an honour, the lowest card is the standard lead. The 10 is an honour, so from 10-x-x, lead the bottom card.

Correct play: East should win the first diamond and switch to a trump. If East wrongly plays a second diamond, declarer can easily ruff the third diamond low in dummy and make two spades, six hearts, one diamond ruff and one club. Likewise, if East switches to a club, South wins and leads a second diamond and will score the diamond ruff. If East switches to a trump at trick 2, South should see that the diamond ruff will vanish: win the ♡A and duck a spade, hoping for a 3-3 spade break, so that the 13th spade will be your tenth trick. Most texts recommend that you count your losers, but a count of winners helps, too. There are only nine tricks and without a diamond ruff, the tenth trick can come only from spades. Note that the spade must be ducked before trumps have been drawn.

CHAPTER 11

THE UNUSUAL 2NT OVERCALL

It is rare to pick up a huge hand after an opponent has opened and so there is little scope for a jump-overcall of 2NT, such as (1 ♡) : 2NT, to show a balanced hand around 20-22 points. Such a hand, when it does arise, can be adequately described by a takeout double followed by a bid in no-trumps later. Accordingly, most partnerships have harnessed the jump-overcall to 2NT after a major suit opening to show a weak hand with both minor suits. As this does not resemble a balanced hand, it has been called the 'unusual 2NT'.

(1 ♡) : 2NT or (1 ♠) : 2NT = About 8-12 HCP and at least 5-5 in the minors.

Each minor suit should contain at least two honour cards if the pattern is 5-5. At favourable vulnerability or if the pattern is 6-5 or more extreme, the strength can be below 8 HCP. You may also take greater liberties with the suit quality when the pattern is at least 6-5. Each of these hands would be worth an overcall of 2NT after an opening bid of (1 ♡) or (1 ♠):

♠ 7 2	♠ 9	♠ 8 3 2	♠ 6	♠ - - -
♡ 9	♡ J 2	♡ - - -	♡ 7	♡ 2
◇ K Q J 6 3	◇ Q J 10 7 2	◇ J 10 7 5 2	◇ Q J 8 6 4 2	◇ K 10 9 7 5 4
♣ K J 9 5 4	♣ A J 7 6 5	♣ A Q J 9 4	♣ Q J 10 5 2	♣ 10 9 8 5 3 2

The function of the unusual 2NT overcall is to suggest a sacrifice to partner if the opponents bid to a game. Accordingly, the 2NT overcall should not be too strong. If you hold 13+ HCP, it is not too likely that the opponents will bid to a game, and if they do, you will have reasonable defensive prospects. Similarly, the 2NT overcall should not have strong defensive prospects against their game. A hand with three likely winners, such as suits headed by A-K and A, is too strong in defence for a 2NT overcall. With 5-5 in the minors and too much strength for the unusual 2NT, content yourself with a simple overcall first and compete again later. With 16+ HCP, you could double first and show the suits later.

If the bidding starts, say, (1 ♠) : 2NT : (4 ♠) . . . fourth player is in a good position to judge whether to defend against 4 ♠ or whether to save ('to save' = 'to sacrifice') in 5 ♣ or 5 ◇ . The advantages of sacrificing are that if the opponents allow you to play in 5 ♣ or 5 ◇ doubled, the cost of the sacrifice may be less than the value of their game, or if the opponents decide to bid 5-in-their-major, that contract might fail. If they are unable to take more than ten tricks, it obviously pays to push them one higher where they can be defeated.

PARTNER'S STRATEGY IF THIRD PLAYER PASSES 2NT

With a weak hand, bid 3 ♣ or 3 ◇ , whichever minor suit holding is longer. It is almost always wrong to pass 2NT and if you have equal length in the minors, bid 3 ♣ . With a strong hand and game chances, you may jump to 4 ♣ or 4 ◇ , or even 5 ♣ or 5 ◇ . You may choose 3NT with a very strong hand and double or triple stoppers in the majors. Remember that partner will have to play the hand in no-trumps and partner will have next to nothing in the majors. A bid of the other major, e. g., (1 ♡) : 2NT : (No) : 3 ♠ , would be a strong hand with a good 6+ suit. Partner should raise with doubleton support.

PARTNER'S STRATEGY IF THIRD PLAYER DOUBLES 2NT

Apply the same strategy as though third player had passed, except that with an equal holding in the minor suits, you should pass and allow the 2NT bidder to choose a suit. If you have a clear preference, bid your longer minor. With equal length, *you* have no preference, so that if one of partner's minors is longer, it will be better to have that suit as trumps. Pass and let partner choose. (This is also a situation where the Eric Murray Principle applies: 'If the contract looks like a disaster, let partner play the hand!')

PARTNER'S STRATEGY IF THIRD PLAYER BIDS 3-MAJOR

Pass with a weak hand *OR* bid 4 ♣ or 4 ◇ as an invitation to game *OR* jump straight to 5 ♣ or 5 ◇ with good chances for game or if you expect to go no more than one off. It is not attractive to sacrifice yet. They may not even bid their game. However, if you are close to game values or if you are sure that they are going to bid their game anyway, a jump to 5-minor puts maximum pressure on opener.

PARTNER'S STRATEGY IF THIRD PLAYER BIDS 4-MAJOR

If they cannot make ten tricks, it does not pay to sacrifice at all. Why should you lose points when they are about to lose points in their contract? Accordingly, the first question is whether you have reasonable defensive prospects. If you have a fair chance of defeating their game, do not sacrifice. In making this assessment, do not count on the 2NT bidder for more than one defensive trick.

It also does not pay to sacrifice if they double you and the penalties cost more than the value of their game. Vulnerability is one factor and the degree of fit with partner's minors is the other. Do not sacrifice on balanced hands – the cost is usually too high. Do not sacrifice if you are vulnerable and they are not, unless you have some hope of making the contract – otherwise, the cost is usually too high. The best holdings for sacrificing are a 4+ holding in one minor and a doubleton or less in the other minor, with very little in the way of defensive tricks. The more balanced the hand, the more you should choose to defend rather than bid on.

ACTION BY THIRD PLAYER AFTER AN OPPONENT'S 2NT OVERCALL

Pass shows a weak hand. Double says you are angling for penalties and shows a strong 4-card holding in at least one of the minors. Then, if fourth player bids the other minor and opener is strong in that suit, opener is able to double for penalties. A bid of 3-of-opener's-major has the same value as a good raise to the 2-level. With support for opener's suit and enough for game, bid 4-in-opener's-major. Bidding 3-of-the-other-major is forcing and shows a good 5+ suit. Bidding 3-of-either-minor cannot be natural. Many play that 3♣ shows a good hand for hearts and 3◇ shows a good hand for spades.

THE UNUSUAL 2NT OVER A MINOR SUIT OPENING

These days opening bids of 1♣ or 1◇ are very often artificial or can be short suits so that it is reasonable to use the unusual 2NT overcall for the minor suits even if they open with a minor suit. That is the arrangement in many regular partnerships. However, another possible arrangement is for the unusual 2NT to show the two cheapest unbid suits, so that (1♣) : 2NT shows diamonds and hearts, while (1◇) : 2NT would show clubs and hearts. The strength would still be weak, normally less than 13 HCP, and the suit texture would be good. Naturally, the partnership will stipulate in advance which approach is to be used.

WHEN IS 2NT NOT FOR THE MINORS?

In most auctions, a bid of 2NT is not for the minors. 2NT normally indicates a balanced hand of a specific strength. The strength varies according to the auction, but if 2NT can have a natural meaning showing a balanced hand, then that meaning is preferred. For example, 1♠ : (2♡) : 2NT would show a heart stopper and about 10-12 points. Likewise, 2NT over their weak 2-opening, e.g., (2♠) : 2NT, shows a balanced hand of about 16-18 points and does not ask for the minors. After (1♡) : No : (2♡) : Double, (No) . . . a bid of 2NT in answer to the double would be a natural bid, showing at least one stopper in the enemy suit.

OTHER SITUATIONS WHERE NO-TRUMP BIDS SHOW THE MINORS

In general, if a no-trump bid *cannot* have a sensible natural meaning in a competitive auction, it is used to show the minor suits. In each of these auctions the final no-trump bid is commonly used for the minors.

WEST	NORTH	EAST	SOUTH	
No	1♡	No	1♠	West's 1NT should not be used in a natural sense. It would be lunacy to compete against two bidding opponents with a weak balanced hand. The 1NT overcall by a passed hand shows the minors, but perhaps not as freakish as 5-5.
1NT . . .				

WEST	NORTH	EAST	SOUTH	
No	1♡	No	2♡	Here, too, as 2NT has been bid by a passed hand, it should be taken as showing both minors. It makes no sense to play 2NT here as a balanced hand.
2NT . . .				

WEST	NORTH	EAST	SOUTH	
1♠	No	2♠	No	North's delayed 2NT shows the minors. It cannot be a huge balanced hand. With that, North would have bid at once over 1♠. North is likely to be 5-4 in the minors, perhaps only 4-4. If 5-5, 2NT might have been bid at once.
No	2NT . . .			

WEST	NORTH	EAST	SOUTH
1♠	No	No	2NT...

As the purpose of the unusual 2NT is to suggest a sacrifice, there is no need to play 2NT in the pass-out seat for the minors. Most pairs use 2NT in the protective position as natural, to show a strong balanced hand, say 17-18 points.

WEST	NORTH	EAST	SOUTH
1♡	1♠	No	2♠
No	No	2NT...	

East's 2NT is for the minors, even though it is by responder, something like ♠6 ♡4 3 ◊J 10 9 4 3 ♣K 7 6 4 2, perhaps. It cannot be a natural bid showing a spade stopper since East failed to bid 1NT or 2NT over 1♠.

WEST	NORTH	EAST	SOUTH
1♡	No	4♡	4NT...

There is no real need here for Blackwood and so 4NT is used to show both minors. Since 4NT commits you to the five-level and you might be doubled, vulnerability and playing-trick potential are important factors.

WEST	NORTH	EAST	SOUTH
3♠	4NT...		

WEST	NORTH	EAST	SOUTH
4♡	4NT...		

Many pairs play that a jump to 4NT over a pre-empt shows both minors. Thus, a 4NT bid over an opening of 3♡, 4♡, 3♠ or 4♠ is for takeout, not an ask for aces. However, this would always be based on a very strong hand and 5-5 in the minors at least. Clearly, such agreements need to be settled by your partnership in advance.

WEST	NORTH	EAST	SOUTH
1♡	2♣	4♡	No
No	4NT...		

North's 4NT is a takeout for the minors, but the failure to bid 2NT over 1♡ marks North with longer clubs than diamonds, 6-7 clubs and perhaps only 4 diamonds. North is anxious to sacrifice and without clear preference for diamonds, South should choose clubs.

EXERCISES: A. At love all. Right-hand opponent opened 1♠. What action do you take on these hands?

1. ♠ 9 5	2. ♠ A	3. ♠ 2	4. ♠ 7 2	5. ♠ - - -
♡ 7 3	♡ A Q	♡ J 3	♡ - - -	♡ J 6 3
◊ A Q 10 6 4	◊ J 9 7 6 4	◊ A K 6 4 3	◊ K Q 8 6 2	◊ A Q J 4 3
♣ K Q 7 3	♣ 9 7 5 3 2	♣ A Q 9 5 4	♣ Q J 9 7 5 2	♣ Q J 8 3 2

6. ♠ A 6 5	7. ♠ - - -	8. ♠ - - -	9. ♠ 7 2	10. ♠ J 2
♡ - - -	♡ K	♡ J 6 2	♡ J	♡ 6
◊ A K Q 6 4	◊ Q 9 7 6 4 2	◊ A K 6 4 3	◊ K Q J 6 2	◊ Q J 10 3
♣ K Q 9 7 3	♣ J 9 8 5 3 2	♣ Q J 10 8 3	♣ A K Q J 7	♣ K Q J 9 7 4

B. Partner opened 1♡ and right-hand opponent overcalled 2NT. What action do you take on these hands?

1. ♠ K 7 6 4 2	2. ♠ A 7	3. ♠ 9 8 3 2	4. ♠ A 7 2	5. ♠ A K 7 2
♡ 7 3	♡ 2	♡ A K J 2	♡ Q J 7 2	♡ K Q 6 3 2
◊ A J 9	◊ Q 9 8 6 4 2	◊ A 7 6 4	◊ K 8 6	◊ 2
♣ 9 7 3	♣ A 7 5 2	♣ 5	♣ 7 5 2	♣ K Q J

C. Left-hand opponent opened 1♡, partner overcalled 2NT and right-hand opponent passed. Your action?

1. ♠ K 8 7 5 4	2. ♠ A 8 7	3. ♠ Q 8 7 4 3	4. ♠ A 7 6 4 3 2	5. ♠ A 8 7 2
♡ 7 6 3	♡ A 9 5 3	♡ K J	♡ J	♡ 6 5 4 3 2
◊ 9 6 4	◊ Q 9	◊ 9 7 6	◊ A K 8 6 2	◊ Q 4
♣ J 7	♣ J 7 3 2	♣ 8 5 4	♣ 7	♣ J 2

6. ♠ A	7. ♠ Q J 10 9 2	8. ♠ A 8 6 3 2	9. ♠ A Q J 8 7 2	10. ♠ A Q 10 9
♡ 9 7 6 3	♡ K Q J 9 3	♡ K Q	♡ J 7 3	♡ A K J 9
◊ A Q 9	◊ 4	◊ A K	◊ A K 8	◊ J 3
♣ K Q J 3 2	♣ 7 2	♣ J 8 5 4	♣ 7	♣ K 3 2

D. What would your answers be in C. if right-hand opponent had raised to 3♡ over 2NT?

PLAY HANDS ON THE UNUSUAL 2NT FOR THE MINORS

Hand 41: The 2NT overcall for the minors – Taking a sacrifice at unfavourable vulnerability

Dealer North : East-West vulnerable

                NORTH
                ♠ J 9
                ♡ K Q 6 4 3 2
                ◇ A K 10 3
                ♣ 7
WEST   **EAST**
♠ A Q 8 7 2   ♠ 6
♡ 8 5   ♡ 7
◇ 5   ◇ Q J 9 6 4 2
♣ 9 8 6 4 2   ♣ A Q J 10 5
                SOUTH
                ♠ K 10 5 4 3
                ♡ A J 10 9
                ◇ 8 7
                ♣ K 3

WEST	NORTH	EAST	SOUTH
	1 ♡	2NT (1)	4 ♡ (2)
5 ♣ (3)	No (4)	No	Dble (5)
No	No (6)	No	

Bidding: (1) Ideal for 2NT with excellent playing strength and little defence. Clearly worth 2NT even at this vulnerability.
(2) Much too strong for just 3 ♡. Worth 13 points for hearts.
(3) Ideal for a save. Great support for one minor and shortage in the other. Such hands make more tricks than the point count suggests. 5 ♣ might actually succeed (as 2NT will not be light at this vulnerability) and should not be more than one off.
(4) Very tough decision. The ◇ A-K suggest defending, but 5 ♡ could be on because of the good shape. 5 ♡ can be beaten, losing two spades and a club, but the defence might slip.
(5) Another tough decision. The absence of a shortage and the likely trump trick with the ♣ K suggest defending.

(6) If you pass the decision to partner and partner elects to double, abide by partner's decision.

Lead: ♡ K. On the ♠ J lead, West can succeed, discarding the heart loser on the second spade. On a trump lead, usually attractive against a sacrifice, declarer could make by taking the ♣ A and having the courage to finesse the ♣ Q, again discarding the heart loser. The ◇ A, dummy's second suit, is not an attractive lead.

Correct play: When West wins the lead, West should lead the singleton diamond. Later West should ruff three diamonds in hand to set up dummy's diamonds. Declarer must not squander dummy's trumps. If dummy's trumps are used too early, dummy will not have an entry later to the diamonds. Going two down will cost 500. Minus 200 is reasonable as 4 ♡ is on, but minus 500 is too expensive.

Hand 42: Bidding over the 2NT overcall – Beware the finesse at trick 1

Dealer East : Game all

                NORTH
                ♠ K 10 9 6 4
                ♡ A J
                ◇ 6 5
                ♣ 7 6 3 2
WEST   **EAST**
♠ A Q J 8 2   ♠ 7 3
♡ Q 10 5 3   ♡ K 9 8 6 4 2
◇ 7 4   ◇ A K 10
♣ K 8   ♣ Q 4
                SOUTH
                ♠ 5
                ♡ 7
                ◇ Q J 9 8 3 2
                ♣ A J 10 9 5

WEST	NORTH	EAST	SOUTH
		1 ♡	2NT (1)
4 ♡ (2)	No (3)	No	No (4)

Bidding: (1) Again an excellent vulnerable 2NT overcall. Note especially the superb suit texture in each minor.
(2) Clearly enough for game. Do not bother with the spades.
(3) Do not sacrifice with a balanced hand or when most of your strength is in the opponents' suits and therefore best for defence. 5 ♣ can be defeated by three tricks, –800, too expensive.
(4) If partner does not wish to sacrifice, neither should you, unless you have something exceptional, such as a 6-6 pattern.

Lead: ◇ Q or ♠ 5. The top of the near sequence is the solid lead, the singleton is the gambling lead which could work.

Correct play: On the ◇ Q lead, East should win and play a low heart to dummy's queen. If hearts are 3-0, the void figures to be with South, and if so, a heart to the queen allows you to finesse against North's jack. On the ♠ 5 lead, declarer must not finesse. North would win with the ♠ K and give South a spade ruff. Now 4 ♡ will go off. As South is 5-5 in the minors, beware of that spade lead. Do not fall for the finesse at trick 1 trap. Take the ♠ A and lead a low heart. This guards against a trump promotion if North began with ♡ A singleton and South with ♡ J-7.

Hand 43: Bidding over the 2NT overcall for the minors – Card combination and card reading

Dealer South : Love all

	WEST	NORTH	EAST	SOUTH
				1♠
	2NT	3♠ (1)	No (2)	4♠ (3)
	No	No	No (4)	

NORTH
♠ K 6 5 4
♡ K Q 5
◊ 7 6 3
♣ J 7 3

WEST
♠ 7
♡ J 10
◊ Q 10 9 8 2
♣ K Q 9 6 5

EAST
♠ Q 10 9
♡ A 9 8 7
◊ 5 4
♣ 10 8 4 2

SOUTH
♠ A J 8 3 2
♡ 6 4 3 2
◊ A K J
♣ A

Bidding: (1) Not a good hand, but it is vital to show support in case opener is very strong. The raise to 3-major over 2NT shows a sound 1-major : 2-major raise, around 7-10 points.
(2) There are no prospects of making 5♣ and the bidding may die out at 3♠. Do not sacrifice if they might not bid the game.
(3) Worth 20 points because of the singleton.
(4) Not worth a sacrifice at equal vulnerability since the hand is balanced and all the strength is in the opposition's suits.

Lead: ♡J or ♣K. Leading Q-x, J-x or 10-x is not attractive, but these are all right if you have the card below, too, i.e., Q-J, J-10 or 10-9. With the touching card, you are not likely to damage your side and may help to build up tricks in partner's hand. The ♣K is a sound alternative and better than the ◊ 10.

Correct play: The normal play in spades with nine trumps is king and ace, hoping that the queen will drop. In view of West's 2NT, the 2-2 break in spades is less likely and you should play a 2NT overcaller to be short in your trump suit. If the ♡J is led to the king and ace and a heart is returned to the queen, West is known to hold five clubs, five diamonds and two hearts and so at most one spade. Therefore, cash the ♣K and lead a spade to the jack. If you play for the drop, you are highly likely to fail. If the lead was the ♣K, play the same way. Firstly, with at least ten cards in the minors, West figures to be short in spades. Secondly, West is likely to hold two hearts and one spade, as West may well have led a singleton heart.

Hand 44: Using 4NT as a minor suit takeout – Competitive decisions

Dealer West : North-South vulnerable

	WEST	NORTH	EAST	SOUTH
	1♡	No	4♡ (1)	4NT (2)
	Dble (3)	5♣ (4)	No	No
	Dble (5)	No	No	No

NORTH
♠ 8 7 6 5
♡ - - -
◊ Q 9 8 4
♣ A 10 4 3 2

WEST
♠ A J 9 2
♡ K Q 6 5 4
◊ A J 6
♣ J

EAST
♠ K Q 10 4 3
♡ 10 9 8 7 2
◊ 7
♣ 9 7

SOUTH
♠ - - -
♡ A J 3
◊ K 10 5 3 2
♣ K Q 8 6 5

Bidding: (1) Standard gambling game raise (see page 7).
(2) In a competitive auction, 4NT as Blackwood is not as valuable as showing a 2-suiter. Locating the best game is more important than aces when nothing is yet known about either partner's hand. 4NT shows a good hand at this vulnerability, but knowing from the auction that North is very short in hearts, South is very confident of locating a fit in one of the minors.
(3) Looking for penalties, mainly because of the diamonds.
(4) Naturally choosing the longer minor suit. With equal length and strength, North could pass and let South make the choice.

(5) This is a common failing. Looking at 16 HCP and having heard partner bid game, West hopes that 5♣ will fail. Yet if the vulnerable opponents are bidding game with so many points missing, they must have excellent shape as compensation. Points do not take tricks when the opponents have voids and singletons. A good guide when you are in doubt in such situations: *If you cannot tell who can make what, bid one more.* If West bids 5♡, this can be defeated by two tricks if North leads a spade or by one trick if North does not lead a spade, but the defence still finds the spade ruff. However, if declarer can draw trumps without the defence finding the spade ruff, 5♡ will make. Any of these results is better than 5♣ doubled, which is unbeatable.
Lead: ◊ 7. From a very weak hand, it is sensible to look for a ruff.
Correct play: ◊ A and another diamond gives the defence its ruff, but declarer easily makes the rest.

CHAPTER 12

PRE-EMPTIVE OPENINGS AND OVERCALLS

The function of pre-emptive openings is to get in the first blow and make it tough for the opposition to gauge their combined assets, because you have taken away their bidding space. Pre-emptive overcalls also aim to force the opponents to guess at the correct contract by robbing them of the space needed to describe their values. Experts fear pre-empts more than any other action because it forces them to guess and they may well go wrong because they lack the information to make an informed judgment. When forced to guess, players may end in the wrong suit, may play in a suit when they should be in no-trumps, play in game when they should be in slam, double you for a small penalty when they could score more by bidding to their best contract. If your hand meets the requirements for a pre-empt, you should bid as high as the guidelines permit at your earliest opportunity. Pre-emptive action almost always occurs only on the first round of bidding and having made a pre-empt, the pre-emptor does *not* bid again unless forced by partner. After pre-empting, let the opponents struggle to find their best fit. They will err often enough.

A pre-emptive opening is based on playing tricks, not on points, but the hand should not be strong. The normal range is 6-10 HCP and a 7+ suit, but in rare cases, a powerful 6-card suit may be suitable if the required number of tricks is present. There can be fewer than six points provided that the playing strength is correct, but only in rare situations should there be more than 10 HCP in first or second seat. If you hold a strong hand, there is less incentive to pre-empt since you may well have more strength than the opponents. The time to pre-empt is when you expect them to hold more points and possibly have a game or slam on. If you pre-empt when holding a strong hand, partner might play you for a weak hand and miss a slam.

WHEN MAY YOU PRE-EMPT WITH A STRONG HAND?

If slam prospects do not exist, you are permitted to pre-empt with a bid of 4♡ or 4♠ with a strong hand, up to about 16 HCP. One situation is when partner is a passed hand (and so cannot be expected to provide more than three tricks for you if too weak to open the bidding). Another situation is after the opponents have opened. It is highly unlikely that you can make a slam, given they have the values for an opening bid. However, when pre-empting with a strong hand, do not pre-empt just to the 3-level, since partner may pass and you could miss a game. With a good hand, either pre-empt to game at once or overcall at a cheaper level to see whether partner has any worthwhile values.

How to count your playing tricks: *In your long suit:* count the ace, king and queen as winners (if the queen is the only honour card in the suit, count it as a ½-trick), and every card beyond the third card as a winner. *In your short suits:* Count the ace as a trick, count the king as a trick unless singleton and count the queen as a trick if it is supported by another honour in a 3-card suit. Count A-Q as 1½ tricks and K-Q as 1 trick.

THE RULE OF THREE AND TWO

When pre-empting, your playing tricks should be three less than your bid when not vulnerable and two less than your bid when vulnerable. The idea of the Rule of 3 and 2 is that if they double and partner produces no tricks at all, the cost will be –500, down three doubled not vulnerable or down two doubled vulnerable. This loss is acceptable, for if partner has no tricks at all, the opponents will often be able to make a slam, not just a game. Minus 500 is a bargain compared with your loss if they can make a slam. If you have a holding which includes a ½-trick, treat it as the next higher number. If not vulnerable against vulnerable opponents, you may shade your pre-emptive openings by a trick for a 3-opening. It is reasonable to shade any 3-level or 4-level pre-emptive opening by a trick in third seat.

A pre-empt skips two or more levels in the bidding, but you should not pre-empt higher than game. If the Rule of 3 and 2 indicates you should open 5♡ or 5♠, choose to open only 4♡ / 4♠ – do not pre-empt beyond game. The pre-emptive suit openings are from 3♣ to 5♦.

Opening 3♣ / 3♦ / 3♡ / 3♠ = seven tricks vulnerable, six tricks not vulnerable, five tricks at favourable.
Opening 4♣ / 4♦ / 4♡ / 4♠ = eight tricks vulnerable, seven tricks not vulnerable.
Opening 5♣ / 5♦ = nine tricks vulnerable, eight tricks not vulnerable.

In other words, given that you hold a long, strong suit and a weak hand, your basic approach is:

- With six playing tricks, open three if not vulnerable, pass if vulnerable.

- With seven playing tricks, open four if not vulnerable, three if vulnerable.

- With eight playing tricks, open 4♡ / 4♠ / 5♣ / 5◇ if not vulnerable, four of any suit if vulnerable.

- With nine playing tricks, open four if your suit is a major, five if it is a minor.

PRE-EMPTIVE OVERCALLS

A pre-emptive overcall skips at least two levels of bidding. (1◇) : 3♡ is a pre-empt (you have skipped over 1♡ and 2♡), but (1◇) : 3♣ is not a pre-empt – in bridge jargon, it is a jump-overcall. Still, a jump-overcall may be a weak bid in the partnership methods – see Chapter 10 for weak jumps. A pre-emptive overcall is not as efficient as a pre-emptive opening, as third player has the advantage of knowing about the opening hand, but pre-emptive overcalls may still make it hard for the opponents to judge their combined values. If your hand is worth a pre-empt, do not lose your nerve. Pre-empt as high as you dare, following the Rule of 3 and 2 which applies to pre-emptive overcalls just as it applies to pre-emptive openings.

RESPONDING TO PARTNER'S PRE-EMPTIVE OPENING OR OVERCALL

1. Assess how many tricks partner has by deducting three if your side is not vulnerable or two if vulnerable.

2. Add to this your supporting tricks: Count the A, K or Q of partner's suit as one trick each. In other suits, count A-K as 2, A-Q as 1½, A as 1, K-Q as 1, and K as ½. If you have support for opener's suit, count an outside singleton as one trick and an outside void as two tricks, since opener will usually have some length, a doubleton at least, where you hold a shortage.

3. If the total is less than partner's bid or just enough for the contract, pass.

4. If the total is more than partner's bid, you should bid on to game (but if partner's bid is already a game, you would pass). If the total is twelve or more, bid to a slam, provided that you are not missing two aces. If you are not sure, use Blackwood over partner's pre-empt to check on aces and, if relevant, kings.

5. Over an opening bid of 3♣ or 3◇, you may try 3NT with a strong balanced hand and at least one stopper in each of the outside suits.

6. Over other opening pre-empts, prefer to stick with partner's suit unless you have a strong hand and a long, powerful suit of your own. A change-of-suit in response to a pre-empt is forcing.

7. Do not 'rescue' partner from a pre-empt. With a weak hand, pass. Let partner suffer.

THE GAMBLING 3NT OPENING

The 3NT opening on a balanced hand of 25-27 points is not used by strong players because it occurs so rarely and there is little room for exploration after the bidding starts so high. It is better to open such powerful hands with a 2♣ demand opening (see Chapter 8) and follow up with a no-trump rebid.

As a result, the 3NT opening becomes available for pre-emptive purposes. One popular usage is the Gambling 3NT Opening, which shows a solid 7+ minor (the suit must be A-K-Q-x-x-x-x or better) and no significant values outside the long suit. Partner is expected to pass with stoppers in the other suits. The theory is that the solid minor will provide seven tricks while partner will provide at least two tricks and simultaneously prevent the opposition cashing a long suit.

Opener should not hold any ace, king or Q-J-x outside the long suit, since this would provide a stopper of which partner would be unaware. Partner would find it very difficult to gauge when to pass 3NT and when to run. If responder cannot provide two tricks or if responder has no stopper in one of the outside suits, responder will bid opener's minor at the 4-level, which opener must pass. If responder cannot tell which minor opener has, responder bids 4♣. If opener has clubs, opener passes, while if opener holds diamonds, opener bids 4◇, which responder can pass. 3NT : 4◇ asks for a singleton. Opener's replies are 4♡ = singleton heart, 4♠ = singleton spade, 4NT = 7-2-2-2, 5♣ = singleton diamond, 5◇ = singleton club.

To play in 5-of-opener's-minor rather than 3NT, bid the minor suit at the 5-level or, if unable to tell which minor opener has, bid 5♣. Opener passes with clubs or corrects to 5♢. Similarly, with enough for a slam, bid opener's suit at the 6-level or 7-level. Opener will pass if holding that suit or convert to the other minor if not.

THE GAMBLING 3NT OVERCALL

The Gambling 3NT is also used as an overcall, e.g., (1♠) : 3NT, but there is a significant difference. As the opponents have opened the bidding, the 3NT overcall contains not only a solid 7+ minor, but also a stopper in the suit opened and usually a stopper in an outside suit, too. This hand would be typical for (1♠) : 3NT –

♠ K 5
♡ A
♢ A K Q 8 7 6 2
♣ 9 5 2

Thus, there is an expectation of making nine tricks on most occasions, particularly if the lead is in the suit opened. The partner of the 3NT overcaller is expected not to run except in absolute desperation. If the opening bidder doubles the 3NT overcall, this requests partner to lead the suit opened despite the 3NT overcall.

EXERCISES

A. You are the dealer. What action do you take on these hands: (a) Not vulnerable? (b) Vulnerable?

1. ♠ Q J 10 8 7 6 3	2. ♠ 2	3. ♠ 2	4. ♠ K J 10 7 6 5 4
♡ 7 3	♡ K Q J 9 7 6 3 2	♡ J 3	♡ - - -
♢ K Q J	♢ 8 4	♢ A K Q 9 8 6 5 3 2	♢ Q J 10 3 2
♣ 3	♣ 9 7	♣ 4	♣ 5

5. ♠ A 6	6. ♠ 9	7. ♠ - - -	8. ♠ A J 7 2
♡ A K 9 8 6 3 2	♡ J 9 7 6 4 3 2	♡ 9 6 2	♡ 3
♢ 4	♢ K Q	♢ J 10 6 4	♢ Q J 9 7 6 5 2
♣ 9 7 3	♣ 6 3 2	♣ A Q J 10 7 5	♣ 3

B. Partner opened 3♡, pass on your right. What action do you take : (a) Not vulnerable? (b) Vulnerable?

1. ♠ A J 9 5 2	2. ♠ A J 9 7 5 2	3. ♠ 2	4. ♠ A 7 2	5. ♠ A K 7 5 2
♡ 7	♡ - - -	♡ K 8 3	♡ 9 3	♡ 9
♢ A Q 10 6 4	♢ Q J 7	♢ A K 6 4 3	♢ K Q 8 6	♢ A K 9 3 2
♣ 6 2	♣ 9 7 3 2	♣ 10 9 5 4	♣ A 9 7 3	♣ 8 3

6. ♠ A K J 9 8 3	7. ♠ 4	8. ♠ A	9. ♠ K Q J 9 8	10. ♠ A K Q 2
♡ 7	♡ K 8 7 3	♡ K J 6 2	♡ K 3	♡ - - -
♢ A Q J	♢ A K Q 8 6 2	♢ A K Q J	♢ K Q	♢ A K 8 3
♣ K 9 6	♣ A 5	♣ A 7 5 4	♣ K Q J 2	♣ Q J 7 4 2

PARTNERSHIP BIDDING: How should these hands be bid? West is the dealer and no one is vulnerable.

SET 25 – WEST	SET 25 – EAST	SET 26 – WEST	SET 26 – EAST
1. ♠ 7 3	1. ♠ A 9 6	1. ♠ 7 2	1. ♠ A K 3
♡ A Q J 7 6 4 3	♡ K 10 8 2	♡ 4 3	♡ K 10 8 2
♢ 9 2	♢ A K Q J 3	♢ 9 5	♢ Q 10 6 4
♣ 9 8	♣ A	♣ A K Q 8 6 4 3	♣ 7 5
2. ♠ 7	2. ♠ A Q 8 3	2. ♠ A K Q 2	2. ♠ 4
♡ 4 2	♡ K Q 10 3	♡ 8 6 4	♡ 9 3
♢ Q J 10 8 6 4 3	♢ K 7	♢ 8 5 3	♢ A K Q J 7 6 2
♣ K 8 3	♣ A J 9	♣ 9 8 3	♣ 7 6 4
3. ♠ 7 2	3. ♠ A K Q J 6 4 3	3. ♠ 7 3 2	3. ♠ 6
♡ 10 9 7 5 3	♡ 2	♡ 4	♡ A K Q 3
♢ K Q J	♢ 6 5 4	♢ 8 7	♢ K Q 6 4 2
♣ K 7 4	♣ Q 6	♣ A K Q 7 6 4 2	♣ 8 5 3
4. ♠ 7	4. ♠ A Q 3 2	4. ♠ 9 2	4. ♠ K 8
♡ 4	♡ A 8 6 5 3	♡ 4 3	♡ A Q 7 2
♢ 6 2	♢ 9	♢ A K Q 8 7 4 2	♢ 9 5 3
♣ A Q J 8 7 5 4 3 2	♣ K 10 6	♣ 6 4	♣ A K Q J

PLAY HANDS ON PRE-EMPTIVE BIDDING

Hand 45: Pre-emptive opening – Card combination – Eliminating a loser – Card reading

Dealer North : Love all

NORTH
- ♠ 9 8
- ♡ 6 5 3
- ◊ A 6 4 2
- ♣ A Q 7 4

WEST
- ♠ Q J 7
- ♡ J 10 9 8
- ◊ K 8 3
- ♣ K J 6

EAST
- ♠ 4
- ♡ A K Q
- ◊ J 10 9 5
- ♣ 10 8 5 3 2

SOUTH
- ♠ A K 10 6 5 3 2
- ♡ 7 4 2
- ◊ Q 7
- ♣ 9

WEST	NORTH	EAST	SOUTH
	No	No	3♠ (1)
No (2)	No (3)	No (4)	

Bidding: (1) Worth about six playing tricks not vulnerable. Not enough for a 4♠ pre-empt.
(2) Much too weak to bid, especially opposite a passed hand.
(3) Worth 2½ tricks in support of spades, not enough to raise. As a non-vulnerable pre-empt is three tricks short of the bid, you need more than three tricks before bidding higher.
(4) Not suitable for any action. For details about competing over a pre-empt, see Chapter 16.

Lead: ♡J. Easy, top of sequence.

Correct play: East wins with the ♡Q (a defender wins as cheaply as possible) and cashes the other hearts, followed by a switch to the ◊J, top of sequence.

South plays the ◊Q, king, ace and should then tackle trumps. With nine trumps missing Q and J, cashing the A and K is normal. Only if left-hand opponent dropped the Q or J might this approach change. When trumps do not break, declarer is faced with five losers. To eliminate the diamond loser, declarer leads a club and finesses dummy's queen. When this holds, the ♣A allows the ◊7 to be discarded and 3♠ is just made.

Even if trumps had been 2-2, declarer should finesse the ♣Q and score an overtrick by eliminating the diamond loser. To make the overtrick would be vital at duplicate. Holding just a singleton, the club finesse might normally be risky, but here East has shown up with A-K-Q in hearts and the ◊J. East cannot hold the ♣K as well, for that would make 13 HCP: East passed originally and would have opened even with 12 HCP.

Hand 46: Raising partner's pre-empt – Setting up a long suit in dummy

Dealer East : Love all

NORTH
- ♠ 4 2
- ♡ K Q 10
- ◊ K 10 8 2
- ♣ Q 7 6 3

WEST
- ♠ K 10 8
- ♡ A J 8 4 3
- ◊ A 5 4
- ♣ J 9

EAST
- ♠ A Q J 9 7 6 5
- ♡ 7
- ◊ 7 6 3
- ♣ 10 4

SOUTH
- ♠ 3
- ♡ 9 6 5 2
- ◊ Q J 9
- ♣ A K 8 5 2

WEST	NORTH	EAST	SOUTH
		3♠ (1)	No (2)
4♠ (3)	No	No	No

Bidding: (1) The best time to pre-empt is first-in-hand, when the opponents know least about each other's hand.
(2) Much too weak to enter the bidding at the 4-level.
(3) There are three sure tricks in the king of trumps and two aces. You need more than three tricks to raise a non-vulnerable pre-empt, but West has potential for a fourth trick, either via a club ruff if East has 3+ clubs or by utilising the heart suit for extra tricks.

Lead: ♣A. An A-K lead is more attractive than a near sequence.

Correct play: South cashes ♣A, ♣K, and should then switch to the ◊Q. Declarer wins the ◊A and needs to eliminate at least one diamond loser.

Counting winners, East has seven spades and two aces. The extra trick can come only from hearts. It is vital to start on hearts before drawing trumps, because dummy's trumps are needed as entries. The correct order is: win the ◊A; cash the ♡A; ruff a low heart; play a trump to dummy's eight (all of dummy's trumps are winners); ruff a low heart. As it happens, the ♡K and ♡Q have now fallen, so dummy's ♡J is high. Cross to dummy's ♠10 and cash the ♡J and the fifth heart, discarding both diamonds and making an overtrick. If North held ♡K-Q-x-x, declarer would have played ♡A; heart ruff; spade to the eight; heart ruff; spade to the ten; heart ruff; spade to the king and the last heart in dummy is high, allowing one diamond discard.

Hand 47: Responding to partner's pre-empt – Play at trick 1 – Setting up a long suit – Change of plan

Dealer South : East-West vulnerable

NORTH
♠ A 8 3
♡ A J 10
◇ A Q J 10
♣ 8 5 3

WEST
♠ J 9
♡ Q 7 5 4 3
◇ K 4 2
♣ A 9 6

EAST
♠ K 10 6 5 4 2
♡ K 9 2
◇ 8 7 6 5
♣ - - -

SOUTH
♠ Q 7
♡ 8 6
◇ 9 3
♣ K Q J 10 7 4 2

WEST	NORTH	EAST	SOUTH
			3♣ (1)
No	3NT (2)	All pass	

Bidding: (1) Worth only 3♣. A drawback to opening 4♣ (or 4◇) is that you bypass 3NT which might be the best spot. (2) With a strong balanced hand and all outside suits stopped, 3NT is a better shot than 5-minor.

Lead: ♠5. It is normal to lead the long suit.

Correct play: Play the ♠Q at once. With Q-x opposite A-x-x or K-x-x, it is best to rise with dummy's queen. The ♠A is one spade trick; playing the ♠Q is the best chance for a second spade trick. After the ♠Q wins, play a top club, intending to set up the clubs. If clubs were 2-1, declarer would force out the ace and have six club winners. If West takes the ♣A early, declarer also has six club winners.

However, West should duck the first club. When East shows out, marking declarer with three clubs, West should not take the ♣A until the third round. If declarer continues clubs and West wins the third round, West returns a spade and dummy's clubs are useless, as dummy has no entry. Declarer can give up a diamond, but can be held to eight tricks. After the first club is ducked and East shows out, declarer should switch plans: win ♠Q; win ♣K; now take the diamond finesse, which wins; play another club to dummy, which West must still duck; repeat the diamond finesse; cash the ◇A and when the ◇K drops, the last diamond is high. North wins two spades, a heart, four diamonds and two clubs, just making 3NT.

Hand 48: Responding to partner's pre-empt – Setting up a long suit in preference to taking a finesse

Dealer West : North-South vulnerable

NORTH
♠ A Q 9
♡ 6 3
◇ 10 9 8
♣ J 9 7 5 3

WEST
♠ 2
♡ K Q J 9 8 7 4
◇ 6 5 4
♣ 8 4

EAST
♠ 8 7 6 5 4
♡ A 2
◇ A K J 2
♣ A K

SOUTH
♠ K J 10 3
♡ 10 5
◇ Q 7 3
♣ Q 10 6 2

WEST	NORTH	EAST	SOUTH
3♡	No	6♡ (1)	All pass

Bidding: (1) West should have strong hearts and six tricks, and East can see five certain winners, plus potential for an extra trick, making slam a reasonable risk. The extra trick can come from a club ruff if West started with three clubs, by finessing the ◇J or by utilising the spade suit. If slam is better than 50%, it is worth bidding. The ◇J finesse on its own is a 50% chance, so that the other chances justify trying for the slam. The spade suit is a risk, but partner might be short in spades (partner is usually short where you are long), or may have a spade winner or may be able to discard spade losers if the opponents do not lead a spade.

Lead: ◇10. Choose the sequence.

Correct play: The ◇10 lead makes it unlikely North has the ◇Q. Declarer should spurn the diamond finesse and aim to set up the spade suit: win ◇A (South signals encouragement with the ◇7); lead a spade; North will probably win and play a second diamond; win the ◇K; ruff a spade; cash the ♡K and lead a heart to dummy's ace; ruff a spade; club to the king and ruff another spade. Dummy's remaining spade is now high. Cross to the ♣A and play the spade winner, discarding the diamond loser. It is vital to start the spade suit early, before drawing trumps. All of dummy's entries, including the ♡A, are vital. You need to be able to cross to dummy four times, three times to ruff the spades and once to cash the fifth spade. When setting up a long suit, use the trump entries first and keep the entries in the side suits for later. It is vital that all the opposition trumps are drawn before you attempt to cash an established winner.

CHAPTER 13

TAKEOUT DOUBLES (1)

If the opponents have opened the bidding and you have a strong hand, you will have a natural desire to enter the bidding. Yet if you lack a long, strong suit to overcall and the hand is not suitable for a 1NT overcall, you should pass even with 13+ HCP unless your hand meets the requirements for a takeout double. Two basic types of doubles are commonly used: The Penalty Double, *which asks partner to pass* (and aims to collect large penalties by defeating the opponents' contract) and the Takeout Double, *which asks partner to bid* (and aims to find the best contract for your side). As the message of these two doubles is opposite, it is clearly vital to know when partner's double is for takeout and when it is for penalties.

WHEN IS A DOUBLE FOR TAKEOUT?

In standard methods, a double is for *penalties* if:

(a) It is a double of a no-trump bid, *or*

(b) It is a double at the 3-level or higher, *or*

(c) It is a double after partner has made a bid.

Some partnerships change these conditions, but unless you and your partner have some specific agreement to the contrary, a double in any of the above situations is intended as a penalty double. Based on this, a double is for takeout if it is a double of a suit bid at the 1- level or the 2-level and partner has not made a bid yet. In the modern style, most partnerships have expanded the range of the takeout double to include:
(a) Doubles of a suit at the 1-level or 2-level even if partner has bid.
(b) A double of a 3-opening or 4-opening is generally played for takeout at duplicate.
(c) A double of a raise to the 3-level or higher, e.g., (1 ◊) : No : (3 ◊) : Double, is for takeout.
(d) A double of a 1NT or 2NT opening is *played for penalties,* but most duplicate players play that a double of a 1NT response is for takeout of the suit opened. For example, (1 ♠) : No : (1NT) : Double is played as a takeout double of 1 ♠ and is equivalent to (1 ♠) : Double.
(e) A double of a suit overcall at the 1-level or 2-level, e.g., 1 ♠ : (2 ◊) : Double, is played for *takeout* by partnerships using negative doubles (see Chapters 30 and 31). According to the standard rules such a double would be for penalties since partner has already bid. If the partnership has not stipulated that negative doubles are to be used, doubles of an overcall can be played for penalties.
(f) Many partnerships have extended the concept of negative doubles to all doubles of suit bids at the 1-level or 2-level. Such doubles are very popular at duplicate since they are so valuable in competitive auctions. Do not adopt such doubles without discussion with your partner, but if these doubles are used, then all doubles whether by opener, responder or an overcaller, of a suit bid at the 1-level or 2-level are for takeout *unless specifically stated to be for penalties.*

A takeout double is usually made at first opportunity, but this need not be so. It is certainly possible to open the bidding and make a takeout double on the second round or to make an overcall initially and follow with a takeout double on the next round, provided that the above conditions for a takeout double are met.

WHAT DOES A TAKEOUT DOUBLE SHOW?

Partner of the doubler can expect the doubler to hold:

● **High card values equivalent to at least an opening bid, generally 12+ HCP,** *and*

● **Support (four cards) or tolerance (three cards) for any unbid suit**

If the doubler is a passed hand, the strength will be 9-11 HCP plus support for the unbid suits.

If the opponents have bid two suits, a double promises 4-card or better support for the unbid suits.

WHAT DO YOU NEED TO MAKE A TAKEOUT DOUBLE?

A takeout double has point count *and* shape requirements. The more strength, the less emphasis on the shape requirements, but if minimum, the shape factors are vital. There are three types of takeout doubles:

Type A: 12-15 HCP. A takeout double with this strength should have 3-4 cards in each unbid suit AND the shortest suit should be the enemy suit, no longer than a doubleton. A double of one major should have four cards in the other major. The double of a minor suit should be no worse than 4-3 in the majors. The hand patterns of 4-4-4-1 and 5-4-4-0 with shortage in the enemy suit are said to have 'classical shape'. With such a pattern you can shade the requirements for a takeout double to about 10-11 HCP.

Type B: 16-18 HCP. If the hand fits a 1NT overcall, prefer that to a double; similarly, prefer a suit overcall if the hand is suitable and has up to 16 HCP; otherwise any hand of this strength starts with a takeout double.

Type C: 19+ HCP and any shape.

TYPE A DOUBLES – THE 12-15 ZONE (including 10-11 with classical shape)

If you have 3+ cards in the opposition suit and are short in an unbid suit, *do not double* with just 11-15 HCP. Either overcall in a strong suit, upgrade a balanced 15 to a 1NT overcall or, if neither of these is available, PASS. There is no obligation to bid after they have opened the bidding. For example:

♠ Q 6	If RHO opens 1♣, 1◊ or 1♡, you should PASS despite your 14 points, because you do
♡ A 9 7 5	not have support or tolerance for spades and you have too many cards in their suit. If
◊ A K 7	their opening bid was 1♠, you are entitled to double. You should open the bidding with
♣ J 8 7 4	12+ HCP, but there is no obligation to enter the bidding later with 11-15 HCP.

WHEN TO DOUBLE & WHEN TO OVERCALL IN THE 12-15 ZONE

Just because you have enough points to double does not mean you must double. A suit overcall can be made on hands with 8-16 HCP (1-level overcall) or 10-16 HCP (2-level overcall), so that there is an overlap in the 12-15 range between doubles and overcalls.

If they have opened with a minor suit and you are in the 12-15 zone:

• With 5-5 or 6-5 in the majors, start by overcalling one of your suits. If partner does not support this suit, you will usually have a convenient opportunity to show the second suit.
• With equal or almost equal length in the majors, 4-3, 4-4 or 5-4, start with a Double.
• With greater difference in length, two cards disparity or more (5-3 or 6-4), overcall in the long major if that suit is strong enough – if it meets the Suit Quality Test – but double if the long major is weak.

If they have opened with a major suit and you are in the 12-15 zone: Overcall with a strong 5+ holding in the other major. Overcall with a strong 5+ holding in a minor *and* three cards or fewer in the other major. Double with a strong 5-card minor *and* 4 cards in the other major.

TYPE B DOUBLES – THE 16-18 ZONE

Do not double if your hand fits a 1NT overcall. With their suit stopped, the balanced 16-18 is best described in one bid by 1NT. With 16-18 balanced, but no stopper in their suit, you may double, but be prepared to pass any minimum reply from partner. After their minor suit opening, with 16-18 balanced and 4-4 in the majors, it usually works better to double even with a stopper in their suit. You are more likely to locate a major suit fit with the double than with the 1NT overcall.

After a weak reply to a double, the doubler shows extra strength by bidding again. Doubler's suit rebid at the cheapest level normally shows 16-18 points and a 5-loser hand.

WEST	NORTH	EAST	SOUTH	North is showing spade support, 16-18 points and 5-6 losers, the
1◊	Double	No	1♠	same values as opener for 1♣ : 1♠, 3♠. The doubler bids only 2♠
No	2♠ ...			as partner has promised no values at all.

WEST	NORTH	EAST	SOUTH	North is showing 5+ spades and about 16-18 points, typically a hand
1♡	Double	No	2◊	with five losers. Double followed by a new suit = 5+ suit. With
No	2♠ ...			support for spades and more than one trick, South should raise to
				3♠ and with 2+ tricks, South should bid 4♠.

TYPE C DOUBLES – 19+ HCP

With 19+ HCP, start with a double and then:

1. If your hand is balanced with 19-21 HCP and you have a stopper in their suit, bid no-trumps at the cheapest available level if unable to support a major suit reply by partner. For example:

♠ Q 5 4	If your right-hand opponent has opened 1 ◊, you should start by doubling and then:
♡ A K J 7	If partner replies 1 ♡, you should raise this to 3 ♡.
◊ A Q	If partner replies 1 ♠, you should rebid 1NT.
♣ K J 4 2	If partner replies 2 ♣, you should rebid 2NT.

2. If your hand is not balanced, make a jump-rebid, either by a jump-raise of partner's suit or a jump-rebid in your own 5+. Suppose you hold :

♠ A Q J 6 5	If your right-hand opponent has opened 1 ◊, you should double and then:
♡ K Q 5 2	If partner replies 1 ♡, you should jump-raise to 3 ♡.
◊ 3 2	If partner replies 2 ♣, jump-rebid in your long suit to 3 ♠.
♣ A K	If partner happens to reply 1 ♠, take a shot at 4 ♠. The jump to game with a 4-loser hand is used only when you hold exceptional support for partner's suit.

WHAT IF YOU HAVE 22+ HCP?

With 22-24 points balanced, double first and then jump in no-trumps (a very rare situation). With 22+ points and unbalanced shape, or with fewer points but no more than three losers, in other words, with a hand worth a 2 ♣ opening, the standard approach is to start by bidding the enemy suit, e.g., (1 ♡) : 2 ♡ . . . This approach is no longer popular, especially at duplicate. Instead, double-first-and-bid-the-enemy-suit-on-the-next-round is used as a force to game, e.g., (1 ♡) : Double : (No) : 2 ♣, (No) : 2 ♡ . . . is artificial and very strong. It is played as forcing for one round.

RESPONDING TO PARTNER'S TAKEOUT DOUBLE

Since the doubler can be expected to have support or tolerance for any unbid major, the doubler's partner, when responding in a major, should count HCP plus 5/3/1 shortage points. If lacking tolerance for the suit chosen, the doubler will be very strong and will bid again to remove an unsuitable reply. If holding a decent 5-card minor, also use the 5/3/1 shortage count when valuing your hand and deciding at which level to show your suit. The doubler will either have tolerance for your suit or will have a strong hand with which further action can be taken.

GENERAL APPROACH WHEN REPLYING TO PARTNER'S DOUBLE

Responder holds	*Responder's action if third player passes*
0-5 points	Bid a suit – No other choice.
6-9 points	Bid a suit *or* Bid 1NT.
10-12 points	Jump-bid a suit *or* Bid 2NT.
13 points or more	Bid game in a major suit *or* Bid 3NT *or* Bid the enemy suit to force to game.

STRATEGY WHEN REPLYING TO THE DOUBLE WITH 0-5 POINTS

For practical purposes, you *must* reply to partner's takeout double when you hold 0-5 points and right-hand opponent passes. (Perhaps once every few years you might pass a takeout double for penalties with 0-5 points. A long and powerful holding in their suit, such as Q-J-10-x-x-x-x, would be acceptable.) *The only reply permitted with 0-5 points is a suit bid. Do not bid 1NT with such a weak hand.*

When you have a choice of suits to bid:
● With a major and a minor, always choose the major even if the minor is longer or better, or both.
● With two majors or two minors, bid the longer. With 5-5 in the suits, bid the higher-ranking suit. With 4-4 in the suits, choose the stronger. You do not expect to bid again unless partner makes a very strong bid.
● If your only 4+ suit is the one bid by the opposition, bid your cheapest 3-card suit. Do not bid a 3-card suit if you hold a 4-card or longer suit elsewhere that you could bid (excluding their suit, of course).

Chapters 14 and 15 deal with replying to partner's double with 6-9 points and 10-12 points respectively.

STRATEGY WITH 0-5 POINTS WHEN THIRD PLAYER DOES NOT PASS THE DOUBLE

(A) THIRD PLAYER REDOUBLES (e.g., 1♠ : Double : Redouble : ?)

Over the redouble, take the same action as though third player had passed. The bidding is no higher, the redoubler has not robbed you of any bidding space and so your task in replying to the double is no tougher. Although your duty to reply to the double ceases if third player bids, this does not apply after a redouble.

One of the reasons you should act over the redouble is that the doubler is usually unsure of the best spot (that is why the double was chosen, to ask you for your best suit) and if you pass it back to the doubler, the doubler may not have a clearcut choice or even an easy choice. Make your normal reply and take the pressure off partner. Another important reason is that with the redouble showing 10+ HCP, your side is in considerable jeopardy and a penalty double is quite feasible. To bid immediately over the double is a show of confidence (even if you feel anything but confident) and the opponents may think twice about doubling a confident bidder. However, if you pass, you are advertising grave weakness and the opponents will be only too pleased to double you or partner now wherever you run. Bidding over the redouble is a psychologically sound show of strength, passing over the redouble gives away your abject weakness. Partner will not be misled by your action. With an opening bid, a takeout double and a redouble, how much can be left for you?

(B) THIRD PLAYER BIDS A NEW SUIT OR RAISES OPENER

You should pass with all hands in the 0-5 range. To bid over intervention promises 6+ points. However, partner may take further action, including another double, and you might be required to bid later.

♠ 7 2
♡ Q 8 6 5
♢ 9 4 3 2
♣ 7 6 2

1. WEST	NORTH	EAST	SOUTH
1♠	Double	No	?

2. WEST	NORTH	EAST	SOUTH
1♠	Double	Rdble	?

3. WEST	NORTH	EAST	SOUTH
1♠	Double	2♣	?

4. WEST	NORTH	EAST	SOUTH
1♠	Double	2♠	?

In auctions 1 and 2, South should bid 2♡, but in 3 and 4, South should pass. In 4, it might continue:

WEST	NORTH	EAST	SOUTH
1♠	Double	2♠	No
No	Double	No	?

North's second double is still for takeout (double of a suit at the 2-level when partner has not bid) and South is obliged to reply. South should bid 3♡. Prefer a major to a minor.

FURTHER ACTION BY THE DOUBLER AFTER A MINIMUM SUIT REPLY

12-15 points, 6-7 losers : Pass. Do not bid again with a minimum double after a weak reply.
16-18 points, 5 losers : Bid again. Raise partner's suit or bid your own 5-card or longer suit.
19 points up, 4 losers : Make a jump rebid. Jump-raise partner's suit or jump bid your own long suit.
19-21 points, balanced : Bid no-trumps at cheapest level unless able to jump-raise partner's major.
22-24 points, balanced : Jump-rebid in no-trumps unless able to raise partner's major suit to game.

With Type A, the doubler is expected to pass any weak suit reply and so has to be prepared for any reply. If doubling with minimum points, the doubler must have support or tolerance for any suit partner might bid. To double and bid again shows a strong doubling hand, at least 16 points or more.

FURTHER ACTION BY THE DOUBLER'S PARTNER

If the doubler raised your suit reply, bid again with prospects for two tricks. By bidding again, the doubler indicates a hand of about five losers. If you have two winners, that will reduce the losers to three, enough for game in a major. Similarly, if the doubler jump-raised your suit, e.g., (1♠) : Double : (No): 1♡ : (No) : 3♡, you should bid on with one sure winner. The doubler's jump indicates a 4-loser hand, one trick short of game. If you have a winner, that should be enough to produce game in a major. With a minor, you would need a little bit more. If the doubler did not have four losers or the equivalent, the doubler should not be bidding for nine tricks opposite a hand which could be worthless. If one trick is not enough for game, the doubler should not follow up with a jump-rebid. That is why with a balanced hand of 19-21 points, the doubler rebids no-trumps at the cheapest level and not with a jump-rebid. A balanced hand has too many losers and makes few tricks opposite a worthless or almost worthless hand. Balanced hands need the full point count quota for game.

EXERCISES

A. Right-hand opponent opened 1 ◊ . What action do you take on each of these hands?

1. ♠ K 8 6 2	2. ♠ A J 7 4	3. ♠ A J 7	4. ♠ A 7 2	5. ♠ A 8 7 2
♡ A Q 7 3	♡ A Q 9 8 3	♡ A Q 9 8 3	♡ J 2	♡ Q 6
◊ 4	◊ 7	◊ 7	◊ A K 8 6 2	◊ A K 9 4
♣ K J 7 3	♣ Q 7 2	♣ Q 7 5 2	♣ Q 9 7	♣ K J 8

B. Partner doubled left-hand opponent's 1 ◊ opening. Right-hand opponent passed. Your action on these hands?

1. ♠ 9 5 4 3	2. ♠ 9 8 7 3 2	3. ♠ 8 7 4 2	4. ♠ J 8 7 2	5. ♠ 6 5 2
♡ 8 3	♡ K 9 5 2	♡ 8 3	♡ J 8 7 2	♡ 9 6 3
◊ 10 6 4 2	◊ 6 4	◊ 6 4	◊ Q 8	◊ A 4 3
♣ 9 7 3	♣ 5 3	♣ K 8 6 4 3	♣ 7 5 2	♣ 9 8 5 3

6. ♠ 7 4 2	7. ♠ 8 7 5 3 2	8. ♠ J 3 2	9. ♠ 8 7 2	10. ♠ 7 4 2
♡ 9 7 3	♡ J 6 5 4 2	♡ 2	♡ J 2	♡ 6 3
◊ Q 8 5 3	◊ 9 7	◊ 8 7 5 4 3 2	◊ Q J 6 2	◊ A J 10 8
♣ 6 5 2	♣ 6	♣ J 7 5	♣ 8 5 3 2	♣ 9 7 4 2

C. You doubled their 1 ◊ opening and partner replied 1 ♠ . The opener passes. Your next action on these hands?

1. ♠ K Q 9 5	2. ♠ K Q 8 4	3. ♠ 3	4. ♠ A Q 7 2	5. ♠ A K 3
♡ A 8 7 3	♡ A K 7 6	♡ A K J 9 3	♡ K Q J 2	♡ A Q J 2
◊ J 4	◊ 3	◊ A K 6	◊ 2	◊ 6 4
♣ K J 7	♣ A Q J 3	♣ A Q 9 5	♣ A J 5 2	♣ J 8 7 3

PARTNERSHIP BIDDING: How should the following hands be bid? The North-South is as indicated.

SET 27 – WEST	SET 27 – EAST	SET 28 – WEST	SET 28 – EAST
1. South opens 1 ◊ .	**1.** South opens 1 ◊ .	**1.** South opens 1 ◊ .	**1.** South opens 1 ◊ .
♠ A K J 8	♠ 6 4	♠ A J 4 3	♠ 8 2
♡ A J 5	♡ Q 7 4 3 2	♡ K Q 7 2	♡ J 9 8 3
◊ Q 8	◊ 9 7 3	◊ A 3	◊ 8 6 2
♣ 8 7 4 3	♣ 6 5 2	♣ K 7 2	♣ Q J 5 4
2. North opens 1 ♣ .	**2.** North opens 1 ♣ .	**2.** North opens 1 ♡ .	**2.** North opens 1 ♡ .
♠ J 7 3 2	♠ K Q 6 4	♠ 8 7 4 2	♠ K Q J 5
♡ 8 3	♡ A 9 7 2	♡ J 6 3	♡ 9
◊ Q 9 8 6 4	◊ A 3 2	◊ 8 5 2	◊ A K 7
♣ 7 3	♣ 8 4	♣ 9 8 4	♣ A K 6 3 2
3. North opens 1 ♠ .	**3.** North opens 1 ♠ .	**3.** South opens 1 ◊ .	**3.** South opens 1 ◊ .
♠ 8 5 3 2	♠ Q 4	♠ A K 7	♠ 9 6 3 2
♡ 7 6 4 3	♡ A J 9 8	♡ K Q J 5	♡ A 6 4 3
◊ 9 8	◊ K Q 7 2	◊ 9	◊ 4 3
♣ 8 4 3	♣ A 9 7	♣ A K 6 3 2	♣ 8 5 4
4. South opens 1 ♡ .	**4.** South opens 1 ♡ .	**4.** North opens 1 ♣ .	**4.** North opens 1 ♣ .
♠ K Q J 6	♠ 10 8 2	♠ 7 6 4 2	♠ A Q 9 8
♡ 7	♡ 6 5 4 3 2	♡ A 2	♡ Q J 9 7 3
◊ A K 9 8	◊ 7 3	◊ 7 6 5	◊ A K
♣ Q J 9 4	♣ K 7 5	♣ 9 8 4 2	♣ 7 3
5. South opens 1 ♠ , North raises to 2 ♠ .	**5.** South opens 1 ♠ , North raises to 2 ♠ .	**5.** South opens 1 ◊ , North responds 1 ♠ .	**5.** South opens 1 ◊ , North responds 1 ♠ .
♠ 8 6 3	♠ 7 2	♠ J 8 7	♠ 6 3
♡ Q 7 5 3	♡ A K J 4	♡ 6 2	♡ A K J 5
◊ 7 2	◊ A Q 8 3	◊ 9 7 4 2	◊ A 6 3
♣ J 7 4 3	♣ K 6 5	♣ 8 6 4 3	♣ A Q J 7

PLAY HANDS ON TAKEOUT DOUBLES (1)

Hand 49: Bidding over a takeout double – Card combinations and card reading

Dealer North : Love all

NORTH
♠ A 7 4 2
♡ A K 6
◇ A 10 7 3 2
♣ 6

WEST
♠ 5
♡ 8 5 4 3
◇ Q 8 4
♣ J 10 5 4 2

EAST
♠ Q 10 8
♡ Q J 10 9
◇ 6 5
♣ A K Q 9

SOUTH
♠ K J 9 6 3
♡ 7 2
◇ K J 9
♣ 8 7 3

WEST	NORTH	EAST	SOUTH
	1◇	Dble (1)	1♠ (2)
No (3)	3♠ (4)	No	4♠ (5)
No	No	No	

Bidding: (1) Worth a double. 14 HCP, short in the suit opened, support for hearts and clubs, tolerance for spades.
(2) Make your normal bid over the double.
(3) If third hand bids over the double, pass with 0-5 HCP.
(4) Too strong for 2♠. Worth 18 points counting the singleton.
(5) With 8+ points, accept opener's game invitation.

Lead: ♣4 or ♡5. The club holding is the stronger, so that the ♣4 is slightly better. A singleton trump lead is usually very poor and so is a suit bid by dummy, hence diamonds are out.

Correct play: East would win the club lead with the queen and switch to the ♡Q.

After winning, declarer should play ♠A, followed by a spade to the jack when East follows with the ten. With nine cards missing the queen, the best chance normally is to cash the ace and king and hope for the queen to drop. As East's double implies tolerance for spades, you should play East to hold three spades, not two. After the ♠J wins, draw the last trump and switch to diamonds. Cash the ◇K and then lead the jack, letting it run if West plays low (there is no benefit for West to cover with the queen). When the ◇J scores, diamonds are continued, and via two working finesses, South makes a lucky twelve tricks. One could finesse East for the ◇Q, but because of the double, East is more likely to be short in diamonds. East could have ◇Q-x, but the odds favour playing the non-doubler for a missing queen in the suit doubled. You should cash the ◇K before taking the diamond finesse, just in case the ◇Q happens to be singleton.

Hand 50: Responding to a double – Doubler's rebid – Card combinations and card reading

Dealer East : North-South vulnerable

NORTH
♠ J 3
♡ K J 4 2
◇ 8 6 5 3
♣ 10 7 5

WEST
♠ 10 9 4
♡ 10 8 6
◇ J 10 9 2
♣ Q 9 2

EAST
♠ 8 7 6 2
♡ Q 9
◇ K Q 7
♣ A K J 6

SOUTH
♠ A K Q 5
♡ A 7 5 3
◇ A 4
♣ 8 4 3

WEST	NORTH	EAST	SOUTH
		1♣	Dble (1)
No	1♡ (2)	No	2♡ (3)
No	No (4)	No	

Bidding: (1) Not ideal for the double because of the shortage in diamonds, but with both majors and better than minimum values, it is better to double than to pass or overcall 1NT.
(2) Show the major, not the minor, in response to a double.
(3) Just all right to raise to 2♡. Worth 18 points for hearts.
(4) With 8+ points or with 2+ tricks, North would bid on.

Lead: ♣A. Leading an A-K suit is very attractive.

Correct play: West plays the ♣9, encouraging. East continues with the ♣K and a third club. West switches to the ◇J. North should take the ◇A and start on trumps. How should declarer manage the hearts?

The ♡Q is marked with East. Dummy has 17 HCP, you have 5 HCP, 18 HCP are missing. West has shown up with the ♣Q and the ◇J. East began with four clubs and so figures to hold a balanced hand (if 4-1-4-4, East would open 1◇). As East opened 1♣ and not 1NT (12-14), all the remaining points will be with East Thus, East figures to hold the ♡Q and finessing the ♡J will fail. Reject the heart finesse and cash the ♡A and ♡K. When the queen drops, lucky you, draw the last trump and run the spades, playing the jack first to make nine tricks. If the ♡Q had not dropped, you would still make eight tricks.

Hand 51: Desperation response to a takeout double – Scrambling for tricks with a poor trump fit

Dealer South : East-West vulnerable

NORTH
- ♠ A 9 5
- ♡ A K J 9 3
- ◇ K 8 5 3
- ♣ Q

WEST
- ♠ 10 7 2
- ♡ 8 6 5 4 2
- ◇ 9 6
- ♣ K 4 3

EAST
- ♠ K Q J 8
- ♡ 7
- ◇ A Q 7 2
- ♣ A 9 8 6

SOUTH
- ♠ 6 4 3
- ♡ Q 10
- ◇ J 10 4
- ♣ J 10 7 5 2

WEST	NORTH	EAST	SOUTH
			No
No	1♡	Dble	No
1♠ (1)	2◇ (2)	2♠ (3)	No
No (4)	No (5)		

Bidding: With no 4+ suit other than the opposition's and 0-5 points, bid your cheapest 3-card suit. 2♣ would be sensible because of the ♣K, but if East raises, you are in *three* clubs, while if East raises spades, you can stop in *two*.
(2) Certainly worth a second bid. Best to show your other suit.
(3) Even over an intervening bid, the doubler's raise promises more than minimum values. It is a mild invitation for game, showing 16+ points and about a 5-loser hand.
(4) Do not panic when raised. Pass and do your best.
(5) If partner cannot raise an effort when you have bid twice, do not persevere without about 19+ points or excellent shape.

Lead: ♡A. An initial trump lead would also be very sensible.

Correct play: North should switch to ace and another trump. When dummy has ruffing potential but no long suit, a trump lead or trump shift is attractive. If North shifts to the ♣Q at trick 2, win with the ♣K, finesse the ◇Q, cash the ◇A, ruff a diamond, ruff a heart and ruff dummy's last diamond. You can then lead a club or a spade. When you are short of trumps, do not draw trumps early, but try to scramble ruffs in both hands.

Hand 52: Doubler's strong rebid – Ruffing a loser in dummy – Ruffing high when you can afford to

Dealer West : Game all

NORTH
- ♠ A 8
- ♡ 8 4 3
- ◇ A 10
- ♣ K Q 10 8 3 2

WEST
- ♠ J 5 4 3 2
- ♡ K 7 5
- ◇ 6 2
- ♣ J 6 5

EAST
- ♠ K
- ♡ A Q J 10 9 2
- ◇ K Q J 7
- ♣ A 7

SOUTH
- ♠ Q 10 9 7 6
- ♡ 6
- ◇ 9 8 5 4 3
- ♣ 9 4

WEST	NORTH	EAST	SOUTH
No	1♣	Dble (1)	No (2)
1♠	2♣ (3)	3♡ (4)	No
4♡ (5)	No	No	No

Bidding: (1) Hands with only four losers are too strong for a simple overcall or a strong jump-overcall. Start by doubling.
(2) With too little to reply normally, do not bid over a double.
(3) Despite the minimum opening, the strong suit justifies 2♣.
(4) The 4-loser hand is shown by doubling first and a jump-rebid later. 3♡ shows 5+ hearts, a huge hand and no fit for spades. It is not forcing, but partner should bid on with a sure trick or a likely trick.
(5) The ♡K counts as a winner in this auction, as partner would be counting its absence as a loser. If the doubler can bid for nine tricks opposite possibly nothing, the king of trumps is worth one trick more.

Lead: ♣9. It is normal to lead partner's suit. Start with the top card when leading from a doubleton.

Correct play: Declarer should win the ♣A, cash the ♡A and then lead the ◇K. North wins and continues clubs. East should ruff the third club high to prevent a possible over-ruff by South. Then cash the ◇Q and ruff the ◇7 with dummy's ♡K. When you can afford to, ruff high. A heart from dummy allows trumps to be drawn and East loses one spade, one diamond and one club. The traps to avoid are drawing three rounds of trumps at the outset (dummy will be without a trump to ruff the diamond), drawing two rounds of trumps (North can lead a third trump when in with the ◇A and again dummy has no trump to ruff the diamond loser), playing the ♡K early (then North can over-ruff dummy on the third diamond) or failing to ruff with the ♡K (again North can over-ruff dummy). It is true that if East plays trumps early and South discards two diamonds, declarer will not need to ruff the diamond loser, but you should not rely on opposition error.

CHAPTER 14

TAKEOUT DOUBLES (2)

STRATEGY WHEN REPLYING TO THE DOUBLE WITH 6-9 POINTS

With 6-9 points, you may reply with a suit bid at the cheapest level, but you may also reply with 1NT, which shows 6-9 points and a stopper in the opposition's suit. With a choice of actions, your priorities are:

• Major suit as first choice   • 1NT as second choice   • Minor suit as the last choice

A 1NT reply denies a 4-card major (other than in their suit, of course). A minor suit bid denies an available major and also denies the ability to reply 1NT (inadequate strength or no stopper or shape too unbalanced). Exceptionally, with 5+ trumps including 3+ honours, you may pass and convert the takeout double to penalties.

With 6-9 points, you are strong enough to bid twice. You can bid quite safely up to the 2-level, and you may bid to the 3-level if necessary to compete against their 2-level contract. Thus, if the auction does become competitive, the doubler with a minimum double can let the bidding come back to you, safe in the knowledge that with 6-9 points, you will not allow the opponents to buy the contract at the 2-level. The basic principle is, *'Do not sell out at the 2-level if you have a trump fit or if they have a trump fit'*.

CHOICE OF SUITS WHEN REPLYING WITH BOTH MAJORS OR BOTH MINORS

When replying to partner's takeout double and obliged to choose between two suits of the same rank: Bid your longer suit first and with 5-5, bid the higher-ranking first. With 6-9 points and 4-4 in suits of the same rank, it is better to bid the higher-ranking suit first, not up-the-line. You may have to bid twice in a competitive auction and rebidding in the lower-ranking suit next time allows partner a cheaper preference.

STRATEGY WITH 6-9 POINTS WHEN THIRD PLAYER DOES NOT PASS THE DOUBLE

(A) THIRD PLAYER REDOUBLES (e.g., 1 ◊ : Double : Redouble : ?)

Over the redouble, take the same action as though third player had passed. You will not be faced with this problem very often with 6-9 points, since if the opening, the double and the redouble are all genuine, you will rarely have 6+ points. Still, the opposition's bidding is not always trustworthy and particularly if the opener was in third seat, you can find yourself in this situation. The reasons for taking the same action as if third player had passed are exactly the same as when you had 0-5 points (see Chapter 13, page 73). Do not be reluctant to bid 1NT over the redouble if that is your normal action. The advantage of 1NT is that it guarantees some values, while a suit bid can be 0-5 points or 6-9. The 1NT reply gives partner a better picture of the values held. If you have enough to bid 1NT, the hand will often belong to your side.

(B) THIRD PLAYER BIDS A NEW SUIT OR RAISES OPENER

With 6-9 points, you are strong enough to bid despite the interference. If your normal reply is still available, make that reply. Bidding over interference will show 6-9 points. You would pass with 0-5 points and you would jump with 10-12 (see Chapter 15). If third player bids a major suit at the 1-level, your 1NT need have a stopper only in the suit opened: you can rely on the doubler for a stopper in the suit bid by third player. If third player changes suit, double for penalties with a strong 4-card holding in that suit. As the doubler should also have tolerance for that suit your side figures to have more trumps than the bidder. It is vital to do so, since this is an area where it is common for third player to psyche ('to psyche' = to make a bluff bid) and they will rob you of your suits if you cannot double for penalties. To expose a psyche, double for penalties and if they revert to opener's suit you then bid your suit at the appropriate level.

FURTHER ACTION BY THE DOUBLER AFTER A 1NT REPLY

The doubler's action over a minimum suit reply was covered in Chapter 13, page 73. Over 1NT, the doubler passes with a minimum hand with no 5-card suit. A suit bid at the 2-level will promise a 5-card suit, but it is not forcing: Pass with a doubleton or with a minimum and 3-card support, but with a maximum and three trumps, raise to the 3-level. The doubler's raise to 2NT is invitational (17-18 points) while a jump to the 3-level in a suit is forcing and promises a 5+ suit. The 1NT bidder raises with 3-card support or bids 3NT with only a doubleton in partner's suit.

EXERCISES

A. The bidding has been (1 ◇) : Double : (Pass) : ? What do you reply to partner's double on each of these hands?

1. ♠ K 8 6 4	2. ♠ 8 4 3	3. ♠ 8 4 3	4. ♠ 8 2	5. ♠ K 8 7 2
♡ Q 7	♡ Q 7	♡ K Q	♡ 9 2	♡ K 9 4 2
◇ K 9 7 3	◇ K 9 7 3	◇ 7 6 4 3	◇ K Q J 10 8	◇ 7 3 2
♣ 8 4 3	♣ K 8 6 4	♣ K 8 6 4	♣ Q J 7 4	♣ Q 7

B. The bidding has been (1 ♠) : Double : (Pass) : ? What do you reply to partner's double with these hands?

1. ♠ 4 2	2. ♠ A J 6	3. ♠ A J 6	4. ♠ A J 6 2	5. ♠ 6 4 3
♡ Q J 6 4	♡ K 9 7 2	♡ 8 4 3 2	♡ 7 6	♡ 9 7
◇ J 3	◇ 8 4 3 2	◇ K 9 7 2	◇ K 9 7 2	◇ A 9 8 3
♣ K 8 7 3 2	♣ 7 5	♣ 7 5	♣ 8 4 3	♣ A 8 7 4

C. After (1 ♡) : Double : (2 ♡) : ? What action do you take on these hands in reply to the double?

1. ♠ K 7 6 4	2. ♠ Q J 7 3 2	3. ♠ A 6	4. ♠ 9 7 2	5. ♠ 9 8 7 2
♡ A 3	♡ 7 4 3	♡ 9 6 3	♡ 8 7 2	♡ 6 2
◇ 8 6 2	◇ 6 4	◇ J 7 6 4 3	◇ 8 6 2	◇ Q 8 6 4 3
♣ 9 6 4 3	♣ 8 3 2	♣ K 8 5	♣ A K 9 7	♣ K Q

D. You doubled 1 ◇ and partner responded 1NT. What is your rebid on each of these hands?

1. ♠ K Q 6 2	2. ♠ A J 7 2	3. ♠ A 9 4 2	4. ♠ A 7 3 2	5. ♠ A Q 8 7 2
♡ A Q 7 3	♡ A Q 4	♡ A K J	♡ A J 9 7 5	♡ K Q J 6
◇ 4	◇ Q 9 7	◇ 8 7 6	◇ 2	◇ A K
♣ K 9 3 2	♣ A K 3	♣ K Q 5	♣ K 9 7	♣ 4 3

PARTNERSHIP BIDDING: There is no North-South bidding other than indicated.

SET 29 – WEST	**SET 29 – EAST**	**SET 30 – WEST**	**SET 30 – EAST**
1. South opens 1 ◇ .	**1.** South opens 1 ◇ .	**1.** North opens 1 ♠ .	**1.** North opens 1 ♠ .
♠ A Q 9 2	♠ K 5	♠ K 9 6 2	♠ 10 3
♡ A 8 7 3	♡ J 6	♡ 7 3	♡ A J 8 4
◇ A 8	◇ 6 4 3 2	◇ A J 7 4	◇ K Q 9
♣ J 4 3	♣ K 8 7 5 2	♣ 7 4 2	♣ A 9 8 6
2. North opens 1 ♣ .	**2.** North opens 1 ♣ .	**2.** South opens 1 ♣ .	**2.** South opens 1 ♣ .
♠ K 7 4	♠ A Q 5 2	♠ K 6 5	♠ A 8 7 3
♡ A 8 3 2	♡ K Q 6 5	♡ A Q 7 2	♡ K 9 6 4
◇ 9 5	◇ A J 7 3	◇ A 7 5 4	◇ J 2
♣ J 9 3 2	♣ 6	♣ 9 6	♣ 7 4 2
3. South opens 1 ♠ .	**3.** South opens 1 ♠ .	**3.** North opens 1 ♣ .	**3.** North opens 1 ♣ .
♠ 7	♠ 8 6 4 3 2	♠ A 8 3 2	♠ K 6 5 4
♡ A J 9 7	♡ K Q 4 3	♡ K 6 5 2	♡ A Q 7
◇ K J 8 3	◇ 7 6	◇ 9 8	◇ A 7 5 4
♣ A 9 6 2	♣ Q 4	♣ 7 5 3	♣ 6 2
4. North opens 1 ♡ .	**4.** North opens 1 ♡ .	**4.** South opens 1 ◇ .	**4.** South opens 1 ◇ .
♠ K 8 2	♠ Q J 6 3	♠ A K 7	♠ 9 5 2
♡ 7 6 4 2	♡ 8	♡ K 9 4 2	♡ A Q 3
◇ Q J 4	◇ K 9 5 2	◇ 7 5 3	◇ K 6 4
♣ Q 8 2	♣ A K 7 5	♣ A K J	♣ 10 6 3 2
5. South opens 1 ◇ , South rebids 2 ◇ .	**5.** South opens 1 ◇ , South rebids 2 ◇ .	**5.** North opens 1 ♠ , North rebids 2 ♠ .	**5.** North opens 1 ♠ , North rebids 2 ♠ .
♠ K J 8 3	♠ 9 7 6 5 4	♠ 6 5 3	♠ 7 2
♡ K 9 7	♡ A Q 3 2	♡ 8 3	♡ K Q 9 7
◇ A 2	◇ 8 6	◇ K 7 5 2	◇ A 8 4 3
♣ Q 7 4 3	♣ 9 8	♣ A Q 6 4	♣ K J 2

PLAY HANDS ON TAKEOUT DOUBLES (2)

Hand 53: NT response to a takeout double – Card-reading for a two-way finesse

Dealer North : North-South vulnerable

WEST	NORTH	EAST	SOUTH
	No	1◊	Dble (1)
No	1NT (2)	No (3)	3NT (4)
No	No	No	

NORTH
- ♠ 6 4 2
- ♡ 8 6 2
- ◊ K 9 4
- ♣ K J 10 3

WEST
- ♠ J 10 8
- ♡ 10 9 7 5 4 3
- ◊ 7 5
- ♣ 9 6

EAST
- ♠ K 9 7 5
- ♡ A
- ◊ Q J 10 8 6
- ♣ Q 8 5

SOUTH
- ♠ A Q 3
- ♡ K Q J
- ◊ A 3 2
- ♣ A 7 4 2

Bidding: (1) If too strong for a 1NT overcall, start by doubling. If no major fit is discovered, rebid in no-trumps. Double and no-trumps later is stronger than 1NT at once.
(2) 1NT is superior to 2♣. If the opening bid had been 1♡ or 1♠, 2♣ would be correct.
(3) Without freakish shape or a strong suit, a minimum opener should not bid again if partner is too weak to find a response.
(4) As the 1NT shows 6-9 points, South has enough to raise to game. Had North replied 2♣, which has a range of 0-9, South could not afford to bid 3NT opposite perhaps 0-2 points. Over 2♣, South would rebid only 2NT.

Lead: ◊ Q. Even though the opponents have a stopper, a long suit headed by a sequence is your best start.

Correct play: Counting dummy's and declarer's points, only 13 HCP are missing, almost all of which must be with East for the opening bid. Knock out the ♡A first. East wins the ♡A and continues with the ◊J. Now tackle the clubs. Without any clues about the location of the high cards, cashing ♣A and then finessing the ♣J is the best play, but here the ♣Q figures to be with East, so cash the ♣K and lead the ♣J (you can afford the jack because you hold the ten). If East covers, capture the ♣Q; if East plays low, let the ♣J run. Even if this lost, West has no more diamonds and East has no entry because you carefully knocked out the ♡A first. You can finesse the ♣Q and make ten tricks (two spades, two hearts, two diamonds, four clubs).

Hand 54: Penalty pass of a takeout double – Opening lead after a penalty pass

Dealer East : Love all

WEST	NORTH	EAST	SOUTH
		No	1◊
Dble	No (1)	No (2)	No (3)

NORTH
- ♠ 10 8 6
- ♡ 7 5 3 2
- ◊ 9 6
- ♣ 9 7 4 3

WEST
- ♠ K Q 9 3
- ♡ A Q 9 4
- ◊ 3
- ♣ A 10 6 2

EAST
- ♠ J 7 5
- ♡ J 10
- ◊ K Q J 10 8
- ♣ J 8 5

SOUTH
- ♠ A 4 2
- ♡ K 8 6
- ◊ A 7 5 4 2
- ♣ K Q

Bidding: (1) Do not bid. Usually East will reply to the double and North-South are off the hook. Bidding on a weak misfit is asking for trouble. It is far riskier for North to bid than to pass.
(2) To justify passing a 1-level double, your trumps should be better than declarer's, normally 5+ trumps with at least three honours. This is logical since to beat 1◊, you have to take 7+ tricks with diamonds as trumps. As partner is likely to be short in diamonds, your diamonds must be superb. Do not pass a takeout double out of weakness or out of fear. Converting a takeout double to penalties by passing is always based on a deliberate intention of massacring their contract.
(3) If South had an escape suit, South would bid it, but West would double any escape attempt, including 1NT.

Lead: ◊ 3. When partner passes your takeout double, a trump lead is expected. Since partner's trumps are better than declarer's, this helps partner draw declarer's trumps.

Correct play: South wins the ◊ A and plays the ♣K or ♣Q. West wins and switches to the ♠K or returns a club (either is safer than a heart switch). South wins, but has no good continuation. On gaining the lead, East will draw South's trumps and switch to the ♡J. Best defence will collect ten tricks, defeating 1◊ doubled by four tricks. South does well to go only three off. Only?

Hand 55: Doubler's rebid after a 1NT response – Leading towards honours to set up a long suit

Dealer South : Game all

NORTH
♠ 10 5 2
♡ 10 9 7 6 2
♢ Q 7
♣ 10 9 5

WEST
♠ K Q 7 6 4
♡ A Q 8 3
♢ 8 2
♣ A K

EAST
♠ 9 3
♡ K 5 4
♢ A 10 5 3
♣ 8 7 3 2

SOUTH
♠ A J 8
♡ J
♢ K J 9 6 4
♣ Q J 6 4

WEST	NORTH	EAST	SOUTH
			1 ◇
Dble (1)	No (2)	1NT (3)	No (4)
3 ♠ (5)	No	3NT (6)	All pass

Bidding: (1) To overcall in spades could miss out on a fit in hearts. With both majors and opening values, choose the double.
(2) Pass with a poor hand over the double.
(3) Shows 6-9 points, a diamond stopper and no 4-card major.
(4) Do not rebid with a modest opening if partner cannot reply.
(5) Forcing and shows five spades. The 1NT denial of a 4-card major means a heart fit does not exist, but East could still hold three spades.
(6) Denies three spades.

Lead: ◇ 6. The long suit is normal, but the ♣ 4 is a sensible alternative, as declarer has indicated that the diamonds are stopped and may not be prepared for clubs.

Correct play: On the ◇ 6 lead, North plays the ◇ Q and East should take the ace. The remaining 10-5-3 is a stopper against South's diamonds and North is unlikely to gain the lead. If you duck the first diamond, North can return a diamond and South's diamonds can be set up.
With only six top winners, spades must be tackled. Lead a spade towards dummy, playing the king if South plays low. Return to hand with a heart to the king and lead another spade, playing the queen if South plays low. A third spade removes the remaining spades and sets up two spade winners. If South plays the ♠ A earlier, declarer's task is easier. South can cash two diamonds, but the ◇ 10 is a stopper on the fourth round.

Hand 56: Competitive bidding after a takeout double – Setting up a winner for a discard

Dealer West : Love all

NORTH
♠ K 3
♡ A 8 7 3 2
♢ J 6
♣ K Q 4 2

WEST
♠ J 10 7 4 2
♡ Q J 10
♢ 10 9 2
♣ A 10

EAST
♠ A Q 9 8
♡ 9
♢ A K 7 5 3
♣ J 8 7

SOUTH
♠ 6 5
♡ K 6 5 4
♢ Q 8 4
♣ 9 6 5 3

WEST	NORTH	EAST	SOUTH
No	1 ♡	Dble (1)	2 ♡ (2)
2 ♠ (3)	No (4)	3 ♠ (5)	No
4 ♠ (6)	No	No	No

Bidding: (1) With four spades and opening values, double rather than overcall in a 5-card or longer minor.
(2) Worth 6 points and a raise because of the doubleton.
(3) It would be very timid to pass. You are not obliged to bid over 2♡, but you are also not forced to pass. 2♠ shows 4+ spades and 6-9 points. Had partner opened 1♠ you would raise to 2♠ – your 2♠ bid here is a similar supporting bid.
(4) In the direct seat, do not bid again with a minimum hand. If East also passes 2♠, partner can compete to 3♡.
(5) 14 HCP plus 3 for the singleton justifies inviting 4♠.
(6) With nine points (one for the doubleton), West is maximum and should accept the game invitation.

Lead: ♣K. Spades are out. It is not attractive to lead from an ace-high suit without the king as well, even if partner has supported your suit, so that eliminates a heart lead (although the ♡ A lead would not cost in this case). Prefer a club lead where the suit has two honours to diamonds with only one honour.

Correct play: Take the ♣ K with the ace, lead the ♠ J for a finesse and draw trumps. A club to the ten forces out the queen. You later discard a diamond loser on the ♣ J and play ◇ A, ◇ K and ruff a diamond, setting up dummy's diamonds. If North starts with the ♡ A lead and continues hearts, ruff in dummy, play ◇ A, ◇ K and give up a diamond. Later, cross to the ♣ A, take the spade finesse, draw trumps and again dummy's diamonds have been set up, giving you eleven tricks.

CHAPTER 15

TAKEOUT DOUBLES (3)

STRATEGY WHEN REPLYING TO THE DOUBLE WITH 10-12 POINTS

With 10-12 points, make *a jump reply* in a suit or in no-trumps. With a choice of actions, the priorities are:

- Major suit as first choice   • 2NT as second choice   • Minor suit as the last choice

With 10-12 points, including shortage points when bidding a major or a good 5-card minor, you have almost enough for a game, but not quite. To show these values, a jump-bid is made to encourage the doubler to push on to game. The jump-bid in a suit is not forcing and does not promise a 5-card suit. If you intend to bid a suit in reply to a double, any quality 4-card suit will do (and in desperation, as we have seen, you may have to bid a 3-card suit). Likewise, any 4-card suit is good enough for a jump-response to a double. A 2NT reply denies a 4-card major (other than in the opposition's suit, of course). A minor suit bid denies an available major and also denies the ability to bid 2NT (incorrect strength or no stopper or shape too unbalanced). With 5+ trumps including 3+ honours, you may pass and convert the takeout double to penalties.

A reply showing 10-12 points is considered strong and if the doubler bids a new suit, that shows at least a 5-card suit and is forcing for one round. If the doubler bids the enemy suit over a jump in a suit, this asks for a stopper. With a stopper, bid no-trumps; with no stopper, make the most descriptive bid available.

CHOICE OF SUITS WHEN REPLYING WITH BOTH MAJORS OR BOTH MINORS

If you are worth a jump reply and have to choose between two suits of the same rank, bid the longer suit first. With 10-12 points and 4-4 or 5-5 in the majors after partner's double of a minor, it is sensible to bid the enemy suit. A cue-bid of opener's suit here is played as forcing to suit agreement. The doubler will usually bid a major which you can raise to the three-level to invite game or you can raise to game with extra shape. With 10-12 points and 4-4 in the minors and no stopper in their suit, jump in your stronger minor.

STRATEGY WITH 10-12 POINTS WHEN THIRD PLAYER DOES NOT PASS THE DOUBLE

(A) THIRD PLAYER REDOUBLES (e.g., 1 ◇ : Double : Redouble : ?)

Over the redouble, give a jump-reply just as though third player had passed. Someone does not have their bid, but you cannot be sure who is foxing, the opener or the redoubler. Trust partner to have the values for the double and give your normal reply. If you bid, but do not jump, partner will place you with 0-9 points (see Chapters 13 and 14) and not with 10-12.

(B) THIRD PLAYER BIDS A NEW SUIT OR RAISES OPENER

1. The bidding is still at the 1-level, e.g., (1 ◇) : Double : (1 ♠) : ?
Give your normal reply with a jump, either in a suit or to 2NT. For a 2NT reply, it is more important to have a stopper in the suit opened (since the doubler is usually weak in the suit opened) than a stopper in the suit bid by third player (since opener has support or tolerance for that suit). With a strong 4+ holding in the suit bid by third player, double for penalties. There is a strong chance that third player is psyching (bluffing).

2. The bidding has reached the 2-level, e.g., (1 ◇) : Double : (2 ◇) : ?
With 10-12 points and a major, jump to 3 ♡ or 3 ♠ . With a no-trump hand, reply 2NT, which still shows 10-12 points. If your suit is a minor, it is not attractive to jump to the 4-level with only 10-12 points, firstly because you do not have the values for the 4-level and secondly, you thereby pass 3NT. With 10-12 points over interference be prepared to bid just 3-minor if no better action is available. Jump to 4-minor only with a very good suit and no prospects for 3NT.

3. The bidding has reached the 3-level, e.g., (1 ◇) : Double : (3 ◇) : ?
The opponents will often try to make things difficult and their jump-raise does make it much tougher for you. With 8-10 points, bid a suit at the 3-level and with 11-12, be prepared to make a mild overbid by jumping a major suit to the 4-level. With 10-12 and a no-trumps hand, including a double stopper, you may try 3NT. With a good minor suit and 10-12, it is better to compete with 4-minor than to pass.

FURTHER ACTION BY THE DOUBLER AFTER A JUMP-REPLY

The jump is not forcing. Pass with a bare 12-13 points. With a good 13-14, invite game by raising partner's suit *or* raise 2NT to 3NT. With 15+, make sure you reach a game either by bidding it *or* by changing suit (forcing after a strong reply) and bidding game on the next round. Change of suit by the doubler logically shows a 5+ suit. If the reply to the double denied a 4+ major, the doubler would not bother showing a 4-card major later. Raise the doubler's major with three trumps or look for 3NT if the doubler bids a minor.

ACTION ON HANDS OF 13 POINTS OR MORE IN REPLY TO THE DOUBLE

With such strength you have enough for game. See Chapters 25 and 26.

EXERCISES

A. The bidding has been (1 ◊) : Double : (Pass) : ? What do you reply to partner's double with these hands?

1. ♠ K 8 6 4	2. ♠ 8 4 3	3. ♠ A 4	4. ♠ 8 2	5. ♠ 8 6 5 2
♡ Q 7	♡ Q 7 6 4 3	♡ K 2	♡ A 2	♡ A K
◊ A J 7 3	◊ A K 7	◊ 7 6 4 3	◊ K Q J 8	◊ 7 3 2
♣ 8 4 3	♣ 6 4	♣ K 8 6 5 4	♣ J 6 4 3 2	♣ Q J 8 7

B. You doubled 1 ◊ and partner responded 2 ♡. What is your rebid on each of these hands?

1. ♠ K Q 6 2	2. ♠ A J 7	3. ♠ A Q J 4 2	4. ♠ A Q 3 2	5. ♠ A 8 4 2
♡ A Q 7 3	♡ K 8 4 2	♡ A J	♡ 7 5	♡ K 6 5 3
◊ 4	◊ 9 7	◊ 8 7	◊ A K J	◊ K 2
♣ K 9 7 3	♣ A 9 7 3	♣ K Q 5 2	♣ K Q 7 2	♣ K 10 7

PARTNERSHIP BIDDING: There is no North-South bidding other than indicated.

SET 31 – WEST	SET 31 – EAST	SET 32 – WEST	SET 32 – EAST
1. South opens 1 ◊ .	**1.** South opens 1 ◊ .	**1.** North opens 1 ♣ .	**1.** North opens 1 ♣ .
♠ A Q 8 7	♠ K 9 6 4	♠ K 9 5	♠ A 8 3 2
♡ A 8 7 2	♡ 6 3	♡ Q J 9	♡ K 7 6 5
◊ J 9	◊ Q 3 2	◊ Q 4 3	◊ K J 5
♣ K 3 2	♣ A Q 9 8	♣ K 9 3 2	♣ Q 4
2. North opens 1 ◊ .	**2.** North opens 1 ◊ .	**2.** South opens 1 ♠ .	**2.** South opens 1 ♠ .
♠ K 2	♠ A J 6 5 4	♠ 4	♠ A 9 3 2
♡ 8 7 3 2	♡ A K 6 5	♡ A K 6 2	♡ Q 7
◊ A J 8	◊ 9 2	◊ A Q J 9	◊ 8 7 5
♣ Q 7 6 5	♣ K 3	♣ K 7 6 4	♣ A 9 5 3
3. South opens 1 ♡ .	**3.** South opens 1 ♡ .	**3.** North opens 1 ◊ .	**3.** North opens 1 ◊ .
♠ A 9 7 4	♠ K 8 5 3	♠ J 7 2	♠ K Q 8 6 3
♡ J 6	♡ Q 2	♡ K Q	♡ A 9 7 2
◊ A K 9	◊ Q 6 4 2	◊ 9 8 2	◊ 7 6
♣ J 7 5 3	♣ A 8 6	♣ K Q 6 4 3	♣ A J
4. North opens 1 ♣ .	**4.** North opens 1 ♣ .	**4.** South opens 1 ♣ .	**4.** South opens 1 ♣ .
♠ 5 4 3	♠ K Q 7 6	♠ A 8 6 5	♠ K 9 4
♡ J 5	♡ A K 3 2	♡ K 9 7 4 2	♡ A 6 5
◊ A K Q 4 3	◊ J 7 6	◊ A K 2	◊ J 8 6 3
♣ J 6 2	♣ 4 3	♣ 8	♣ K 9 7
5. South opens 1 ♠ , North raises to 2 ♠ .	**5.** South opens 1 ♠ , North raises to 2 ♠ .	**5.** North opens 1 ♡ , South raises to 2 ♡ .	**5.** North opens 1 ♡ , South raises to 2 ♡ .
♠ 7	♠ J 3 2	♠ K 9 7 3	♠ A 8 6 4
♡ A 7 3 2	♡ K Q 5 4	♡ 7 4 3	♡ 6
◊ K Q 8 7 6	◊ 4	◊ A Q	◊ K 6 5 3
♣ A 9 8	♣ K J 5 3 2	♣ J 6 5 2	♣ A Q 8 4

PLAY HANDS ON TAKEOUT DOUBLES (3)

Hand 57: Jump-reply to a double – Leading towards honours when drawing trumps – Ruffing finesse

Dealer North : East-West vulnerable

```
              NORTH
              ♠ 9
              ♡ A J 10
              ◇ Q 10 7 2
              ♣ A K 9 8 7
WEST                        EAST
♠ K 2                       ♠ A J 8 7
♡ 8 7 6 3 2                 ♡ K Q 5 4
◇ K 3                       ◇ A 9 6 4
♣ Q J 10 2                  ♣ 4
              SOUTH
              ♠ Q 10 6 5 4 3
              ♡ 9
              ◇ J 8 5
              ♣ 6 5 3
```

WEST	NORTH	EAST	SOUTH
	1♣	Double	No (1)
2♡ (2)	No (3)	4♡ (4)	All pass

Bidding: (1) With a very weak hand, pass.

(2) Decide first what to bid and then how high to bid. West is clearly going to bid hearts rather than no-trumps. In hearts, the hand is worth 11 points, counting one for each doubleton. With 10-12 points, give a jump-reply to the double. If South had unwisely bid 1♠, West should jump to 3♡.

(3) Do not rebid with a minimum opposite a passing partner.

(4) Worth 17 points in hearts, counting three for the singleton, and thus enough for game opposite 10-12 points.

Lead: ♣A. There is no urgency to lead the singleton spade. Firstly, you have trump control and can lead the singleton later if that seems best. Secondly, with such strong trumps you are usually not looking for a ruff. After the ♣A, the switch to the ♠9 looks the best continuation.

Correct play: Declarer should win the spade lead in hand with the king and lead a trump towards dummy's K-Q. Without a solid sequence, lead towards honours rather than lead the honours themselves. If North plays low, play the king. When it wins, do not lead another heart from dummy. That will cost a trick. Come to hand with the ◇K and lead a second heart from hand towards the queen. If North plays low and the queen wins, abandon trumps. If North takes the ace, win any switch and draw North's last trump. Cross to hand via a spade ruff or a diamond ruff and lead the ♣Q. The lead marks the king with North. If North plays low, let the queen run. If North covers with the king, ruff it and your remaining clubs are high.

Hand 58: No-trumps reply to a takeout double – Card combinations and card reading

Dealer East : Game all

```
              NORTH
              ♠ 7 4 3
              ♡ A 9 3 2
              ◇ A Q 8 4
              ♣ J 8
WEST                        EAST
♠ 9 5                       ♠ K 8 6 2
♡ 8 6 5                     ♡ K Q J 10 7
◇ J 7 6 3                   ◇ 10
♣ 9 6 4 3                   ♣ A 10 5
              SOUTH
              ♠ A Q J 10
              ♡ 4
              ◇ K 9 5 2
              ♣ K Q 7 2
```

WEST	NORTH	EAST	SOUTH
		1♡	Double
Pass	2NT (1)	No (2)	3NT (3)
No	No	No	

Bidding: (1) Prefer no-trumps to diamonds. With 11 points, you have enough for a jump to 2NT, showing a balanced hand of 10-12 points with hearts covered and denying four spades.

(2) Not worth any action with minimum values.

(3) With 15 HCP opposite 10-12, game is likely. If your side could hold 26 points, keep bidding. With no long suit and relying on partner to have a stopper in hearts, South's best bid is 3NT. 5◇ is a good spot, but most would reach 3NT. It is tempting to double 3NT with five probable winners, but four heart winners are not sure and they might make nine tricks before you can make your five.

Lead: ♡K. May all your leads be so easy.

Correct play: Win the ♡A. There is no point holding up as East's opening bid must include the ♣A, which will always be an entry. Do not tackle clubs (instant demise). The missing points indicate the ♠K is with East. Finesse the ♠Q; play the ◇K and a diamond to the ◇A; repeat the spade finesse; as East showed out on the second diamond, finesse the ◇8; repeat the spade finesse. Making nine tricks via four spades, one heart and four diamonds. You must start on the spades while you still have diamond entries and you must note the fall of East's ◇10.

Hand 59: Doubler's rebid after a jump-response – Hold-up and avoidance play

Dealer South : Love all
          NORTH
          ♠ K Q J
          ♡ 10 9 5 4
          ◇ K Q J 10 8
          ♣ 7
WEST   EAST
♠ 8 4   ♠ A 10 9 3
♡ A Q   ♡ K J 8 2
◇ 9 4 3 2   ◇ A 6
♣ K 10 8 5 4   ♣ A J 2
          SOUTH
          ♠ 7 6 5 2
          ♡ 7 6 3
          ◇ 7 5
          ♣ Q 9 6 3

WEST	NORTH	EAST	SOUTH
			No
No	1◇	Dble (1)	No
3♣	No	3NT (2)	All pass (3)

Bidding: (1) East has the values for a 1NT overcall, but with both majors and only one stopper in diamonds, double is a better initial action. If partner bids a major, raise to 2-major, and if partner is unable to make a jump-reply, game is not very likely. If East does overcall 1NT, West is worth a raise to 3NT.
(2) West has no major to call and no stopper in diamonds, so that leaves only a reply in clubs. West is worth 11 points for clubs, counting the two doubletons.
(3) As 3♣ denies a 4-card major, there is no point introducing hearts or spades. East's 17 points are enough to take shot at game and with a stopper in diamonds, 3NT is the best chance. Even with just one stopper, prefer 3NT to 5-of-a-minor.

Lead: ◇ 7. Partner's suit is normal. Top from a doubleton.

Correct play: Duck the first diamond. With A-x or A-x-x, it is best not to take the ace early if all the other suits are well covered. After winning the ◇ A at trick 2, East should tackle the clubs. In the abstract the normal play with this combination is ♣ A first, followed by the ♣ J, intending to let it go if South plays low. However, North is likely to hold the ♣ Q on the bidding and you do not want to give the lead to North, who could cash the other diamond winners. Cross to the ♡ A and lead a low club to your jack. If the jack wins, cash the ♣ A. If they break, you have eleven tricks, while if South shows out, you have nine tricks. As it happens, South wins with the ♣ Q, but has no more diamonds. (If South had another diamond, the suit would be 4-3 and you would lose at most three diamonds and a club.) If South switches to a spade, win with the ♠ A, cross to the ♡ Q, back to the ♣ A, cash the ♡ K and ♡ J, followed by the rest of the clubs. Ten tricks.

Hand 60: Competitive bidding after a double – Card combination and the Rule of Restricted Choice

Dealer West : North-South vulnerable
          NORTH
          ♠ A K 9 5
          ♡ 7 2
          ◇ K Q 8
          ♣ Q 10 7 4
WEST   EAST
♠ J 8 6   ♠ Q
♡ A Q J 10 6   ♡ K 8 5 4
◇ A 10 7   ◇ 9 6 5 4 3
♣ 8 5   ♣ 9 3 2
          SOUTH
          ♠ 10 7 4 3 2
          ♡ 9 3
          ◇ J 2
          ♣ A K J 6

WEST	NORTH	EAST	SOUTH
1♡	Double	2♡ (1)	3♣ (2)
No (3)	4♠ (4)	All pass	

Bidding: (1) With support and the values for a raise, give a normal raise over a double.
(2) Spades is the suit to bid, not clubs. Worth the jump because of the doubletons. If worth a jump-reply, bid it even over a bid by third player. 2♠ here would show only 6-9 points.
(3) Not worth any further action in the direct seat.
(4) Worth 15 points and as partner's range is 10-12, there could be 26 points between you. If that is possible, keep bidding. To pass is risky, to bid 4♠ is risky. If both actions are risky, choose the action which yields the greater reward if successful.

Lead: ♣ 8. Spades are out. It is not attractive to lead from an ace-high suit without the king as well, so the red suits are excluded. That leaves only clubs. Lead top from a doubleton.

Correct play: Win the ♣ A and play a spade to the ace. Is East's queen a singleton or from Q-J doubleton? When an honour drops, the odds favour it to be a singleton (Rule of Restricted Choice). In addition, as West failed to lead a heart, West would not have A-K or K-Q in hearts. That marks East with at least the ♡ K. With only 17 HCP missing, virtually all the other points must be with West. Without the ♠ J, West has 11 HCP, possible but not likely. Lead a low diamond to the jack and ace (if they do not cash their hearts now, you can discard one). When you regain the lead, play a spade to dummy's nine. Making 4♠ when the nine wins.

CHAPTER 16

DEFENDING AGAINST PRE-EMPTS

1. OVER THEIR WEAK TWOS

Weak two openings, used normally only in the majors, are based on a strong 6-card suit and 6-10 HCP. You are less likely to meet weak twos in rubber bridge, but they are very popular and common at duplicate. The recommended defence is to treat a weak two as a 1-opening and to use the same style of defence. Thus:

2NT = 16-18 points, balanced, with at least one stopper in opener's suit (the same as a 1NT overcall over a 1-opening). With a double stopper, the strength may be shaded to 15 points. After 2NT, partner's new suit at the 3-level is droppable. Bidding the suit opened, e.g., (2 ♡) : 2NT : (No): 3 ♡ = Stayman.

Suit bid = a strong 5+ suit and opening hand values at least, up to a maximum of about 16 points. With more than 16 points, double first and bid the suit later or jump-bid your suit later with a 4-loser hand. Jump-overcalls, e.g., (2 ♡) : 3 ♠, are strong, about 16+ HCP and five losers, even if the partnership uses weak jump-overcalls over 1-openings.

Double = for takeout. The double promises a sound opening with four cards in the other major. Treat it like the double of a 1-opening, e.g., (2 ♠) : Double is equivalent to (1 ♠) : Double *or* (1 ♠) : No : (2 ♠) : Double. In reply to the double, bid a suit at the cheapest level with 0-5 points. With 6-9 points, bid your suit at the cheapest level or bid 2NT with a stopper in their suit and not four cards in the other major. With 10-12 points, make a jump-reply and with 13+ points, bid game or, if uncertain of the best game, bid their suit. Bidding their suit, e.g., (2 ♡) : 3 ♡ = an artificial game-force, equivalent to the demand 2 ♣ opening.

2. OVER THEIR 3-OPENINGS

When you hold a good hand, a sound working approach is to bid on the assumption that partner has about 6-8 points. As the pre-emptor has a weak hand, it is unlikely, although possible, that partner has a worthless hand. Say you hold 20 HCP; assume the pre-emptor has about eight; you can place partner with 6 HCP, half of the points missing. If 6-8 points is enough for game, bid the game. If you need more than eight points for game, bid a suit below game or make a takeout double. While this will not always work out, it is dangerous to be too conservative over a pre-empt, as you may easily miss a game. Pre-empts work well since they force you to guess, but the following guidelines will assist you in guessing correctly more often than not.

3NT = 16+ points, balanced, at least one stopper in their suit.

Suit at the 3-level = About 14-17 points, strong 5-card or 6-card suit, around six losers.

Minor at the 4-level = Strong, 17-20 points, excellent suit around five losers.

Jump to 4-major = Strong, 17-20 points, excellent suit, around five losers. A 4-loser hand with a strong suit can be shown by doubling first and bidding game in your suit on the next round.

Jump to 4NT over 3 ♡ or 3 ♠ = Takeout for the minors, not Blackwood. See Chapter 11, page 62.

Bid their suit, e.g., (3 ♡) : 4 ♡ ? = Artificial game force. Equivalent to a 2 ♣ demand, around three losers.

Double = For takeout, the popular, recommended approach, although other methods exist. Double for takeout over a 3-level pre-empt includes these benefits: partner's reply can be at the 3-level *or* at the 4-level; partner can choose 3NT as a contract; partner can pass the double for penalties with a strong holding in their suit; it frees all other actions for natural bidding, so that you do not lose 3NT or some suit bids. The only immediate loss when using double for takeout is the inability to make a penalty double. Even so, you will still collect penalties a lot of the time when they are available, since partner can pass a takeout double for penalties. If you have the penalty double type hand, you should either bid 3NT and forego the penalties if your hand justifies 3NT, or pass and hope that partner might be able to rake up a takeout double in fourth seat so that you can then pass and convert the double to penalties. Even if you do occasionally miss doubled penalties, the advantages of using the double for takeout far outweigh the disadvantages. Part of the superiority of the takeout double is its greater frequency. If they pre-empt, which do you pick up more often, a strong holding in their suit or a shortage in their suit? Catering for the shortage makes more sense.

WHEN SHOULD YOU DOUBLE FOR TAKEOUT?

With a good hand with support or tolerance for the missing suits, it is highly likely that a trump fit exists for your side, and so you may anticipate this fit and value your hand by counting HCP plus shortage in their suit at once, using three for a void, two for a singleton and one for a doubleton. Count nothing for an unsupported queen or jack in their suit or for a singleton king in their suit. There is also a distinction between bidding in the direct seat (second seat) and bidding in the pass-out seat (fourth seat). It is riskier to take action in second seat since third player might have a very strong hand and you can be caught by a penalty double, but if it has gone (Pre-empt) : No : (No) to you, third player is not that strong. You can reduce the requirements for action in fourth seat by about three points.

After a 3-opening an immediate takeout double should be worth 17+ points, calculated as above, while a double in fourth seat should be worth 14+ points. If you find this too limiting and want to be more daring, shade the requirements, but by one point only. The double should include support for any unbid major unless you have a safe haven if partner makes an unwelcome reply. In fourth seat, you should be quick to double with modest values and shortage in opener's suit, because partner could have a penalty-type hand and might be delighted to pass out your takeout double for penalties. Be wary of taking action in fourth seat, however, when third player trances for some time, thus indicating strength but uncertainty about what to bid. Do not protect on moderate values against a trancer.

RESPONDING TO A SUIT OVERCALL AT THE 3-LEVEL

With 9+ HCP, you are worth some action, but with less than 9 HCP or less than three winners, pass. With three winners or more, bid on. Support partner's major as first priority, with 3NT as the second choice.

RESPONDING TO THE TAKEOUT DOUBLE

With 0-8/9 points and 9 losers or worse, bid a suit at the cheapest level. Prefer a major to a minor. With 9/10 points or more and either three winners or eight losers, or better, bid game in a major or bid 3NT if you have a stopper in their suit and no major to bid. With a 2-suited hand and not certain of the best game, you can bid the enemy suit, e.g., (3 ◇) : Double: (No) : 4 ◇ asks partner to choose the contract. Slam is possible with a strong trump fit and five winners or a 6-loser hand, or better. After a pre-empt, however, it pays to be conservative about slam bidding. In view of the pre-empt, bad breaks in the other suits are quite likely.

REBIDS BY THE DOUBLER

After a weak reply to the double, the doubler should usually pass unless holding a total of about 20+ points, or five losers, or better. Do not bid the same values twice. In answer to a double or in answer to a suit overcall, partner is expected to bid game with about 9+ HCP, or the equivalent counting distributional values. If partner has not bid game, you should not have to bid partner's cards as well as your own.

3. OVER THEIR 4-LEVEL PRE-EMPTS

There is no ideal method for coping with high-level pre-empts. Many pairs prefer to use a double as being 'Co-operative', suggesting a very strong, balanced type of hand. Others prefer to use double for takeout (and that use is recommended for duplicate). Partner is always entitled to pass a co-operative double or a takeout double for penalties with values in the opener's suit. Over a 4♡ or a 4♠ pre-empt, many pairs like to use 4NT as a takeout bid, but you should settle with partner whether it is a 3-suited takeout or a 2-suited takeout. For duplicate, a sensible approach is to use double as a 3-suited takeout and 4NT as a 2-suited takeout, although many pairs do use double of a 4-major opening for penalties. Suit bids over a 4-level pre-empt are natural and very strong hands. Bidding the enemy suit is a gigantic takeout bid, looking for a slam.

4. OVER THE GAMBLING 3NT (see Chapter 12, page 66)

If you pass a gambling 3NT, lead an ace or a K-Q combination to take a look at dummy and then decide on the best way to continue the defence. Once they obtain the lead, they usually have at least nine tricks available. If you wish to bid over their 3NT, a sensible method is:

Double = a strong, balanced hand, looking for penalties. A double of 3NT followed by a double of their run to 4♣ or 4 ◇ is also for penalties.

4♣ = takeout for the major suits, equal length suits or hearts are preferred.

4 ◇ = takeout for the major suits, emphasis on spades which will be the longer suit or the stronger suit.

4♡ or 4♠ = 1-suited hands, no interest in the other major.

If you wish to bid in fourth seat after the bidding has started (3NT) : No : (4♣ or 4 ◇) . . . use the same methods that the partnership uses over a 4♣ or a 4 ◇ opening bid.

EXERCISES

A. Neither side is vulnerable. Your right-hand opponent opens 3 ◇. What action do you take with these hands?

1. ♠ K 5	2. ♠ A 9 8 2	3. ♠ A Q J 7 6 2	4. ♠ A 2	5. ♠ A 2
♡ 7 3	♡ A Q 4 3	♡ J 3	♡ K 4 3	♡ Q J 3
◇ A Q 10 6 4	◇ 9	◇ 4 3	◇ 8 6 2	◇ A Q 2
♣ K Q 7 3	♣ A J 3 2	♣ K Q 9	♣ K Q J 7 5	♣ K Q J 3 2

6. ♠ A K 5	7. ♠ K Q J 2	8. ♠ A Q 8 2	9. ♠ A J 8 7	10. ♠ K Q J 9
♡ A J 2	♡ A Q J 8 3	♡ J 6 2	♡ A K 8	♡ A K Q J
◇ A K 4	◇ 9	◇ Q J 9 7	◇ 6 2	◇ 3
♣ A J 9 7	♣ A K 6	♣ A 9	♣ A Q 5 2	♣ A K J 9

B. Neither side is vulnerable. The bidding has been (3 ♡) : Double : (No) to you. Your action with these hands?

1. ♠ 9 5 3 2	2. ♠ 6	3. ♠ K Q 7 2	4. ♠ A Q 9 7 4 2	5. ♠ 8 2
♡ 7 3	♡ 4 3 2	♡ J 3	♡ 8	♡ K 6 3
◇ Q 10 6 4	◇ J 9 7 6 4	◇ A 9 6 4	◇ Q 8 6 2	◇ A Q J 4
♣ Q 7 3	♣ 9 7 5 3	♣ J 9 5	♣ 5 2	♣ Q 9 8 3

C. Neither side is vulnerable. The bidding has been (3 ♣) : Double : (No) to you. Your action with these hands?

1. ♠ 9 6 4 3 2	2. ♠ 4	3. ♠ 9 5 2	4. ♠ Q 8 7 2	5. ♠ A Q 7 2
♡ Q J 7 3	♡ A Q 2	♡ J 3	♡ Q 9 5 3	♡ K Q 6 3
◇ 6 4	◇ J 10 7 6 4	◇ A K 6 4 3	◇ Q 8 2	◇ J 4 3
♣ 7 3	♣ Q J 9 3	♣ A 8 4	♣ 4 3	♣ 3 2

PARTNERSHIP BIDDING: No North-South bidding other than indicated. Two-openings are weak twos.

SET 33 – WEST	SET 33 – EAST	SET 34 – WEST	SET 34 – EAST
1. North opens 2 ♠.	**1.** North opens 2 ♠.	**1.** South opens 3 ♣.	**1.** South opens 3 ♣.
♠ J 4 2	♠ 7 6	♠ K J 9 7	♠ 8 5
♡ K 8 5 3	♡ A 9 7 4	♡ A Q 9 6	♡ J 7 5 3 2
◇ 6 4	◇ A Q 9 8	◇ A J 8 3	◇ 7 6 5 2
♣ 7 6 5 2	♣ K Q J	♣ 7	♣ Q 5
2. South opens 2 ♠.	**2.** South opens 2 ♠.	**2.** North opens 3 ♣.	**2.** North opens 3 ♣.
♠ 3	♠ 7 6 4	♠ K 9 8 3 2	♠ 7 6
♡ Q 8 6 2	♡ A J 10 3	♡ K 4 3	♡ A Q J 8 6 2
◇ A K Q 9 3	◇ 8 5	◇ A 7 5	◇ K Q J
♣ K 8 5	♣ A Q 4 2	♣ 8 5	♣ Q 4
3. North opens 2 ♡.	**3.** North opens 2 ♡.	**3.** South opens 3 ◇.	**3.** South opens 3 ◇.
♠ K 7 4	♠ A Q	♠ A Q 6 4	♠ 5 3
♡ 7 3	♡ K Q 9	♡ K Q 8 3	♡ A 7 6 5 4
◇ J 5 3	◇ A K 7 6	◇ 7	◇ J 8 3
♣ A Q 9 7 5	♣ 6 4 3 2	♣ A 9 8 3	♣ K Q 5
4. South opens 2 ♡.	**4.** South opens 2 ♡.	**4.** North opens 3 ♡.	**4.** North opens 3 ♡.
♠ 5 4 3	♠ K Q 7 6	♠ A K 8 3	♠ 7 6
♡ J 5	♡ A K 3 2	♡ 7	♡ K Q 9 3
◇ A K Q 4 3 2	◇ J 7 6	◇ K 5 4 3	◇ A Q 2
♣ A 6 2	♣ 4 3	♣ A 9 6 2	♣ 8 7 4 3
5. North opens 2 ♠.	**5.** North opens 2 ♠.	**5.** North opens 3 ◇.	**5.** North opens 3 ◇.
♠ Q 5 4	♠ 3	♠ A Q 8 4	♠ K 9 7 2
♡ 7 3 2	♡ K Q J 8 6 4	♡ A 7 4 2	♡ K Q 6
◇ 8 7 5	◇ A K Q	◇ 8 6	◇ J 2
♣ Q 9 6 5	♣ K J 2	♣ Q 9 8	♣ A K J 3

PLAY HANDS ON DEFENDING AGAINST PRE-EMPTS

Hand 61: Jump-reply to a double of a pre-empt – Signalling – Defensive technique

Dealer North : Love all

```
              NORTH
              ♠ A K 10 4 2
              ♥ 10 8
              ◇ Q 10 3
              ♣ J 10 6
WEST                        EAST
♠ Q 5                       ♠ 7 3
♥ K J 9 7 5 2               ♥ 6
◇ J                         ◇ A K 9 8 5 4 2
♣ 9 8 7 4                   ♣ 5 3 2
              SOUTH
              ♠ J 9 8 6
              ♥ A Q 4 3
              ◇ 7 6
              ♣ A K Q
```

WEST	NORTH	EAST	SOUTH
	No	3 ◇	Dble (1)
No (2)	4♠ (3)	All pass	

Bidding: (1) This is all right for a takeout double, although it is a minimum. Support for both majors and shortage in their suit are vital when you compete at the 3-level on minimum values. The double allows partner to bid 3-major or 4-major, while inferior takeout methods (such as 3NT or cheaper minor 4♣) commit you to the 4-level.
(2) Do not consider 'rescuing' a pre-empt with a weak hand.
(3) Too strong for just 3♠ with an excellent 5-card major and better than two winners. Even allowing for the doubtful value of the ◇ Q, the hand is too good for just 3♠.

Lead: ◇ A. When West drops the ◇ J, East should continue with the ◇ K.

An honour-card signal denies the next honour up (with ◇ Q-J, West would drop the queen under the king, not the jack). West shows out on the second diamond and West should discard the ♥ 2 to discourage a switch to hearts. A signal does not show or deny high cards; it is meant to tell partner what to do. If West wanted a heart switch now, a high heart would ask for a heart *now*. As West wants another diamond, West should discourage hearts. On the third diamond, declarer ruffs high in dummy, but West over-ruffs and exits in a black suit. Ultimately West scores the ♥ K for one down. If East leads a heart or switches to a heart at trick 2 or trick 3, North should win with dummy's ace. It would be an error to play the queen, as a lead or a shift by a pre-emptor is so likely to be a singleton. If the ♥ Q were played, West would win and give East a heart ruff, but if you win with the ♥ A and draw trumps, the contract is home.

Hand 62: Takeout double after a pre-empt — Penalty pass — Signalling and defensive technique

Dealer East : Love all

```
              NORTH
              ♠ A Q J 3
              ♥ A J 7 6 2
              ◇ 10
              ♣ J 8 2
WEST                        EAST
♠ K 10 9 4 2                ♠ 7 5
♥ K Q 10 8                  ♥ 5
◇ 5                         ◇ A K 8 7 4 3 2
♣ 7 6 5                     ♣ Q 9 4
              SOUTH
              ♠ 8 6
              ♥ 9 4 3
              ◇ Q J 9 6
              ♣ A K 10 3
```

WEST	NORTH	EAST	SOUTH
		3 ◇	No (1)
No (2)	Dble (3)	All pass (4)	

Bidding: (1) Much too weak to take any action here.
(2) Do not bid with a weak hand after partner's pre-empt.
(3) In the direct seat, these values would be too skimpy for action, but in fourth seat, you have enough. With both majors, choose the takeout double.
(4) South could choose 3NT, but to pass the double is superior. 3NT may or may not make, but with excellent trumps, playing for penalties is bound to score a plus result You might score penalties when 3NT is failing, while if 3NT is on, you could find that the penalties are greater than the value of the game.

Lead: ♣ A. An A-K suit lead is highly attractive.

Correct play: On the ♣ A, North discourages with the ♣ 2. South should switch to the ♠ 8, as North is marked with strength in the majors. (It would be an error to cash the ♣ K at trick 2. North would not discourage clubs if holding the ♣ Q. Cashing the ♣ A sets up declarer's ♣ Q.) North captures the ♠ 9 with the ♠ J and returns the ♣ J. South cashes a third club and reverts to spades: ten – queen – seven. North should cash the ♥ A next (else East discards a heart on the ♠ A) and then play the ♠ A. If East ruffs low, South over-ruffs. South exits with the 13th club, North ruffs with the ◇ 10, an 'uppercut' (so called because it knocks out a high trump), which sets up an extra trump trick for South. That takes 3 ◇ doubled five down.

Hand 63: Action after a pre-empt – Defensive technique – Card reading and countermeasures

Dealer South : North-South vulnerable

```
            NORTH
            ♠ 6 5
            ♡ A 7
            ◇ 8 4
            ♣ K Q 10 9 8 7 3
WEST                    EAST
♠ K J 9 7              ♠ A 10 4 2
♡ J 2                  ♡ K Q 10 8
◇ K J 9 7             ◇ A Q 10
♣ J 6 5               ♣ 4 2
            SOUTH
            ♠ Q 8 3
            ♡ 9 6 5 4 3
            ◇ 6 5 3 2
            ♣ A
```

WEST	NORTH	EAST	SOUTH
			No
No	3♣ (1)	Dble (2)	No
4♠ (3)	No	No	No

Bidding: (1) The clubs are worth six tricks, the ace makes it seven, which is what is needed for a vulnerable 3-opening.
(2) Just enough for a takeout double.
(3) Even discounting the ♣J completely, the hand is worth 10 points for spades, too good for just 3♠, which would be a very timid effort. East would pass and a game missed. Prefer to reply to the double with a major than a minor.

Lead: ♣K. Far more likely to be productive than the ♡A, hoping for a ruff. The ♡K is highly likely to turn up in dummy because of the double.

Correct play: South is obliged to win the ♣A and returns a heart. North wins the ♡A and cashes the ♣Q, noting that South shows out and that West holds another club. North's best defence is to play a third club, particularly when South discourages diamonds with the ◇2.

The best chance for no trump loser with K-J-x-x opposite A-10-x-x is to finesse for the queen through the player likely to have greater length in that suit. After a pre-empt, it is a sound approach to place significant high cards outside the pre-empt suit with the partner of the pre-emptor, not with the pre-emptor. There is confirmation that South has the ♠Q. North has shown up with the ♡A and ♣K-Q, 9 HCP. The ♠Q would make it 11 HCP, usually too much for a pre-empt. Once you decide to play South for the ♠Q, do not ruff low in dummy on the third club – South will over-ruff. Ruff the third club with the ♠A and lead the ♠10, letting it run if not covered. Repeat the spade finesse and draw trumps. Making ten tricks.

Hand 64: Action after a vulnerable pre-empt – Card reading to avoid a fatal ruff

Dealer West : East-West vulnerable

```
            NORTH
            ♠ A 9 4 2
            ♡ 10 7 4
            ◇ K 10
            ♣ 10 6 5 2
WEST                    EAST
♠ K Q J 10 7 6 5       ♠ - - -
♡ 3 2                  ♡ 6 5
◇ Q J 9              ◇ 8 7 6 5 4 2
♣ 9                  ♣ K Q J 7 3
            SOUTH
            ♠ 8 3
            ♡ A K Q J 9 8
            ◇ A 3
            ♣ A 8 4
```

WEST	NORTH	EAST	SOUTH
3♠ (1)	No	No (2)	4♡ (3)
No	No	No	

Bidding: (1) Six tricks in spades, one in diamonds = seven, the number needed for a vulnerable pre-empt at the 3-level.
(2) Do not panic with a weak hand just because you are void in partner's suit Do not try to rescue partner with weakness. A new suit is forcing and you are in sufficient peril at the 3-level without going any higher.
(3) It is reasonable to play partner for about 6-8 points or about two tricks after they pre-empt. With eight tricks in hand and hoping for two tricks from partner, 4♡ is the obvious choice.

Lead: ♠K. Prefer the solid sequence in spades rather than the near sequence in diamonds.

Correct play: The instinctive play is to rise with dummy's ♠A, and only after East ruffs this does it dawn on declarer that it was almost certain that the ♠A would be ruffed. West would have seven spades for the 3♠ opening, dummy has four spades and South has two, leaving East with a marked void. It is vital to count the spades *before* playing from dummy. Once you realize the ♠A will be ruffed, it is clear that you must not play the ace. Duck the first spade, duck the second spade, win the next lead in hand and draw trumps. Later cross to dummy with a diamond to the king or a trump to the ten and cash the valuable, preserved ♠A on which you discard one of your club losers. You lose two spades and one club. Making ten tricks.

REVISION TEST ON PART 2

The answers to all these questions can be found in Chapters 9-16. Give yourself 1 mark for each correct answer. If you score less than 40, it will profit you to revise the relevant sections.

A. Your right-hand opened 1 ◊ . What action do you take with each of these hands?

1. ♠ K Q 2	2. ♠ A J 3 2	3. ♠ - - -	4. ♠ A 9 7	5. ♠ A 8 7 2
♡ 7 2	♡ 3	♡ A K J 8 7 6 2	♡ A J 3	♡ A 2
◊ A Q 9 6 4	◊ A 9 7	◊ 7 6	◊ K 9 8	◊ 3
♣ Q J 7	♣ Q 9 7 4 2	♣ K J 10 4	♣ A K J 2	♣ A K Q 8 6 3

B. Right-hand opponent has opened 1 ♠ . What action do you take with each of these hands?

1. ♠ 3	2. ♠ 7	3. ♠ A	4. ♠ 3	5. ♠ A 10 4
♡ A Q J 3 2	♡ 3	♡ 7 3	♡ A Q 7	♡ A K 9
◊ 8 6	◊ Q J 9 6 3 2	◊ A Q 10 6 2	◊ K Q 3 2	◊ J 6 4 3
♣ K Q 10 5 4	♣ K J 10 8 6	♣ A 10 8 5 2	♣ K 9 8 4 2	♣ K Q 2

C. The bidding has been (1 ◊) : 1 ♠ : (No) to you. What action do you take in reply to partner's overcall?

1. ♠ 8 7	2. ♠ J	3. ♠ A 8 5 3 2	4. ♠ J 8 2	5. ♠ J 8 7 5
♡ K 7 3	♡ A Q 8 5 4 3	♡ K Q 6 2	♡ A Q 10	♡ 6
◊ A Q 9 2	◊ 7 6 4	◊ A 7 6	◊ K Q 10 3	◊ J 9 4 3
♣ A 10 5 2	♣ K J 3	♣ 4	♣ A J 10	♣ A K Q J

D. The bidding has been (1 ♡) : Double : (No) to you. What action do you take with these hands?

1. ♠ K 9 4 2	2. ♠ A 7	3. ♠ A 5 3	4. ♠ 3 2	5. ♠ 2
♡ A Q 7 3	♡ A Q 3 2	♡ J 7 2	♡ 9 6 4 3 2	♡ K 8
◊ J 9	◊ 7 6 4	◊ 8 7 2	◊ 9 6 2	◊ 9 7 5 3 2
♣ 9 5 2	♣ J 7 3 2	♣ J 8 5 4	♣ Q 9 7	♣ J 8 6 3 2

E. The bidding has been (1 ♡) : Double : (1 ♠) to you. What action do you take with these hands?

1. ♠ Q 7	2. ♠ A J 7 5 2	3. ♠ A Q J 2	4. ♠ Q 7	5. ♠ A 8 3 2
♡ Q 8 4	♡ 6 4	♡ 8 2	♡ A J 9	♡ K J 6 4
◊ 7 6	◊ 9 7	◊ 6 3 2	◊ K J 6 2	◊ 9 4 2
♣ 9 8 7 5 3 2	♣ A 8 3 2	♣ J 8 5 4	♣ 9 7 3 2	♣ 6 2

F. What would your answers be on the hands in E. if the bidding had started (1 ♡) : Double : (2 ♡) to you?

G. What are your answers for the hands in E. if the bidding had started (1 ◊) : Double : (Redouble) to you?

H. The bidding has started (1 ♠) : Double : (Redouble) to you. What action do you take with these hands?

1. ♠ 9 7 4 2	2. ♠ K 7 5 2	3. ♠ A 9 7 2	4. ♠ A Q 2	5. ♠ 8 7 4
♡ 6 3 2	♡ 9 6 4 2	♡ K J 6 4 3	♡ J 3 2	♡ Q 10
◊ 6 4	◊ Q 9	◊ 8	◊ Q 7 2	◊ K 3
♣ J 8 3 2	♣ 7 3 2	♣ 9 5 4	♣ 8 7 5 3	♣ K Q 9 8 5 2

I. Right-hand opponent has opened 2 ♠ , weak. What action do you take with each of these hands?

1. ♠ 9 7	2. ♠ A J 8 7 3	3. ♠ A	4. ♠ A Q 2	5. ♠ 2
♡ K 3	♡ A Q	♡ A K J 2	♡ A 8	♡ 6
◊ A Q 9 6 4	◊ Q 9 7 6	◊ 8 7 6 4	◊ A K 8 6 2	◊ K J 9 4 3
♣ K 9 7 3	♣ J 7	♣ K 8 5 4	♣ K Q 7	♣ K Q J 8 6 2

J. The bidding has been (3 ◊) : Double : (No) to you. What action do you take with these hands?

♠ K 7 5 2	2. ♠ A 7	3. ♠ 9 7 5 4 2	4. ♠ A 7 2	5. ♠ Q 8 5 2
♡ K 8 7 3	♡ 8 7 5 3 2	♡ 8 6 4 3 2	♡ 9 7	♡ 6
◊ A	◊ 6 4	◊ K 7	◊ A K 8	◊ 9 4 3
♣ 9 8 5 3	♣ A K 3 2	♣ 4	♣ 9 6 5 4 2	♣ K 9 8 6 4

PART 3

EXPAND YOUR
CONSTRUCTIVE BIDDING

If you ever become satisfied with your level of competence and your mastery of the game, you will have reached a plateau and will remain at that level or fall below it. The true enthusiast is constantly aiming to improve the skills already acquired and to add new dimensions to the existing store of knowledge. This part delves further into actions after your side has opened the bidding and deals with areas which are considered part and parcel of being a competent bidder. If you propose to 'grow up' as a bridge player, you will want to rise beyond the basics and learn how to solve the problems and challenges which each new deal thrusts upon you. You will want to master the vital techniques, which enable you to get the most out of the cards when they are running your way. Both partners need to be conversant with the principles in this section. If you have any doubts about your partner's expertise in any of these areas, make sure that you and your partner go through the relevant sections together thoroughly. A little study by both of you will repay you tenfold when you can cope with trouble situations confidently and competently.

In many parts of this book, hands are discussed in terms of losers. If you are not yet familiar with counting losers, take another look at Chapter 12, page 65 on 'How to count your playing tricks' and also have a preview run through the text of Chapter 23 on 'The Losing Trick Count'. Assessing the playing strength of a hand in terms of losers is a very useful valuation technique.

Chapter 17 deals with fourth-suit forcing; when to use it; when it is unnecessary; how the bidding develops after fourth-suit-forcing has been used; the effect of fourth-suit forcing on other auctions which become non-forcing.

Chapter 18 is concerned with reverses and jump-shifts; opener's requirements and responder's weak and strong continuations; opener's rebids; the forcing status of opener's and responder's subsequent actions; types of hands suitable for a jump-shift; rebids after a jump-shift.

Chapters 19 and 20 cover how to show specific hand patterns; how to let partner know that you have a 5-5, a 6-5, a 6-6, a 5-4 or a 6-4 pattern; how to recognise partner's pattern and how to choose the correct contract after the pattern is revealed; how to play such hands to best advantage as declarer.

Chapter 21 explores stopper-showing and stopper-asking; how to discover whether the partnership holds the stoppers vital to make 3NT the best spot; how to avoid 3NT and locate the best alternative contract when the stoppers necessary for no-trumps are not present.

Chapter 22 examines responder's problems with a weak hand; the use of Stayman on weak hands; when you can afford to use Stayman with junk in order to rescue the partnership from 1NT and when you should subside in 1NT and suffer the consequences; how to recognise the weak actions by responder in order to bail out in a part-score superior to 1NT; further, the use of the 1NT response when holding a long suit in a hand too weak to respond at the 2-level is covered; how to handle the later bidding; when to show the long suit and when to stick with partner's suit.

Chapter 23 provides an outline of the Losing Trick Count, a valuation technique superior to the point count when a trump fit has come to light; when to use it and when to avoid it; how the LTC operates; its limitations; how to calculate the number of losers expected in partner's hand.

Chapter 24 is on long suit trials; how to recognise a long suit trial; when to use it; when to accept partner's invitation and when to reject it. The ability to use long suit trials will be invaluable in reaching major suit games (and occasionally slams as well) when the fit is just right even though the point count is minimal.

CHAPTER 17

FOURTH-SUIT FORCING

The concept of fourth-suit forcing introduced by the Acol system is now common to all standard bidding systems, whether one uses 4-card suits or 5-card majors, weak no-trumps or strong, and so on. Fourth-suit forcing is a valuable adjunct to natural bidding methods because it enables one to explore the nature and strength of partner's hand without fear of being dropped. Without fourth-suit forcing, one would be forced to jump to game and gamble on the correct contract instead of consulting and co-operating with partner.

After the partnership has bid three suits (e.g., 1 ◇ : 1 ♠, 2 ♣), the following principles apply:

1. A 2NT or 3NT bid *promises* at least one stopper in the unbid suit. It is attractive for a 1NT rebid by responder also to have a stopper in the unbid suit (e.g., after 1 ♣ : 1 ♡, 1 ♠), but it is not vital.

2. A rebid of 2NT by responder suggests around 11-12 points and is invitational, not forcing. This applies whether 2NT is a simple rebid (e.g., 1 ◇ : 1 ♠, 2 ♣ : 2NT or 1 ♠ : 2 ♣, 2 ♡ : 2NT) or whether it is a jump-rebid (e.g., 1 ♣ : 1 ◇, 1 ♡ : 2NT). With more than 12 points, bid 3NT or use the fourth suit.

3. If there is a clearcut, natural bid, make that bid and do not use fourth-suit-forcing.

4. If responder raises opener's *second* suit, that *promises* 4-card support and is not forcing.

5. A jump-rebid in responder's suit (e.g., 1 ◇ : 1 ♠, 2 ♣ : 3 ♠) *promises* a 6-card suit and is not forcing.

6. Responder's jump to the 3-level in opener's suit shows 10-12 points and is not forcing if opener's rebid has not promised a strong opening. Thus 1 ◇ : 1 ♠, 2 ♣ : 3 ◇ = 10-12 points. Likewise, 1 ♣ : 1 ♡, 1 ♠ : 3 ♣ is highly invitational, and responder's 3 ♡ or 3 ♠ rebid after the same start would also be a strong invitation, *but not forcing.* To create a forcing auction, responder must use the fourth suit. Where only two suits have been bid, responder's jump-rebid is still recommended as 10-12, invitational, (e.g., 1 ♣ : 1 ♠, 2 ♣ : 3 ♠). With 13-15 points, responder must rebid in game (e.g., 1 ♣ : 1 ♠, 2 ♣ : 4 ♠) or manufacture a new suit rebid, which is forcing (e.g., 1 ♣ : 1 ♠, 2 ♣ : 2 ◇). Not perfect, but it is the least of evils.

7. A jump-rebid in the fourth suit is *natural* and shows a 5-5 or 6-5 pattern with at least game expectations. For example, after 1 ♣ : 1 ♡, 1 ♠ . . . responder's 3 ◇ shows 5+ hearts and 5+ diamonds and enough for game. Similarly, 1 ♣ : 1 ◇, 1 ♠ : 3 ♡ promises five hearts and six diamonds at least, with enough strength for game. The jump-rebid in the fourth suit is a rare creature, but a valuable descriptive technique.

A bid of the fourth suit is *artificial*, shows game-going values and the inability to make a clearcut, natural bid. Perhaps responder has no stopper in the fourth suit. Perhaps responder is too strong to bid just to game and is worth a slam invitation. Perhaps responder's suit is five cards long, and not six cards, and thus responder cannot make a minimum rebid in that suit (which would show a weak hand) or a jump-rebid in that suit (which would promise a 6-card suit). Perhaps it is a combination of these problems. Whatever the reason, responder needs more information about opener's values and the nature of opener's hand.

Responder's bid of the fourth suit is forcing to game and both partners must keep bidding until at least game is reached. That can cause some difficulty for responder with some 11-12 point hands, but cope as best you can. To resolve conflicts with hands in this point range, prefer to overbid, and force to game if need be, than to bid too little and perhaps miss a game. Fourth-suit forcing to game tends to keep the bidding lower for very strong hands and thereby assists greatly in slam bidding.

OPENER'S USE OF FOURTH-SUIT FORCING

When opener rebids the suit opened and responder changes suit (e.g., 1 ◇ : 1 ♠, 2 ◇ : 2 ♡), opener can use fourth-suit forcing (by bidding 3 ♣ in this sequence). Here opener is not showing any extra strength (the 2 ◇ rebid already showed a minimum opening), but is indicating a strong hand in context, one which is unable to support either of responder's suits and has no stopper in the fourth suit (otherwise no-trumps would be a convenient bid). Opener's use of fourth-suit forcing can also arise after a strong auction where responder's suit has been rebid. After 1 ◇ : 1 ♡, 3 ♣ : 3 ♡, a 3 ♠ rebid by opener is not genuine, but denies support for hearts and denies a spade stopper. Perhaps something like ♠ 8 6 4   ♡ J   ◇ A K J 8 4   ♣ A K Q J.

AFTER RESPONDER'S FOURTH-SUIT FORCING

Opener has a choice of actions. In order of preference, opener should:

1. Give delayed 3-card support for responder's suit. Where responder's suit is a major suit, this delayed 3-card support takes precedence over other actions. Responder might hold a strong hand with a 5-card major and also enough for 3NT. Responder is unable to jump-rebid in the major, as that would show 10-12 points and a 6-card suit. To check whether opener holds 3-card support for the major, responder uses fourth-suit forcing, planning to rebid 3NT if 3-card support is not forthcoming. In a sequence like 1 ◇ : 1 ♡, 1 ♠ : 2 ♣ (fourth suit), 2 ♡ tends to show doubleton support and a jump to 3 ♡ = 3-card support.

2. Bid no-trumps with at least one stopper in the fourth suit. If responder's suit is a minor, bidding no-trumps takes priority over giving delayed support for responder's suit.

3. Raise the fourth suit (but never beyond 3NT). If opener could genuinely hold the fourth suit, raising the fourth suit shows a 4-card holding in that suit. If opener has previously denied holding the fourth suit, raising the fourth suit shows a strong hand, too good to make the weakest rebid of opener's first suit, *but with no stopper in the 4th suit*. For example, after 1 ◇ : 1 ♠, 2 ♣ : 2 ♡ (fourth-suit), 3 ♡ by opener would show four hearts and either a 1-4-4-4 or a 0-4-5-4 pattern, since the 2 ♣ rebid did not deny four hearts. However, after 1 ◇ : 1 ♡, 2 ♣ : 2 ♠ (fourth suit), 3 ♠ by opener cannot show four spades – opener would have rebid 1 ♠ over 1 ♡. Here 3 ♠ says, 'I have a strong opening (normally 15+ HCP), but with no stopper in spades and no 3-card support for hearts.' Again, this situation is not common, but very useful when a problem hand occurs.

4. Rebid opener's second suit with at least five cards in that suit.

5. Rebid opener's first suit with 5+ cards in that suit.

AFTER OPENER'S REPLY TO THE FOURTH SUIT

If opener did not support responder's major and responder rebids the major, that will be a good 6+ suit. Opener should now support the suit with a doubleton or a high singleton (queen or better). If responder supports a suit bid by opener, this is strong and suggests slam prospects. For example, 1 ♡ : 1 ♠, 2 ♣ : 2 ◇ (fourth-suit), 2NT : 3 ♡ is stronger than 4 ♡ over 2 ♣.

If opener bids 2NT and responder raises to 3NT, that does not show extra strength. Opener is entitled to bid further if very strong, as responder's expected strength is 13+ points. If responder's suit is a major and opener does not support the major after fourth-suit, 3NT by responder does not show extras. Responder was seeking support for the major and planned to rebid 3NT if support was not forthcoming. If opener does show delayed support for responder's major and responder then bids 3NT, this is very strong, usually 16-19 points and invites a slam. This auction would be such an example: 1 ◇ : 1 ♡, 2 ♣ : 2 ♠ (fourth-suit), 3 ♡ : 3NT. Why didn't responder simply jump to 3NT over 2 ♣? That would show a stopper in spades and about 13-15 points. Using fourth-suit first and then bidding 3NT despite support for the major implies a stronger hand.

AFTER OPENER'S USE OF FOURTH-SUIT FORCING

Responder will bid no-trumps with a stopper in the fourth suit. With no stopper, responder may give delayed support for opener or rebid one of responder's suits. Delayed support will depend on what has been shown or denied so far. For example, after 1 ♠ : 2 ◇, 3 ♣ : 3 ◇ , 3 ♡ (fourth suit) responder's 3 ♠ is based on a doubleton only, because of the failure to support spades earlier, and denies a stopper in hearts. However, delayed support with a jump-rebid shows genuine support and a hand too strong to support earlier. For example, in the above auction, if responder bid 4 ♠ over 3 ♡, that would promise 3-card support, strong diamonds and suggest slam. If weaker with no slam interest, responder should bid 4 ♠ over 3 ♣. Responder's 3 ◇ rebid was forcing since opener's 3 ♣ rebid created a game-force, but choosing 3 ◇ when holding spade support indicates that more than just game is in responder's mind.

THE 1 ♣ : 1 ◇, 1 ♡ : 1 ♠ AUCTION vs THE 1 ♣ : 1 ◇, 1 ♡ : 2 ♠ AUCTION

Modern style is to use the 1 ♠ rebid as a *natural* rebid, promising four spades, and forcing for one round. The 1 ♠ rebid does not promise more than six points, although it could be a very strong hand, just like an immediate 1 ♠ response to 1 ♣ shows 6+ points. Subsequent bidding is natural. The jump to 2 ♠ over 1 ♡ is artificial and is used as fourth-suit forcing, promising enough for game and specifically denying four spades. Bidding over 2 ♠ continues as after any fourth-suit-forcing rebid.

A. Partner opened 1 ◊ and rebid 2♣ over your 1 ♡ response. What action do you now take on these hands?

1. ♠ 8 4 3 2
   ♡ A K 9 8
   ◊ K Q
   ♣ J 4 3

2. ♠ K Q 8
   ♡ K 9 8 6 3
   ◊ Q 9
   ♣ J 4 3

3. ♠ 8 4 3
   ♡ A K 9 8
   ◊ K 6
   ♣ J 8 6 3

4. ♠ 8 4 3
   ♡ A K J 3
   ◊ K 6
   ♣ K 8 6 3

5. ♠ K 8 6
   ♡ K Q 7 6 2
   ◊ A Q
   ♣ 8 4 2

6. ♠ 7 3
   ♡ A J 7 2
   ◊ K Q 4 3
   ♣ J 8 5

7. ♠ 7 3
   ♡ A K 7 2
   ◊ K Q 4 3
   ♣ K 7 6

8. ♠ 8 6
   ♡ A Q J 6 5 2
   ◊ 9 7
   ♣ 9 4 3

9. ♠ J 6
   ♡ A Q J 6 5 2
   ◊ K 7
   ♣ 8 4 3

10. ♠ 8 6
    ♡ A Q 8 6 4 2
    ◊ A 3
    ♣ A 7 2

B. With silent opponents, the bidding has been 1 ◊ : 1 ♡, 2♣ : 2♠ (fourth suit). What is opener's next action?

1. ♠ 6 5 2
   ♡ 8
   ◊ K Q J 3 2
   ♣ A Q 5 4

2. ♠ K Q 8
   ♡ 3
   ◊ K J 8 6 4
   ♣ A K 3 2

3. ♠ 3
   ♡ K 9 8
   ◊ A K 6 5 2
   ♣ A Q 6 3

4. ♠ 8 4
   ♡ K
   ◊ K Q 6 5 2
   ♣ A J 7 4 3

5. ♠ 6
   ♡ 2
   ◊ A Q 9 7 3 2
   ♣ A K J 5 2

6. ♠ Q J 6
   ♡ 2
   ◊ K Q 5 3 2
   ♣ A J 5 4

7. ♠ 7 3
   ♡ 8 4
   ◊ K Q 9 3 2
   ♣ A K J 2

8. ♠ J 6
   ♡ 5 2
   ◊ A K 8 5 2
   ♣ A K Q 9

9. ♠ J 6
   ♡ 2
   ◊ A K 7 5 3 2
   ♣ A 8 4 3

10. ♠ 8 6 2
    ♡ Q
    ◊ A K J 9 6
    ♣ A Q J 7

PARTNERSHIP BIDDING: How should the following hands be bid? West is the dealer on all hands.

SET 35 – WEST	SET 35 – EAST	SET 36 – WEST	SET 36 – EAST
1. ♠ A Q 8 7 ♡ K 3 ◊ 7 6 ♣ K Q 9 8 5	1. ♠ K 9 3 ♡ 7 6 2 ◊ A Q 4 3 2 ♣ A 4	1. ♠ A Q 8 6 ♡ 7 3 2 ◊ 9 ♣ K Q J 7 3	1. ♠ K 4 ♡ 8 5 ◊ A Q J 3 2 ♣ A 8 2
2. ♠ A J 8 4 ♡ A Q 2 ◊ 6 ♣ K Q 9 8 4	2. ♠ K 5 2 ♡ 7 6 ◊ A K J 7 3 ♣ J 3 2	2. ♠ A Q 10 8 7 ♡ A K 9 3 ◊ 7 4 ♣ 6 3	2. ♠ K 2 ♡ 8 7 2 ◊ 9 8 6 ♣ A K Q 5 4
3. ♠ K Q 4 2 ♡ 3 2 ◊ A 9 ♣ K Q 7 3 2	3. ♠ A 3 ♡ K J 8 6 4 ◊ 7 4 3 ♣ A 6 5	3. ♠ - - - ♡ 8 3 2 ◊ A K 7 3 2 ♣ A Q 9 8 3	3. ♠ K Q 8 7 4 ♡ A J 10 7 4 ◊ Q ♣ J 2
4. ♠ A K Q 7 ♡ 8 4 3 ◊ 9 ♣ A Q 9 6 3	4. ♠ 6 4 ♡ A Q J 7 5 ◊ J 3 2 ♣ K J 2	4. ♠ A K J 7 ♡ 6 4 ◊ A Q 7 5 4 ♣ 9 3	4. ♠ 8 3 2 ♡ A K 9 8 3 2 ◊ K 8 ♣ 7 4
5. ♠ K Q 9 8 3 ♡ A ◊ 2 ♣ A 9 8 6 3 2	5. ♠ A 6 2 ♡ K Q 7 3 2 ◊ Q 4 ♣ J 4 2	5. ♠ A K J 7 ♡ 7 3 2 ◊ 8 ♣ A Q 9 8 5	5. ♠ Q 8 3 ♡ J 5 ◊ A Q 7 4 3 2 ♣ K J
6. ♠ - - - ♡ A J 4 2 ◊ K Q 8 6 3 ♣ K J 5 2	6. ♠ A J 10 9 6 ♡ 10 5 ◊ A 5 2 ♣ A 9 3	6. ♠ A K 9 8 5 ♡ K Q 3 2 ◊ 3 ♣ Q 7 6	6. ♠ 6 4 ♡ A 9 8 ◊ 7 6 ♣ A K J 5 3 2

PLAY HANDS ON FOURTH-SUIT FORCING

Hand 65: Fourth-suit forcing – Avoidance technique (keeping the danger hand off lead)

Dealer North : Love all

NORTH
- ♠ K Q 7 2
- ♡ K J 6
- ◊ K 8
- ♣ K 7 3 2

WEST
- ♠ J 8 4 3
- ♡ 10 7 4
- ◊ Q J 6
- ♣ Q 9 8

EAST
- ♠ 10 9 6
- ♡ A Q 8 5 3
- ◊ 10 5 2
- ♣ 5 4

SOUTH
- ♠ A 5
- ♡ 9 2
- ◊ A 9 7 4 3
- ♣ A J 10 6

WEST	NORTH	EAST	SOUTH
	1♣	No	1◊ (1)
No	1♠ (2)	No	2♡ (3)
No	2NT (4)	No	3NT (5)
No	No	No	

Bidding: (1) Too strong to jump to 3♣. With 13-15 points and not balanced, change suit and await developments.
(2) Do not bypass a 4-card major. 1♠ is better than 1NT.
(3) Fourth-suit forcing. A jump to 3♣ would show only 10-12 points. South wants to find 3NT, but cannot bid no-trumps with no stopper in the unbid suit.
(4) Shows a stopper in hearts.
(5) No interest in any spot other than 3NT.

Lead: ♡ 5. Do not be put off by the fact that North is known to hold a stopper in hearts. Your job is to knock out that stopper and set up your long suit.

Correct play: West plays the ♡ 10 and North wins with the ♡ J. With one trick in and seven more in top cards, North needs to set up one more trick. The club suit will provide that. North must keep West off lead and it would be an error here to cash the ♣K and finesse the ♣J. West would win and a heart from West gives the defence four more tricks. North's remaining ♡ K-6 provides a stopper if East is on lead, but not if West is on lead. West is thus the danger hand and North plans to keep West off lead. Play a club to the ace and lead the ♣J, playing low if West plays low. Even if this finesse lost to East, the hearts would not be at risk and North would have nine tricks. As it is, finessing clubs the safe way nets ten tricks.

Hand 66: Fourth-suit forcing – Delayed support – Setting up dummy's long suit – Ruffing finesse

Dealer East : North-South vulnerable

NORTH
- ♠ 8 6 5
- ♡ J 10 5
- ◊ A K 9 8 2
- ♣ 10 5

WEST
- ♠ K 3 2
- ♡ A K 7 6 2
- ◊ Q J 4
- ♣ 4 3

EAST
- ♠ A J 9 4
- ♡ 9 8 4
- ◊ 7
- ♣ A K 7 6 2

SOUTH
- ♠ Q 10 7
- ♡ Q 3
- ◊ 10 6 5 3
- ♣ Q J 9 8

WEST	NORTH	EAST	SOUTH
		1♣	No
1♡ (1)	No	1♠	No
2◊ (2)	No	3♡ (3)	No
4♡ (4)	No	No	No

Bidding: (1) It would be dreadful to respond 3NT, as some players do, ('just to show my points, partner'). Choose a major suit response when available.
(2) Fourth-suit forcing. West has enough for 3NT, but should check whether opener has 3-card support for hearts. If West does not receive delayed support for hearts after fourth-suit, time enough then to bid 3NT.
(3) Shows 3-card support for hearts. With only a doubleton heart and no diamond stopper, East would bid 2♡.
(4) Note how poor 3NT is on the marked diamond lead.

Lead: ◊ A. An A-K suit is highly attractive, but a trump lead would also be sensible here.

Correct play: North should not continue diamonds, but should switch to a spade or a trump. If the switch is to a spade, West should win with the ♣K, cash ♡ A-K and then play ♣A, ♣K and ruff a club. North can over-ruff and continue spades, but declarer wins with the ♠A and ruffs another club to set up the last club in dummy as a winner. Now lead the ◊ Q: if North plays low, run the queen (the ◊ K should be with North on the initial ◊ A lead). If North covers the ◊ Q, ruff in dummy and cash the last club on which the spade loser is discarded. West has a trump and the ◊ J left. Making eleven tricks. Note declarer's timing of the play.

Hand 67: Hunting for the best spot when one suit is unguarded – Keeping control of the trump suit

Dealer South : East-West vulnerable

NORTH
- ♠ A Q 5
- ♡ 9 3 2
- ◇ A J 10 6 3
- ♣ Q 8

WEST
- ♠ 4 2
- ♡ K Q J
- ◇ Q 9 8 5
- ♣ 10 9 4 3

EAST
- ♠ 9 8 7 3
- ♡ A 10 7 6 5
- ◇ K 4
- ♣ 7 2

SOUTH
- ♠ K J 10 6
- ♡ 8 4
- ◇ 7 2
- ♣ A K J 6 5

WEST	NORTH	EAST	SOUTH
			1♣
No	1◇	No	1♠
No	2♡ (1)	No	3♣ (2)
No	4♠ (3)	All pass	

Bidding: (1) 3NT is risky unless partner has something in hearts. Note that a heart lead quickly puts paid to 3NT. North has enough for a game, but the best contract is not clear. 3NT is appealing only if the hearts are covered. If South does have a stopper in hearts, it might be best if South declares no-trumps. To discover more, North uses fourth-suit forcing.
(2) No stopper in hearts, 0-2 diamonds, 5+ clubs.
(3) North discounts no-trumps now that the hearts are known to be unprotected. While a 4-3 trump fit is not particularly desirable, it is acceptable if no-trumps is out of the question. With a strong hand for spades, North would rebid 3♠.

Lead: ♡ K. The unbid suit is the normal lead.

Correct play: Hearts are continued and South must resist the natural inclination to ruff the third round. If South does ruff the third heart and then leads three rounds of trumps, East would be left with the last trump plus two heart winners for two down. With six trumps missing, a 4-2 break is more likely than a 3-3. To protect the trump position, South discards a diamond on the third heart. If a fourth heart came, dummy could ruff. It is fine to ruff with the short trump hand, but risky to ruff with the long trump hand. On anything but a heart at trick 4, declarer wins, draws four rounds of trumps and cashes the ◇ A and the five club winners. Play the ♣ Q first when starting the clubs (high-from-shortage when cashing winners). Making ten tricks.

Hand 68: Bidding when 1♠ is the fourth suit – Keeping control of the trump suit

Dealer West : Game all

NORTH
- ♠ 10
- ♡ J 10 9 6
- ◇ 9 8 4 3 2
- ♣ K 10 6

WEST
- ♠ A K 7 6
- ♡ K Q 5 3
- ◇ 6
- ♣ A 5 4 2

EAST
- ♠ 5 4 3 2
- ♡ A 8 7
- ◇ K Q J 10 7
- ♣ 8

SOUTH
- ♠ Q J 9 8
- ♡ 4 2
- ◇ A 5
- ♣ Q J 9 7 3

WEST	NORTH	EAST	SOUTH
1♣	No	1◇ (1)	No
1♡ (2)	No	1♠ (3)	No
3♠ (4)	No	4♠ (5)	All pass

Bidding: (1) Longest suit first is the normal response. It would be abnormal to respond 1♠.
(2) 4-card suits are shown up-the-line, even on the rebid.
(3) This is superior to a rebid in diamonds. In modern style, this shows four spades even though it is the fourth suit, since 2♠ over 1♡ can be used as fourth suit when not holding 4+ spades. Even if 1♠ as fourth suit would not guarantee a spade suit, opener still raises spades with 4-card support, just in case responder does have spades. Without spades, responder could always revert to no-trumps over a spade raise.
(4) Shows four spades and a strong opening.
(5) 4♠ is the best spot. 3NT is beaten on a club lead.

Lead: ♣ Q. Top of a near sequence is best when all suits have been bid.

Correct play: It is instinctive to win with the ♣ A and tackle trumps next, but this is risky. The normal split with five trumps missing is 3-2, but a 4-1 break occurs about a quarter of the time. If East were to play off the ♠ A-K first, South would get in with the ◇ A, draw declarer's trumps and cash clubs. Declarer should play a diamond before starting trumps to knock out the ◇ A and set up diamond winners in hand. Any return can be won, followed by ♠ A, ruff a club, ♠ K, ruff a club and then play the diamond winners. This produces ten tricks in comfort.

CHAPTER 18

REVERSES AND JUMP-SHIFTS

REVERSES

The concept of the reverse is common to all standard bidding systems, whether one uses 5-card majors or 4-card majors, weak no-trump or strong no-trump, and so on. The reverse allows the opener to reveal a strong hand without a jump-rebid. A reverse is a *non-jump* rebid in a new suit beyond opener's barrier (see page 8 on the Barrier Principle).

Opener's simple reverse is a new suit at the two-level and higher-ranking than opener's first suit.

Opener's high reverse is a bid in a new suit at the three-level after a two-level response.

Opener's rebids in these sequences are examples of a simple reverse:

WEST	EAST	WEST	EAST	WEST	EAST	WEST	EAST	WEST	EAST
1♣	1♠	1♦	1NT	1♣	1♥	1♥	2♦	1♦	2♣
2♥ . . .		2♠ . . .		2♦ . . .		2♠ . . .		2♥ . . .	

Examples of sequences which do not constitute a reverse include 1♣ : 1♥, 1♠ (opener's rebid is at the 1-level), 1♦ : 1♠, 2♣ (opener's second suit is *lower*-ranking), 1♣ : 1♥, 2♠ (opener's rebid is a jump), 1♥ : 2♥, 2♠ (a game try as hearts have been raised), and so on.

WHAT DOES A REVERSE SHOW?

A reverse promises better than a minimum opening (since it breaks the Barrier Principle).

A simple reverse is normally made on a 5-4, 6-4, 6-5 or other pattern where the first bid suit is longer than the second. For example, the expectancy for 1♣ : 1♠, 2♥ is 5+ clubs, 4+ hearts and 17+ points. A simple reverse is never made with a 5-5 pattern, since the higher suit is opened first with a 5-5 pattern. A high reverse is at least a 5-4 pattern and may be a 5-5, 6-5, 6-6 or freakier.

The usual strength for a reverse is 17+ points (16 HCP with one length point for a 5-4 pattern, or 15 HCP with two length points for a 6-4 pattern, or 13-14 HCP and a 6-5 pattern). A hand worth a reverse bid normally contains five losers, but a 4-loser hand even with only 12 or 13 HCP would be strong enough for a reverse.

SUBSEQUENT BIDDING AFTER A REVERSE

After a 1-level response, opener's reverse is forcing for one round. After a 2-over-1 response, opener's reverse is forcing to game.

It is logical that a reverse showing 17+ points should be game-forcing after a 2-level response which showed 10+ points. Subsequent bidding after a reverse over a 2-level response follows standard principles: a bid of no-trumps promises a stopper in the missing suit and a bid of the fourth suit asks for a stopper in that suit or for further description of opener's shape and values.

If you decided to respond with a hand of 0-4 total points, when you should have passed, you may pass a reverse or jump-shift. Otherwise, you must bid again. After a 1-level response, responder has four weak actions, each of which indicates about 5-8 HCP and is not forcing.
1. Raise opener's second suit, e.g., 1♣ : 1♠, 2♦ : 3♦ . . . not forcing.
2. Rebid 2NT with a stopper in the fourth suit, e.g., 1♣ : 1♠, 2♦ : 2NT . . . not forcing.
3. Give preference to opener's first suit, e.g., 1♦ : 1NT, 2♥ : 3♦ . . . not forcing.
4. Rebid responder's suit, e.g., 1♦ : 1♠, 2♥ : 2♠ . . . not forcing.

All other actions by responder are strong, indicating 9+ HCP and therefore are logically forcing to game, as opener should have the equivalent of 17+ points. Responder's strong actions will be:
1. Fourth-suit forcing, shows 9+ points after a reverse, e.g., 1♦ : 1♠, 2♥ : 3♣ . . . forcing to game.
2. Any jump-rebid, e.g., 1♣ : 1♥, 2♦ : 3♥ or 1♣ : 1♥, 2♦ : 4♣ . . . forcing to game.

Suppose the bidding starts 1 ◊ : 1 ♠ , 2 ♡ ... Responder's possible rebids are: 3 ♡ (6-8 points and support for hearts), 2NT (6-8 points, stopper in clubs, denies support for hearts), 3 ◊ (6-8 points, preference for diamonds, at least 3-card support), 2 ♠ (6-8 points, 6-card spade suit or, at the worst, a very good 5-card suit; the rebid of your own suit is used as a last resort with only a 5-card suit), 3 ♣ (fourth-suit forcing, game-force; opener will support spades with three trumps, bid 3NT with a stopper in clubs, or otherwise make some other descriptive bid; if nothing clearcut is available, opener can rebid 3 ◊). 3 ♠ or 3NT or 4 ◊ or 4 ♡ are all natural and game-going. A bid of game is not forcing; a jump-rebid below game after a reverse is a game-force.

After responder has shown a weak hand, 6-8 points, opener with 16-17 HCP and a 5-4 pattern should not bid on, especially when responder has given preference to opener's minor. With a hand of 18 points or so, opener may make one more effort to reach game. For example, after 1 ◊ : 1 ♠ , 2 ♡ : 3 ◊ , a 3 ♠ rebid by opener would show 3-card support and indicate extra strength, because opener bid again despite responder's minimum rebid. Responder can pass, but with 7-8 points would bid again over 3 ♠ , choosing 4 ♠ with five spades or even with a strong 4-card suit, or chancing 3NT with a club stopper (unlikely as responder failed to bid 2NT over 2 ♡) or reverting to diamonds.

EXAMPLES

♠ 2 ♡ A Q 9 6 ◊ A K J 8 6 ♣ K 4 3	You open 1 ◊ . If partner responds 1 ♠ or 1NT, you should rebid 2 ♡ (a reverse). You have the right shape (first suit longer) and enough points. If partner then rebids 3 ◊ or 2 ♠ or 2NT, a weak rebid showing 6-8 points, you should pass. Over responder's 3 ♣ or 3 ♠ rebid, you should rebid 3NT.
♠ 2 ♡ A Q 9 6 ◊ A K J 8 6 ♣ 7 4 3	You open 1 ◊ . If partner responds 1 ♠ or 1NT or 2 ♣ , you should rebid 2 ◊ . You have the correct shape for a reverse (the first suit is longer than the second suit), but your hand is too weak for a reverse. 2 ◊ shows a minimum opening, while 2 ♡ would show a strong hand since it goes beyond your 2 ◊ barrier (see page 8).
♠ 2 ♡ A Q 9 8 4 ◊ A K 8 7 5 2 ♣ 8	You open 1 ◊ . If partner responds 1 ♠ or 1NT or 2 ♣ , you should rebid 2 ♡ . Although your HCP count is not high, you are strong enough to reverse, as you have a 4-loser hand, very powerful playing strength. Over any weak rebid by responder, you should rebid 3 ♡ to show that you hold five hearts and hence at least six diamonds, as you bid diamonds first. Partner will now realize that your strength might be below 16 HCP.

WHEN IS A REVERSE NOT A REVERSE?

If the bidding is beyond opener's barrier (see page 8) before opener has a chance to rebid, opener may bid a new suit at the 2-level without the normal requirements for a reverse. There are two common situations: after a jump-shift or after a competitive auction. For example, after 1 ♣ : 2 ♡ , a rebid of 2 ♠ shows four spades, but does not promise a strong hand or long clubs. The sequence is like 1 ♣ : 1 ♡ , 1 ♠ but one level higher. Similarly, if the bidding has been, say, 1 ♣ : (1 ♠) : 2 ◊ a rebid of 2 ♡ by opener need not have extra strength. Responder's 2 ◊ was already beyond opener's 2 ♣ barrier. Likewise, after 1 ◊ : (2 ♣) : 2 ♡ , a rebid of 2 ♠ by opener can be made with minimum values.

JUMP-SHIFT BY OPENER

Opener's jump-shift is based on a hand that is worth game opposite a 1-level response and hence should contain 19+ points or the equivalent. A 4-loser hand with about 16-18 HCP will normally warrant a jump-shift. If the partnership plays that a 1-level change of suit is forcing, opener's jump-shift to the 2-level (such as 1 ♣ : 1 ♡ , 2 ♠) can be used to guarantee at least a 5-4 pattern (5+ clubs, 4+ spades). It would not be a balanced hand (rebid 1 ♠ or with a jump in no-trumps) or a 4-4-4-1 since the forcing 1 ♠ rebid would be available for that pattern. To play auctions like 1 ♣ : 1 ♡ , 1 ♠ as forcing is no hardship. If partner was able to respond to 1 ♣ , partner will be able to respond to 1 ♠ also (imagine the 1 ♠ rebid was the opening bid).

After a 2-level response, change of suit is forcing, so that there is less need for opener's jump-shift. Hence many partnerships sensibly play that a jump-shift after a 2-over-1 response (e.g., 1 ♠ : 2 ♣ : 3 ◊) shows a strong 5-5 pattern. With a strong 5-4 or a weak 5-5, opener can simply change suit (e.g., 1 ♠ : 2 ♣ : 2 ◊) and rebid the second suit with the 5-5 (thus a weak 5-5, because of the failure to jump-shift earlier) or rebid strongly with a powerful 5-4.

After the jump-shift, responder will rebid naturally, supporting opener's second suit with 4-card support *or* giving delayed support for opener's first suit *or* giving jump-support below game for opener's first suit with 4-card support and prospects for slam (e.g., 1 ♢ : 1 ♠, 3 ♣ : 4 ♢) *or* rebidding responder's suit with a 6-card suit or a very strong (three honours) 5-card suit *or* bidding 3NT with the fourth suit stopped. With no clearcut action or needing more information from opener, responder can make use of fourth-suit forcing (e.g., 1 ♡ : 1 ♠, 3 ♣ : 3 ♢ = fourth-suit forcing). However, this fourth-suit forcing does not promise any extra strength since opener's jump-shift created a game-force already. To justify the 3 ♢ fourth-suit forcing here, responder may have a weak 5-card suit, too weak to rebid (e.g., ♠Q 7 6 4 2 ♡7 2 ♢Q 6 3 ♣Q 8 2), or perhaps responder has no stopper in the fourth suit (e.g., ♠A J 3 2 ♡5 3 ♢6 4 3 2 ♣J 8 6).

RESPONDER'S JUMP-SHIFT

Responder's jump-shift is particularly useful with suitable hands in the 16-18 zone. In this area, it is best to describe your values and allow opener to move on to a slam if opener has better than minimum values. The high card content can be shaded to 14-15 HCP if responder has a solid suit. A hand with A-K-Q-J-x-x in a major and an outside ace would justify a jump-shift, followed by a rebid of game in the major. With a solid 7-card suit, such as A-K-Q-x-x-x-x and an outside A or K-Q, again it is best to jump-shift initially. If you jump-shift first then, if a slam is feasible, opener will take over the reins. With a much stronger hand, say 19+ HCP and a good suit, responder should also jump-shift initially. However, as responder can create an initial force with a change of suit and can later force again either via fourth-suit forcing or via a jump-rebid in some auctions, responder may choose not to jump-shift initially. Provided that responder can control the subsequent auction, responder may choose to bid at the cheapest level in order to find out more about opener's hand. It is usually preferable for the stronger hand to find out about the weaker than vice versa.

THE JUMP-SHIFT TO THE 3-LEVEL AFTER PASSING

After passing, a 2-level response shows 10-12 points and a 5-card suit (see page 26). What then should one make of a jump-shift to the 3-level after passing (e.g., No : 1 ♠, 3 ♣)? It cannot show more points . . . how much more can you have if you could not open? Most partnerships, especially at duplicate, utilize the jump-shift after passing to show a maximum pass + a strong 5-card suit + support for opener's suit. The support will depend on the length promised by the opening bid. If playing normal 4-card suits, responder's 3 ♣ in this sequence would promise five good clubs, 10-11 points and 4+ spades. If the club suit is not strong, responder should choose No : 1 ♠, 3 ♠. Do not bother to show a weak secondary suit.

It follows that auctions like No : 1 ♠, 2 ♣ deny support for opener's suit and opener would be less inclined to repeat an ordinary suit or to bid at all with a minimum opening and tolerance for responder's suit.

It also cannot be rational for responder to make a *natural* jump-response to 3NT after passing. For example, Pass : 1 ♡, 3NT is logically impossible. If you had enough to warrant 3NT, you would have had enough to open the bidding. Some partnerships use this sequence to promise very strong support for opener's suit and a hand too good to jump to 3-of-opener's-suit, which could be dropped. The jump to 3NT after passing says, 'I have exceptional support for your suit and an absolutely maximum passed hand. It is so good that I cannot risk being dropped below game. If you have extra values, there could even be a slam on.' Consequently, after passing, responder's raises of opener's major in order of strength would be to the 2-level (6-9 points), to the 4-level (pre-emptive, 6-9 HCP, seven losers), to the 3-level (10-12 points, eight losers), a passed hand jump-shift (10-11 points, good outside suit) and to 3NT (10-12 points, 7 losers or better).

FAKE REVERSES AND FAKE JUMP-SHIFTS

Opener may choose to reverse or to jump-shift into a mere 3-card suit when holding strong support for responder's suit. Since the reverse or jump-shift is forcing, opener will have another chance to show the nature of the hand, including the support held. This is revealed if opener bids game in responder's suit without responder having shown more than 4-card length. For example, 1 ♢ : 1 ♠, 3 ♣ : 3NT, 4 ♠. Opener certainly has four spades, but might have only three clubs. Indeed, opener's most likely pattern is 4-1-5-3 with a hand too good to jump to 4 ♠ over 1 ♠. Likewise, after 1 ♣ : 1 ♠, it would be safe for opener to reverse into 2 ♡ with a strong hand and a 3-3-1-6 or 3-3-2-5 pattern, even though there are only three hearts. If responder raises hearts to show 4-card support, responder must hold five spades to have bid 1 ♠ ahead of four hearts and so opener will be able to revert to spades over any heart raise.

EXERCISES

A. You opened 1♣ and partner responded 1♠. What is your rebid with these hands?

1. ♠ A 4	2. ♠ 7 3	3. ♠ 3	4. ♠ 4 3	5. ♠ 8 6
♡ A K 9 8	♡ A Q J 6	♡ A K 9	♡ A K J 3	♡ Q J 6 2
◊ Q 6	◊ 9 2	◊ K 7 4 2	◊ K 6 2	◊ A
♣ J 8 6 4 3	♣ A Q 9 8 2	♣ A K J 6 4	♣ A K 9 3	♣ A K Q 8 6 3

B. With silent opponents, the bidding has been 1◊ : 1♠, 2♡. What is responder's next action?

1. ♠ K J 6 3	2. ♠ J 8 6 4 2	3. ♠ Q J 9 7 3 2	4. ♠ J 9 8 5	5. ♠ Q J 9 8
♡ Q 5	♡ K 8 6 3	♡ A K	♡ 7 3	♡ 9 2
◊ 7 6 4	◊ Q 6	◊ 6 5 2	◊ 6 5	◊ 7 5 3
♣ 9 8 4 2	♣ 8 2	♣ J 6	♣ A J 7 4 3	♣ A K J 5

6. ♠ 9 8 7 6 4 2	7. ♠ A K 7 3	8. ♠ K Q 8 4 3	9. ♠ A 8 6 2	10. ♠ A K 8 6 2
♡ 2	♡ K 4	♡ 5 2	♡ 2	♡ K Q 7 3 2
◊ 3 2	◊ 9 3 2	◊ 8 3	◊ K Q 7 3	◊ 9 6
♣ A Q 5 4	♣ 7 6 3 2	♣ A 9 6 2	♣ K 8 4 3	♣ 7

C. The bidding has started 1◊ : 1♠, 3♣. What action should responder now take with these hands?

1. ♠ K Q 7 4	2. ♠ A 9 8 6 3	3. ♠ J 8 6 4 3	4. ♠ Q 10 9 8 3 2	5. ♠ Q J 8 6 5 2
♡ 9 7 3	♡ 8 5 4	♡ J 3	♡ 8 7 4	♡ K J 9 8 6 3
◊ Q 10 6	◊ 6 4	◊ A K 6 4	◊ 6 2	◊ 3
♣ 6 5 2	♣ Q 5 2	♣ Q 9	♣ A 2	♣ - - -

PARTNERSHIP BIDDING: How should the following hands be bid? West is the dealer on all hands.

SET 37 – WEST	SET 37 – EAST	SET 38 – WEST	SET 38 – EAST
1. ♠ K 8 7 3 2	1. ♠ 4	1. ♠ A 7 6 2	1. ♠ K 4
♡ K 4	♡ A Q 9 6	♡ J 3 2	♡ K Q 7 6
◊ 7 5 4	◊ A K J 8 6	◊ 5 4	◊ A K Q 3 2
♣ 6 5 2	♣ K 4 3	♣ A J 10 8	♣ 9 3
2. ♠ K 8 7 3 2	2. ♠ 4	2. ♠ J 6	2. ♠ K 9 7 4 2
♡ K 4	♡ A Q 9 6	♡ A K 3 2	♡ 6 5
◊ 9 5	◊ A K J 8 6	◊ 7 6	◊ A 9 8
♣ 9 8 5 2	♣ 7 4 3	♣ A K Q 4 3	♣ 7 6 5
3. ♠ 3 2	3. ♠ A 8 7 5 4	3. ♠ Q 7 6 2	3. ♠ K 8 3
♡ A 9 8 6	♡ K 4 3 2	♡ 6 5 3	♡ K Q J 2
◊ A K J 8 6 4	◊ 5	◊ A J 10	◊ 8
♣ 7	♣ A 9 4	♣ 7 5 3	♣ A K Q 4 2
4. ♠ A Q	4. ♠ J 8 6	4. ♠ 4 3	4. ♠ A K 7 2
♡ 7 3	♡ K Q 8 6 5 4	♡ A K Q 2	♡ 7 6 5
◊ K Q 7 2	◊ 9 3	◊ A Q 8 6 2	◊ K 4 3
♣ A J 10 4 3	♣ 7 5	♣ K 3	♣ 8 6 2
5. ♠ A 10	5. ♠ 7 3	5. ♠ Q 10 6 5 2	5. ♠ A 8 3
♡ 7 3	♡ A Q 8 6 5 4	♡ A 5	♡ K Q J 2
◊ K Q J 3	◊ A 2	◊ J 4 2	◊ 8
♣ A Q 8 7 4	♣ 5 3 2	♣ K 5 3	♣ A Q J 4 2
6. ♠ A J 9 6	6. ♠ K 7 4	6. ♠ 4 2	6. ♠ A 9 6 5 3
♡ A K Q 8 6	♡ 3 2	♡ A K Q 3	♡ 9 6
◊ K 5	◊ 8 7 4 3	◊ K Q J 5 3 2	◊ A 8 7 6
♣ 7 2	♣ A K J 9	♣ Q	♣ A 6

PLAY HANDS ON REVERSES

Hand 69: Rebidding after a reverse – Discarding a loser and ruffing in dummy

Dealer North : North-South vulnerable

	WEST	NORTH	EAST	SOUTH
		No	No	No
	1 ◇	No	1 ♠	No
	2 ♡ (1)	No	3 ◇ (2)	All pass (3)

NORTH
- ♠ A 9 6
- ♡ 10 8 3 2
- ◇ Q 10 3
- ♣ Q J 10

WEST
- ♠ 4
- ♡ A Q 9 6
- ◇ A K J 8 6
- ♣ K 4 3

EAST
- ♠ K 8 7 3 2
- ♡ K 4
- ◇ 7 5 4
- ♣ 6 5 2

SOUTH
- ♠ Q J 10 5
- ♡ J 7 5
- ◇ 9 2
- ♣ A 9 8 7

Bidding: (1) West has the right shape for the reverse (2-suiter, with the first suit longer) and the right strength, 16+ HCP or five losers, or better.
(2) With a minimum responding hand, East should choose a minimum rebid. 2 ♠ is possible, but 3 ◇ is better: play in the known trump fit (as 2 ♡ showed four hearts and 5+ diamonds).
(3) With a minimum reverse (only 17 HCP, no better than five losers) West should respect East's sign-off. Although 3NT has some chance, the odds for success in 3NT are poor. The club lead is marked and the defence can take three clubs, one spade and one diamond. 3NT requires diamonds to break with the queen onside, less than a 50% chance.

Lead: ♣ Q. The unbid suit and top of sequence.

Correct play: South wins the first trick with the ♣ A and West should win the club return. Rather than tackle trumps at once, declarer can discard the club loser: heart to the king, heart to the ace and discard dummy's third club on the ♡ Q. You could ruff the club loser in dummy next, but a sound move before ruffing the club is to lead the singleton spade. If North plays low, you have stolen a spade trick; if North takes the ♠ A and returns a spade, discard a heart, play a diamond to the ace and ruff the club. North's best defence is to take the ♠ A and lead a heart, allowing South to over-ruff dummy. From the bidding, North knows that West began with four hearts and so South must now be void. On best defence, declarer makes just nine tricks.

Hand 70: Ducking a side suit to retain control and prevent trumps being drawn

Dealer East : East-West vulnerable

	WEST	NORTH	EAST	SOUTH
			No	1 ♣
	No	1 ♠ (1)	No	2 ♡ (2)
	No	3 ♣ (3)	All pass (4)	

NORTH
- ♠ A J 6 4
- ♡ 7 5 2
- ◇ J 9 2
- ♣ 10 8 3

WEST
- ♠ Q 8 7
- ♡ Q 10 8 6
- ◇ K 7 5
- ♣ Q J 9

EAST
- ♠ K 10 9 5 2
- ♡ J 9
- ◇ A 6 4 3
- ♣ 7 2

SOUTH
- ♠ 3
- ♡ A K 4 3
- ◇ Q 10 8
- ♣ A K 6 5 4

Bidding: (1) 1 ♠ is much better than a 1NT response.
(2) South's 2 ♡ shows four hearts and longer clubs. The 2 ♡ rebid not only indicates the 4-card heart length, but also simultaneously clarifies that the club opening was not only genuine but also at least a 5-card suit.
(3) With no stopper in the unbid suit, North should give preference to partner's longer suit rather than passing 2 ♡.
(4) With no extra values, South should accept the sign-off.

Lead: ◇ 5. It is natural to lead the unbid suit, diamonds, and the correct card from K-x-x is the bottom card.

Correct play: The defence takes the first two diamonds and declarer wins the third round. It is tempting to draw two rounds of trumps and then play ace, king and a third heart. This plan would work if hearts were 3-3 or the player who wins the third heart does not hold the last trump. However, as the cards lie, West would win the third heart, draw dummy's trump with the ♣ Q and then cash the heart winner for one off. In situations like these, where a heart has to be lost anyway, concede a heart before touching trumps. Then you can win any return, cash A-K of trumps, A-K of hearts and ruff the heart loser in dummy. On this line South loses only two diamonds, one heart and one club.

Hand 71: Discarding a loser before touching trumps – Double finesse

Dealer South : Game all

	WEST	NORTH	EAST	SOUTH
				No
	1♣	No	1♡	No
	2◊ (1)	No	3♡ (2)	No
	4♡ (3)	No	No	No

NORTH
♠ K 10 8 4 2
♡ J 9
◊ 9 7 6 5
♣ 9 8

WEST
♠ A J
♡ 7 3
◊ K Q 8 2
♣ A Q 10 4 3

EAST
♠ 7 3
♡ A Q 8 6 5 4
◊ A 3
♣ 6 5 2

SOUTH
♠ Q 9 6 5
♡ K 10 2
◊ J 10 4
♣ K J 7

Bidding: (1) 2◊ shows four diamonds, 5+ clubs and 16+ HCP (or if below 16 HCP, then five losers or better).
(2) As 2♡ would be a weak rebid, showing just 6-8 points, East must take stronger action. With 9+ HCP opposite a reverse, either jump-rebid or bid the fourth-suit to make a forcing bid. 3♡ shows 9+ points with at least six hearts.
(3) West could rebid 3NT since West has a stopper in spades, but 4♡ is better. West has doubleton support for the 6-card suit shown by East's 3♡ rebid. 3NT can be made on the normal spade lead, but it is a poor prospect.

Lead: ♣ 4. The unbid suit is the normal lead.

Correct play: You can make eleven tricks because of the lucky club position: win the ♣ A, play a diamond to the ace, diamond to the king and discard the spade loser on the ◊ Q. Then finesse the ♡ Q. This loses, but declarer ruffs the spade return, cashes the ♡ A and leads a club, finessing the ten. (With A-Q-10 opposite x-x-x, finesse the ten first unless you need only one extra trick.) After regaining the lead, East can finesse the ♣ Q, thus losing no club tricks. (As a heart trick must be lost in any event, the technically superior line is: ♣ A; ♡ A; ◊ A; ◊ K; ◊ Q, discarding the spade loser; heart to the queen, and so on.)

Hand 72: Strong action after a reverse – Ruffing a loser – Coping with a bad trump break

Dealer West : Love all

WEST	NORTH	EAST	SOUTH
No	1◊	No	1♠ (1)
No	2♡	No	4◊ (2)
No	4NT	No	5♣
No	5NT (3)	No	6◊
No	7◊ (4)	All pass	

NORTH
♠ K 2
♡ A K Q 3
◊ K Q J 9 3
♣ 7 5

WEST
♠ Q J 10
♡ 8 7
◊ 10 5 4 2
♣ 9 8 3 2

EAST
♠ 9 8 7 4
♡ J 10 5 4 2
◊ - - -
♣ Q J 10 6

SOUTH
♠ A 6 5 3
♡ 9 6
◊ A 8 7 6
♣ A K 4

Bidding: (1) South has enough for game at least, but which game is not clear. Start with the major.
(2) Better than 4NT, since with only aces and kings, it is better to answer Blackwood than to ask for aces yourself. If North were to bid 5◊ next, South is worth 6◊ simply on values.
(3) Confirms all the aces are held and shows grand slam ambitions. If South shows no king, North will settle in 6◊.
(4) North can count twelve top tricks for no-trumps via two spades, three hearts, five diamonds and two clubs. The chance of ruffing a heart for the extra trick makes the grand slam in diamonds attractive.

Lead: ♣ Q. Top of a solid sequence is always attractive, especially in an unbid suit.

Correct play: Win the lead and play a diamond to the king. With no possible trump losers, keep the trump suit 'fluid' by keeping a top trump in each hand. If trumps were 2-2 or 3-1, the hand would be child's play. Simply draw trumps and ruff the heart loser. With the 4-0 break, North must ruff the heart loser before drawing all the trumps, so switch to the ♡A, ♡K and then the ♡3, *ruffing with the ace of diamonds*, finesse the nine of diamonds, draw trumps and claim. Traps to avoid include playing off the ace, king *and queen* of hearts *or* failing to ruff the ♡3 high *or* drawing four rounds of trumps at once *or* playing the ◊A on the first round of trumps.

CHAPTER 19

SHAPE-SHOWING: 5-5, 6-6 AND 6-5 PATTERNS

Balanced hands are generally described with one or two bids, but for unbalanced hands it frequently takes three bids to convey the hand pattern to partner. Consequently, one should be reluctant to jump to game, particularly 3NT, if partner has not yet had the chance to reveal the shape of the hand.

Certain hand patterns are described in a standard way, almost regardless of the system being played and it is important to be aware of the technique to show specific hand patterns. Shape-showing bids continue, provided that the hands are strong enough to keep bidding, until either a trump fit has been located or one partner's shape has been fully revealed. The other partner should then be able to decide on the contract. Once a trump suit has been agreed, shape-showing is usually discontinued and the value of the hand is then bid (pass, invite game, bid game, explore slam, and so on).

THE 5-5 PATTERN

OPEN WITH THE HIGHER RANKING SUIT (regardless of suit quality)

NEXT BID THE LOWER-RANKING SUIT

THEN REBID THE LOWER SUIT

There is controversy whether you should follow the same approach when the two suits are spades and clubs. It is recommended that you do. If the opponents promise to remain silent it would work fine to open 1♣ with 5-5 in the black suits. If there is opposition bidding, there is a risk that you lose the major suit fit. Therefore even with five spades – five clubs, start by opening 1♠.

You can train your ear to listen for the sequence: first suit, second suit, second suit again (Code : ABB). These are typical auctions where the opener has revealed at least a 5-5 pattern:

WEST	EAST		WEST	EAST
1◇	1♠		1♠	2◇
2♣	2NT		2♡	3♣
3♣ ...			3♡ ...	

West has at least five diamonds and five clubs.　　West has at least five spades and five hearts.

While this is the most common approach, one can also jump to game in a new suit. The second suit must be a 5-card suit and so West is showing at least a 5-5 pattern in the major suits in each of these auctions:

WEST	EAST		WEST	EAST
1♠	1NT			1♣
4♡ ...			1♠	2NT
			4♡ ...	

THE 6-6 PATTERN

The description of the freak 6-6 pattern commences the same way as the 5-5 (Higher Suit, Lower Suit, Repeat Lower Suit), but if suit agreement has still not been reached after the first three shape-showing bids, the 6-6 hand rebids the lower suit once more. A jump to 5-of-a-minor is also often indicative of the 6-6 pattern, for example, 1◇ : 1♠, 5♣.

THE 6-5 PATTERN

OPEN WITH THE 6-CARD SUIT (regardless of suit quality)

NEXT BID THE 5-CARD SUIT

THEN REBID THE 5-CARD SUIT

The sequence to show a 6-5 pattern is also first suit, second suit, second suit again (Code: ABB). Where the 6-card suit is also higher-ranking than the 5-card suit, the sequence will follow the same path as for 5-5s. Each of the auctions in the 5-5 section is consistent with West holding a 6-5 pattern. Where the 6-card suit is lower-ranking, there will be no ambiguity and partner will be able to identify the pattern as 6-5.

WEST	EAST		WEST	EAST
1♦	1♠		1♦	1♥
2♥	2NT		1♠	2♣
3♥ ...			2♠ ...	

West has at least six diamonds and five hearts.   West has at least six diamonds and five spades.

West's rebid of the second suit confirms five cards in the second suit, but had the pattern been 5-5, the higher-ranking suit would have been opened. The logical explanation is that the lower suit must be longer.

Since a jump to game in a new suit promises five cards in that suit, West is also taken as showing at least a 6-5 pattern in each of these auctions:

WEST	EAST		WEST	EAST
1♣	1♠			1♣
4♥ ...			1♦	1NT
			4♥ ...	

EXERCISE

Assuming you do not find a trump fit early and partner forces you to keep bidding, which three bids should you make to show the following hand patterns?

1. ♠ 7	2. ♠ A	3. ♠ A 8 6 4 3 2	4. ♠ 7	5. ♠ A J 6 5 2
♥ 7 3	♥ Q	♥ A	♥ A J 9 8 4 2	♥ 6
◇ A Q 9 6 4	◇ Q J 7 6 4	◇ K 8 7 6 4 3	◇ A K 8 6 2	◇ A K 9 5 3 2
♣ A K J 3 2	♣ A K 8 7 3 2	♣ - - -	♣ 7	♣ J

PARTNERSHIP BIDDING: How should these hands be bid? West is the dealer on all hands.

SET 39 – WEST	SET 39 – EAST	SET 40 – WEST	SET 40 – EAST
1. ♠ K Q 8 7 6	1. ♠ 3	1. ♠ K Q 9 4 3	1. ♠ A 5 2
♥ A K 9 4 3	♥ J 5 2	♥ 8	♥ K J 9 7 4
◇ J 3	◇ A K 9 7	◇ A Q J 6 4 2	◇ 7 3
♣ 2	♣ A J 6 4 3	♣ 3	♣ A J 6
2. ♠ A 2	2. ♠ K Q 8 6 4	2. ♠ 8 3 2	2. ♠ A K 7 5 4
♥ Q 9 2	♥ J 10 8 6 5	♥ A K J 8 5 3	♥ 4
◇ 7 6	◇ A J 3	◇ 8 7 2	◇ 5
♣ A K 9 8 7 3	♣ - - -	♣ A	♣ K Q 7 6 4 3
3. ♠ J 2	3. ♠ A 9 7 6 5	3. ♠ A Q J 6 2	3. ♠ 5
♥ 9 8	♥ A K 7 3 2	♥ K Q 9 8 6 5	♥ A 2
◇ A Q 8	◇ J	◇ - - -	◇ J 8 7 6
♣ A K 9 8 7 3	♣ 4 2	♣ J 2	♣ K Q 8 5 4 3
4. ♠ J 3 2	4. ♠ K Q 9 7 4	4. ♠ 6 4	4. ♠ A K 8 3 2
♥ K 6	♥ A 9 5 4 2	♥ 3 2	♥ K Q 7 6 5 4
◇ A Q 7 6 3 2	◇ 8	◇ A Q 2	◇ 5
♣ K 2	♣ A 3	♣ A K 8 7 4 2	♣ 3
5. ♠ 3 2	5. ♠ Q J 8 7 6 5	5. ♠ 4 3	5. ♠ A Q 9 6 5
♥ 2	♥ K Q 3	♥ J 2	♥ 7 3
◇ A K 8 4 3	◇ 5	◇ K 8 7	◇ A Q 9 5 4 2
♣ K Q 9 6 2	♣ 4 3 2	♣ A K Q 10 4 2	♣ - - -
6. ♠ - - -	6. ♠ Q 9 8 6 5 4	6. ♠ A Q 8 6 4	6. ♠ 7 3 2
♥ J 3 2	♥ A 8 7	♥ 3	♥ K Q 9 8
◇ A K 8 4 3	◇ 6	◇ 7	◇ Q 4 3 2
♣ K Q 9 6 2	♣ J 5 4	♣ A Q 9 6 5 2	♣ 4 3

PLAY HANDS ON SHAPE-SHOWING: 5-5 AND 6-5 PATTERNS

Hand 73: 5-5 Pattern – Misfit – Ducking to set up a long suit

Dealer North : East-West vulnerable

NORTH
♠ 9 3
♡ Q 10 6 5
♢ K 7 6 4
♣ Q 6 3

WEST
♠ A 7 6 5 4
♡ A K 7 3 2
♢ J
♣ 4 2

EAST
♠ J 2
♡ 9 8
♢ A Q 8
♣ A K 9 8 7 5

SOUTH
♠ K Q 10 8
♡ J 4
♢ 10 9 5 3 2
♣ J 10

WEST	NORTH	EAST	SOUTH
	No	1♣	No
1♠	No	2♣	No
2♡	No	2NT	No
3♡ (1)	No	3NT (2)	All pass

Bidding: (1) Repeating the hearts to confirm the 5-5.
(2) With no fit for either major and the diamonds well stopped.

Lead: ♢ 3. As declarer and dummy have at least five cards in spades, hearts and clubs, it is normal to lead the unbid suit.

Correct play: North plays the ♢ K and declarer wins the ace. With seven top tricks, declarer sees that the club suit offers the best chance for extra tricks. ♣A, ♣K and give up a club might work if the opponents continue diamonds, but if not and they lead either major instead, declarer would have no entry to hand and three club winners and the ♢ Q would be stranded.

It does not pay to rely on the opponents to help you, particularly when you can help yourself. Since a club trick has to be lost anyway, declarer should simply 'duck' a club (play a low club from both hands) at trick 2. Now even if the opponents fail to continue diamonds, dummy has a club to reach declarer's hand. As long as the clubs divide 3-2, declarer has an easy path to ten tricks (one spade, two hearts, two diamonds and five clubs). Declarer could also have attempted to establish the hearts, but it is better to go for the clubs since you have more of them. A favourable break in clubs is more likely than in hearts or in spades.

Hand 74: How to handle a 2-suiter in the play – Setting up the second suit early

Dealer East : Game all

NORTH
♠ 9 2
♡ K 7 6
♢ A 8 3
♣ A Q 7 4 3

WEST
♠ J 4
♡ Q J 5 2
♢ Q 10 6 4
♣ J 8 5

EAST
♠ A 10 8 5
♡ 10
♢ J 9 7 5
♣ K 10 9 6

SOUTH
♠ K Q 7 6 3
♡ A 9 8 4 3
♢ K 2
♣ 2

WEST	NORTH	EAST	SOUTH
		No	1♠
No	2♣	No	2♡
No	3♢ (1)	No	3♡ (2)
No	4♡ (3)	All pass	

Bidding: (1) Fourth-suit forcing, planning to rebid 3NT over a 1♠ rebid by opener. 2NT instead of 3♢ would not be adequate since 2NT would not be forcing.
(2) Confirms the 5-5 by rebidding the lower-ranking suit.
(3) The 5-3 heart fit is now known. 4♡ is far superior to 3NT, which is almost hopeless on a diamond lead. 4♡ can be made by skilful play despite the bad trump break and the poor split in spades.

Lead: ♢ 4. The unbid suit is the natural lead.

Correct Play: The best way to play a pronounced 2-suiter is to set up the second suit if it is not already high. Where losers in the second suit need to be ruffed and dummy has only a few trumps, it is normal to set about the second suit early, usually before drawing trumps. It also does not pay you to ruff in the long trump hand unless this is unavoidable. Declarer's trump length will be needed later as entries for the established second suit. Win the ♢ A and lead a spade to the king (East should duck). Play a heart to the king in order to lead dummy's last spade, taken by East who will return a diamond. Win the diamond and play the ♡ A, followed by a low spade to ruff in dummy. It would be an error to lead the ♠ Q first, since West could ruff this high and lead the other top trump, eliminating dummy's last trump and leaving you with an extra spade loser. When you regain the lead, just keep on playing spades, forcing West to ruff.

Hand 75: 6-5 pattern – Setting up the second suit before drawing trumps

Dealer South : Love all

NORTH
- ♠ A K 7 5 4
- ♡ A 8 6 5 3 2
- ◇ 6
- ♣ 5

WEST
- ♠ Q 10 9 2
- ♡ K J 9
- ◇ K 10 4 2
- ♣ 6 3

EAST
- ♠ J
- ♡ Q 10 4
- ◇ Q J 9 8 3
- ♣ Q 10 9 2

SOUTH
- ♠ 8 6 3
- ♡ 7
- ◇ A 7 5
- ♣ A K J 8 7 4

WEST	NORTH	EAST	SOUTH
			1 ♣
No	1 ♡	No	2 ♣
No	2 ♠ (1)	No	2NT (2)
No	3 ♠ (3)	No	4 ♠ (4)
No	No	No	

Bidding: (1) New suit by responder is forcing.
(2) Merely confirms a stopper in diamonds and no support yet for either of responder's suits.
(3) The spade rebid confirms five spades and therefore six hearts, as hearts were bid first. With 5-5, spades are bid first.
(4) It is clearcut to support now that partner has shown five spades. It would have been premature to raise spades over 2 ♠, as it might then have been only a 4-card suit. With a doubleton in each major, responder would support hearts here. Note that 3NT is hopeless on the obvious diamond lead.

Lead: ◇ Q. The unbid suit is normal. Top of a near-sequence.

Correct play: Win the ◇ A and continue with the ♡ A, ruff a heart, spade to the ace and ruff another heart. When hearts divide 3-3, declarer's remaining hearts are high. Ruff a diamond to hand and cash the ♠ K. When spades do not break, keep on leading hearts. Do not play a third trump. If hearts had not been 3-3, you may hope that a defender who over-ruffs is using what would have been a trump winner anyway. It would also have been an error to play trumps early, as dummy's trumps are needed to ruff hearts. Another error would be to ruff clubs or diamonds in hand. It is normally wrong to shorten the long trump hand. Ruffing with the long trump hand is appropriate if you need an entry to hand, or you are playing on a cross-ruff, or you are in the process of setting up a long suit in dummy.

Hand 76: 6-5 Pattern – Setting up the second suit early

Dealer West : North-South vulnerable

NORTH
- ♠ J 10 8 7
- ♡ A 9 2
- ◇ 10
- ♣ Q 9 8 7 4

WEST
- ♠ K Q 9 4 3
- ♡ 8
- ◇ A Q J 6 4 2
- ♣ 3

EAST
- ♠ A 5 2
- ♡ K J 10 7 4
- ◇ 7 3
- ♣ A J 6

SOUTH
- ♠ 6
- ♡ Q 6 5 3
- ◇ K 9 8 5
- ♣ K 10 5 2

WEST	NORTH	EAST	SOUTH
1 ◇	No	1 ♡	No
1 ♠	No	2 ♣ (1)	No
2 ♠ (2)	No	4 ♠ (3)	All pass

Bidding: (l) Fourth-suit-forcing, planning to rebid 3NT unless opener shows a significant shape feature. It is unnecessary to rebid the hearts. If opener holds three hearts, such secondary support will be shown in response to fourth-suit forcing.
(2) Confirms the 6-5 shape with at least six diamonds. Also shows a minimum opening. With a stronger hand, 3 ♠ would be bid here, and if even stronger, West would have rebid 2 ♠ over 1 ♡.
(3) With support for both the major and the minor, prefer to support the major.

Lead: ♣ 7. The unbid suit is normal. The ◇ 10 is a poor lead. With a natural trump trick, it is rarely desirable to lead a singleton to try for a ruff. Also, it is almost always poor strategy to lead declarer's second suit.

Correct play: Win the ♣ A and finesse the ◇ Q. Cross to dummy's ♠ A and finesse the ◇ J. If North ruffs and returns a club, you ruff, cash the ♠ K, ♠ Q and continue with the ◇ A and another diamond, setting up your diamonds. You lose one spade, one heart and one diamond. It is an error to draw trumps early (you may need dummy's trumps to ruff diamonds) or to ruff a club in hand (do not shorten the long trump hand). If West leads a heart, North should rise with the ace, as the ♡ 8 must be a singleton. As West's bidding has shown six diamonds, five spades and West followed to the first club, West cannot hold more than one heart.

CHAPTER 20

SHAPE-SHOWING: 6-4 AND 5-4 PATTERNS

Showing the 6-4 and 5-4 patterns is not as cut and dried as the 5-5 and 6-5 patterns, because the way to treat them will depend on which is the long suit and also the strength of the hand. One of the major obstacles to revealing the complete shape is the inability to 'reverse' when the hand is minimum (see Chapter 18 on Reverses). *Bidding a new suit at the 2-level higher-ranking than your first suit shows a better-than-minimum hand.* Therefore, if opener's hand *is* minimum, opener should not bid the second suit at the 2-level when the second suit is higher-ranking. For example, 1 ◇ : 1 ♠, 2 ♡ is a reverse and promises extra values, while 1 ◇ : 1 ♠, 2 ♣ does not. Similarly, after a 2-level response, opener should not proceed to the 3-level with minimum values: *opener's rebid at the 3-level after a 2-level response shows a better-than-minimum hand.* Therefore, if the hand *is* minimum, opener can bid a new suit at the 2-level lower than the suit opened or, if this is not possible, opener will have to rebid the original suit. For example, 1 ♠ : 2 ◇, 3 ♣ shows extra values, while 1 ♠ : 2 ◇, 2 ♡ does not promise more than a minimum, because the rebid is at the 2-level and lower than the suit opened. **The Barrier Principle**: The 2-level rebid of the suit opened is a notional barrier and opener's rebids higher than the barrier show a strong opening (see Chapter 2, page 8).

THE 6-4 PATTERN: If the hand is not minimum, the standard approach is:

Start with the 6-card suit – Next bid the 4-card suit – Then rebid the 6-card suit

The order this time is first suit, second suit, first suit again (Code: ABA). These are typical auctions where the opener has revealed at least a 6-4 pattern :

WEST	EAST		WEST	EAST
1 ◇	1 ♡		1 ♠	2 ◇
2 ♣	2NT		2 ♡	3 ◇
3 ◇ ...			3 ♣ ...	

West has at least six diamonds and four clubs.　　West has at least six spades and four hearts.

Where the opener has a minimum hand, it will depend on which suits are held. With a 6-card minor and a 4-card major, open the 6-card minor and bid the 4-card major next at the 1-level if possible. If this is not possible (e.g., you hold six clubs and four hearts and the bidding starts 1 ♣ : 1 ♠), repeat the 6-card minor. Do not bid your 4-card major at the 2-level with minimum values, as that is beyond your barrier.

With a 6-card major and a 4-card minor, open the major and bid the minor next if possible at the 2-level. If the 2-level is not possible (e.g., you have six spades and four clubs and the bidding starts 1 ♠ : 2 ♡), repeat your 6-card major. Do not rebid at the 3-level with minimum values. Also if your 6-card major is very strong and your 4-card minor is very weak, do not show the minor. Prefer to repeat the major suit.

With six spades – four hearts, follow the normal order (spades, hearts, then spades again) unless a fit has been found earlier. With four spades and six hearts, you open 1 ♡, but with minimum values, you are not strong enough to reverse with 2 ♠ over a 1NT or 2 ♣ or 2 ◇ response. Simply rebid 2 ♡ to confirm the minimum opening.

THE 5-4-4-0 PATTERN: Open with the 5-card suit and if the hand is not minimum, show the cheaper 4-card suit next and, if still no trump fit has been found, bid the third suit (e.g., 1 ♡ : 1 ♠, 2 ♣ : 2NT, 3 ◇). The same applies if the hand is minimum except that you must not make a reverse bid or bid a new suit at the 3-level over a 2-level response. For example, with four hearts, four diamonds, five clubs you open 1 ♣. If partner responds 1 ♠, you can rebid 2 ◇ (a reverse) if better than minimum, but should rebid only 2 ♣ if the hand is minimum. Likewise, if you hold five spades, four diamonds and four clubs and open 1 ♠, if partner responds 2 ♡, you can rebid 3 ♣ if better than minimum, but should rebid 2 ♠ with a minimum.

THE 5-4-2-2 PATTERN: It is normal to open the 5-card suit and then bid the 4-card suit. However, if the hand is minimum, the rebid in the second suit must not be a reverse or a bid at the 3-level. When opener's hand is minimum, the 5-card suit is a minor and almost all of the points are in the doubletons, you may choose to open 1NT with the right strength. Otherwise prefer the suit opening.

THE 5-4-3-1 PATTERN: Open with the 5-card suit. With 15+ HCP, bid your second suit. With a minimum opening, you may raise responder's major with three trumps, otherwise bid your 4-card suit, provided that this is not a reverse. If neither of these choices is available, repeat your 5-card suit. With four spades, three hearts and a 5-card minor, prefer to rebid 1 ♠ over a 1 ♡ response. With 15+ HCP, bid your second suit.

If no fit has been found after you have shown both your suits and you are obliged to bid again, then if your 3-card holding is in partner's original suit, support that suit ('delayed support'), but if your 3-card holding is in the unbid suit, accept your partner's suggestion for no-trumps or bid no-trumps yourself if the 3-card holding amounts to a stopper (Q-x-x or better = a stopper). If your 3-card suit is J-x-x or worse and partner has not bid no-trumps, rebid your 5-card suit as a last resort.

EXERCISES

A. You opened 1 ◇ and partner responded 1 ♠. What is your rebid with each of these hands?

1. ♠ 8 2	2. ♠ A 2	3. ♠ A 2	4. ♠ A 2	5. ♠ A 8 7 2
♡ 3	♡ 3	♡ K J 6 4	♡ K J 6 4	♡ 6
◇ A Q J 8 6 4	◇ A K J 9 7 2	◇ A J 6 4 3 2	◇ A J 6 4 3 2	◇ A K J 4 3 2
♣ K Q 9 3	♣ 8 7 3 2	♣ 7	♣ A	♣ A 3

6. ♠ K 7	7. ♠ K	8. ♠ A 6 3	9. ♠ - - -	10. ♠ - - -
♡ K J 7 3	♡ A K Q	♡ K Q 7 2	♡ A J 7 2	♡ A Q 7 2
◇ A Q 9 6 3	◇ Q 9 7 6 4	◇ K 8 6 4 3	◇ A K 8 6 2	◇ A K 9 4 3
♣ 4 2	♣ J 7 3 2	♣ 4	♣ Q 8 6 4	♣ K Q 7 6

PARTNERSHIP BIDDING: How should the following hands be bid? West is the dealer on all hands.

SET 41 – WEST	SET 41 – EAST	SET 42 – WEST	SET 42 – EAST
1. ♠ K Q 8 7 4 3	1. ♠ J 6	1. ♠ Q 6 5	1. ♠ K J 9 3 2
♡ A K 9 2	♡ Q 4	♡ 6	♡ A J 4 3
◇ J 3	◇ K Q 5 4 2	◇ A K J 4 3	◇ Q 7
♣ 7	♣ A 8 6 3	♣ K Q J 6	♣ 3 2
2. ♠ 8 4	2. ♠ K Q J 2	2. ♠ K 5 3	2. ♠ 9 6 2
♡ K 8 6 4	♡ 7 3	♡ A 8 6 3	♡ 7
◇ 5 4 2	◇ A Q 9 8 7 3	◇ 7 4 3	◇ A K Q 6 2
♣ A J 8 7	♣ 2	♣ A 9 8	♣ K Q J 5
3. ♠ A 2	3. ♠ K 8 7 6 4 3	3. ♠ K 9	3. ♠ A Q 7 2
♡ 7 6	♡ A Q J 2	♡ J 6 3	♡ A 10 8 4
◇ A 9 3	◇ K 8	◇ A 7 4 3 2	◇ - - -
♣ K Q 8 5 4 2	♣ 3	♣ 7 6 2	♣ K Q 9 8 4
4. ♠ 8 6	4. ♠ K 7 3 2	4. ♠ J 6 2	4. ♠ A Q 8 7 4
♡ A 9 5 3	♡ 6	♡ A K 8 7 2	♡ - - -
◇ K 7 6 2	◇ A Q	◇ K J 9 3	◇ Q 5 4 2
♣ Q 9 2	♣ A K 8 7 4 3	♣ 8	♣ A J 9 2
5. ♠ K Q	5. ♠ J 8	5. ♠ 9 8 3 2	5. ♠ K Q
♡ K 7 3 2	♡ Q J 6 4	♡ J 7 5 2	♡ A Q
◇ A 9 8 6 5 3	◇ 7	◇ Q 3	◇ J 7 6 4 2
♣ 7	♣ A K 8 6 5 2	♣ A 5 4	♣ K 10 3 2
6. ♠ A Q 9 8 6 4	6. ♠ 2	6. ♠ 8 3	6. ♠ A Q 9 6 5
♡ 4 2	♡ K Q J 7 5 3	♡ 4 2	♡ A 10 8 7
◇ K Q 7 3	◇ A J 9 8	◇ A Q 8 7 4	◇ K 3
♣ Q	♣ K 3	♣ A Q J 6	♣ 4 3

PLAY HANDS ON SHAPE-SHOWING: 6-4 AND 5-4 PATTERNS

Hand 77: 6-4 pattern – Establishing an extra winner in dummy for a discard

Dealer North : Game all

NORTH
- ♠ J 6
- ♡ K 6 2
- ◇ K Q 8 6 5
- ♣ Q 4 3

WEST
- ♠ A 10 5 2
- ♡ 8 5
- ◇ A 10 3 2
- ♣ 10 9 2

EAST
- ♠ 9
- ♡ J 10 9 7
- ◇ J 9
- ♣ K J 8 7 6 5

SOUTH
- ♠ K Q 8 7 4 3
- ♡ A Q 4 3
- ◇ 7 4
- ♣ A

WEST	NORTH	EAST	SOUTH
	No	No	1♠
No	2◇ (1)	No	2♡ (2)
No	2NT (3)	No	3♠ (4)
No	4♠	All pass	

Bidding: (1) A 2-over-1 by a passed hand shows 10-12 points and a 5+ suit (see Chapter 4, page 26), but change of suit by a passed hand is not forcing.
(2) Change of suit by opener after a 2-over-1 response is forcing, even where responder is a passed hand.
(3) Confirms a stopper in clubs, the unbid suit, and denies support for either major, i.e., not three spades, not four hearts.
(4) The ABA Pattern showing six spades and four hearts. 3NT would be defeated easily on a club lead, followed by a club continuation when West wins the lead with either ace.

Lead: ♣ 10. Lead the top card from a 3-card suit, if the top cards are touching *and* include an honour.

Correct play: Win the ♣ A and lead a spade to dummy's jack, followed by a spade to your king. Had trumps divided 3-2. you would not lose more than one spade, one heart and one diamond. Ruff the club return and play the ♠ Q. Do not play a fourth spade and do not start on the hearts yet. Lead a diamond to dummy's king, cross back to your ♡ A and lead another diamond, playing low if West takes the ace, or playing the queen if West plays low again. Either you lose no diamond or the ◇ Q is high for a heart discard. The ♡ K in dummy is your entry to the established queen of diamonds if West takes the ◇ A on the second round of diamonds.

Hand 78: How to handle the 5-4-3-1 – Setting up the stronger suit

Dealer East : Love all

NORTH
- ♠ 7 3
- ♡ Q 8 7
- ◇ K Q 10 8 7
- ♣ A 10 8

WEST
- ♠ A J 10 5
- ♡ 9 5 3
- ◇ 9 5 3 2
- ♣ 7 6

EAST
- ♠ 4 2
- ♡ J 10 6
- ◇ A 6 4
- ♣ K J 9 5 2

SOUTH
- ♠ K Q 9 8 6
- ♡ A K 4 2
- ◇ J
- ♣ Q 4 3

WEST	NORTH	EAST	SOUTH
		No	1♠
No	2◇ (1)	No	2♡ (2)
No	2NT (3)	No	3NT (4)
No	No	No	

Bidding: (1) Bid a good 5-card suit rather than 2NT which implies no powerful suit and diminishes your chances of reaching a possible diamond slam.
(2) Change of suit after a 2-over-1 response is forcing.
(3) Showing a club stopper and giving the opener a chance to show five hearts (3 ♡) or six spades (3 ♠).
(4) Holding a 5-4-2-2 pattern, opener would choose 3NT. Similarly, with a 5-4-3-1 and a singleton in responder's suit, go for 3NT, which makes easily here, while 4♠ is easily beaten.

Lead: ♣ 5. With nothing of significance elsewhere, the unbid suit is the natural lead.

Correct Play: With honour-ten in hand, play low from dummy, not the honour. As it happens the ten wins and you should set up the diamond winners, making at least ten tricks. Although you have more spades and hearts than diamonds, play a diamond to the jack, a heart to the queen and then top diamonds to force out the ace. The diamond suit is more solid and can provide more tricks. Declarer should make ten or eleven tricks (four hearts, four diamonds and two clubs, plus a spade later perhaps). If declarer plays a spade before the diamonds (error), West can win and return a club, setting up East's clubs, which East cashes on winning the ◇ A.

Hand 79: 5-4-3-1 pattern – Tend to be highly suspicious when dummy's long suit is led

Dealer South : North-South vulnerable

WEST	NORTH	EAST	SOUTH
			No
1♡	No	1♠	No
2♢ (1)	No	2NT (2)	No
3♠ (3)	No	4♠	All pass

NORTH
♠ 9 2
♡ K J 10 3 2
♢ 9 6
♣ A 6 5 4

WEST
♠ Q 4 3
♡ A Q 9 8 4
♢ K Q J 2
♣ K

EAST
♠ A J 10 6 5
♡ 7 6
♢ A 4 3
♣ Q 9 7

SOUTH
♠ K 8 7
♡ 5
♢ 10 8 7 5
♣ J 10 8 3 2

Bidding: (1) With a minimum, West might bid 2♠. With a strong opening, prefer 2♢ and support spades later.
(2) 2NT is better than repeating the spades. 2♠ would show the five spades but only a weak hand (6-9), while 3♠ would show a strong hand, but it promises six spades. 2NT shows a club stopper and allows opener to reveal any further shape.
(3) This now shows three-card support, a better-than-minimum opening and is forcing.

Lead: ♡5. The jack of clubs, the unbid suit, would be reasonable, but a singleton is very attractive when you have a weak hand (as partner then will have an entry) and you have trump control (A-x, A-x-x or K-x-x prevents declarer drawing trumps quickly).

Correct play: Win the ♡A and lead the ♠Q for a finesse. If South wins and leads a club to the ace and North plays king and another heart, East ruffs high. East then draws trumps and discards a club on the fourth diamond. **Trap:** Do not take the heart finesse at trick 1. If declarer succumbs to the lure of the heart finesse, North can win with the ♡K and give South a heart ruff. Declarer still has to lose to the ♠K and ♣A. Be very suspicious when an opponent leads dummy's long suit. The lead is usually a singleton.

Hand 80: 6-4 pattern – Jump-shift – Utilizing the ruffing finesse

Dealer West : East-West vulnerable

WEST	NORTH	EAST	SOUTH
1♡	No	1♠	No
3♣ (1)	No	4♣ (2)	No
4♡ (3)	No	No (4)	No

NORTH
♠ K 9 8 4 3
♡ 9 7 5
♢ Q 10 5 2
♣ 7

WEST
♠ 2
♡ A K J 8 6 4
♢ A K
♣ K 8 6 3

EAST
♠ A Q J 6
♡ Q 3
♢ 6 4 3
♣ 9 5 4 2

SOUTH
♠ 10 7 5
♡ 10 2
♢ J 9 8 7
♣ A Q J 10

Bidding: (1) The jump-shift is normally based on at least a 5-4 pattern, 19+ points and is forcing to game. 3♣ is superior to 4♡ (the hand is too strong for 3♡), since partner could have a singleton or void in hearts and have four or five good clubs, making a club slam possible.
(2) Bidding 3♢ (fourth-suit) would also be reasonable since the club support is not strong.
(3) Showing 6-4 and allowing partner to revert to 5♣ if 4♡ is out of the question.
(4) Very happy to pass 4♡. 3NT is best, but not easy to reach.

Lead: ♣7. Although it is usually unattractive to lead declarer's suit and the ♢2 lead, the unbid suit, is normal, the singleton club is a reasonable gamble with a weak hand.

Correct play: South wins with the ♣A and continues with the ♣Q. North ruffs declarer's king. North exits with a trump or a diamond. How can declarer make 4♡ safely with two losing clubs in each hand?

Win the red suit exit in hand and do not draw trumps yet. Play a spade to the ace and lead the ♠Q. If South were to produce the king, you would ruff, cross to the ♡Q and discard a club loser on the ♠J. When South plays low on the ♠Q, do not ruff – discard a club instead. Even though North wins, North has no club to cash and the ♠J is established as a winner to allow you to discard the other club loser, with the ♡Q as the required entry. This play in the spade suit is known as a 'ruffing finesse' and the manoeuvre of discarding a loser while setting up an extra trick goes by the name of 'loser-on-loser play'.

CHAPTER 21

FINDING THE STOPPERS FOR 3NT

There are many situations where you feel no-trumps is best, but you are worried about a particular suit. The suit might be completely unguarded or partner might have it stopped. If partner has already bid no-trumps indicating a balanced hand, it is reasonable to take your chances in raising no-trumps, but in a suit auction partner might have no stopper or be very short in that suit. The real risk in 3NT is not an unguarded suit but shortages. You are more likely than not to make 3NT if your only danger is a suit where you hold x-x-x opposite x-x-x, since the opponents may not lead that suit. If they do, it is about 60% likely that the suit will divide 4-3 so that the defence can take only four tricks. When you have an unguarded suit with x-x opposite x-x, or x-x-x opposite a singleton, then you have real problems. Even one stopper, such as A-x-x opposite a singleton, may prove to be insufficient unless you can run nine tricks.

The technique of searching for a stopper will differ according to what has taken place in the auction so far.

1. The opponents have bid a suit – you would like to bid no-trumps, but have no stopper in their suit.

Solution: Bid their suit. Bidding the enemy suit is covered in detail in Chapter 25, but one of its functions is to *ask partner for a stopper in their suit*. See Chapter 25 for further information.

2. Your side has bid three suits – you want to bid no-trumps, but have no stopper in the fourth suit.

Solution : Use fourth-suit forcing. Fourth-suit forcing was the subject matter of Chapter 17. One of its functions is to *ask partner for a stopper in the fourth suit*. Partner has a specific set of priorities in replying to fourth-suit forcing. See Chapter 17 for further information.

3. Your side has found a minor suit fit and has the values for a game – you want to be in 3NT rather than 5-of-a-minor, but do not hold a stopper in every outside suit. An outside suit might be wide open.

Solution: After minor suit agreement, bidding a new suit below 3NT is forcing and shows a stopper.

For example, after 1♡ : 2♣, 3♣ a rebid of 3◊ by responder would *show* a stopper in diamonds and thus indicate that the worry for 3NT is spades. Likewise, after 1♡ : 2♣, 3♣ a rebid of 3♠ by responder would *show* a stopper in spades and indicate that diamonds is the worry. If partner has the danger suit held, partner will bid 3NT, but with no stopper in the danger suit, partner will take some other descriptive action.

After 1♣ : 2♣, a rebid of 2◊ is forcing and *shows* a diamond stopper. Responder should now show a stopper in a major if possible (the 2♣ response already denied a 4-card major), *or* bid 2NT (minimum) or 3NT (maximum) with a stopper in both majors, *or* 3♣ with no major stopper.

After 1♣ : 3♣, a rebid of 3◊ is forcing and *shows* a diamond stopper. Responder should now bid 3♡ or 3♠ with a stopper in the suit bid, or bid 3NT with stoppers in both majors. After 1♣ : 3♣, a rebid of 3♡ is forcing, *shows* a stopper in hearts and *denies* a stopper in diamonds. Stoppers are shown up-the-line and bypassing a suit denies a stopper in the suit passed. Over 3♡, responder must not bid 3NT without a stopper in the danger suit, diamonds. After 1♣ : 3♣, a rebid of 3♠ is forcing, *shows* a stopper in spades and *denies* a stopper in hearts and in diamonds (both suits bypassed). With stoppers in hearts and diamonds, responder will bid 3NT, while with no stopper in one of the danger suits, responder will revert to clubs.

After minor suit agreement and a stopper bid by partner at the 3-level (e.g., 1♡ : 2♣, 3♣ : 3◊), if you have no stopper in the danger suit, the options are:

● Repeat your major suit with a powerful holding in that suit (at least three honours) which partner may then raise to the major suit game with just a doubleton, *or*

● Revert to 4-of-the-agreed-minor with a two or three cards (no stopper) in the danger suit. Partner may pass or push on to 5-of-the-minor, *or*

● Jump to 5-of-the-agreed-minor with a singleton in the danger suit. Partner may pass or push on to slam. The jump to 5-minor to show a singleton applies only if there is one danger suit. Where there are two danger suits (e.g., 1♣ : 3♣, 3♠), a jump to 5-minor simply shows maximum values, not a specific singleton.

After major suit agreement, stopper-showing is not used, since the assumption is that the partnership will finish in the major suit at some level. After 1-Major: 2-Major, a change of suit is forcing and is a trial bid (see Chapter 24 on Long Suit Trials), while after 1-Major : 3-Major, a new suit is looking for slam.

Because *stopper-asking* is the approach when bidding the enemy suit or when using fourth-suit forcing, some partnerships use *stopper-asking* after minor suit agreement. If you have agreed to play *stopper-asks*, a new suit at the 3-level after a minor suit has been raised (e.g., 1♡ : 2♣, 3♣ : 3◇) *asks for a stopper in the suit bid*. With a stopper in that suit, bid 3NT. With no stopper, your options are to rebid a powerful 5-card major, bid 4-of-the-agreed-minor with no stopper in the asked suit or bid 5-of-the-agreed-minor with a singleton in the asked suit. Asking-for-stoppers has definite advantages over stopper-showing methods and is recommended at duplicate for serious and regular partnerships.

EXERCISES

A. The bidding has started 1♡ : 2♣, 3♣ . . . How should responder continue with these hands?

1. ♠ K 7	2. ♠ 9 7	3. ♠ A 8 2	4. ♠ 7 2	5. ♠ A 2
♡ 7 3	♡ 5 2	♡ J	♡ Q J 3	♡ 6
◇ A Q 9 6	◇ A K 3	◇ 6 4 3	◇ A K 8	◇ A K 9 4
♣ K J 7 3 2	♣ A J 8 7 3 2	♣ A K J 8 5 4	♣ K 9 7 4 3	♣ K Q 9 7 5 2

B. The bidding has begun 1♠ : 2♣, 3♣ : 3♡ . . . How should opener continue with these hands?

1. ♠ Q J 8 5 2	2. ♠ Q J 8 5 2	3. ♠ A Q J 10 2	4. ♠ A Q 7 5 2	5. ♠ A 8 7 4 2
♡ 7	♡ A 2	♡ J 3	♡ A 7 2	♡ 9 6
◇ A Q 9	◇ 6 4	◇ 8 7	◇ 2	◇ K 2
♣ K J 7 3	♣ A J 3 2	♣ A J 5 4	♣ A 8 6 3	♣ K Q J 4

PARTNERSHIP BIDDING: West is the dealer on all hands. How should the bidding go:
(a) Using stopper-showing methods, and (b) Using stopper-asking methods?

SET 43 – WEST	SET 43 – EAST	SET 44 – WEST	SET 44 – EAST
1. ♠ A Q J 8 6	1. ♠ 7 4	1. ♠ J 6	1. ♠ 8 4 2
♡ K 3	♡ 9 6 2	♡ A 9 8 4 3	♡ K
◇ 9 5	◇ A K J	◇ 9 2	◇ A K Q 3
♣ K 8 4 3	♣ A Q 9 7 5	♣ A K 8 6	♣ Q J 9 5 4
2. ♠ J 4 3	2. ♠ A Q 7	2. ♠ A K J 10 3	2. ♠ Q 5
♡ J 5	♡ A K 6 4 2	♡ 7 6	♡ 8 3
◇ A K	◇ 7 5 4	◇ 8 4	◇ K Q 7 2
♣ A K J 8 6 2	♣ 9 3	♣ K J 9 7	♣ A Q 8 6 5
3. ♠ 7 2	3. ♠ A 4 3	3. ♠ K J 8 6 2	3. ♠ A
♡ K 5	♡ A 8 7 2	♡ K Q 3	♡ A J 2
◇ K Q J	◇ 6 2	◇ 7	◇ 8 6 3 2
♣ A J 8 7 5 3	♣ K 9 4 2	♣ A J 9 2	♣ K Q 10 8 7
4. ♠ K Q 9 8 5	4. ♠ J 4 2	4. ♠ A K J	4. ♠ 9 2
♡ Q 4	♡ A K	♡ 7 6	♡ 5 2
◇ A J 8 3	◇ K Q 9 7 5 2	◇ 9 4	◇ A K 3 2
♣ 7 5	♣ 8 2	♣ A Q 9 8 3 2	♣ K 7 6 5 4
5. ♠ 7 3	5. ♠ Q J 4	5. ♠ K Q	5. ♠ 7 6
♡ A Q 9 8 2	♡ 6 5	♡ A J 10 3 2	♡ 9 6 4
◇ A J	◇ K Q 6	◇ 8 7	◇ K Q J
♣ K 8 6 3	♣ A Q 10 7 5	♣ K 9 3 2	♣ A Q J 7 5
6. ♠ K Q 2	6. ♠ 7 6	6. ♠ 8 3	6. ♠ 7 6
♡ 8	♡ K Q 3	♡ A J	♡ K Q
◇ A J 6 4	◇ K Q 8 7 3	◇ A J 6 4	◇ K Q 9 7 3 2
♣ K Q 6 4 3	♣ A 8 2	♣ K Q J 6 3	♣ A 8 7

PLAY HANDS ON STOPPER-SHOWING

Hand 81: Stopper-showing for no-trumps – Catering for a bad split

Dealer North : Love all

```
            NORTH
            ♠ A J 10 8 6
            ♡ K 10
            ◇ 9 6
            ♣ A 8 4 3
WEST                    EAST
♠ Q 9 5 2              ♠ K 3
♡ Q 8 5               ♡ A J 7 4 3
◇ Q 10 7 5 4 3        ◇ 8 2
♣ - - -               ♣ J 10 6 2
            SOUTH
            ♠ 7 4
            ♡ 9 6 2
            ◇ A K J
            ♣ K Q 9 7 5
```

WEST	NORTH	EAST	SOUTH
	1♠	No	2♣ (1)
No	3♣ (2)	No	3◇ (3)
No	3NT (4)	All pass	

Bidding: (1) Keen on no-trumps but worried about hearts.
(2) Minimum with club support. Far better than rebidding 2♣.
(3) Shows a stopper in diamonds and pinpoints hearts as the problem suit. (Using stopper-asks, South would bid 3♡ here to ask for a stopper in hearts. North would reply 3NT.)
(4) Shows at least one stopper in hearts. K-x is quite adequate as a stopper. The expectation is that there will be nine tricks to run as long as the opponents cannot take five tricks first.
Lead: ♡4. The long suit is normal. As East seems to have the clubs stopped, East can afford to give up a trick to North's stopper in hearts. Without club values, East might try a diamond, hoping for West to gain the lead and lead hearts through North. This could work when West has ♡Q-10-x and North ♡K-x.

Correct play: When 3NT looks easy, ask yourself what could go wrong. Here a 4-0 club break could make life difficult. Just in case, cash the ♣A first, not the ♣K or ♣Q. With two honours missing, you need two honours to capture them and so keep dummy's two club honours intact on the first club lead. If clubs are 2-2 or 3-1, the rest is easy. When the bad break appears, lead another club. East will play the ten (else you finesse the nine) and the ♣Q wins. Back to hand via the ♠A and another club allows you to finesse against East's J-x. On a diamond lead, win ◇A, club to the ace, club to East's ten taken by the ♣Q, finesse the ♠J, win the diamond exit with the ◇K, finesse the ♠10, cash the ♠A and lead a club to finesse dummy's nine.

Hand 82: Finding the right spot after a stopper auction – Catering for a bad break

Dealer East : North-South vulnerable

```
            NORTH
            ♠ 10
            ♡ Q J 10 5 4
            ◇ 10 9 6 3
            ♣ 10 8 5
WEST                    EAST
♠ K 9 8 5 4           ♠ A 3 2
♡ 7 6 3              ♡ 9 2
◇ A J 4 2            ◇ K Q
♣ K                  ♣ A Q J 6 4 3
            SOUTH
            ♠ Q J 7 6
            ♡ A K 8
            ◇ 8 7 5
            ♣ 9 7 2
```

WEST	NORTH	EAST	SOUTH
		1♣	No
1♠	No	3♣ (1)	No
3◇ (2)	No	3♠ (3)	No
4♠ (4)	No	No	No

Bidding: (1) Shows 6+ clubs and about 16-18 points, denies support for responder and denies a second suit.
(2) Shows a stopper in diamonds and focuses attention on the heart suit as the problem for 3NT. Even though clubs have not been raised here, a new suit is still treated as a stopper, since 3♣ denied a second suit. (With stopper-asks, West would bid 3♡ to ask for a heart stopper. The rest would be identical.)
(3) Delayed 3-card support for spades.
(4) If West held only four spades and did not wish to play in a 4-3 spade fit, West could choose 5♣ if 3NT is not feasible.

Lead: ♡Q. Top of sequence.

Correct play: After two heart tricks, declarer wins any switch. The ♠A is cashed and when North drops the ♠10, West can guard against a 4-1 break. On the next spade, South should play low (to insert an honour makes it easier for declarer) and West should play the ♠9. If this lost to the ♠J or ♠Q with North, the ♠K would draw the last trump later. As it is, the ♠9 wins. Cash the ♣K, ♣K, cross to the ◇K and play club winners, discarding the heart loser and diamonds. South can score one spade trick but no more. If the defence takes two hearts and West later plays ♠A and ♠K, 4♠ would fail, as South scores two trump tricks.

Hand 83: Stopper location for 3NT – Catering for a bad break

Dealer South : East-West vulnerable

	NORTH		
	♠ 5 3		
	♡ 8 4 3		
	◊ A K 5 2		
	♣ A K 8 4		
WEST		EAST	
♠ Q 10		♠ K 9 8 6	
♡ J 10 6 5 2		♡ Q 9 7	
◊ J 6		◊ 10 9 8 7 4	
♣ J 10 7 2		♣ Q	
	SOUTH		
	♠ A J 7 4 2		
	♡ A K		
	◊ Q 3		
	♣ 9 6 5 3		

WEST	NORTH	EAST	SOUTH
			1♠
No	2♣ (1)	No	3♣ (2)
No	3◊ (3)	No	3NT (4)
No	No	No	

Bidding: (1) 4-card suits are bid up-the-line. It does not appeal to respond 3NT with the hearts unguarded.
(2) 3♣ is better than 2♠. Support partner when you can.
(3) Showing a stopper and emphasizing the need for hearts to be covered before trying 3NT. (Using stopper-asks, North would bid 3♡, asking for a stopper in hearts and South would reply 3NT.)
(4) Delighted to bid 3NT with hearts well held.

Lead: ♡ 5. The natural lead.

Correct play: Declarer can count eight tricks on top. The best chance for a ninth is from the club suit. Any 3-2 split will produce an extra trick. So, win the ♡ A and a lead a club to the ace. As a trick has to be lost in clubs no matter what, a low club at trick 3 cannot harm your chances. When an honour has dropped from East, it is vital to continue with a low club to your nine. If the suit does break 3-2, the ♣ K will later capture the missing club and the fourth round of clubs will be high. If clubs break 4-1 with East holding the ten, jack or queen, the low club to your nine forces an honour from West. When you regain the lead, you can lead a club and finesse dummy's eight. Note that if you play off the ♣ A and ♣ K, 3NT should be defeated.

Hand 84: Bidding after a stopper auction – Ruffing losers in dummy before drawing trumps

Dealer West : Game all

	NORTH		
	♠ 8 7 4		
	♡ 7 5 3		
	◊ K Q 8 7 5 4		
	♣ 4		
WEST		EAST	
♠ K Q 3		♠ A J 2	
♡ K 10 8 6 2		♡ A	
◊ 10		◊ 9 6 3 2	
♣ A J 9 2		♣ K Q 10 8 7	
	SOUTH		
	♠ 10 9 6 5		
	♡ Q J 9 4		
	◊ A J		
	♣ 6 5 3		

WEST	NORTH	EAST	SOUTH
1♡	No	2♣	No
3♣ (1)	No	3♠ (2)	No
5♣ (3)	No	6♣ (4)	All pass

Bidding: (1) Not quite strong enough for 4♣.
(2) Showing the spade stopper and indicating concern about diamonds. Here 3NT succeeds, but it is a risk since partner could be short in diamonds. On different diamond layouts, 3NT could fail and if 3NT is right, partner will usually be able to bid it over 3♠. (If using stopper-asks, East bids 3◊ over 3♣ – the rest is the same.)
(3) The jump to 5♣ indicates a singleton in the danger suit.
(4) Although 6♣ might not be laydown, it figures to be a good chance with only one diamond loser. Rag cards facing shortage mean the high cards should be in the right place.

Lead: ♠ 5 or a trump. If declarer needs ruffs in dummy, a trump lead is often best.

Correct play: Whether a trump or a spade is led, the best plan is to ruff two diamonds in dummy and discard a diamond on the ♡ K. Therefore, win the lead in dummy and lead a diamond at trick 2. Win any return in hand and ruff a diamond. Cross to hand, ruff another diamond and then proceed to draw the remaining trumps. It would be an error to draw trumps early because if you draw three rounds of trumps, you cannot ruff two diamonds in dummy. A different line of play does work on this hand: ♡ A, play a trump to dummy, ruff a heart and eventually set up the fifth heart suit by ruffing two low hearts. This plan is inferior and could fail if the heart split is unfriendly.

CHAPTER 22

PART A: USING STAYMAN WITH WEAK HANDS

The primary function of Stayman is to reach the best game or slam contract by locating a 4-4 major fit (see Chapter 6). When Stayman is used for this purpose, responder will hold 11+ points if facing a 12-14 1NT. However, simple Stayman may also be used on very weak hands when there is no chance for game at all and the object is to find a safer part-score than 1NT. There are three hand types where Stayman can be safely used for rescue purposes even though responder has a hand in the 0-10 range:

1. *Responder has 6+ clubs and judges 3♣ to be a better spot than 1NT.* With this type, respond 2♣ and rebid 3♣ over opener's reply to Stayman. The 3♣ rebid is an absolute sign-off – opener must pass 3♣.

2. *Responder has at least 5-4 in the majors.* With this type, respond 2♣ and then if opener bids a major, you pass, while if opener bids 2◊, you rebid 2-of-your-5-card-major. Your 2-major rebid is not encouraging and opener should pass. With game values and a 5-card major, you would rebid 3-major over the 2◊ reply.

3. *Responder has a 3-suiter (5-4-4-0 or 4-4-4-1) with clubs as the short suit.* With this type, respond 2♣ and pass opener's reply, whatever it is. You have judged that this figures to be a better spot than 1NT.

EXAMPLES

♠ 8 ♡ 9 4 ◊ 8 6 2 ♣ Q J 8 6 5 3 2	What action do you take if partner opens 1NT? Unless partner has A-K-x in clubs, your hand is likely to be useless in no-trumps. Clubs is a far safer part-score. You cannot stop in 2♣ (that is the price for using the Stayman Convention), but you can stop in 3♣. Respond 2♣ and rebid 3♣ over any reply to 2♣. Opener must pass 3♣.
♠ 9 7 5 3 2 ♡ J 9 6 4 ◊ 8 ♣ Q 4 2	What action do you take if partner opens 1NT? Your hand looks better in a suit contract and you could reply 2♣, a weakness takeout. However, that risks playing in 2♠ when partner has two spades and four hearts and 2♡ would be better. Respond 2♣ and pass a 2♠ or 2♡ reply. Over 2◊, rebid 2♠ which opener is expected to pass.
♠ J 6 4 2 ♡ K 7 5 3 ◊ 9 7 6 4 3 ♣ - - -	What action do you take if partner opens 1NT? You could bid 2◊, a weakness takeout, but 2♣ is superior, planning to pass any reply by opener. If opener bids 2♡ or 2♠, you are in a better spot than 1NT and perhaps a better spot than 2◊, while if opener bids 2◊, you are better off since opener is playing the 2◊ contract.

PART B : THE 1NT RESPONSE WITH A LONG SUIT

♠ 6 ♡ K 8 6 5 3 2 ◊ Q J 4 ♣ 8 7 2	If partner opens 1♣ or 1◊, you have an easy 1♡ response, and if partner opens 1♡, you are worth 4♡, but what do you do after a 1♠ opening? You are not strong enough for 2♡, which shows 10+ points. You might fudge by one point, but not by four points. The solution is respond 1NT and hope for another bid later.

Hands with 5-8 HCP and a 6+ suit respond 1NT when the suit cannot be shown at the 1-level. It is better to respond 1NT and show the weak strength even if the hand is not suitable for no-trumps than to respond at the 2-level and promise 10+ points when you are nowhere near that. With 9 HCP and a 6-card suit (or 8 HCP and a 7-card suit), you have enough to respond at the 2-level and below 5 HCP, it is better to pass.

If partner passes 1NT, do the best you can. You can console yourself that you never could have stopped in 2-of-your-suit, as your new suit response would have been forcing. If partner bids again over 1NT, you may be able to show your suit then, depending on opener's rebid, or you may be happy to pass opener's rebid.

The 1NT response followed by a new suit rebid shows 5-8 HCP and a 6+ suit

In addition, responder will not have a fit for opener's suit(s), since responder would be happy to play in opener's suit if a fit existed. If opener bids a second suit, opener will be at least 5-4 in the two suits, while if opener rebids the suit opened, that will be at least a 6-card suit, which responder will often be happy to pass. After opener rebids the suit opened, you have to decide whether to pass or whether to show your own suit. With a void in partner's suit and six in your own *or* with a singleton in partner's suit and seven in your own, bid your own suit (i.e., bid your own suit if the difference in lengths is six or more). With doubleton support for opener or with a difference in lengths of five or less, pass opener's rebid. Even if opener's rebid was a reverse, responder's 1NT-then-new-suit is still weak and indicates no fit for opener's suits. If opener's rebid was 2NT, about 17-18 points, responder can show the long suit at the 3-level, as a degree of tolerance will exist.

If responder bids 1NT and later a new suit, *opener should almost always pass*. The hand is a misfit and will usually play better in responder's suit. With a significant fit for responder, opener may raise the suit if game chances still exist despite responder's announced weakness via 1NT. Opener should not rebid a suit previously bid by opener unless opener has both greater length in that suit than already promised *and* absolutely no tolerance for responder's suit, such as a void. Opener should not rebid 2NT as a rescue or 3NT over responder's 3-level bid without significant extra strength. 3NT on a misfit needs lots of HCP.

EXERCISES

A. The bidding has been 1♠ : 1NT, 2◇ . What action should responder now take with each of these hands?

1. ♠ 8 2	2. ♠ 8 2	3. ♠ - - -	4. ♠ 7	5. ♠ - - -
♡ Q J 8 6 4 2	♡ Q J 8 6 4	♡ K 9 6 4 3	♡ K Q 6	♡ J 8 4
◇ 4	◇ 5 4	◇ J 6 4	◇ 3 2	◇ 9 8 4 3
♣ K 9 7 3	♣ K 9 7 3	♣ Q J 7 3 2	♣ J 9 7 5 4 3 2	♣ K Q 9 6 4 3

B. What would your answer be on the hands above if the bidding had started 1♠ : 1NT, 2♠?

PARTNERSHIP BIDDING: How should the following hands be bid? West is the dealer on all hands.

SET 45 – WEST	SET 45 – EAST	SET 46 – WEST	SET 46 – EAST
1. ♠ A Q 9 8 4	1. ♠ 6	1. ♠ 9 4 3	1. ♠ 6 2
♡ 3 2	♡ Q J 8 7 6 4	♡ 5	♡ A K J 8 7 6
◇ 6 4	◇ A 9 3 2	◇ K 8 7 6 4 2	◇ A 3
♣ K Q J 9	♣ 6 2	♣ A 8 3	♣ 7 6 4
2. ♠ 3	2. ♠ A Q 7 5 4	2. ♠ K 5 4	2. ♠ A 3 2
♡ 9 7 4 3	♡ K 6 2	♡ A K 8 5 4 3	♡ 2
◇ A Q 10 8 6 5	◇ 3	◇ A 8 4	◇ J 2
♣ 9 5	♣ K Q 8 3	♣ 6	♣ Q 9 8 7 5 4 2
3. ♠ A Q 9 6 5	3. ♠ 4 2	3. ♠ 8 5	3. ♠ K Q 9 3 2
♡ 5 3	♡ A 8 7 6 4 2	♡ K J 7 4	♡ A 3 2
◇ A 8 6 5 2	◇ K	◇ Q J 9 8 7	◇ 4
♣ K	♣ 8 7 5 3	♣ 9 5	♣ A Q 6 2
4. ♠ - - -	4. ♠ A Q J 10 8 5	4. ♠ A K 8 7 4	4. ♠ 3
♡ A 6 3 2	♡ 9 5 4	♡ A 4 3	♡ K Q 9 8 6 2
◇ 9 7 4 2	◇ A J	◇ A Q 9 2	◇ 7 5
♣ K J 8 6 2	♣ 7 4	♣ 6	♣ J 7 4 3
5. ♠ J 3 2	5. ♠ A K 6	5. ♠ A K 9 8 2	5. ♠ 5
♡ J	♡ A K 6 4 2	♡ K Q J 4	♡ A 2
◇ 7 5 3	◇ Q 6 4	◇ 7 3	◇ 8 4 2
♣ A 8 7 6 4 3	♣ Q 2	♣ A Q	♣ K 9 8 7 6 4 3
6. ♠ J 6 2	6. ♠ Q 7	6. ♠ J 10 5 4	6. ♠ A 9 8
♡ A 9 6 4	♡ 7	♡ Q 9 5 3	♡ K 7 6 4
◇ A J 9 7	◇ Q 5 2	◇ 8 7 5 2	◇ A Q 3
♣ A 7	♣ J 9 8 6 5 3 2	♣ Q	♣ J 7 2

PLAY HANDS ON RESCUE STAYMAN

Hand 85: Removing 1NT into a club part-score – Leading towards honours

Dealer North : North-South vulnerable

```
             NORTH
             ♠ A J 3
             ♡ Q 6 5 3
             ◇ A Q J
             ♣ 8 7 2
WEST                      EAST
♠ 10 7 2                  ♠ Q 9 8 5
♡ K 10 7                  ♡ A J 9 4 2
◇ K 8 7 4                 ◇ 9 6 2
♣ A Q 6                   ♣ J
             SOUTH
             ♠ K 6 4
             ♡ 8
             ◇ 10 5 3
             ♣ K 10 9 5 4 3
```

WEST	NORTH	EAST	SOUTH
	1NT	No (1)	2♣ (2)
No	2♡ (3)	No	3♣ (4)
No	No (5)	No	

Bidding: (1) Too weak to overcall, even at this vulnerability.
(2) It would be an error to pass 1NT which would be easily beaten, starting with the ♡4 lead to the king and the ♡10 return. With a weak hand and a long suit, responder should rescue partner from 1NT.
(3) Four hearts. Opener gives the normal reply to Stayman.
(4) Sign-off. Shows 6+ clubs and no prospects for game.
(5) Opener *must* pass this 3♣ sign-off.

Lead: ♠2, lowest from three to an honour. There is no attractive lead.

Correct play: You should play the jack of spades, hoping that West has led from the queen. East plays the ♠Q and you win the king. Finesse the jack of diamonds and lead a club from dummy, covering East's jack with the king. There are two club losers, plus one spade and one heart to lose.

Hand 86: Using Stayman on a weak hand with both majors – Ruffing losers in dummy

Dealer East : East-West vulnerable

```
             NORTH
             ♠ A J 10 8
             ♡ Q 7
             ◇ 7 5
             ♣ K J 9 5 2
WEST                      EAST
♠ K 9                     ♠ Q 7 6 5 2
♡ A K 3 2                 ♡ 9 6 5 4
◇ Q J 10 2               ◇ K 4 3
♣ 7 6 4                   ♣ 8
             SOUTH
             ♠ 4 3
             ♡ J 10 8
             ◇ A 9 8 6
             ♣ A Q 10 3
```

WEST	NORTH	EAST	SOUTH
		No	No
1NT	No	2♣ (1)	No
2♡	No (2)	No (3)	No (4)

Bidding: (1) It would be an error to pass 1NT, which would fail by one or two tricks on straightforward defence. 2♠ over 1NT is better than passing, but not best, as it puts all your eggs in one basket. 2♣ allows you to play in hearts or spades. Against 2♠, the ♡J would be led and as the cards lie, declarer figures to lose three spades, one heart, one diamond and one club for one off.
(2) If South were to double 2♣, which would be a lead-directing double, North would later bid 3♣, which makes.
(3) Had West bid 2◇, East would now sign off in 2♠.
(4) A delayed 2NT, takeout for the minors, is not clearcut on a balanced hand, but it is reasonable as the opponents have stopped in 2♡ and it would put North-South into 3♣, making.

Lead: ◇7 or ♣5. Neither major is attractive.

Correct play: While trumps are likely to divide 3-2, it is risky to play off the ♡A and ♡K early. If the hearts are 4-1, an opponent may draw the rest of your trumps when you give up the lead later. It is better to set up the club ruff as well as the diamond and spade winners before cashing the ♡A-K. Against a diamond lead and return, West should immediately lead a club. Even though the defence can take a diamond ruff, West can arrange to ruff two clubs in dummy and lose just one spade, one heart, one diamond, a diamond ruff and one club. On a club lead and trump switch, win the ♡A, ruff a club and lead a diamond. Ruff your other club at your first opportunity and then lead another diamond if they are not yet set up, or lead a spade if the diamonds are high.

PLAY HANDS ON THE 1NT RESPONSE WITH A LONG SUIT

Hand 87: Removing opener's rebid to a safer part-score – Ruffing finesse – Compulsory duck

Dealer South : Game all

NORTH
- ♠ - - -
- ♡ 8 6 4
- ◊ A J 9 5 3 2
- ♣ Q 7 4 3

WEST
- ♠ A J 10 8
- ♡ J 7 5
- ◊ K 7
- ♣ J 8 6 5

EAST
- ♠ 9 5 3
- ♡ K Q 10 9
- ◊ Q 10 8
- ♣ K 10 9

SOUTH
- ♠ K Q 7 6 4 2
- ♡ A 3 2
- ◊ 6 4
- ♣ A 2

WEST	NORTH	EAST	SOUTH
			1♠
No	1NT (1)	No	2♠ (2)
No	3◊ (3)	All pass (4)	

Bidding: (1) Too weak for 2◊, which shows 10+ points up.
(2) Repeating spades over 1NT promises a 6+ suit.
(3) To pass 2♠ is possible, but not recommended. In 2♠ South might manage six tricks at best (and no-trumps is even worse). 3◊ denies tolerance for spades and shows 6+ diamonds.
(4) It would be very poor for South to bid again.

Lead: ♡K. King from K-Q suits is normal in a trump contract.

Correct play: Win the ♡A and lead the ♠K (ruffing finesse), planning to discard a heart if West plays low, thus setting up the ♠Q as a winner. When West plays the ♠A, you ruff, cross to the ♣A and discard a heart loser on the ♠Q.

It is still too soon to lead trumps as you need to ruff clubs. Lead the ♣2 from dummy. When West plays low on this club, you should assume East has the ♣K (West would rise with the king when the last club from dummy is played), and so there is no point playing the ♣Q, which would be taken by the king. Duck the club, won by East who would cash a heart and might play a third heart. You ruff this, lead a low club and ruff in dummy, noting with satisfaction the fall of the ♣K, which makes your ♣Q high. Now lead a diamond to your ace and a diamond back, clearing two rounds of trumps. You later lose another diamond, but make your contract, losing one heart, two diamonds and one club.

Hand 88: Responding 1NT with a long suit – Compulsory duck – Card combination

Dealer West : Love all

NORTH
- ♠ 10 9 8 2
- ♡ K 4 2
- ◊ A 9 6 4
- ♣ A 5

WEST
- ♠ A Q 7 5 4
- ♡ 3
- ◊ K Q 8 3
- ♣ K 6 2

EAST
- ♠ 3
- ♡ A Q 10 8 6 5
- ◊ J 5
- ♣ 9 7 4 3

SOUTH
- ♠ K J 6
- ♡ J 9 7
- ◊ 10 7 2
- ♣ Q J 10 8

WEST	NORTH	EAST	SOUTH
1♠	No	1NT (1)	No
2◊	No	2♡ (2)	All pass (3)

Bidding: (1) Much too weak to respond 2♡.
(2) No tolerance for West's suits; shows 6+ hearts, 5-8 HCP.
(3) It would be poor for West to bid again. West has already shown five spades, four diamonds. A 2NT rebid suggests about 17-18 HCP, still looking for game. 2NT is not a rescue move and is not an attractive spot if the hands are weak and misfits.

Lead: ♣Q. Top of the sequence in the unbid suit is natural.

Correct play: Do *not* play the ♣K at trick 1. The lead marks North with the ♣A and you will just lose dummy's king if you play it. If the ♣K is played, 2♡ is beaten easily: ♣A wins; a club to South, who continues the clubs. Dummy ruffs the fourth club and whether North over-ruffs or not, declarer will fail, losing another two hearts and the ◊A.

Play low in dummy on the ♣Q lead (North's ace might be singleton). If South continues clubs, play low in dummy again. When North's ace falls, the ♣K is high. With a tough lead to make, North might switch to a heart or cash the ◊A and lead a second diamond. On a heart switch, East should play the queen from hand, not the ten. With only one finesse available with an A-Q-10 combination, choose the queen finesse. When the ♡Q wins, cash the ♡A and then lead the ◊J or a third heart. If North had switched to ace and another diamond, win the ◊J, cross to the ♠A, cash ◊K to discard one club, and then lead a heart to your queen, cash the ♡A and play a third heart. Careful play restricts the losers to one heart, one diamond and two clubs.

CHAPTER 23

THE LOSING TRICK COUNT

The Losing Trick Count is a more accurate guide than point count in assessing the playing potential of the partnership hands when a good trump fit exists. Players who count their points at the outset and do not change that total as the bidding progresses fail to get an accurate picture of their assets. Counting HCP is best for balanced hands and misfit hands. The Losing Trick Count is not used for opening the bidding, for no-trump hands or for misfit hands. It becomes useful only after a trump fit has been established, but once the trump fit exists, it can be used by opener, responder or the overcalling side. You are able to use the LTC even though partner has never heard of it. The LTC is not a convention, but a technique for valuation. Using the LTC replaces the use of the 5-3-1 shortage point count because the trick-taking capacity revealed by the LTC is more accurate more often than that indicated by point count. The following is a brief summary of how the LTC works and how you can use it to value your trump fit hands, but for a complete treatment, you should acquire a copy of the book that covers the topic thoroughly, *The Modern Losing Trick Count.*

THE LTC FORMULA

Count Your Losers – Add Partner's Losers – Deduct This Total From 24

The answer is the number of tricks the partnership will win most of the time when playing in the known trump fit. The answer is correct almost all of the time when suits break normally and half of your finesses work. If trumps split 4-0 or every finesse is wrong, clearly you will not make the number of tricks expected.

COUNTING YOUR OWN LOSERS

3-card or longer suit: Count losers only in the top three cards of the suit; everything beyond the third card counts as a winner. *No suit ever counts more than three losers.* In the top three cards, count the ace and king as winners and everything lower than the queen as a loser. Count the queen as a winner if there is a second honour card in the suit; if the queen is the only honour card in the suit, count the queen as half a winner, half a loser. For example, A-6-4-2 is two losers, A-K-5-4-2 is one loser, 8-6-3-2 is 3 losers, Q-J-5-4 is 2 losers, but Q-7-6-3 is 2½ losers.

Short suit holdings: A void is no losers (since you are playing in your trump fit), a singleton counts as one loser, except for ace-singleton which is no losers, and a doubleton is two losers, except for A-x (one loser), K-x (one loser) and A-K (no loser). K-Q-doubleton, A-Q-doubleton, and K-singleton are all one loser holdings.

ASSESSING PARTNER'S LOSERS

Just as an average minimum opening is around the 13-point mark, so the average minimum opening in terms of the LTC is 7 losers. This applies to a normal, balanced opening. The more freakish the shape, the fewer losers the hand will have. Note that when opening with a 1-bid, use the point count, not losers.

♠ A 7 ♡ K Q 7 4 ◇ K 9 5 ♣ 8 6 4 2	This is minimum 1-opening in almost any standard system, but you will note that it contains just seven losers. There is one loser in spades, one loser in hearts (the fourth card counts as a winner), two in diamonds and three in clubs (in the LTC, no suit counts more than three losers). Thus, seven losers is a good estimate for a minimum opening hand.

Just as a minimum opening may be 14-15 points or occasionally 10-11 points, so a minimum opening may have 6½ losers or 7½ or 8 losers. An extra loser is common when the hand pattern is 4-3-3-3.

If partner's bidding promises minimum opening strength, play partner to hold a 7-loser hand.

For example, if the bidding has started 1♣ : 1♡, 2♡ opener has a minimum opening and you should play opener for seven losers. The 12-14 1NT opening usually has 7-8 losers. For auctions such as 1♣ : 1♠, 1NT, showing 15-16 points balanced, opener will have around 6½ losers and for a sequence like 1◇ : 1♠, 2NT (17-18 points, balanced) take opener to have as six losers. A minimum takeout double would be seven losers, and so on. Where opener rebids the suit opened, e.g., 1♡ : 1♠, 2♡, normally a 6-card suit, opener will often have seven losers, but might have only six losers because of the significant extra length.

If partner shows more than a minimum opening, play partner to have fewer than seven losers.

The number of losers depends on how strongly partner has bid, but if you can work out partner's points, you have a good basis for assessing partner's losers, (work on 16-18 points six losers, 19-21 points five losers and 22-24 points four losers). A reverse has 5-6 losers, a jump-shift has four losers, a jump-rebid of opener's suit (1♣ : 1◊, 3♣) has 5-6 losers, the 2♣ opening has about three losers, the 2♠, 2♡ and 2◊ openings have 3½-4½ losers, and so on. When raising partner, opener's single raise (1◊ : 1♠, 2♠) shows seven losers, a jump-raise to the 3-level show six losers and a jump-raise to game would be a 5-loser hand.

If partner's bidding shows less than opening strength, play partner to hold more than seven losers.

Play a hand of 10-12 points to hold eight losers, a hand of 7-9 points to hold nine losers, and worse hands to have ten or more. If partner is a passed hand, assume partner to hold eight losers at best. A jump-raise shows 10-12 points and eight losers. A single raise (1♠ : 2♠) has about 6-9 points, and thus 8-9 losers. A 2-level response (1♠ : 2♡) has at least 10 points and so will hold eight losers or better, while a 1-level response should be played for nine losers or better. Whenever partner has a long suit, there are fewer losers. Expect a weak 2-opening to have eight losers if minimum, seven if maximum. A 3-level pre-empt has seven losers not vulnerable, six losers vulnerable, while a 4-level pre-empt should have six losers not vulnerable, five losers vulnerable (see Chapter 12). A 1-level overcall should be eight losers or better, and an overcall at the 2-level is normally seven losers or better. Playing weak jump-overcalls, your methods would be:

Weak jump-overcall, e.g., (1◊) : 2♠ = Good 6-card suit, 6-10 HCP, 7-8 losers.

Simple overcall at the 1-level = 6-8 losers; simple overcall at the 2-level = 6-7 losers.

Overcall-type hand with 5 losers: Double, then bid your suit next.

Overcall-type hand with 4 losers: Double, then jump bid your suit.

Overcall-type hand with 3 losers: Force to game.

Responding to a takeout double with a suit bid: With 9-10 losers, bid your suit at the cheapest level; with eight losers you can jump-bid your suit, and with seven losers you can bid game if a trump fit is certain.

WHY 24?

Why is the total of your losers and partner's losers deducted from 24? As there are at most three losers per suit, there are at most 12 losers in a hand. The maximum possible number of losers in your hand and partner's hand is therefore 24, and by deducting the actual losers from the maximum possible, the difference is the number of tricks the partnership figures to win.

KEY FIGURES TO REMEMBER

1. If partner opens and you have a 7-loser hand: Game in a major should be bid if a good fit is found.

2. If partner opens and you have a 5-loser hand: There is slam potential if a good fit is found, but you still must check whether the partnership has sufficient controls (Blackwood for aces, etc.).

3. Partner opens and shows better than a minimum opening. If you have a 7-loser hand or better, there is slam potential if a good trump fit can be found.

COVER CARDS

The concept of cover cards, devised by George Rosenkranz, works very well in conjunction with the LTC. Where you have a trump fit and have ruffing potential, use the LTC as above, but where a trump fit exists and either you have no ruffing value for partner or you hold the long trump suit and know you are facing a balanced hand (e.g., partner has opened 1NT), it is better to estimate the partnership potential through cover cards. The method is quite simple. If you have the balanced hand:

Estimate partner's losers – Count your cover cards – Deduct the cover cards from the losers

If you have the long suit or the freakish shape and partner has the balanced hand:

Count your losers – Estimate partner's cover cards – Deduct the cover cards from the losers

Deduct this answer from thirteen (the number of cards held) to arrive at the number of tricks the hand with the long suit figures to win. For example, if partner is expected to hold six losers, you have three cover cards. 6 – 3 = 3, so that the partnership has three losers and hence 13 – 3 = ten winners.

The cover card approach works well when partner is known to have a long, strong suit (as after a weak two opening or after a pre-empt) or when partner's shape is clearly revealed (as after a reverse, 5-4 at least, or when the shape has been shown to be 5-5, 6-5, 6-4 etc. as in Chapters 19 and 20).

A cover card is any card that eliminates or is likely to eliminate a loser in partner's hand. In partner's known long suit or suits, each ace, king or queen counts as a cover card. Outside partner's known long suits, the lower the honour the less valuable it is as a cover card. An outside ace is almost always a cover card (it might not be if partner is void in that suit), a king might cover a loser, but an outside suit headed by the queen or jack is of limited value for partner. For example, facing a pre-empt you would not count Q-J-x-x-x as removing any of partner's losers. A-K will usually cover two losers and K-Q will cover one loser unless partner has a singleton in that suit. The more you know about partner's hand pattern, the more accurate will be your assessment of the cards that will count as cover cards.

A 13-15 point opening will usually contain 3-4 cover cards. You can expect 4-5 cover cards from a 16-18 point hand, 5-6 cover cards from 19-21, and so on, while 2-3 cover cards will be normal for a 10-12 point hand, 1-2 cover cards for 7-9 points and 0-1 cover cards for a hand below seven points.

EXERCISES

A. How many losers do each of these card combinations contain?

1. J 7 3 2	**4.** K Q 7 5 4 3	**7.** A K 6 3 2	**10.** Q J 8 6 4 2	**13.** 8 3	**16.** A 8 4
2. A Q 9 5 4 2	**5.** K Q 7 3	**8.** Void	**11.** Q 8 7 5 4 2	**14.** Q 3	**17.** A K 3
3. A Q 6	**6.** Q 10 6	**9.** A K Q 8 5 3	**12.** 10 9 7 4 3	**15.** K 3	**18.** K Q

B. For these hands, state (a) the number of losers   (b) The number of cover cards for a spade contract.

1. ♠ K 4	2. ♠ 9 7 5 4 2	3. ♠ A	4. ♠ Q 7 2	5. ♠ 2
♡ A 3 2	♡ A K	♡ A K	♡ A J	♡ A 9 6
◊ A 9 6 2	◊ Q 9 7 6	◊ 8 7 6 4 3 2	◊ A K 8 6 2	◊ A K 9 4 3
♣ A 9 7 3	♣ J 7	♣ K Q 5 4	♣ 10 9 7	♣ A K 5 2

PARTNERSHIP BIDDING: How should these hands be bid? West is the dealer unless stated otherwise.

SET 47 – WEST	SET 47 – EAST	SET 48 – WEST	SET 48 – EAST
1. ♠ K Q 6 5 4	1. ♠ A 8 3 2	1. ♠ A 7 6 3	1. ♠ K 9 8 5 4 2
♡ K 8	♡ 6 3	♡ 9 8	♡ 6 4
◊ 7 6 4	◊ 9	◊ K Q	◊ A 7 5 4
♣ A 8 3	♣ K 9 7 6 5 4	♣ K 8 6 5 4	♣ 7
2. ♠ 7 5 4 2	2. ♠ 8	2. ♠ K 8 4 2	2. ♠ A J 6 3
♡ A 7 6 2	♡ K Q 9 4 3	♡ Q 10	♡ J 9 8
◊ K 5 4	◊ A Q 8 7 6	◊ J 2	◊ K 7 4
♣ 3 2	♣ Q 10	♣ A K 7 4 2	♣ Q 6 3
3. ♠ K 8 6 4	3. ♠ A Q 9 7 5 3	3. ♠ A 10 7 4 2	3. ♠ K Q 6 3
♡ K 4	♡ A 6	♡ A 6 4 2	♡ 10
◊ A 10 8 3	◊ 2	◊ A 9	◊ K 8 3 2
♣ 7 5 4	♣ A K 6 2	♣ 7 4	♣ A K Q J
4. ♠ 9 6 3	4. ♠ A K 8 7 5 4 2	4. ♠ A 6 3 2	4. ♠ K Q 9 8 5
♡ Q 8 4 3	♡ 7 5 2	♡ 7	♡ A K Q 8 6 2
◊ A K	◊ 9 8	◊ A J 9 3 2	◊ 4
♣ A 9 8 3	♣ 5	♣ A 4 2	♣ 3
5. South opens 1 ♣.	5. South opens 1 ♣.	5. South opens 1 ♡.	5. South opens 1 ♡.
♠ A Q 8 3 2	♠ K 9 7 5 4	♠ A 9 7 4	♠ K 8 5 3
♡ 7 5	♡ A K 8 3 2	♡ Q 9	♡ J 4
◊ K 9 4	◊ 8 2	◊ A K 9	◊ Q J 7 3
♣ 8 6 2	♣ 7	♣ J 7 5 3	♣ A 8 6

PLAY HANDS ON THE LOSING TRICK COUNT

Hand 89: Hand valuation after a 2-over-1 response – Card combination – Setting up a long suit

Dealer North : East-West vulnerable

NORTH
♠ A K Q 8 6 4
♡ K 8 6 5 2
◇ 7
♣ 2

WEST
♠ J 10 5
♡ - - -
◇ Q 6 5 4 3 2
♣ K Q 10 7

EAST
♠ 9 7
♡ Q 10 9
◇ K J 10 9
♣ A 6 5 3

SOUTH
♠ 3 2
♡ A J 7 4 3
◇ A 8
♣ J 9 8 4

WEST	NORTH	EAST	SOUTH
	1♠	No	2♡ (1)
No	4NT (2)	No	5♡
No	6♡ (3)	All pass	

Bidding: (1) Shows 10+ points and 5+ hearts (see page 25).
(2) With an excellent fit for hearts, North heads for slam, counting four losers in hand and assessing responder as eight losers or better for the 2♡ response, 10+ points (10-12 points = about eight losers). 4 + 8 = 12; 24 – 12 = 12 tricks potential. With two singletons, asking for aces is the best approach. It would be wrong to jump straight to 6♡, as two aces could be missing. It would be a serious underbid to jump to 4♡. This would miss a slam, as responder would surely pass 4♡.
(3) With one ace missing, bid a small slam if the LTC potential indicates twelve tricks. You can afford to lose one trick.

Lead: ♣K. King from a K-Q-10 suit is an attractive start.

Correct play: The defence wins the first trick, but South wins the next trick and should draw trumps. With only three trumps missing, the split will usually be 2-1, but the correct play is to cash the ♡K first to guard against three hearts with East. (If West has the three hearts, a trick will have to be lost, no matter what.) When the ♡K reveals the bad break, South finesses the ♡J. The third round draws the missing trump and then declarer runs the spade suit. If West had not led a club, declarer would draw trumps as above and then discard all the clubs on the spade suit and ruff the diamond loser in dummy.

Hand 90: Hand valuation for a grand slam – Suit combination – Ruffing losers and discarding losers

Dealer East : Game all

NORTH
♠ J 9 8
♡ Q J 8
◇ Q 7 6 5
♣ 10 6 3

WEST
♠ K Q 6 2
♡ 10
◇ K 8 4 3
♣ A K Q J

EAST
♠ A 10 7 4 3
♡ A 6 4 2
◇ A 2
♣ 7 4

SOUTH
♠ 5
♡ K 9 7 5 3
◇ J 10 9
♣ 9 8 5 2

WEST	NORTH	EAST	SOUTH
		1♠	No
3♣ (1)	No	3♡ (2)	No
4NT (3)	No	5♠	No
5NT (4)	No	6♣	No
7♠	No	No	No

Bidding: (1) Jump-shift, 16+ points, game force.
(2) Shows 4+ hearts and therefore 5+ spades.
(3) When East opens 1♠, West recognizes the grand slam potential. West knows there is a strong spade fit and West has four losers. Crediting East with a 7-loser hand for the opening bid, West calculates 4 + 7 = 11; 24 – 11 = 13 tricks potential.
(4) Once East shows three aces, West can count 13 tricks (five spades, four clubs, two diamonds, one heart and a heart ruff). If the LTC potential is 13 tricks and you have all the aces and the K-Q of trumps, bid your grand slam. West can bid 7♠ over 5♠, but asks for kings with 5NT. If East has the ♡K, West can bid 7NT. When the ♡K is missing, West is content with 7♠. Note that there are only twelve tricks in no-trumps.

Lead: ◇J. Top of sequence is normal.

Correct play: Cash the ♠K first, not the ♠A, just in case North has ♠J-9-8-5. When all follow to the first round of trumps, draw the remaining trumps, cash ♡A, ruff a heart and discard the other heart losers on the clubs. Had South been void in spades, then after winning ♠K, East would play ♡A and ruff a heart before drawing all the trumps. Then ♠Q and a finesse of the ♠10 allows declarer to draw trumps.

Hand 91: Hand valuation for slams – Setting up a long suit – Managing your entries

Dealer South : Love all

NORTH			
♠ K 8 7 6 5 3			
♡ 4			
◊ 6 3			
♣ A 5 4 2			

WEST	NORTH	EAST	SOUTH
			1 ◊
No	1 ♠	No (1)	4 ♠ (2)
No	4NT (3)	No	5 ♡
No	6 ♠	All pass	

WEST
♠ J 10 4
♡ Q 9 6 5 3 2
◊ 9 8
♣ Q 3

EAST
♠ - - -
♡ A K 8 7
◊ Q 10 5 2
♣ J 10 8 7 6

SOUTH
♠ A Q 9 2
♡ J 10
◊ A K J 7 4
♣ K 9

Bidding: (1) Despite the low count, a takeout double would not be unreasonable because of the excellent shape.
(2) With five losers, two tricks better than a minimum opening, South bids two tricks more than a minimum 2 ♠. Another path: South has five losers, a 1-level response is usually nine losers or better. 5 + 9 = 14; 24 – 14 = ten tricks.
(3) North has seven losers and counts South for a 5-loser hand 7 + 5 = 12; 24 – 12 = twelve tricks potential. With a singleton in hearts, Blackwood is best (but if North had a rag doubleton in hearts, a cue-bid of 5 ♣ would be a better approach). With one ace missing, North bids the small slam.

Lead: ♡ A. It is natural to try to cash two tricks against a slam.

Correct play: North ruffs the second heart and should draw trumps. If trumps were 2-1, the hand would be over very quickly, drawing trumps and ruffing two club losers in dummy. When trumps break 3-0, North should still draw all the trumps. Trap: If you try to ruff a club in dummy before trumps have been drawn, West over-ruffs. After trumps have been drawn, set up the diamond suit via ◊ A, ◊ K, ruff a diamond, club to the king, ruff a diamond. The fifth diamond is now a winner. Cash the ♣ A, ruff a club to reach dummy and discard the club loser on the fifth diamond. You could finesse the ◊ J, which works, but it is not the best play. Note that diamonds must be started before playing ♣ K, ♣ A and ruffing a club. The ♣ K and the club ruff are vital entries to dummy to utilize the diamonds.

Hand 92: Grand slam valuation – Suit combination – Setting up a long suit – Timing

Dealer West : North-South vulnerable

NORTH			
♠ J 10 7			
♡ J 9			
◊ K Q 7			
♣ J 10 8 6 5			

WEST	NORTH	EAST	SOUTH
1 ◊	No	1 ♡ (1)	No
1 ♠ (2)	No	4NT (3)	No
5 ♣	No	7 ♠ (4)	All pass

WEST
♠ A 6 3 2
♡ 7
◊ A J 9 3 2
♣ A 4 2

EAST
♠ K Q 9 8 5
♡ A K Q 8 6 2
◊ 4
♣ 3

SOUTH
♠ 4
♡ 10 5 4 3
◊ 10 8 6 5
♣ K Q 9 7

Bidding: (1) Prefer not to jump-shift with a two-suiter unless one of the suits is opener's suit.
(2) Always show the major. 1 ♠ is far superior to 2 ◊.
(3) Once West introduces spades, East applies the LTC since it was not until then that a good trump fit had come to light. East has three losers, West's opening indicates seven or fewer, so that there is potential for a grand slam (3 + 7 = 10; 24 – 10 = 14 tricks potential!). With second round control in all suits, asking for aces is best. 4 ♠ would be a gross underbid.
(4) Because it may be necessary to ruff one or two hearts, 7 ♠ is much better than looking for 7NT.

Lead: ♣ J. The ◊ K is more dangerous, as West bid diamonds.

Correct play: Win the ♣ A and draw trumps, starting with the ace, just in case North holds J-10-7-4. When all follow, draw the trumps in three rounds and then play ♡ A, ♡ K, ♡ Q and ruff a heart. This sets up the remaining hearts as winners. If North did have J-10-7-4 in spades, then after ♠ A, a second spade would see North play the ten, taken by the king. Then cash the ♡ A and ruff a heart to set the hearts up before all of West's trumps have gone. This would be followed by a spade to finesse against North's remaining J-x, and trumps would be drawn, after which the rest is easy.

CHAPTER 24

LONG SUIT TRIAL BIDS

WEST A	EAST A	WEST B	EAST B	WEST C	EAST C
♠ A Q 8 5 4	♠ K J 9 2	♠ A Q 8 5 4	♠ K J 9 2	♠ A Q 8 5 4	♠ K J 9 2
♡ A 8 6 3	♡ K 5	♡ A 8 6 3	♡ 9 5 4	♡ A 8 6 3	♡ 9 5 4
◇ A 7	◇ 9 5 4	◇ A 7	◇ K 5	◇ A 7	◇ 8 6 5 3
♣ Q 2	♣ 8 6 5 3	♣ Q 2	♣ 8 6 5 3	♣ Q 2	♣ K 5

It is worth studying the above hands. On Hand A, 4♠ is a very good contract. Declarer would plan to ruff two hearts in the East hand before drawing trumps and could afford to ruff the fourth round of hearts with a top trump. Hands B and C, however, offer no prospects of game. Yet the West hand is identical in all three cases and the East hand in each case has the same number of points and the same number of losers. How can we account for this difference and how can we reach the good game while avoiding the hopeless ones? The *location* of key high cards and short suits is also vital for accurate assessments. Long Suit Trial Bids can discover whether partner's high cards or short suits are 'in the right place', whether the fit is excellent.

WHAT IS A LONG SUIT TRIAL BID?

A long suit trial bid is *a change of suit after a major suit has been raised to the 2-level,* whether it is opener or responder who makes the change of suit. The final bid in each of these auctions is a long suit trial bid:

Long suit trial bids by opener:

Opener	Responder	Opener	Responder
1♡	2♡	1♡	2♡
3♣		2♠	

Long suit trial bids by responder:

Opener	Responder	Opener	Responder
1♣	1♡	1◇	1♠
2♡	3◇	2♠	3♡

WHAT DOES THE TRIAL BID MEAN?

The long suit trial bid is an invitation to game *in the agreed major suit.* The suit in which the trial bid is made is known as 'the trial suit'. A long suit trial bid promises 3+ cards in the *trial suit* and asks for help in the trial suit. For example, 1♠ : 2♠, 3♣ means, 'I am interested in 4♠, but I need help in clubs.'

STRENGTH OF THE TRIAL SUIT

A long suit trial bid is always made in a weak suit, typically a suit with two or three losers. The trial suit should not be headed by A-K, A-Q, K-Q or A-J-10 (these holdings make the trial suit too strong, as there could be no losers or just one loser in that suit even if partner has no helpful cards in the trial suit). The typical trial suit contains three or four cards either with no top honour at all or with at most one top honour of the ace, king or queen. If there are two trial suits available, choose the weaker suit. If the suits are about equal, make the trial bid in the cheaper suit.

WHEN TO MAKE A TRIAL BID

After 1♡ : 2♡ or 1♠ : 2♠, opener makes a trial bid with an invitational hand, usually with about 16-18 points (including the 5-3-1 shortage count) or a hand with six losers. With a 7-loser hand in the 12-15 point range, opener should pass, while with a sound 5-loser hand, opener has enough to bid game without inviting. Responder's raise to the 2-level can be expected to be around the 8 to 9 loser mark.

After responder has been raised to the 2-level (e.g., 1♣ : 1♡, 2♡), responder may trial with around 10-12 points, about 7-8 losers. With a 7-loser hand or 13+ points, responder has enough to bid straight to game without inviting. Even with eight losers and 10-12 points, responder should try for game. Although opener will usually have seven losers, opener might have a bit extra, such as 6½ losers, or six losers, but in a hand of only 12-13 HCP. Even if opener has seven losers, opener's values may be just in the right spot for responder. That is exactly what the long suit trial bid is trying to discover: *whether partner's values cover your losers.*

Occasionally, responder will have slam interest after a raise to the 2-level and can use a trial bid to find out whether opener has help in responder's second suit. Responder intends to bid to slam if opener can show help in the required suit or to bid only to game if opener's reply indicates no help in the trial suit.

REPLYING TO THE LONG SUIT TRIAL BID

    No losers in the trial suit: Bid game in the agreed major suit.
    1 loser in the trial suit: Bid game in the agreed major suit.
    2 losers in the trial suit: Bid game if maximum, but sign off in 3-of-your-major if minimum.
    3 losers in the trial suit: Sign off in 3-of-your-major.

NO LOSERS IN THE TRIAL SUIT

Holdings which are 'no losers' are a void, ace-singleton, A-K-doubleton or A-K-Q in the trial suit.

ONE LOSER IN THE TRIAL SUIT

Holdings which count as one loser are a singleton, A-x or K-x, or 3-card or longer suits including two of the top three honours, i.e., A-K-x, A-Q-x or K-Q-x. With one loser in the trial suit, bid the major suit game.

TWO LOSERS IN THE TRIAL SUIT

Holdings which count as two losers are any doubleton headed by the queen or worse, or any 3+ suit which contains one of the top three honours, such as A-x-x, K-x-x or Q-J-x. Tend to upgrade holdings like A-J-x or K-J-x in the trial suit (give a huge upgrade to A-J-10), but tend to downgrade Q-x-x without either the jack or ten as well. With two losers in the trial suit, bid 3-of-your-major if your hand is minimum for the raise, but if you have maximum values for the raise, accept the invitation and bid 4-of-your-major.

THREE LOSERS IN THE TRIAL SUIT

Holdings which count as three losers are any 3+ suit headed by the jack or weaker. With three losers in the trial suit, normally sign off in 3-of-your-major suit, which partner is expected to pass (unless, of course, responder made the trial bid with slam in mind, which is revealed when responder bids on to game despite the intended sign-off in 3-of-the-major).

PARTNERSHIP BIDDING: How should the following hands be bid? West is the dealer on all hands.

SET 49 – WEST	SET 49 – EAST	SET 50 – WEST	SET 50 – EAST
1. ♠ 8 7 3 2 ♡ K 7 6 2 ◇ 7 5 4 ♣ K 5	**1.** ♠ 9 6 ♡ A Q J 5 4 ◇ A 2 ♣ A 6 3 2	**1.** ♠ 7 ♡ A K Q 6 2 ◇ 7 6 5 ♣ A J 8 2	**1.** ♠ K Q ♡ J 10 8 4 ◇ 9 8 4 ♣ K 7 6 4
2. ♠ 8 7 3 2 ♡ K 7 6 2 ◇ K 5 ♣ 7 5 4	**2.** ♠ 9 6 ♡ A Q J 5 4 ◇ A 2 ♣ A 6 3 2	**2.** ♠ 9 8 4 3 ♡ 7 6 5 ◇ 4 ♣ K Q 9 8 2	**2.** ♠ Q J 10 6 5 2 ♡ A 8 ◇ A 7 3 ♣ A 4
3. ♠ 8 7 3 2 ♡ K 7 6 2 ◇ 7 5 ♣ K 5 4	**3.** ♠ 9 6 ♡ A Q J 5 4 ◇ A 2 ♣ A 6 3 2	**3.** ♠ A J 7 2 ♡ Q ◇ A Q 2 ♣ J 8 6 4 2	**3.** ♠ K 9 8 4 3 ♡ A J 9 ◇ 10 5 4 3 ♣ 7
4. ♠ A K 9 7 3 ♡ K 6 ◇ A Q ♣ 9 8 3 2	**4.** ♠ Q 10 4 2 ♡ A 4 ◇ 10 6 5 3 ♣ Q J 10	**4.** ♠ 8 3 ♡ A J 4 2 ◇ A J 8 3 2 ♣ K 4	**4.** ♠ A 2 ♡ K 10 9 8 6 ◇ 7 ♣ A Q 7 3 2
5. ♠ A K 9 7 3 ♡ K 6 ◇ A Q ♣ 9 8 3 2	**5.** ♠ Q 10 4 2 ♡ Q 4 ◇ 10 6 5 3 ♣ Q J 10	**5.** ♠ A Q J 8 6 ♡ 7 ◇ A 8 6 4 2 ♣ Q 5	**5.** ♠ K 7 5 2 ♡ 9 5 3 ◇ K 3 ♣ 8 6 4 2
6. ♠ A K 9 7 3 ♡ K 6 ◇ A Q ♣ 9 8 3 2	**6.** ♠ Q 10 4 2 ♡ Q J 10 7 ◇ 10 6 5 3 ♣ J	**6.** ♠ A Q J 8 6 ♡ 7 ◇ A 8 6 4 2 ♣ Q 5	**6.** ♠ K 7 5 2 ♡ 8 6 4 2 ◇ 9 5 3 ♣ K 3

PLAY HANDS ON LONG SUIT TRIAL BIDS

Hand 93: Bidding after a trial bid – Ruffing losers in dummy – Delaying trumps

Dealer North : Love all

NORTH
- ♠ 9 6
- ♡ A Q J 5 4
- ◇ A 2
- ♣ A 9 3 2

WEST
- ♠ Q J 10 4
- ♡ 9
- ◇ K Q 10
- ♣ J 10 7 6 4

EAST
- ♠ A K 5
- ♡ 10 8 6
- ◇ J 9 8 6 3
- ♣ Q 8

SOUTH
- ♠ 8 7 3 2
- ♡ K 7 3 2
- ◇ 7 5 4
- ♣ K 5

WEST	NORTH	EAST	SOUTH
	1♡	No	2♡
No	3♣ (1)	No	4♡ (2)
No	No	No	

Bidding: (1) Long suit trial bid. North is worth 17 points and has six losers. On either basis, North is worth an invitation to game and the 3♣ trial is more precise and more co-operative than a simple raise to 3♡ (which South would pass).
(2) With just one loser in the trial suit South accepts the invitation by bidding 4♡ even though South is minimum for the 2♡ raise. With one loser, the strength of the hand is not relevant.

Lead: ♠A. It is natural for East to start with three rounds of spades. On the ♠A, West should signal with the ♠Q. The queen signal on an ace lead is either a singleton or promises the jack and lets partner know that it is safe to lead low next. East has no reason to want West on lead urgently and so continues with ♠K and a third spade.

Correct play: After ruffing the third spade, North should not draw trumps yet. North needs to ruff two clubs in dummy. North could draw two rounds of trumps, using the ace and queen, but this also has some risk (East's ♡10 might be promoted). Either draw no trumps at all or draw just one round with the ace before clubs: club to the king, club to the ace and a third club. If East discards, ruff low; come to the ◇A and ruff the fourth club, followed by trumps. If East ruffs in on the third club, over-ruff with the ♡K, draw the trump still out with a heart to hand and then ruff the last club. North should lose only two spades and one diamond.

Hand 94: Rejecting a trial bid – Leading towards honours to set up winners rather than take a finesse

Dealer East : Love all

NORTH
- ♠ A 9 5 4
- ♡ 9 7 3
- ◇ K Q 4
- ♣ Q 10 8

WEST
- ♠ 7
- ♡ A K Q 6 2
- ◇ 7 6 3
- ♣ A J 4 2

EAST
- ♠ K Q 8
- ♡ J 10 8 4
- ◇ 9 8 5
- ♣ K 7 6

SOUTH
- ♠ J 10 6 3 2
- ♡ 5
- ◇ A J 10 2
- ♣ 9 5 3

WEST	NORTH	EAST	SOUTH
		No	No
1♡	No	2♡	No
3◇ (1)	No	3♡ (2)	All pass

(1) Trial bid. West is worth 17 points (three for the singleton) and has six losers. Either way, the hand warrants an invitation to game. West could make a trial bid in clubs or in diamonds. Choose the suit where help is needed most.
(2) With three losers in the trial suit, East reverts to 3♡, even though East has a maximum raise to the 2-level.

Lead: ◇K. The K-Q combination is the most attractive holding in North's hand, but the trial suit is often the most attractive lead anyway if a trial bid invitation is rejected. The trial bid shows a weak suit and if the reply indicates no help in the trial suit, the defence figures to be strong in that suit. South encourages and the defence takes three rounds of diamonds.

Correct play: South is likely to win the third diamond and might switch to clubs, dummy's weaker suit outside trumps, or might lead a trump, the safest option. West wins a club or a trump exit and draws trumps, ending in hand. Before tackling the clubs (club to the king, club back and finesse the jack), declarer should lead the singleton spade. If North has the ace and ducks, dummy wins and there is no spade loser, and now the club finesse can be taken. If North takes the ♠A, dummy's ♠K-Q are high and will provide discards for West's clubs without needing the club finesse. If it turns out that South has the ♠A, so that the ♠K loses to South and dummy has only one spade winner, then the club finesse is needed.

Hand 95: Playing safe – Playing for an overtrick at duplicate – Setting up a long suit for discards

Dealer South : North-South vulnerable

WEST	NORTH	EAST	SOUTH
			1♠
No	2♣	No	3◊ (1)
No	4♠ (2)	All pass	

NORTH
♠ 9 8 4 3
♡ 7 6 5
◊ J
♣ K Q 9 7 6

WEST
♠ A
♡ Q J 10 4
◊ Q 9 8 6
♣ 10 8 5 4

EAST
♠ K 7
♡ K 9 3 2
◊ K 10 5 4 2
♣ J 3

SOUTH
♠ Q J 10 6 5 2
♡ A 8
◊ A 7 3
♣ A 2

Bidding: (1) Long suit trial bid. South is worth 17 points and has six losers. 3◊ is the best invitation.

(2) With only one loser in the trial suit North accepts the game invitation, even though North's raise is minimum in high cards.

Lead: ♡Q. Top of the sequence is most attractive.

Correct play: South can make 4♠ safely: win the ♡A and lead a trump, losing only one heart and two spades. South later ruffs a diamond in dummy and discards the other diamond loser on the third club. This would be the correct play at rubber bridge where the emphasis is on making your contract. It would be risky to play clubs first, in case an opponent ruffs the second round of clubs with the ♠7 and 4♠ might then fail.

At duplicate pairs, however, you are rewarded for outscoring other pairs and it is worthwhile to try for an overtrick to obtain a higher score. Win the ♡A and play ♣A, club to the king and lead the ♣Q. If East were to follow suit or discard, South would pitch the heart loser. If East ruffs with a top spade, South again discards the heart loser and concedes only two trump tricks. If East ruffs with the ♠7, South has a choice: (1) Discard the heart loser and hope the trumps are now 1-1 (which they are) so that both trumps fall when South later leads a trump, or (2) Over-ruff East, play ◊A and ruff a diamond and lead another club. If East ruffs high, discard the heart loser; if East discards, ruff the club, ruff a diamond and then discard the heart loser on the fifth club. No matter who ruffs, South loses only two trump tricks.

Hand 96: Slam exploration via a long suit trial – Suit combination – Using a long suit for a discard

Dealer West : East-West vulnerable

WEST	NORTH	EAST	SOUTH
1◊	No	1♡	No
2♡	No	3♣ (1)	No
4♡ (2)	No	4NT (3)	No
5♡	No	6♡	All pass

NORTH
♠ 10 9 7 6 5 4
♡ 10
◊ K 9
♣ J 9 8 5

WEST
♠ 8 3
♡ A J 4 2
◊ A J 8 3 2
♣ K 4

EAST
♠ A 2
♡ K 9 8 6 5
◊ 7
♣ A Q 7 3 2

SOUTH
♠ K Q J
♡ Q 7 3
◊ Q 10 6 5 4
♣ 10 6

Bidding: (1) With only five losers, East is worth a slam try and could simply ask for aces. The 3♣ trial bid is better. If West rejects the game try (thus indicating that the ♣K is probably missing) and it turns out later that an ace is also missing, East should avoid the slam.

(2) With one loser in the trial suit, bid the major suit game.

(3) Checking on aces and bidding the excellent small slam. With five losers opposite a likely seven losers, a grand slam is unlikely and to attempt a grand slam, East would need to find West with the ♡Q as well. Do not bid a grand slam with nine trumps missing the queen or king. The chance of losing a trump trick is too great.

Lead: ♣K. Top of sequence is best.

Correct play: Win the ♠A and draw trumps, playing the ♡K and a heart to the ♡A. Even though the trump finesse does in fact work here, it is not the best play. If the trump finesse were to lose to North's queen, the defence could cash a spade and defeat the slam. After the ♡A does not drop the ♡Q, leave the trump queen out and start on the clubs: ♣K; club to the ace and then the ♣Q, pitching the losing spade from dummy. South can ruff this with the ♡Q, but that is the only trick for the defence. It was far more important to eliminate the spade loser from dummy on the club suit than to concern yourself about a possible trump loser.

REVISION TEST ON PART 3

The answers to all these questions can be found in Chapters 17-24. Give yourself 1 mark for each correct answer. If you score less than 40, it will profit you to revise the relevant sections.

A. The bidding has been 1♠ : 2♣, 2♥ : 3♦. What should opener do next with each of these hands?

1. ♠ A 9 7 4 3	2. ♠ A J 8 3 2	3. ♠ K Q 8 6 3	4. ♠ A J 9 7 2	5. ♠ A K 8 7 2
♥ K J 7 2	♥ K Q 9 6 4	♥ A K J 8	♥ A 9 7 2	♥ A J 9 7
♦ A Q	♦ 9	♦ 7 6	♦ 8	♦ K 3
♣ 9 7	♣ K 3	♣ J 4	♣ A Q 2	♣ 5 2

B. The bidding has started 1♦ : 1NT, 2♠. What should responder do now with each of these hands?

1. ♠ K 5 3	2. ♠ 7 5 2	3. ♠ J 2	4. ♠ 9 3 2	5. ♠ K Q
♥ Q J 3	♥ K J 9	♥ 7 3 2	♥ K Q 10	♥ 8 6 2
♦ 8 6 3	♦ 6 3 2	♦ 9 4	♦ 8 3 2	♦ A 9 4
♣ 10 5 4 2	♣ Q J 10 8	♣ K Q 9 8 6 3	♣ K J 10 4	♣ K 7 5 3 2

C. The bidding has been 1♦ : 1♥, 1♠ : 2NT. What should opener do next with each of these hands?

1. ♠ A J 8 7	2. ♠ Q 10 7 6 2	3. ♠ A 8 5 3	4. ♠ Q J 8 2	5. ♠ A 8 7 5
♥ K 7 3	♥ 3	♥ Q 6	♥ Q 2	♥ - - -
♦ A Q 10 9 2	♦ A K 9 8 3 2	♦ A Q 9 6 2	♦ A K Q 8 6 3	♦ A Q J 4 3
♣ 2	♣ A	♣ K 5	♣ 5	♣ K J 7 3

D. The bidding has started 1♦ : 1♠, 3♦. What should responder do now with each of these hands?

1. ♠ K 9 4 2	2. ♠ A J 7 4 2	3. ♠ A Q 9 7 2	4. ♠ K J 9 7 3 2	5. ♠ A J 8 2
♥ 8 7 3	♥ K Q 3 2	♥ A 7 2	♥ 3 2	♥ K 8 3
♦ 9 2	♦ 7 6	♦ 8 7 2	♦ 9 6 2	♦ 9 7
♣ K 9 5 2	♣ 8 4	♣ 5 4	♣ A J	♣ Q J 3 2

E. The bidding has started 1♣ : 2♣, 2♦. What should responder do now with each of these hands?

1. ♠ J 7	2. ♠ A J 10	3. ♠ K 7 2	4. ♠ 6 5 2	5. ♠ 3 2
♥ J 6 4	♥ K 9 6	♥ Q J 4	♥ A K 9	♥ 6 4
♦ K 6	♦ 9 7	♦ 6 3	♦ 6 2	♦ A 4 2
♣ J 8 7 5 3 2	♣ 9 8 5 3 2	♣ J 8 5 4 2	♣ J 9 7 3 2	♣ K 9 8 6 3 2

F. The bidding has started 1♠ : 1NT, 2♣. What should responder do now with each of these hands?

1. ♠ 9 7	2. ♠ 4	3. ♠ - - -	4. ♠ 9 2	5. ♠ 7
♥ K 6 3	♥ 4 2	♥ Q 4	♥ J 3	♥ A 9 8 6 3
♦ K J 9 7 4 2	♦ K 9 7 6 3 2	♦ 9 8 6 5 4 3 2	♦ Q J 7 6 4 2	♦ A 3
♣ 3 2	♣ Q J 3 2	♣ A 9 5 4	♣ K 3 2	♣ 9 8 6 5 2

G. What are your answers for the hands in F. if the bidding started 1♠ : 1NT, 2♥?

H. What are your answers for the hands in F. if the bidding started 1♠ : 1NT, 2♠?

I. The bidding has started 1♠ : 2♠. What action should opener now take with each of these hands?

1. ♠ J 7 6 5 3 2	2. ♠ A J 8 7 3	3. ♠ A Q 7 6 3 2	4. ♠ A 9 8 5 2	5. ♠ A Q J 8 4
♥ A K 2	♥ A Q	♥ A K J 9	♥ A K	♥ 6
♦ K Q	♦ 7 6	♦ 4	♦ 9 7 6 2	♦ A Q J 4 3
♣ K 2	♣ J 7 5 2	♣ 9 6	♣ K J	♣ 6 2

J. The bidding has been 1♠ : 2♠, 3♥. What should responder do now with each of these hands?

1. ♠ Q 7 5 2	2. ♠ A 7 4	3. ♠ 9 7 5 4	4. ♠ A 7 4 2	5. ♠ Q 8 5 2
♥ K Q 7	♥ K 7 6 5 3 2	♥ 6 4 3	♥ K 7	♥ 6
♦ 9 3	♦ 6 4	♦ Q 7	♦ 8 6 3	♦ 9 4 3
♣ 9 8 5 3	♣ 3 2	♣ K J 4 2	♣ 9 6 5 4	♣ K 9 8 6 4

PART 4

EXPAND YOUR COMPETITIVE
AND DEFENSIVE BIDDING

This part covers more advanced situations where the opponents have opened the bidding or where your side has opened the bidding and the opponents intervene, situations which you and your partner must get right to score what is rightfully yours or to avoid a horrible debacle. Here also, both partners need to be conversant with the relevant principles and rather than wait until a calamity occurs at the table, make sure that you and your partner go through the relevant areas together thoroughly. The groundwork by both of you will be well rewarded by success when the difficult situations do arise.

Chapter 25 deals with bidding the enemy suit: what it means if you bid the enemy suit directly over an opponent's opening bid and what it means later in the auction or in response to partner's action, and how the bidding proceeds after a bid of the enemy suit has been used.

Chapter 26 is concerned with responder's strong hands after a takeout double, how responder conveys enough strength for game and how the bidding then develops; also how opener can use the takeout double to show various types of strong hands, particularly the strong balanced types.

Chapter 27 covers actions by the third player after an opponent makes a takeout double, including the redouble and subsequent bidding after the redouble, as well as the 2NT Convention (Truscott) over an opponent's takeout double which has become an integral part of most standard systems.

Chapter 28 comprises overcalling their 1NT opening (what conventions are commonly used and what you need to implement them) and coping with opposition interference over your partner's 1NT (which bids are merely competitive, which are invitational and which are forcing).

Chapter 29 deals with bidding in fourth seat after a 1-level or 2-level bid by an opponent is passed back to you: when to pass, when to reopen the bidding and how such actions differ from bidding in the direct seat.

Chapters 30 and 31 illustrate the use of negative doubles: how to recognise them, when to use them and how the bidding continues after a negative double has been made. Chapter 30 covers responder's hands in the 6-9 and 10-12 zone, while Chapter 31 deals with responder's game-going hands of 13+ points and opener's rebids when holding game-invitational or game-forcing values after responder has made a negative double.

Chapter 32 concludes by treating penalty doubles: what do you need to make a penalty double of 1NT, of a suit overcall, of opponents' games and slams and how to collect penalties even though your partnership is playing negative doubles.

CHAPTER 25

BIDDING THE ENEMY SUIT

Bidding the enemy suit is sometimes called 'cue-bid of the enemy suit'. A cue-bid implies control of a suit, such as a void or ace in the suit. Cue-bids are often used in slam going auctions *after suit agreement*. For example, after 2 ♠ : (3 ◇) : 3 ♠ : No, a bid of 4 ◇ by opener would, in standard methods, indicate the ◇ A or a diamond void and interest in slam. Bidding the enemy suit before your side has agreed on a suit does not promise the ace or a void in their suit. 'Cue-bid of the enemy suit' is still used because it once was a requirement that a bid of the enemy suit did imply such control even before your side had agreed on a suit.

Today, bidding the enemy suit *before suit agreement* is played in standard methods as an artificial, strong action, normally forcing to game. The meaning will vary depending on how the auction has started. The principles are not difficult as long as you realize that bidding the enemy suit is a strong, artificial action. The concept of bidding the enemy suit by responder later in the auction is very similar to fourth-suit forcing (see Chapter 17) and if the fourth-suit forcing area has been absorbed, this chapter will pose no difficulties.

BIDDING THE ENEMY SUIT DIRECTLY OVER THEIR OPENING BID e.g., (1 ♡) : 2 ♡

(A) STANDARD APPROACH: Whether it is a major or a minor, bidding their suit directly over the opening is artificial, forcing to game and shows values equivalent to a 2 ♣ opening (23+ HCP or a hand with three losers or fewer). All further bidding is natural and a no-trump bid by either partner promises a stopper in the enemy suit. Bidding must continue until game is reached or a penalty double is made if the opponents bid again. All doubles by either player after bidding the enemy suit are for penalties.

(B) MICHAELS CUE-BID: Popular at duplicate, this convention shows a 2-suiter, similar in strength and shape to the unusual 2NT, about 7-12 HCP and at least a 5-5 pattern (see Chapter 11). The suits shown, however, are not the minors. (1 ♣) : 2 ♣ or (1 ◇) : 2 ◇ shows both majors. (1 ♡) : 2 ♡ or (1 ♠) : 2 ♠ promises five cards in the other major and a 5+ minor. The minor suit is not disclosed. With no fit for the major, you can ask for the minor suit with 2NT. After using Michaels, any double by you or partner is for penalties.

(C) MICHAELS OVER MAJORS, NATURAL OVER MINORS: In this method, the Michaels Cue-Bid is used only if the opponents open with a major suit, while (1 ♣) : 2 ♣ and (1 ◇) : 2 ◇ are played as natural overcalls, just as though the bidding had started (1 ♡) : 2 ♣ or (1 ♠) : 2 ◇ and later bidding is exactly the same as after a natural overcall. This approach is sensible, but not very popular in duplicate circles. Most pairs prefer to use (1 ♣) : 2 ♣ and (1 ◇) : 2 ◇ to show both majors. The advantage is that both suits are shown at once and it puts partner in a strong position to judge which suit to support and how high to bid.

What do you do then if they open 1 ♣ or 1 ◇ and you have a reasonable hand with length and strength in their suit? If not especially strong or with only five cards in their suit, pass and perhaps bid the suit later if the bidding is not too high. Passing and bidding an opponent's suit on the next round is natural if partner has not bid. With 11-15 HCP and a decent 6-card holding in their minor suit, make a jump-overcall: (1 ♣) : 3 ♣ or (1 ◇) : 3 ◇. These overcalls are not played as weak.

The jump-overcall in their major suit, (1 ♡) : 3 ♡ or (1 ♠) : 3 ♠, is not played as natural. This bid is used to ask partner to bid 3NT with a stopper in their suit. The overcaller will have a strong hand with 8+ winners.

Obviously the partnership must agree which of the above approaches is to be used. If you and partner adopt either (B) or (C), then the game-forcing demand after they open is shown by doubling first and bidding their suit after partner's reply to the double. Double first, bid their suit next, is forcing to suit agreement.

BIDDING THE ENEMY SUIT LATER IN THE AUCTION

(A) AFTER YOUR SIDE OPENED 1NT: This is covered in Chapter 28 (Interference Over 1NT). Basically, bidding the enemy suit here, e.g., 1NT : (2 ♡) : 3 ♡, is used to replace Stayman.

(B) AFTER PARTNER MADE A TAKEOUT DOUBLE: See Chapter 26 (Takeout Doubles: Strong Replies & Strong Rebids). Bidding the enemy suit in response to a takeout double, e.g., (1 ◇) : Double : (No) : 2 ◇, confirms a strong hand. Some play it as 13+ points, and forcing to game. A more popular treatment for bidding the enemy suit in this situation is 10+ points and forcing only until suit agreement has been reached.

(C) AFTER A MAJOR SUIT HAS BEEN RAISED TO THE 2-LEVEL: Bidding the enemy suit in this situation, e.g., 1♠ : (2◊) : 2♠ : (No), 3◊, is a long suit trial bid (see Chapter 24). It is forcing for one round, like any normal long suit trial, and so does not commit the partnership to game.

(D) OTHER SITUATIONS: Bidding the opposition's suit in other cases is primarily a strong action, normally leading to a game somewhere and denies an available clearcut action. If you have an obvious, natural bid, make the natural bid and do not bid the enemy suit. Bidding their suit is almost always used when you have enough points for a game, but you cannot tell yet which is the correct contract. Perhaps your natural bid would go beyond 3NT and yet 3NT could be the correct spot. Perhaps you would like to play in 3NT, but you do not have a stopper in the enemy suit, yet partner could have a stopper. After partner has bid the enemy suit, your priorities are:

- Give delayed support for partner's suit if it is a major.
- Bid no-trumps with a stopper in the enemy suit.
- Without a stopper, give delayed support for partner's suit if it is a minor.
- Without a stopper and without delayed support, make the most descriptive bid possible. You must not pass, so cope as best you can.

PARTNERSHIP BIDDING: How should the following hands be bid? West is always the dealer unless otherwise stated and there is no opposition bidding other than that given.

SET 51 – WEST	SET 51 – EAST	SET 52 – WEST	SET 52 – EAST
1. South opens 1◊.	**1.** South opens 1◊.	**1.** N. overcalls 2◊.	**1.** N. overcalls 2◊.
♠ 6 5	♠ K 10 9	♠ 7 6	♠ A K 5 3 2
♡ K 3	♡ A Q 5	♡ 4 2	♡ A J 10
◊ A 4 3	◊ 6 5 2	◊ K Q 3	◊ 4 2
♣ K Q 10 9 8 4	♣ A J 7 2	♣ A K J 8 7 4	♣ Q 5 3
2. South opens 1♡.	**2.** South opens 1♡.	**2.** S. overcalls 2♣.	**2.** S. overcalls 2♣.
♠ K Q J 3	♠ A 9 8	♠ 7 4 3	♠ Q J 2
♡ K J	♡ 4 3	♡ A Q 7	♡ 9 5
◊ A Q J 10 7 5	◊ K 9 3	◊ K Q 2	◊ A 9 7 5 4 3
♣ 9	♣ Q J 5 3 2	♣ A K J 10	♣ 7 5
3. South opens 3♣.	**3.** South opens 3♣.	**3.** S. overcalls 1♠.	**3.** S. overcalls 1♠.
♠ K 9 6 5 4	♠ A 7 3 2	♠ 7 4 3	♠ 6 2
♡ A J 7 3	♡ K 6 4 2	♡ K 7 2	♡ A 9 6 4 3
◊ K Q J	◊ A 5	◊ A K Q 3	◊ 6 4 2
♣ 6	♣ J 4 2	♣ A K 2	♣ Q 5 4
4. N. overcalls 2◊.	**4.** N. overcalls 2◊.	**4.** S. overcalls 2♣.	**4.** S. overcalls 2♣.
♠ A Q 9 5 4	♠ 7	♠ K Q	♠ 4
♡ K 2	♡ A Q 8 6 4 3	♡ Q J 4 2	♡ K 9 6 5
◊ 5 2	◊ 9 8 4	◊ A J 8 3 2	◊ K 6 5
♣ Q J 8 4	♣ A K 3	♣ 7 2	♣ A K 6 4 3
5. N. overcalls 2♡.	**5.** N. overcalls 2♡.	**5.** South opens 1♡.	**5.** South opens 1♡.
♠ A Q 7 6 3	♠ 2	♠ A Q 9 8 6 2	♠ - - -
♡ K 2	♡ 7 4 3	♡ - - -	♡ J 10 9 3
◊ A J 9 4 2	◊ Q 5 3	◊ A K Q J 2	◊ 10 7 4 3
♣ 9	♣ A K Q J 7 2	♣ A J	♣ 10 7 6 4 2
6. S. overcalls 2♡.	**6.** S. overcalls 2♡.	**6.** South opens 1♠.	**6.** South opens 1♠.
♠ A 9 7 4 3	♠ K	♠ 7 6 3	♠ 4
♡ 7 6	♡ 8 4 3	♡ - - -	♡ A K Q 7 3 2
◊ A Q 5	◊ K J 2	◊ A 9 6 4 2	◊ 7
♣ K 4 2	♣ A Q J 9 5 3	♣ J 7 6 5 4	♣ A K Q 9 3

PLAY HANDS ON BIDDING THE ENEMY SUIT

Hand 97: Bidding the enemy suit – Leading a high card for a finesse

Dealer North : Love all

	WEST	NORTH	EAST	SOUTH
NORTH		1♡	Dble (1)	No
♠ 10 7	3♣ (2)	No	3◇ (3)	No
♡ A Q 10 9 6 5	3♡ (4)	No	3NT (5)	All pass

NORTH
♠ 10 7
♡ A Q 10 9 6 5
◇ K 8 4
♣ A 10

WEST
♠ A 9
♡ 8 3 2
◇ 10 3 2
♣ K Q 7 4 3

EAST
♠ K Q J 3
♡ K J
◇ A Q J 7 6 5
♣ 9

SOUTH
♠ 8 6 5 4 2
♡ 7 4
◇ 9
♣ J 8 6 5 2

Bidding: (1) Unsuitable for a strong jump-overcall because of the four spades.
(2) Shows 10-12 points, 4+ clubs and denies four spades.
(3) East could bid 3NT here, but this is too hasty. 3◇ is forcing and does not preclude 3NT. 5◇ could be the best spot.
(4) With a balanced hand, West prefers to look for 3NT. 3♡ *asks* East for a stopper in hearts.
(5) With a stopper, East bids 3NT. Without a stopper, East would bid 3♠ or 4◇. As the cards lie, 5◇ is on, but 3NT is safer. You also score more for eleven tricks in 3NT.

Lead: ♡ 7. Partner's suit and top of a doubleton.

Correct play: North wins the ♡ A and returns a heart. As East-West hold 26 HCP, North-South have 14 HCP. The ◇ K is thus almost certainly with North, who opened the bidding. Otherwise North would have opened with 11 HCP, possible but not likely. Win the ♡ K, cross to the ♣ A and lead the ◇ 10, playing low from hand when North plays low. Repeat the diamond finesse and claim six diamonds, four spades and one heart. It is an error to lead a low diamond from dummy instead of the ten. The finesse wins, but you would be stuck in hand without another entry to dummy to repeat the finesse.

Hand 98: Searching for a stopper in the enemy suit – High cards from shortage – Marked finesse

Dealer East : North-South vulnerable

	WEST	NORTH	EAST	SOUTH
NORTH			No	1♣ (1)
♠ Q J 2	No	1◇ (2)	1♠ (3)	2♣ (4)
♡ 9 5 3	No	2NT (5)	No	3NT (6)
◇ A 9 7 4 3	No	No	No	

NORTH
♠ Q J 2
♡ 9 5 3
◇ A 9 7 4 3
♣ 5 4

WEST
♠ 8 5
♡ J 8 4 2
◇ J 8 6 5
♣ Q 9 2

EAST
♠ A K 10 9 7
♡ K 10 6
◇ 10
♣ 8 7 6 3

SOUTH
♠ 6 4 3
♡ A Q 7
◇ K Q 2
♣ A K J 10

Bidding: (1) South's standard approach with a balanced 19 is to open and rebid 3NT. If East had not bid, the bidding would be 1♣ : 1◇, 3NT (although some prefer to rebid 2NT with 18-19 and 1NT with 15-17).
(2) Prefer a 1◇ response to 1NT. If no-trumps is to be the contract, allow the stronger hand to bid no-trumps first.
(3) Although just short of an opening, the hand is ideal for an overcall with length and strength in the spades.
(4) Do not bid no-trumps with no spade cover. With enough for game, but unsure of the best spot, bid their suit.
(5) Confirms at least one stopper in spades.
(6) Exactly what South wanted to hear. 5◇ can be defeated via ♣ A, ♠ K and a spade ruff.

Lead: ♠ 10. Prepared to give North a trick and hoping East or West can regain the lead before North can win nine tricks.

Correct play: North wins the first spade trick and should tackle the diamonds. The correct order is to play off the ◇ K and ◇ Q first (high cards from shortage). East drops the ten on the first round and when East shows out on the second round, continue with a low diamond and finesse the nine if West plays low. Play off the remaining diamonds. If North cashes the ◇ A on the first or second round of diamonds, West's J-8-6-5 cannot be captured and 3NT should then be defeated.

Hand 99: Playing safe – Playing for an overtrick at duplicate – Setting up a long suit for discards

Dealer South : East-West vulnerable

NORTH
♠ 10 6 4 3 2
♡ 9 5 2
◇ 10 7 5 3
♣ J

WEST
♠ A Q
♡ 7 4
◇ 9 4 2
♣ A Q 10 9 6 2

EAST
♠ K J 8 7
♡ J 6
◇ A K Q 8
♣ 8 7 5

SOUTH
♠ 9 5
♡ A K Q 10 8 3
◇ J 6
♣ K 4 3

WEST	NORTH	EAST	SOUTH
			1♡
2♣	No	2♡ (1)	Dble (2)
3♣ (3)	No	4♣ (4)	No
5♣ (5)	No	No	No

Bidding: (1) A sound opening hand opposite a 2-level overcall is usually enough for game in no-trumps or a major. 2♡ is the best action. 2♠ or 2◇ would indicate a 5+ suit. Opposite a minor suit overcall, bidding the enemy suit primarily asks for a stopper in their suit. If West bid 2NT, East would raise to 3NT. (2) Confirms very strong hearts and asks partner to be sure to lead a heart if West becomes declarer. (3) Denies a stopper in hearts and denies four spades. (4) This is no longer forcing. While East has enough for 3NT, East's values may not be enough for 5-in-a-minor. 4♣ allows West to pass if minimum for the 2♣ overcall.

(5) Just worth a shot at 5♣ West figures that if either black king is missing, the finesse is almost sure to work, since South opened the bidding.

Lead: ♡ 5. Partner's suit and M.U.D. to deny a doubleton.

Correct play: After cashing two hearts, South might switch to a spade or continue with a third heart. Declarer's only problem is the trump suit. With A-Q-10-x-x-x opposite x-x-x, it is normal to finesse the queen, not the ten. This wins against (K-x) and (J-x), as well as against (K-x-x) and (J). The ♣K is marked with South for the opening bid, but with 14 points missing, the ♣J could be in either hand. With no strong reason to go against the normal line, cross to dummy and lead a club to the queen. When North's jack drops, return to dummy and lead another club, finessing the ten, and then cash the ♣A, picking up South's king.

Hand 100: Locating the best trump fit – Loser count – Slam exploration – Setting up a long suit

Dealer West : Game all

NORTH
♠ 10
♡ A K Q 8 6 4
◇ 9
♣ A K Q 7 6

WEST
♠ A K Q 9 5 3
♡ J 5 3
◇ Q J 7
♣ 9

EAST
♠ 7 6 4
♡ 10 9 7 2
◇ K 10 4 3
♣ 10 3

SOUTH
♠ J 8 2
♡ - - -
◇ A 8 6 5 2
♣ J 8 5 4 2

WEST	NORTH	EAST	SOUTH
1♠	2♠ (1)	No	3◇ (2)
No	3♡ (3)	No	4♣ (4)
No	4NT (5)	No	5◇
No	6♣	All pass	

Bidding: (1) North has only two losers and so insists on game. To jump to 4♡, as some would do, is very lazy. Firstly, the correct contract can be in clubs, not hearts. Secondly, more than just game might be possible. The challenge is to locate the best trump fit and to get the most out of your cards. 2♠ insists on game, but if the partnership uses the bid of the enemy suit here for other purposes (e.g., Michaels Cue-Bid), North doubles first and rebids 2♠ over South's 2◇ reply. The 2♠ rebid would then create a game force and when South rebids 3♣ North would Blackwood with 4NT and bid 6♣. (2) With 5-5, show the higher suit first. (3) Longer suit first. 3♡ is forcing because of the 2♠ bid.

(4) It is natural to show the second suit. 3NT is out with no spade stopper. If desperate, 3♠ could be used. (5) With the club fit known and only two losers, North asks for aces, planning to pass 5♣ if South has none.

Lead: ♠A. Another spade hoping partner can over-ruff if dummy ruffs low is about the only hope to beat 6♣.

Correct play: Draw trumps in two rounds, ending in dummy. Continue with the top hearts, ruffing the fourth round of hearts. Dummy's remaining hearts are winners. 6♣ made.

CHAPTER 26

TAKEOUT DOUBLES: STRONG REPLIES & STRONG REBIDS

After a takeout double, responding with 0-5, 6-9 or 10-12 points was covered in Chapters 13,14 and 15.

PARTNER DOUBLES FOR TAKEOUT: REPLYING WITH 13 POINTS OR MORE

With 13+ points, you have enough for game opposite the double. Therefore:

BID GAME   or   **BID THE ENEMY SUIT**

With a long, strong major, bid 4 ♡ or 4 ♠. With a balanced hand, no 4+ major and their suit well stopped, bid 3NT. With a weak major *or* with a choice of contracts or with no obvious game at this stage, bid the enemy suit. This is forcing to suit agreement (i.e., until a suit has been bid and raised). 13-14 points opposite a double does not mean that game in a minor must be a good bet. For example, the 4 ◇ bid in this auction is encouraging, but not forcing– (1 ♠) : Double : (No) : 2 ♠, (No) : 3 ◇ : (No) : 4 ◇.

Unless your game bid is clearcut, choose the bid of the enemy suit. If the opponents have bid two suits, such as (1 ◇) : Double : (1 ♠) or (1 ◇) : No : (1 ♠) : Double, a bid of their first suit (2 ◇) is natural, but a bid of their second suit (2 ♠) is artificial and game-going. If third player raises opener's suit, you can still bid their suit to ask the doubler to choose a contract, e.g., (1 ◇) : Double : (3 ◇) : 4 ◇ asks partner to bid a major.

AFTER PARTNER BIDS THEIR SUIT IN REPLY TO YOUR DOUBLE

Bidding continues until game is reached or a suit is bid and raised. Suits are shown in normal order: longest first; higher first with a 5-5; cheapest first with 4-card suits. Higher suit followed by lower suit shows at least a 5-4 pattern, as usual. After the enemy suit has been bid, 2NT is still forcing, shows a stopper in their suit and suggests 3NT. If stuck later for a bid below 3NT, you can bid the enemy suit again. This asks partner to bid 3NT with a stopper in their suit or to make a descriptive bid with no stopper in their suit.

OPENER'S POWERFUL DOUBLING HANDS

After partner's suit reply showing 0-9 points: Pass below 16 points. Otherwise:

Doubler's holding	Doubler's rebid	Doubler's holding	Doubler's rebid
Long suit, 5-loser hand	Bid suit (not forcing).	19-21, balanced	1NT if possible, else 2NT.
Long suit, 4-loser hand	Jump suit (not forcing).	22-23, balanced	Jump rebid no-trumps.
3-loser hand or better	Bid game or enemy suit.	24 up, balanced	Rebid 3NT.

A no-trump rebid by the doubler promises a stopper in the enemy suit. With 19+ HCP and no long suit, no support for partner's suit and no stopper in their suit, the doubler has a serious problem. Best is to bid their suit and play it by ear from there. You may then elect to pass partner's rebid below game.

THE DOUBLE AND SUBSEQUENT 1NT REBID

WEST	NORTH	EAST	SOUTH
1 ◇	Double	No	1 ♠
No	1NT ...		

North's rebid does not *sound* strong, but it shows 19-20-21 points, balanced, with a stopper in their suit. With 12-15 points, North would pass South's 1 ♠ reply.

Double and bid again opposite a weak reply always shows more than a minimum double. With 16-18 points balanced and a diamond stopper, North would have bid 1NT at once rather than double. Therefore, to double and rebid 1NT, North must be stronger than 18 points.

After partner's reply showing 6-9 points (1NT or a suit bid over interference): A new suit by the doubler shows a 5-card suit and is encouraging, but not forcing. Jump in a new suit, showing a 5+ suit, or a bid of the enemy suit, asking for a stopper in their suit, is a game-force. Where partner has bid 1NT, already showing a stopper in their suit, bidding the enemy suit shows a strong hand with a void or singleton in their suit. This warns partner against no-trumps unless the enemy suit is well covered, at least a double stopper.

After partner's reply showing 10-12 points (a jump-response to the double): A new suit by the doubler shows a 5+ suit and is forcing. A rebid of 2NT by the doubler is also forcing and promises a stopper in their suit. If the doubler bids the enemy suit, this is forcing to game and asks for a stopper in their suit. If partner's reply was a jump to 2NT, a bid of the enemy suit by the doubler shows a void or singleton in the enemy suit. It warns partner against no-trumps unless partner has the enemy suit well stopped.

A. Partner has doubled their 1 ♡ opening, pass on your right. What is your reply on each of these hands?

1. ♠ Q J 7	**2.** ♠ A J 9 8 6 3	**3.** ♠ 7 2	**4.** ♠ 8 7 6 4 2	**5.** ♠ A Q 7
♡ 8 6	♡ 7 6	♡ A Q J	♡ A J	♡ 8 6 4 3
◊ A Q 8 6	◊ K 9 2	◊ K Q 7 2	◊ K Q	◊ A K
♣ K J 9 3	♣ A 2	♣ J 9 8 4	♣ K 9 4 3	♣ J 7 6 2

B. You have doubled their 1 ◊ opening and partner replied 2 ◊. What is your rebid on each of these hands?

1. ♠ K 8 7 4	**2.** ♠ A 9 7 4 2	**3.** ♠ K 7 6 4 2	**4.** ♠ Q 7 3 2	**5.** ♠ A Q 3
♡ 8 6 4 3	♡ K Q 9 3	♡ Q 9 4 3 2	♡ A 8 3	♡ K Q 6
◊ A 7	◊ 7	◊ A K	◊ 9 6	◊ 8 7 3 2
♣ A Q 3	♣ K J 2	♣ 7	♣ A K 5 4	♣ A Q 4

PARTNERSHIP BIDDING: How should these hands be bid? There is no bidding other than that given.

SET 53 – WEST	**SET 53 – EAST**	**SET 54 – WEST**	**SET 54 – EAST**
1. South opens 1 ♡.	**1.** South opens 1 ♡.	**1.** South opens 1 ♣.	**1.** South opens 1 ♣.
♠ A 8 7 2	♠ Q J 10 9 4 3	♠ K Q 8 5	♠ 9 3
♡ 8 2	♡ A K 7	♡ A J	♡ 8 7 6 5 4 2
◊ K 5 4	◊ 6	◊ A 8 2	◊ 6 4
♣ K Q 7 3	♣ 9 4 2	♣ A Q 9 2	♣ 8 6 3
2. (a) S. opens 1 ♠.	**2.** (a) S. opens 1 ♠.	**2.** (a) S. opens 1 ♣.	**2.** (a) S. opens 1 ♣.
♠ A	♠ 8 6	♠ K 9	♠ A 3 2
♡ K Q 9 3	♡ J 7 5 4 2	♡ A K 3 2	♡ 6 5 4
◊ A 7 6 5 2	◊ K 8 3	◊ K Q 9	◊ J 10 4 3 2
♣ J 7 3	♣ A K Q	♣ A J 5 4	♣ Q 2
(b) South opens 1 ♣.	(b) South opens 1 ♣.	(b) South opens 1 ◊.	(b) South opens 1 ◊.
3. South opens 1 ◊.	**3.** South opens 1 ◊.	**3.** South opens 1 ◊.	**3.** South opens 1 ◊.
♠ K Q 4 3	♠ A 2	♠ A Q 9 7 2	♠ J 4 3
♡ A 9 3 2	♡ 8 7	♡ A K 4 3	♡ 8 2
◊ A 8	◊ 7 6 4 2	◊ 8	◊ A Q 9 7
♣ 7 4	♣ A K Q 8 6	♣ K Q 10	♣ 9 7 6 4
4. South opens 1 ♣.	**4.** South opens 1 ♣.	**4.** South opens 1 ♣.	**4.** South opens 1 ♣.
♠ A Q 4 3	♠ K 9 7 6	♠ 6 5	♠ J 8 2
♡ A 8 2	♡ K 9 7 6	♡ A Q 8 7 6 4	♡ K 9 5
◊ A 9 8 3	◊ K Q J	◊ A K	◊ 8 7 4 3 2
♣ 7 5 4	♣ J 3	♣ K Q J	♣ 8 6
5. South opens 1 ◊.	**5.** South opens 1 ◊.	**5.** South opens 1 ♡.	**5.** South opens 1 ♡.
♠ A Q 6 5	♠ K 7	♠ A 7	♠ J 8 4 2
♡ K 9 7 4	♡ A 8 3	♡ 6 4	♡ 7 3
◊ 8 2	◊ Q J 4 3	◊ A K 3	◊ 8 5 4 2
♣ A J 10	♣ K 4 3 2	♣ A K Q 8 6 2	♣ 7 5 3
6. South opens 1 ♣.	**6.** South opens 1 ♣.	**6.** South opens 1 ♡.	**6.** South opens 1 ♡.
♠ Q J 5 4 2	♠ K 7 3	♠ A 2	♠ J 7 6 5
♡ A Q J 3	♡ K 6 5	♡ 7 6	♡ A 3
◊ K 4 3	◊ A 7 2	◊ A K Q 8 6 2	◊ 7 5 3
♣ 9	♣ A 8 4 2	♣ A K 3	♣ 8 5 4 2

PLAY HANDS ON STRONG DOUBLES & STRONG REPLIES TO DOUBLES

Hand 101: Bidding the enemy suit – Counting your tricks – Card combination

Dealer North : North-South vulnerable

NORTH
- ♠ Q 9
- ♡ Q J
- ◇ A Q J 10 7
- ♣ Q 9 8 5

WEST
- ♠ A 4
- ♡ K 6 3
- ◇ K 6 4 3
- ♣ K 7 3 2

EAST
- ♠ K 8 6 5
- ♡ A 7 4 2
- ◇ 9 5
- ♣ A J 10

SOUTH
- ♠ J 10 7 3 2
- ♡ 10 9 8 5
- ◇ 8 2
- ♣ 6 4

WEST	NORTH	EAST	SOUTH
	1 ◇	Dble	No
2 ◇ (1)	Dble (2)	2 ♡ (3)	No
2NT (4)	No	3NT (5)	All pass

(1) Artificial, showing enough values for game.
(2) Shows a strong suit and asks partner to lead diamonds. Double of an artificial bid is usually lead-directing.
(3) 4-card suits are bid up-the-line.
(4) Promises a diamond stopper and denies four spades.
(5) No point showing the spades, as partner's 2NT rebid denied four spades. East would rebid 3 ♡ with a 5-card suit.

Lead: ◇ Q. Prepared to concede a trick to the ◇ K in order to set up the rest of the diamonds.

Correct play: Take the ◇ K. If not, North may switch and then even with four club tricks, West does not have enough winners.

West needs the ◇ K in order to score nine tricks. Continue with a low club and finesse the ♣ 10. Return to hand with a heart to the king and lead another low club, finessing the ♣ J. Cash the ♣ A, come to hand with the ♠ A and cash the ♣ K. Making two spades, two hearts, one diamond and four clubs. It would be an error to cash the ♣ K before the club finesse. That would limit you to three club tricks if North has Q-singleton, Q-x, Q-x-x-x or Q-x-x-x-x in clubs. Taking the first round finesse scores four club tricks whenever North has the ♣ Q, regardless of length. Playing the ♣ A first and then leading the ♣ J is not as good. This scores four tricks only if clubs are 3-3 and South has the ♣ Q. The ♣ Q is far more likely to be with North, the opening bidder.

Hand 102: Exploring for the best game – Card reading and counting – Endplay

Dealer East : East-West vulnerable

NORTH
- ♠ K 10 4
- ♡ A 5 4
- ◇ A 4 3
- ♣ Q 7 4 3

WEST
- ♠ 6 5
- ♡ J 10 8 2
- ◇ Q 10 8 7 2
- ♣ 10 5

EAST
- ♠ A 8 2
- ♡ 9 7
- ◇ 9 5
- ♣ A K J 8 6 2

SOUTH
- ♠ Q J 9 7 3
- ♡ K Q 6 3
- ◇ K J 6
- ♣ 9

WEST	NORTH	EAST	SOUTH
		1 ♣	Dble (1)
No	2 ♣ (2)	Dble (3)	2 ♠
No	2NT (4)	No	3 ♡
No	4 ♠ (5)	All pass	

Bidding: (1) With 5-4 in the majors, prefer double to overcall.
(2) Artificial and showing values for game.
(3) Shows strong clubs. Lead-directing.
(4) Shows a stopper in clubs and seeks further information.
(5) South's 2 ♠ then 3 ♡ shows 5+ spades and 4+ hearts. Therefore, North elects to play in the spade game.

Lead: ♣ 10. Partner's suit. Top from a doubleton.

Correct play: South should play low from dummy and East encourages with the ♣ 8. The next club is ducked in dummy and the ♣ J is ruffed. A spade to the ten loses to East's ace, and East's ♣ K is ruffed high by South, West discarding a diamond.

West's ♣ 10 then ♣ 5 shows a doubleton. South ruffs high to avoid the risk of an over-ruff. Trumps are drawn, West discarding another diamond. West must retain all four hearts, as South bid hearts: *keep length with declarer.* If West lets a heart go, South has four heart tricks instead of three. Having lost two tricks, it seems that South needs hearts 3-3 or the ◇ Q onside. However, South can survive, even though neither hearts nor diamonds are favourable. Play off the top hearts. When they do not break 3-3 and West has the last heart, play the fourth heart and put West on lead. West is out of clubs and spades. With only diamonds left, West has to lead into South's ◇ K-J-6. The losing diamond finesse is avoided by *endplaying* West.

Hand 103: Doubling with a powerful hand – Bidding the enemy suit – Creating an entry to dummy

Dealer South : Game all

NORTH
♠ Q 9 7 4
♡ A
◇ K 9 8 3
♣ A 8 3 2

WEST
♠ 8 3
♡ 10 9 8 3
◇ A 7 5
♣ Q J 10 5

EAST
♠ A K 6 2
♡ K Q J
◇ Q J 4
♣ K 7 4

SOUTH
♠ J 10 5
♡ 7 6 5 4 2
◇ 10 6 2
♣ 9 6

WEST	NORTH	EAST	SOUTH
			No
No	1 ◇	Dble (1)	No
1 ♡ (2)	No	1NT (3)	No
3NT (4)	No	No	No

Bidding: (1) Too strong for a 1NT overcall.
(2) Show the major first in reply to a double.
(3) The 1NT rebid after doubling shows 19-21 balanced.
(4) Certainly worth a shot at 3NT. 2NT would be too timid.

Lead: ◇ 2. Bottom from three to an honour is the standard lead even if the honour is the ten. Reject partner's suit only when you have a good long suit and outside entries.

Correct play: Win the ◇ A at once – do not duck. Lead *hearts* next, not clubs, to knock out the ♡ A. On regaining the lead, cash your hearts.

Continue by leading the ♣ K (North should duck this) and a second club to dummy. When you reach dummy, now or later, cash the heart winner and, if North had switched to spades after winning the ♡ A, lead a diamond. You win three hearts and two tricks in the other suits. Traps to avoid: (1) If you duck the first diamond, North could take the ◇ K and switch to spades. On winning the ♣ A or ♡ A, North could lead another spade. The defence then scores two spades, the ◇ K and two aces before declarer comes to nine tricks. (2) Ducking the first diamond, winning North's diamond return (it is not easy for North to find the spade switch) and tackling clubs next. If North ducks the first two club leads, declarer cannot reach the extra heart winner in dummy and makes only eight tricks. When declarer is trying to set up dummy's long suit and dummy has no outside entry, it pays you to hold off with the ace in dummy's suit.

Hand 104: Doubling with a powerful hand – Bidding the enemy suit – Creating an entry to dummy

Dealer West : Love all

NORTH
♠ A 5 3
♡ A K Q J 10 8
◇ A Q 3 2
♣ - - -

WEST
♠ K Q 10 9 8
♡ 7 2
◇ K 10 7
♣ K Q 9

EAST
♠ J
♡ 9 6 5 3
◇ 9 8 5 4
♣ 10 8 5 4

SOUTH
♠ 7 6 4 2
♡ 4
◇ J 6
♣ A J 7 6 3 2

WEST	NORTH	EAST	SOUTH
1 ♠	Dble (1)	No	2 ♣
No	3 ♡ (2)	No	3 ♠ (3)
No	4 ♡ (4)	All pass	

Bidding: (1) Much too good for an overcall, even a strong jump-overcall, or a pre-emptive jump to 4 ♡.
(2) North has eight obvious tricks and the ◇ Q could be a ninth trick. For 4 ♡ to be a good chance, South needs to produce at least one trick. Double then jump-rebid is the way to show a hand which is just one trick short of game.
(3) South has the trick needed, but no clear idea which game is best. Bidding the enemy suit solves the problem.
(4) 4 ♡ is safer than 3NT because of the club void. If South has the values to allow 3NT to make (such as the ◇ K or ♠ K), 4 ♡ should make as well. However, 4 ♡ may be on where 3NT cannot be managed, because of only one stopper in spades.

Lead: ♠ J. Partner's suit. The ♠ J would be considered clearcut and automatic by almost everyone and yet it is a trump lead that can defeat 4 ♡. Bridge is a tough game!

Correct play: West should overtake the ♠ J with the ♠ Q and North wins (else East ruffs the ♠ A). North must not play trumps next. Instead, North leads the ◇ Q to create an entry to dummy (via the ◇ J) to reach the ♣ A. If West ducks the ◇ Q, cash the ◇ A and ruff a diamond. Then discard a loser on the ♣ A for eleven tricks. If West takes the ◇ Q, North will ruff high on the fourth round of spades. Trumps are drawn in four rounds and a diamond to dummy's jack allows declarer to play the ♣ A and discard a diamond loser.

CHAPTER 27

BIDDING OVER AN OPPOSITION TAKEOUT DOUBLE

After partner has opened with a suit bid and second player doubles, e.g., 1 ◊ : (Double) : to you, different methods exist. It is recommended that you and your partner(s) adopt the Modern Style (see below).

STANDARD TREATMENT

1. All hands with 10+ HCP redouble (the 'omnibus redouble').

2. Change of suit is 6-9 points and non-forcing, whether the new suit is at the 1-level or at the 2-level.

3. Jump-shift = 6-9 points and an excellent suit. Not forcing.

4. With 0-5 points, pass is normal, but with decent support and 4-5 points, a raise to the 2-level is acceptable.

5. A jump-raise, e.g., 1 ♡ : (Double) : 3 ♡, is pre-emptive with less than 10 HCP.

BARON OVER THE DOUBLE: In this method, which is not recommended, redouble with 10+ HCP, pass with 6-9 HCP and bid with 0-5 HCP. Bidding with 0-5 points and passing with 6-9 points may occasionally trap the unwary, but it is unsound against competent opposition. It is especially risky to bid with 0-5 points and a misfit after partner has opened with a major. The penalties can be severe.

MODERN STYLE

1. Change of suit retains its normal meaning and is forcing. The same applies to a jump-shift.

2. 1NT is 6-9 points, as usual.

3. 2NT is not used in its normal sense, 11-12 points balanced. With a hand suitable for a natural 2NT reply, redouble first and bid no-trumps later if a penalty double is not appropriate.

4. The structure for raising opener is:
- Raise to the 2-level = 4-9 HCP and 9 losers.
- Raise to the 3-level = 6-9 HCP and 8 losers.
- Raise to the 4-level = 6-9 HCP and 7 losers.
- With support and 10+ HCP, bid 2NT over the double, e.g., 1 ♠ : (Double) : 2NT. This artificial strong raise over their double is known as the Truscott 2NT Convention.

5. Without support for opener and 10+ HCP, redouble if you wish to make a penalty double of a bid by an opponent. If your hand is not suited for a penalty double, make your normal response (except for 2NT). Hands suitable for a penalty double are covered in Chapter 32.

Bidding after a new suit response, a jump-shift, a raise or a 1NT response follows normal lines.

BIDDING AFTER THE TRUSCOTT 2NT RESPONSE

The Truscott 2NT Response after a takeout double is very sensible. It allows responder to distinguish between weak, shapely hands (raise according to the number of losers) and raises backed by high card strength. It also usually shuts out the fourth player. If the bidding starts 1 ♡ : (Double) and you have to *redouble* to show a strong hand with support, you allow fourth player an easy entry to the auction. Over your redouble, fourth player can make a cheap lead-directing bid or suggest a sacrifice. By contrast, if you bid 2NT over the double to show support plus strength, fourth player is rarely strong enough to come in at the 3-level.

The Truscott 2NT is forcing and promises support for opener's suit. Support depends on what length was promised by the opening bid. It will guarantee 4-card support opposite a possible 4-card suit.

With a minimum opening, opener signs off in 3-Major. Responder can still bid game with 13+ HCP, or even with less if holding seven losers. With game possibilities, opener can bid a new suit as a trial bid (see Chapter 24), e.g., 1 ♡ : (Double) : 2NT: (No), 3 ♣ . . . The trial bid must be below 3-of-the-agreed-major. With enough for game but no slam interest, opener bids 4-Major over 2NT. With slam values after 2NT, opener may cue-bid a new suit higher than 3-of-the-agreed-major, e.g., after 1 ♡ : (Double) : 2NT : (No), opener's 3 ♠, 4 ♣ or 4 ◊ is a cue-bid. A new suit below 3-Major is a trial bid and a new suit above 3-Major is a cue-bid. It is even sensible to use 3NT over Truscott 2NT as Blackwood.

Where opener's suit is a minor, Truscott 2NT denies a major. For example, 1♣ : (Double) : 2NT shows club support, 10+ HCP and no 4-card major. With support and a major suit as well, bid the major.

If your right-hand opponent bids 2NT over partner's takeout double, you are worth a bid with a 4-card major or a 5-card minor and about an 8-loser hand. With fewer losers, you may make a jump-bid.

BIDDING AFTER THE REDOUBLE

1. *The doubler's partner should bid.* Say the bidding has started (1♠) : Double : (Redouble) . . . Do not pass the redouble even if very weak. The bidding has shown that fourth player has very little. However, it is best for fourth player to bid for psychological reasons. A pass reveals weakness and will encourage the opponents to double later actions for penalties. A bid *sounds* stronger even though a bid does not promise any strength at all. Fourth player should also bid to take pressure off partner. The doubler usually has no clear idea of the best trump suit – after all, that is why the double was chosen. Fourth player should therefore indicate the desired suit. The best principle is: *After partner's takeout double, bid over a redouble as you would bid over a pass.* The bidding over a redouble is no higher, so that there is no greater difficulty. If you would have bid over a pass, what is so tough about bidding over a redouble? Unlike a bid, the redouble has not cancelled the double, so that fourth player should take out the double. If fourth player is worth a jump-reply to the double, make the jump-reply. The redoubler could be bluffing or maybe the opening was a 'psyche'.

2. *The opener should pass unless able to make a penalty double.* After a redouble, all doubles are for penalties. A strong 4+ holding in a suit they bid is adequate for a penalty double. If opener is unable to make a penalty double, opener should pass on any normal hand. The redouble promises another bid, so that partner will not let the bidding die out. The redoubler may want to double for penalties and if opener bids first, the opponents are off the hook. A bid by opener ahead of the redoubler shows a weak, distributional hand.

Suppose the bidding has started 1♠ : (Double) : Redouble : (2♣) to the opener. With 4+ strong clubs, double for penalties. With other normal opening hands, pass. A new suit bid such as 2♡ or 2♢ would suggest a weak 5-5 or 6-5 with only 10 or 11 HCP, unsuitable to defend for penalties. Rebidding the suit opened – 2♠ – ahead of the redoubler would suggest 6-7 spades, 10 or 11 HCP and unsuited for defence.

Opener may pass fourth player's bid and later bid a new suit to remove a penalty double by the redoubler. This shows a shapely hand, usually 5-5, but not a weak, sub-minimum opening. Opener is suggesting that game chances offer a better reward than defence.

3. *The doubler takes normal action.* Suppose the bidding has been (1♡) : Double : (Redouble) : 1♠, (No) to you. You would bid now only if you would normally have bid over a weak reply to your double. Any further action by the doubler shows a strong doubling hand.

4. *The redoubler must take action if fourth player's bid is passed around.* Suppose partner opened 1♡ and you redoubled RHO's takeout double. LHO bids 2♣, passed back to you. You may double 2♣ for penalties with 4+ good clubs. A misfit with opener makes penalties attractive. A new suit by the redoubler is natural and forcing, and subsequent bidding is natural. Reverting to opener's suit (2♡ in the given auction) suggests only delayed, secondary support because of the failure to use 2NT over the double. A 2NT rebid by the redoubler is not forcing and shows 10-12 points and at least one stopper in their suit. Bidding the enemy suit (3♣ above) is forcing to game and asks for a stopper for 3NT.

OPENER'S REDOUBLE WHERE THE FOURTH PLAYER MAKES A TAKEOUT DOUBLE

If partner changes suit over your opening and fourth player doubles, e.g., 1♢ : (No) : 1♠ : (Double), opener's rebids have the normal meaning. Redouble by the opener indicates 16+ HCP, denies support for responder and suggests a desire for penalties. All doubles following the redouble are for penalties.

The function of the redouble by responder or by opener is to indicate that your side holds the balance of power (12 + 10 or 16 + 6). If the hand is also a misfit and you have a strong 4+ holding in their suit, you will usually score more via a penalty double than by bidding on. Redoubles suggest penalties.

AFTER THE DOUBLE OF PARTNER'S 1NT RESPONSE

The double of a 1NT *response* is commonly played as a takeout double these days (see page 70). For example, 1♡ : (No) : 1NT : (Double) is used as a takeout double of 1♡. Opener takes normal action here just if fourth player had passed 1NT. Redouble by opener indicates 16+ HCP, asks the responder to pass 1NT redoubled with any normal 1NT response and suggests penalties if either opponent bids again.

A. Partner opened 1♡, next player doubled. What action do you take, in the modern style, on these hands?

1. ♠ K 7 4 3	**2.** ♠ 7	**3.** ♠ A J 9 8 4	**4.** ♠ - - -	**5.** ♠ A Q 6 3
♡ A 2	♡ K 7 4 3	♡ 2	♡ K 8 4 3 2	♡ K 8 6 4
◇ A 9 8 4	◇ A 9 4 3	◇ A Q 10 2	◇ 8 6 4 3 2	◇ Q 7
♣ Q 6 3	♣ J 5 3 2	♣ 8 6 4	♣ K 7 5	♣ 9 8 3

B. Partner doubled their 1♡ opening and next player redoubled. What should you do now with these hands?

1. ♠ Q 9 5 2	**2.** ♠ 9 7	**3.** ♠ A Q 9 5 4	**4.** ♠ 8 6 3	**5.** ♠ A Q 6
♡ 7 6	♡ 6 5 3 2	♡ 6 4 3	♡ 7 4 3 2	♡ Q 7
◇ 8 5 3 2	◇ 6 4	◇ Q J 7	◇ Q 7 6	◇ Q 9 4 3
♣ 8 7 3	♣ 9 6 5 3 2	♣ 5 3	♣ 8 4 2	♣ K J 7 6

C. The bidding has been 1♡ : (Double) : Redouble : (1♠), back to opener. What should the opener do now?

1. ♠ A 7	**2.** ♠ A K 10 9	**3.** ♠ K 5 4	**4.** ♠ 7	**5.** ♠ 9
♡ A 9 7 4 3	♡ K Q 8 7 3	♡ A J 7 4 3	♡ K 9 8 6 4 2	♡ A K Q 8 6 3
◇ K Q 6 2	◇ 4	◇ K Q 3	◇ A Q J 6 3	◇ J 8 4
♣ 8 3	♣ J 10 2	♣ 9 2	♣ 4	♣ J 5 2

D. The bidding has been 1♠ : (Double) : Redouble : (2♡), No : (No) : back to you, the redoubler. What now?

1. ♠ 7	**2.** ♠ 8 6	**3.** ♠ 5 2	**4.** ♠ 7 2	**5.** ♠ 6
♡ A J 9 3	♡ Q J 4	♡ K 8 4	♡ 8 6 3	♡ 7 2
◇ K Q 7	◇ A 9 8 2	◇ A J 8 6	◇ A K 4 3	◇ A Q 8 3
♣ J 10 7 4 2	♣ K Q J 2	♣ Q J 7 4	♣ K Q J 4	♣ K Q 9 7 4 2

PARTNERSHIP BIDDING: How should these hands be bid? There is no bidding other than that given.

SET 55 – WEST	**SET 55 – EAST**	**SET 56 – WEST**	**SET 56 – EAST**
1. N doubles W's 1♡.	**1.** N doubles W's 1♡.	**1.** N doubles W's 1♣.	**1.** N doubles W's 1♣.
♠ 7 2	♠ 8 5	♠ K Q 7 4	♠ A 2
♡ A Q 7 6 2	♡ K 9 4 3	♡ 8 3	♡ K Q 9 6 5 2
◇ K 3	◇ A Q J 5	◇ A 2	◇ J 3
♣ K Q 8 4	♣ J 9 2	♣ A Q 9 3 2	♣ 8 6 4
2. S doubles E's 1♠.	**2.** S doubles E's 1♠.	**2.** N doubles W's 1◇.	**2.** N doubles W's 1◇.
♠ 9 7 6 4	♠ A K 8 5 2	♠ A Q 7 5	♠ 6 4
♡ 7	♡ A K 9 4	♡ 7	♡ A 9 6
◇ A K 4 3	◇ 7 6	◇ A K 8 6 4	◇ Q J 7 3 2
♣ 8 6 4 2	♣ 5 3	♣ K Q 3	♣ A 8 5
3. N doubles W's 1♣.	**3.** N doubles W's 1♣.	**3.** S doubles E's 1♣.	**3.** S doubles E's 1♣.
♠ 8 3	♠ K Q J	♠ A 9 7 4 2	♠ K 8
♡ A J 4 2	♡ 7 3	♡ 7 6 4	♡ K J 2
◇ 7 2	◇ Q 4 3	◇ Q 9 5	◇ 7 2
♣ A Q J 6 4	♣ K 8 5 3 2	♣ J 5	♣ A Q 7 6 3 2
4. N doubles W's 1♡.	**4.** N doubles W's 1♡.	**4.** N doubles W's 1♠.	**4.** N doubles W's 1♠.
South bids 2♣.	South bids 2♣.	South bids 2♡.	South bids 2♡.
♠ K J 8	♠ Q 9 5 2	♠ A Q J 6 4 3	♠ 8 7
♡ A Q 7 5 4	♡ 2	♡ 7 4	♡ J 3
◇ K 9 3 2	◇ A 6 4	◇ A J 4	◇ K 10 8 3
♣ 7	♣ A J 8 6 2	♣ 8 2	♣ A K Q 6 4
5. N doubles W's 1♠.	**5.** N doubles W's 1♠.	**5.** N doubles W's 1♠.	**5.** N doubles W's 1♠.
South bids 2◇.	South bids 2◇.	South bids 2♣.	South bids 2♣.
♠ A K 9 7 2	♠ 6 3	♠ K Q 8 7 3 2	♠ 5
♡ 7	♡ A Q 8 5 3	♡ A J 9 5 4	♡ K 10 8 2
◇ K Q 10 6	◇ 7 2	◇ J 2	◇ A 9 7 4
♣ J 6 2	♣ K Q 9 3	♣ - - -	♣ A 7 4 3

PLAY HANDS ON BIDDING OVER AN OPPOSITION TAKEOUT DOUBLE

Hand 105: Truscott 2NT – Defensive technique – Signalling with a queen – Cashing out

Dealer North : East-West vulnerable

NORTH
♠ 4 3 2
♡ 4 2
◊ Q J 10 7 4
♣ 9 5 4

WEST
♠ K 10 7 6
♡ A Q J 6 5
◊ 9 3
♣ 7 2

EAST
♠ A Q J 9 5
♡ K 8
◊ 6 5
♣ K J 10 6

SOUTH
♠ 8
♡ 10 9 7 3
◊ A K 8 2
♣ A Q 8 3

WEST	NORTH	EAST	SOUTH
	No	1♠	Dble
2NT (1)	No (2)	4♠ (3)	All pass

Bidding: (1) 10+ HCP plus support for opener's suit.
(2) Not strong enough for 3 ◊ .
(3) East with 16 points, six losers, is better than minimum. Either way East is worth game opposite the 2NT values.

Lead: ◊ A. An A-K suit is attractive. It lets you see dummy, partner's signal and decide whether to continue or whether to switch. On a spade or a heart lead, East wins, draws trumps and discards two diamond losers and a club on the hearts.

Correct play: If South continues with the ◊ K at trick 2, East will discard three club losers on the hearts after trumps are drawn and lose only two diamonds and one club.

It does not help South to switch to ♣ A at trick 3. To defeat 4 ♠ , the defence must take two diamonds and two clubs before declarer comes in. To do this North must play a club through East. To help South find the defence, North signals with the *queen* of diamonds on the ◊ A lead. The Q-signal on the ace promises the jack or the queen is a singleton. In either case, it tells partner you will win if partner leads low, away from the king. Either you have the jack or you will ruff. Do not signal with the queen from Q-doubleton (except Q-J doubleton). The defence goes: ◊ A lead, ◊ Q from North; ◊ 2 from South, North's ◊ 10 wins; North shifts to the ♣ 5 – jack – queen, ♣ A cashed; one off. If North signalled with ◊ 10 on the ◊ A, South might lead a low diamond at trick 2, but the ◊ Q signal makes it easier.

Hand 106: The queen signal on the ace – Recognizing the danger of a ruff – The scissors coup

Dealer East : Game all

NORTH
♠ Q 10 5 2
♡ A 7 6
◊ 3
♣ A K 8 4 2

WEST
♠ 8 3
♡ K Q 10 8 3
◊ 10 7 5 4
♣ 10 5

EAST
♠ A K J
♡ J 9 5 2
◊ A K Q J
♣ 6 3

SOUTH
♠ 9 7 6 4
♡ 4
◊ 9 8 6 2
♣ Q J 9 7

WEST	NORTH	EAST	SOUTH
		1 ◊ (1)	No
1♡ (2)	Dble (3)	4♡ (4)	All pass

Bidding: (1) Not quite enough to open 2NT.
(2) Too good to pass. Bid 1 ♡ rather than support diamonds.
(3) Better to double with the unbid suits than to overcall 2♣ .
(4) With 20 points in support of hearts, East is worth game.

Lead: ♣ A. An A-K suit appeals greatly.

Correct play: South should signal with the *queen* of clubs under the ♣ A. On seeing that, North should switch to the singleton ◊ 3 at trick 2. This is North's plan: If declarer leads a trump, North takes the ♡ A, leads a low club to South and South returns a diamond for North to ruff, one down.

If the ♣ Q were singleton, this defence would still work as long as South started with two hearts: South ruffs when North leads a low club and gives North a diamond ruff. Declarer should realize what is happening after the ♣ Q signal and the switch to diamonds, an obvious singleton. Declarer can do nothing if South has the ♡ A entry, but might be able to remove the club entry via a loser-on-loser play. Win the ◊ A at trick 2 and play ♠ A, ♠ K and lead the ♠ J. When South follows low on the ♠ J, discard your club (loser-on-loser). North wins the ♠ Q, but South can no longer gain the lead. Declarer later forces out the ♡ A and draws trumps, losing one spade, one heart and one club. This technique is called the 'scissors coup' because it *cuts* the communications (entries) between the defenders.

Hand 107: Truscott 2NT – Using a strip-and-throw-in to avoid tackling Q-x-x opposite J-x-x

Dealer South : Love all

NORTH
- ♠ K Q 6 5
- ♡ 8 6 4
- ◊ Q 6 2
- ♣ A 9 3

WEST
- ♠ 10 9
- ♡ Q 10 7 5
- ◊ A 10 9
- ♣ K Q J 7

EAST
- ♠ 8
- ♡ J 9 2
- ◊ K 8 7 3
- ♣ 10 8 6 4 2

SOUTH
- ♠ A J 7 4 3 2
- ♡ A K 3
- ◊ J 5 4
- ♣ 5

WEST	NORTH	EAST	SOUTH
			1♠
Dble (1)	2NT (2)	No	4♠ (3)
No	No	No	

Bidding: (1) Just enough for a double.
(2) Truscott 2NT, showing 10+ HCP and support for opener.
(3) Only seven losers, suggesting a 3♠ rebid, but because of the extra trump length and the singleton, South is worth 4♠.

Lead: ♣K. Clearcut.

Correct play: There is a danger of losing three diamonds and one heart. Correct technique can limit the opposition to two diamond tricks by forcing an opponent to start the diamond suit or concede a ruff and discard.

Win the ♣A and ruff a club high. Cash a top spade and lead a spade to dummy, which draws trumps. Ruff dummy's last club, creating a void opposite a void. Then play ♡A, ♡K and exit with a heart. You have now 'stripped' the hearts also (void opposite void) and the third heart forces an opponent on lead ('throw in'). No matter who wins the third heart, declarer is safe. A heart or a club gives declarer a ruff and discard, while a diamond guarantees one diamond trick as long as declarer plays second hand low. If declarer starts diamonds, the defence can come to three diamonds, plus a heart. If the defence can be forced to start diamonds, declarer loses only two diamonds and a heart.

Hand 108: Sign-off after Truscott 2NT – Card combination – Throw-in to avoid guessing a finesse

Dealer West : East-West vulnerable

NORTH
- ♠ K J 6 4 3
- ♡ 8 6 3
- ◊ A 10 4
- ♣ A 8

WEST
- ♠ Q 10 8
- ♡ 10 9 7
- ◊ Q 8 6
- ♣ 10 7 5 4

EAST
- ♠ - - -
- ♡ K Q J 2
- ◊ 9 7 5 2
- ♣ K Q J 6 3

SOUTH
- ♠ A 9 7 5 2
- ♡ A 5 4
- ◊ K J 3
- ♣ 9 2

WEST	NORTH	EAST	SOUTH
No	1♠	Dble (1)	2NT (2)
No	3♠ (3)	No	4♠ (4)
No	No	No	

Bidding: (1) Much better to double than to overcall 2♣.
(2) Truscott 2NT, 10+ points with support for opener.
(3) Sign off with a minimum opening and no extra length and no singleton or void as compensation.
(4) South has enough to bid game despite opener's sign-off. Opening + opening = game. If South had a stronger hand and slam ambitions, South could continue with a cue-bid, as 2NT already agreed spades as trumps, or with 4NT for aces.

Lead: ♡K. With two sequences, lead the stronger, but with equal sequences, lead the shorter suit. On the actual hand, it is immaterial whether ♡K or ♣K is led. However, declarer or dummy figures to be shorter in clubs than in hearts. Therefore you are likely to take more tricks in hearts than in clubs.

Correct play: Win the ♡A. There is no benefit here in ducking. Cash the ♠A and when East shows out, finesse the ♠J and cash the ♠K to draw trumps. It would be an error to cash the ♠K first as a trump loser can be avoided only if trumps are 2-1 or West has Q-10-8. If Q-10-8 is with East, a trump loser is inevitable. If South held ♠A-10-7-5-2, so that there is a two-way finesse in spades, cashing the ♠A first would still be correct. East is more likely to be short in spades because of the takeout double.

After drawing trumps, cash the ♣A and exit with a heart or a club. After two hearts and one club, the defence must lead a diamond (thus eliminating a diamond loser if you play second-hand low) or give you a ruff and discard. Either way you lose only three tricks. Avoid the temptation of finessing against East for the ◊Q. The ◊Q is *likely* to be with East because of the double, but the throw-in play makes game a *certainty*.

CHAPTER 28

COMPETING AFTER A 1NT OPENING

THEY OPEN 1NT – YOUR ACTIONS

1. DOUBLE: It is standard to play a double of their 1NT opening for penalties. After a weak 1NT opening (12-14, 12-15 or 13-15 points), the strength for a double should be 15+ HCP. With a long, strong suit and 7+ potential winners, you may double with fewer than 15 HCP. A suitable holding might be a suit such as K-Q-J-10-8-4-2 and an outside ace. With a solid suit, such as A-K-Q-J-x or better, but fewer than seven winners, pass. Do not double and do not bid your suit in second seat. You have ideal defence and you are on lead against no-trumps. If third player bids and a no-trumps contract no longer seems likely, bid your solid suit later, if you can do so at a convenient level. For example, with ♠A K Q J 7 2 ♡8 6 ◇7 4 3 ♣6 2, you would pass RHO's 1NT opening. If the bidding continues (1NT) : No : (2♡) : No, (No) to you, you should bid 2♠. Likewise, if responder had bid 2♣ Stayman and the 1NT opener rebid 2♡, it would be opportune to bid 2♠ now. It is clear that third player was certainly not looking for a spade fit and if you do not bid 2♠, 2♡ might end the bidding. Again, if responder had bid 2◇ as a transfer to 2♡ and opener duly bid 2♡, you should bid 2♠. While the bidding might continue to a higher level, there is too great a risk that 2♡ will be the contract if you pass.

In fourth seat, after (1NT) : No : (No), double is still for penalties, but it should be based on the 15+ HCP hand. Since you are not on lead, it is too risky to double with just a long, strong suit and one or two entries if your suit needs to be set up. Partner is unlikely to lead your long suit and declarer might make seven tricks before your long suit is established. Your entries could be knocked out and you might be unable to regain the lead later when your suit is established. Holding ♠A 9 3 ♡8 2 ◇K Q J 8 7 4 2 ♣6 in fourth seat, bid 2◇ or 3◇, according to vulnerability. Similarly, with a solid suit such as A-K-Q-J-x or better in fourth seat, bid the suit. You are not on lead and partner is bound to make a worse lead unless you indicate your suit.

After partner doubles 1NT, you normally pass with 6+ HCP, regardless of shape. However, with 9+ HCP and a 6+ major, you may score more in a major suit game. Jump to 3♡ or 3♠ with a 6-card major and 9+ HCP, and 4♡ or 4♠ with a 7-card suit (or a 6-card suit with four honours).

With 0-5 HCP, pass the double if your hand is balanced, but bid a 5+ suit if unbalanced. A 2-level suit bid after partner's penalty double is a very weak action. If third player redoubles, remove the redouble on any hand with 0-5 points. If they make 1NT redoubled (quite probable if your hand is so weak), they score a game. It is usually better to concede a penalty at the 2-level than to let them make 1NT redoubled. In addition, redoubled overtricks score very heavily. See Chapter 32 on the S.O.S. Redouble for further information on this and related areas.

2. BIDDING A MAJOR AT THE 2-LEVEL: This shows a powerful 5-card suit or a strong 6-card suit. The suit needs to conform to the Suit Quality Test (see Chapter 9, page 50). The strength is about 9-14 HCP and good playing strength: 5½-6 tricks if not vulnerable (7-7½ losers) *or* 6-6½ playing tricks vulnerable (6½-7 losers) *or* 7-7½ playing tricks when vulnerable against not vulnerable (six losers or better). A raise is invitational. A new suit is strong (not a rescue) and is forcing (except if third player doubled the 2-Major bid for penalties). 2NT is strong and encouraging, but shows only doubleton support.

3. BIDDING A SUIT AT THE 3-LEVEL: The suit will be a broken 6+ suit. With a solid suit, prefer to defend against no-trumps. The hand will have about 9-14 HCP and should contain 6½-7 playing tricks not vulnerable, 7-7½ playing tricks vulnerable and 8-8½ tricks at adverse vulnerability.

4. JUMPS TO 4♡ OR 4♠: These are based on playing strength and at least a strong 7+ suit. The basic minimums are 7½ tricks not vulnerable, 8+ tricks vulnerable and 8½+ tricks at adverse vulnerability.

5. 2NT OVER THEIR 1NT: This shows a freak 2-suiter, at least a 5-5 pattern and no more than three losers. It may contain any two suits, not just the minors. Bidding continues until at least game.

6. 2♣ OR 2♢ OVER 1NT: There are many possible uses for 2♣ and 2♢. You and partner need to agree on which method the partnership should adopt. Possibilities include:

(a) Natural overcalls: In this case, the hand type is the same as bidding a major at the 2-level. See #2 above.

(b) 2♣ for the majors – The Landy Convention: In this method, (1NT) : 2♣ shows at least 5-4 in the majors. The strength is about 8-14 HCP, but at the lower end, the pattern should be at least 5-5. Partner chooses the major where longer support is held. Bid hearts with equal support. With a total misfit, you may pass 2♣ with 6+ clubs or bid 2♢ with 6+ diamonds. With game chances, jump to 3♡ or 3♠ to invite game with 4+ support. A 2NT response to 2♣ is strong and asks for further information. A sensible structure of replies to 2NT could be: 3♣: any minimum (then 3♢ asks for the longer major, bid 3NT if 5-5); 3♢: maximum with 5-5 in the majors; 3♡ or 3♠: maximum with 5+ cards in the suit bid.

(c) The Astro Convention: In this method, 2♣ shows hearts and another suit, 2♢ shows spades and a minor suit, 2♡ and 2♠ are natural bids, while 2NT is a freakish two-suiter, forcing to game.

Over 2♣, 2♡ is a sign-off and 3♡ is invitational. 2♢ asks for partner's cheaper 5-card suit and partner can pass 2♢ with 5+ diamonds. 2NT over 2♣ is artificial, strong, asking for partner's second suit. Similarly over 2♢, advancer's 2♡ is a non-forcing enquiry for the cheaper 5-card suit and 2NT is a strong relay.

Other methods exist over 1NT and no method is wholly satisfactory. You and partner need to settle in advance the methods you will adopt. The Astro Convention is the best of the above.

7. AFTER THIRD PLAYER RESPONDS TO 1NT

(a) Stayman: After (1NT) : No : (2♣), fourth player should double to show a strong 5+ club holding. It asks partner to lead a club. The club suit should contain three of the four top honours, at least K-Q-J-x-x. After 1NT : (No) : 2♣ : (Double), opener should make the normal reply to Stayman if holding a stopper in clubs and should pass with no stopper in clubs. If opener passes, a redouble by the 2♣ bidder asks opener to make the normal reply. This allows the partnership to avoid a silly 3NT when the club suit is wide open.

(b) Other artificial bids: Double of an artificial response by third player shows a strength in the suit bid. For example, (1NT) : No : (2♡ Transfer) : Double shows strong hearts. Partner should lead the suit doubled.

(c) Natural bids: Double of a natural bid is for takeout in the direct seat or the pass-out seat. For example, (1NT) : No : (2♡) : Double or (1NT) : No : (2♡) : No, (No) : Double. Both doubles are for takeout.

YOUR SIDE OPENS 1NT – THEY INTERVENE

1. They double your 1NT: After a penalty double, your first concern is self-preservation and all suit bids at the 2-level are natural. They show a weak hand and a 5+ suit. In particular, 1NT : (Double) : 2♣ = 5+ clubs and is *not* Stayman. With 1NT 12-14, you should redouble with 10+ HCP, since your side has more strength than theirs. You will thus make 1NT redoubled more often than not, and if they flee to a suit at the 2-level, you and partner should be alert for penalty doubles. Jumps to the 3-level over a penalty double are based on 9-11 HCP and a 6+ suit. With a fit *and* a maximum, opener should bid on. With a freak 2-suiter and game chances more profitable than penalties, bid 2NT over the double. Subsequent bidding is natural, showing the suits held, until the best fit is found.

2. They intervene with a natural suit bid, e.g., 1NT : (2♢)

(a) *Suit bids at the 2-level are competitive and non-forcing.* The strength is about 7-10 points. Opener may raise responder's suit with a fit *and* maximum values.

(b) *A minor suit bid at the 3-level lower-ranking than their suit is not forcing,* e.g., 1NT : (2♢) : 3♣.

(c) *A major suit at the 3-level is forcing.* For example, 1NT : (2♠) : 3♡ is forcing and shows a 5-card suit.

(d) *Jumps to game are normal.* The jump to 3NT does *not* promise a stopper in their suit. No stopper is needed since their suit will not be solid (they would pass and defend with a solid suit). Therefore, opener figures to hold the missing honours and thus has a stopper in their suit. While a stopper in opener's hand is not guaranteed, this is a sound working assumption. Do not be afraid of bidding 3NT with no stopper.

(e) *Double is for penalties.* With 9+ HCP *and* a strong 4-card holding in their suit, be quick to double.

(f) *2NT is invitational, as usual.* As with 3NT, the 2NT response need not contain a stopper in their suit.

(g) *Bidding the enemy suit is Stayman and forces to game.* For example, 1NT : (2♡) : 3♡ promises four spades and 1NT : (2♠) : 3♠ shows four hearts. For 1NT : (2♣) : 3♣ or 1NT : (2◊) : 3◊ responder has at least one 4-card major. Opener now bids a 4-card major or bids 3NT with no major. With both majors, bid 3♡. Responder will raise to 4♡ with support or bid 3NT with four spades. Over this 3NT, opener bids 4♠ with four spades or passes 3NT with 2-3 spades. Responder promised a major by bidding the enemy suit and 3NT denies hearts. Note that 1NT : (2♣) : Double is for penalties, not Stayman.

3. They intervene with an artificial suit bid

(a) *Double is for penalties.* The double suggests a desire to play for penalties in the suit(s) actually shown.
(b) *Bidding the artificial suit is natural and non-forcing.* For example, 1NT : (2◊ Transfer) : 3◊ shows real diamonds and is not Stayman. A 5-card or longer suit is promised and about 9-11 HCP. If their overcall is natural, bidding that suit is artificial. If their overcall is artificial, bidding that suit is natural.
(c) *Bidding the suit actually shown is artificial, game-forcing and replaces Stayman.* For example, after 1NT : (2♣), if 2♣ shows hearts and a minor, 2♡ by responder is artificial and takes the place of Stayman. Similarly, after 1NT : (2♡), if 2♡ is a transfer showing 5+ spades, 2♠ by responder replaces Stayman.
(d) Other actions have the same meaning as over a natural overcall.

A. Partner opened 1NT and next player overcalled a natural 2♡. What action do you take on these hands?

1. ♠ A	2. ♠ A Q 7 2	3. ♠ K J 8 6 4 3	4. ♠ A Q 6	5. ♠ A 9 7 4 3
♡ K 10 8 3	♡ 7 4	♡ 7 2	♡ 6 4 2	♡ 6
◊ 9 7 4 2	◊ K 9 3	◊ 8 6	◊ K Q 3	◊ A 8 5
♣ K 6 4 3	♣ A 8 5 4	♣ Q J 2	♣ Q 8 4 2	♣ K J 5 2

B. Partner opened 1NT and next player bid 2♡, an artificial transfer, showing 5+ spades. Your action?

1. ♠ 8 7	2. ♠ 9 3	3. ♠ A J 8 7	4. ♠ 9 7 2	5. ♠ 6
♡ K 4	♡ A Q 6 2	♡ K 8 7 2	♡ J 4 3	♡ A Q J 7 4 3
◊ K 3 2	◊ K 8	◊ 7	◊ A K 8 6	◊ A 9 4 2
♣ Q J 8 7 4 2	♣ K J 4 3 2	♣ Q 9 4 2	♣ K Q 4	♣ 6 2

PARTNERSHIP BIDDING: West is the dealer on all hands. Bid the hands with the interference given. All bids by North or South are natural.

SET 57 – WEST	SET 57 – EAST	SET 58 – WEST	SET 58 – EAST
1. South bids 2♡.	**1.** South bids 2♡.	**1.** North bids 2♡.	**1.** North bids 2♡.
♠ K J 9 8 4	♠ 10 7 3	♠ K 8 6 4	♠ Q J 5 2
♡ K 5	♡ J 3	♡ A J	♡ 8 7 2
◊ 9 6 5 3	◊ K Q 7 2	◊ 9 8 7	◊ A Q
♣ 6 4	♣ A K 10 3	♣ A Q 3 2	♣ K J 6 4
2. North bids 2◊.	**2.** North bids 2◊.	**2.** North bids 2◊.	**2.** North bids 2◊.
♠ A K J 4	♠ 8 7 2	♠ J 9 7 4	♠ A 3
♡ 8 7 5 4	♡ A Q 2	♡ A K 2	♡ Q J 8 7
◊ K 5 3	◊ 7	◊ 9 7 2	◊ A 5
♣ K 9	♣ Q J 10 7 4 3	♣ A J 5	♣ K 10 6 4 2
3. North bids 2♠.	**3.** North bids 2♠.	**3.** North bids 2◊.	**3.** North bids 2◊.
♠ A 9 7	♠ 8 2	♠ J 8	♠ K Q 7 5
♡ A Q 3	♡ K J	♡ K 10 7 4	♡ A 8
◊ Q 7 5	◊ A K 6 4 3 2	◊ A K 6	◊ 8 3 2
♣ Q 8 6 3	♣ J 5 2	♣ Q 7 4 2	♣ A J 9 6
4. South bids 2♡.	**4.** South bids 2♡.	**4.** North bids 2◊.	**4.** North bids 2◊.
♠ Q 9 2	♠ A J 7	♠ Q 9 6 2	♠ A J 7 4
♡ A J 8 7	♡ 9 3 2	♡ 8 7 5 3	♡ A K
◊ 3	◊ A K 5 4	◊ K 7	◊ 9 3 2
♣ K 6 5 3 2	♣ J 7 4	♣ A K J	♣ Q 9 4 3

PLAY HANDS ON COMPETING OVER 1NT

Hand 109: Coping with interference over 1NT – Throw-in to increase chances of a vital finesse

	Dealer North : Game all		

Dealer North : Game all

```
              NORTH
              ♠ A J 3
              ♡ K 9 8 6
              ◊ A 7
              ♣ Q 4 3 2
WEST                        EAST
♠ 10 8 5 4                  ♠ Q 7 6
♡ 5 3                       ♡ A 4 2
◊ Q 8 5                     ◊ K J 10 9 6 4
♣ J 10 9 7                  ♣ 8
              SOUTH
              ♠ K 9 2
              ♡ Q J 10 7
              ◊ 3 2
              ♣ A K 6 5
```

WEST	NORTH	EAST	SOUTH
	1NT	2 ◊ (1)	3 ◊ (2)
Dble (3)	3 ♡ (4)	No	4 ♡ (5)
No	No	No	

Bidding: (1) Just enough for 2 ◊ vulnerable because of the good suit quality.

(2) Bid the enemy suit when you would have used Stayman.

(3) Double of an artificial bid asks partner to lead that suit.

(4) Answering Stayman.

(5) 3NT could be defeated on a diamond lead even if clubs were 3-2 and the spade finesse worked. 4 ♡ can be made even though clubs are 4-1 and the ♠Q is offside.

Lead: ♣8 or ◊ J. The ♣8 is better, looking for a ruff if West holds the ◊ A, distinctly possible after the double of 3 ◊ .

Correct play: North wins with the ♣Q and leads a low heart. East wins the first or second heart and switches to the ◊ J, taken by North. Trumps are drawn and the top clubs are cashed. When the clubs split 4-1, declarer has a loser in clubs, diamonds and hearts. Declarer cannot afford a spade loser as well. The simple line is to finesse the ♠J, a 50% line. A superior move is to exit with a diamond. If East wins, the hand is over: East leads a spade into North's A-J-3 or concedes a ruff and discard. If West wins the diamond exit, West cashes a club and then leads a low spade (a diamond gives a ruff and discard). North plays low from hand and East must insert the queen to beat dummy's nine. If the ♠Q and ♠10 were reversed, East's ♠10 would be taken by the king and then the ♠J finessed. Forcing West to lead a spade increases the chances of no spade loser from 50% to 75%. If West exits with ♠10, North plays the ♠J to ensure no loser.

Hand 110: Interference over 1NT – Elimination and throw-in to force a ruff and discard

Dealer West : Love all

```
              NORTH
              ♠ Q 10 8
              ♡ A K 9 6 5 3
              ◊ 9
              ♣ J 10 2
WEST                        EAST
♠ J 5 4 2                   ♠ A K 9 6 3
♡ Q 8                       ♡ 7 2
◊ A 7 4 3                   ◊ K 8 6 2
♣ A Q 4                     ♣ K 7
              SOUTH
              ♠ 7
              ♡ J 10 4
              ◊ Q J 10 5
              ♣ 9 8 6 5 3
```

WEST	NORTH	EAST	SOUTH
1NT	2 ♡ (1)	3 ♠ (2)	No
4 ♠ (3)	No	No	No

Bidding: (1) Certainly worth 2 ♡ not vulnerable.

(2) Forcing to game with five spades, just like 1NT : 3 ♠ with no overcall.

(3) 3NT fails even if West wins with the ♡Q on a low heart lead by North.

Lead: ♡ J. Partner's suit and top card from J-10-x.

Correct play: After taking two heart tricks, North should shift to the ◊ 9. Declarer wins and plays ♠A, ♠K. When South shows out, leave North with the ♠Q – do not play a third spade yet. Cash the ♣K, lead a club to the ace and discard a diamond on the ♣Q. Hearts and clubs have been stripped – you are void in each suit in both hands.

Now play your other top diamond. If North ruffs, North must give you a ruff and discard. If North discards on the top diamond, do not play another diamond. You have lost two hearts and you are bound to lose a spade – you cannot afford to lose a diamond as well. The solution is to throw North in with a spade. Out of diamonds, North has to give you a ruff and discard. You ruff in dummy and discard the last diamond from hand. Make sure you do not ruff in hand, for that still leaves you with a diamond loser. The recommended line also works if North began with a doubleton diamond. Make sure you strip the clubs before you play the second diamond, else North can ruff the second diamond and exit safely with a club.

Hand 111: Bidding the enemy suit as Stayman – Setting up a long suit – Keeping the danger hand off lead

Dealer South : North-South vulnerable

	WEST	NORTH	EAST	SOUTH

NORTH
- ♠ J 9 4 2
- ♡ 10
- ◇ A Q 4
- ♣ A K 8 6 3

WEST
- ♠ A 7
- ♡ K 9 8 6 5 3 2
- ◇ 8 2
- ♣ Q 9

EAST
- ♠ Q 10 8 6
- ♡ Q 7
- ◇ 10 9 7 5
- ♣ J 10 5

SOUTH
- ♠ K 5 3
- ♡ A J 4
- ◇ K J 6 3
- ♣ 7 4 2

WEST	NORTH	EAST	SOUTH
			1NT
2♡ (1)	3♡ (2)	Dble (3)	3NT (4)
No	No	No	

Bidding: (1) With seven losers, this is worth only 2♡ despite the 7-card suit and the favourable vulnerability.
(2) Forcing to game and Stayman enquiry.
(3) Lead-directing. Shows a top honour in hearts.
(4) Denies four spades and confirms hearts are stopped. With no heart stopper and no four spades, South would pass the double and leave it to North to decide what to do next.

Lead: ♡ 6. Especially after partner's lead-directing double.

Correct play: South must capture East's ♡ Q with the ace. If South ducks, East continues hearts and West's hearts are set up, with the ♠ A as entry. South could then be held to seven tricks. After the ♡ A, South must prevent East from gaining the lead. It is disastrous to play ♣ A, ♣ K and a third club. East is in and a heart lead through South's J-4 gives West six heart tricks. However, South's ♡ J-4 operates as a stopper against West. After the ♡ A, lead a low club. If West plays the ♣ 9, take the ace. Do *not* cash the ♣ K. Return to hand with a diamond to the ace and lead another club. When West plays the ♣ Q, leave West on lead. You would also duck the first round of clubs if West plays the ♣ Q. With West on lead, you are safe and you now make at least one heart, four diamonds and four clubs. An overtrick is yours if West cashes ♡ K or ♠ A.

Hand 112: Coping with interference over 1NT – Keeping the danger hand off lead

Dealer West : East-West vulnerable

NORTH
- ♠ A Q 9 6 5 3
- ♡ 8 7
- ◇ K Q 2
- ♣ J 7

WEST
- ♠ K J 10
- ♡ K J 4 3
- ◇ 8 7 5
- ♣ A 9 2

EAST
- ♠ 4 2
- ♡ A Q 5
- ◇ A 6 3
- ♣ K 10 6 4 3

SOUTH
- ♠ 8 7
- ♡ 10 9 6 2
- ◇ J 10 9 4
- ♣ Q 8 5

WEST	NORTH	EAST	SOUTH
1NT	2♠ (1)	3NT (2)	All pass

Bidding: (1) The spades are not strong enough to justify 3♠, despite the favourable vulnerability.
(2) Enough for game and 3NT is the only attractive game. 3♣ is out, as that is not forcing. 3♠ is unsuitable, since that would be Stayman and you are not looking for a 4-4 major fit. 3NT is not 100% safe, but it is a sound practical bid. With solid spades, North would pass and defend 1NT. Therefore, North's spades are not solid and the 1NT opening is highly likely to include a spade stopper. 4♡ would be defeated easily on the ◇ K lead.

Lead: ♠ 6. This is the best chance, hoping that partner can gain the lead early and lead a spade back. The ◇ K is a reasonable second choice.

Correct play: Win trick 1 with the ♠ J. It is clear that North's spades are headed by the A-Q. You must develop club tricks, but you cannot afford to let South in. ♣ A, club to the king and a third club would be a disaster. South wins and a spade through your K-10 is curtains. It is not good enough to play ♣ A and then a low club, planning to duck if North plays the ♣ Q. With ♣ Q-x, North could pitch the ♣ Q under the ace to avoid coming on lead. The best chance is the ♡ 3 to the ace and a low club back, finessing the 9. This works whenever clubs are 3-2 and the ♣ Q and ♣ J are split, whenever North has ♣ Q-J-x or longer and whenever South holds a singleton honour. It fails if South has ♣ Q-J-x or longer, but then nothing works. On this line North wins the club with the jack, but a spade lead *by North* gives you an extra trick. If North exits with the ◇ K, take the ◇ A, play a club to the ace and cash three more clubs. You make ten tricks. (If North leads ◇ K originally and continues with the ◇ Q, duck the first two diamonds and later play the clubs as above.)

CHAPTER 29

RE-OPENING THE BIDDING

When the bidding is at a low level and it goes No : (No) to you, there are many situations where it is unsound to pass, even with the most modest values. Finding an action in the pass-out seat is known as 'balancing', 'protecting' or 're-opening the bidding', for if you pass, the auction is over.

1. (1NT) : No : (No) to you. Bid in this auction only if you would have bid in the direct seat. There is no urgency to compete against 1NT and it is not advisable to balance with light values or weak suits. Any action taken over 1NT in fourth seat has the same meaning as that action in the direct seat.

2. (1-suit) : No : (1NT) : No, (No) to you. Again it is not worthwhile finding heroic bids here on light values and weak suits. The balancing double of a 1NT response indicates about 13-15 points and strength in opener's suit. It suggests penalties, but partner can remove the double with a long suit. It does not demand the lead of opener's suit, but such a lead is acceptable if partner has no good, long suit available.

If the bidding has started (1 ◇) : No : (1NT) : No, (No) to you, it is reasonable to bid a 6-card major, one which is too weak for an immediate overcall, such as J-x-x-x-x-x or x-x-x-x-x-x. Do not back in with 2 ♣ in this auction, however. The 1NT responder is marked with length in clubs because of the failure to bid a major or raise diamonds. Consequently, a re-opening 2 ♣ risks a hefty penalty.

3. (1-suit) : No : (No) to you: With length and strength in the suit opened, pass and defend, but otherwise you should be reluctant to pass. Find some action or other, even on slender values.

(a) *Overcall a suit at the 1-level:* A 5+ suit need not conform to the Suit Quality Test (see page 50) and a strong 4-card suit is also acceptable. The strength may be as little as 7 HCP.

(b) *Overcall a suit at the 2-level:* The Suit Quality Test does not apply, but a 5+ suit is expected. The hand should contain at least 9 HCP, a fraction less than the normal 2-level overcall.

(c) *Jump-overcalls.* Even if you use weak jump-overcalls in the direct seat, they are not appropriate in the pass-out seat. A hand with 11-15 HCP and a good 6+ suit is suitable for a fourth seat jump-overcall. If the suit qualifies via the Suit Quality Test, it is strong enough for a fourth seat jump-overcall.

(d) *1NT and 2NT in fourth seat:* There are several different structures and the partnership should choose the method preferred. For maximum action with reasonable safety, method (i) is recommended.

(i) 1NT is 9-12 points balanced. 2NT is 17-18 points balanced, with a stopper in their suit. The unusual 2NT does not apply in fourth seat after two passes. With 13-16 points balanced, double, and with 19+ balanced, double and jump-bid in no-trumps later. One advantage of this method is that a fourth seat double will have good shape if it contains less than 13 HCP.

(ii) 1NT is 11-14 points, balanced, with a stopper in their suit. With no stopper, double. Below 11 points, pass or double. Bid 2NT with 19-20 points balanced. With 15-18 points balanced, double first and rebid 1NT if no fit is found. If partner bids at the 2-level, pass with 15-16 and rebid 2NT with 17-18. With 21+ points and balanced, double first and jump-rebid in no-trumps.

(iii) 1NT is 11-16, balanced and 2NT is 17-18 balanced. A 2 ♣ reply to 1NT asks for partner's range and a reply of 2 ◇ or 2 ♡ or 2 ♠ shows 11-12 points, 2NT shows 13-14 and 3-level rebids show 15-16.

(iv) 1NT is 15-18 points balanced, much the same as a 1NT overcall in the direct seat. One advantage of this approach is that you do not need to learn a new set of point ranges for overcalling 1NT, but it also means that you are likely to sell out at the 1-level with 9-10 point hands when both sides can make a low contract. However, until you are confident in other areas of your system, it is not a bad idea to have the same range in second seat and fourth seat. If so, bid 2NT with 19-20 balanced. Below 15 or above 20, double first.

Each of the above methods can present problems and gaps. None is perfect, but whichever 1NT range you select, other than (iii), a 2 ♣ reply should be Stayman, 2-level suit replies are weak and jumps force to game.

(e) *Double in fourth seat:* The double includes all the hands usually covered by a takeout double in second seat, plus the hands not covered by the 1NT and 2NT re-openings in (d). As you are anxious not to sell out at the 1-level, your fourth-seat doubles can easily drop to 10 HCP or even 9 HCP with good shape. Partner should be conservative in making a jump-reply to a fourth-seat double when holding only a weak 4-card suit.

The desire to compete creates a loss of accuracy and definition after a fourth-seat double. It is quite normal to take action in fourth seat on hands with 2-3 HCP less than required in the direct seat. If in doubt, *bid.*

(f) *Bidding their suit in fourth seat:* This can be used as a game-force takeout, even though it might be used as a weak 2-suiter in the direct seat (Michaels Convention). If the bidding has stopped at the 1-level, you have no need for pre-empts or unusual weak 2-suiter re-openings. The hand probably belongs to you.

4. You open, LHO bids a suit, passed back to you: For example, 1 ◊ : (1 ♠) : No : (No) to you. If LHO's overcall was at the 1-level or 2-level, you should be reluctant to pass, unless you have length and strength in the suit overcalled. If LHO made a strong jump-overcall, you may pass. You may also pass any jump-overcall to the 3-level – bid again only with extra values. If LHO made an *intermediate* jump-overcall and you hold K-x-x or Q-x-x or better in that suit, pass unless you have better than a minimum opening. On all other hand types, be quick to compete – do not sell out.

With any ordinary competing hand, re-open with a double. It is the most efficient and most flexible action. A new suit, lower-ranking, normally implies a 5-5 pattern, e.g., 1 ◊ : (1 ♠) : No : (No), 2 ♣. Re-opening with 1NT shows 17-19 points, the values for a jump-rebid in 1NT, e.g., 1 ◊ : (1 ♠) : No : (No), 1NT.

5. They open, you overcall, LHO raises opener's suit and this is passed back to you: For example, (1 ♡) : 1 ♠ : (2 ♡) : No, (No) to you. With most hands worth another action, compete via a takeout double. To repeat your suit, you should have at least a 6-card suit. A new suit, lower ranking, usually indicates a 5-5 pattern. Be wary of doubling with strength in their suit if unable to stand a particular new suit by partner. A double would be misguided in the above auction if you could not handle a 3 ◊ reply. Double would be all right if you were short in clubs and could bid 3 ◊ over an unwelcome 3 ♣ response from partner.

6. They bid and raise a suit to the 2-level, passed back to you: For example, (1 ♠) : No : (2 ♠) : No, (No) to you. Be reluctant to sell out when they find a fit and stop at the 2-level. In these situations, it is almost always correct to compete, even on very light values and even when vulnerable. Your options are:

Delayed overcall: This promises a 5+ suit not good enough for an immediate overcall.

Delayed double: Promises any unbid major and tolerance for other unbid suits. Will be less than 12 HCP as you did not double on the previous round.

Delayed 2NT: This cannot be a strong, balanced hand, as you would have bid earlier. It promises 4-4 or more in the minor suits. It could be 5-5 in the minors, but this is not likely, as you did not use the unusual 2NT on the first round. It will not contain four cards in an unbid major, since you would prefer to double with that.

Whichever delayed action you choose, partner will be conscious of the limited nature of your values because of your failure to bid on the first round. Accordingly, partner will not compete beyond the 3-level.

7. Other competitive situations: Whenever the auction reveals that the opponents have a primary trump fit and the bidding is dying out at the 2-level, you should be reluctant to sell out. Under these conditions, your partnership should use takeout doubles and the unusual 2NT even on minimal values.

WEST	NORTH	EAST	SOUTH	
1 ♡	Double	No	2 ♠	What action should East take with J-x-x-x-x in each minor and nothing more? Rather than sell out, bid 2NT, which must be for the minors. You would have bid 1NT earlier with 6-9 balanced or redoubled with 10+ points.
No	No	?		

WEST	NORTH	EAST	SOUTH	
1 ♡	1 ♠	2 ♡	2 ♠	Almost regardless of values, East should compete to 3 ♡. It is tactically unsound to pass. If you have only 3-card support for hearts, bid a new suit with 5-6 cards. The meek may inherit the earth but they lose at bridge!
No	No	?		

Once the bidding is at the 3-level, pass and defend with most hands where you have only an 8-card trump fit, but bid 3-over-their-3 with a 9-card trump fit. Do not compete a part-score to the 4-level.

A. You opened 1 ◇, LHO overcalled 1 ♡, passed back to you. What action do you take in the pass-out seat?

1. ♠ K 7 6 3	**2.** ♠ K 9 8 6	**3.** ♠ 7	**4.** ♠ K 7 2	**5.** ♠ 2
♡ 7	♡ 6 2	♡ A K 9 2	♡ A Q J	♡ 6
◇ A Q 8 5	◇ A Q 7 5	◇ 8 7 6 4 3 2	◇ A K 8 6	◇ K Q 9 4 3 2
♣ A K 4 3	♣ A K 2	♣ A Q	♣ Q 9 7	♣ A Q J 6 4

B. You opened 1 ♡, LHO overcalled 2 ♣, passed back to you. What action do you take in the pass-out seat?

1. ♠ K 7 3	**2.** ♠ A 7 2	**3.** ♠ A	**4.** ♠ A Q 7 2	**5.** ♠ 7 2
♡ A Q 8 6 2	♡ A Q 8 5 4 2	♡ A K J 8 7	♡ A J 9 8 6 2	♡ A J 9 7 2
◇ Q J 6 4	◇ Q 9 7	◇ 9 3 2	◇ A 2	◇ A
♣ 3	♣ 2	♣ Q 8 5 4	♣ 7	♣ K Q 8 6 2

C. Partner opened 1 ♡, your RHO overcalled 2 ◇, passed back to opener who re-opened with a double, passed to you. What action do you take now with each of these hands?

1. ♠ Q 7 4	**2.** ♠ A 7 5 3 2	**3.** ♠ K 8	**4.** ♠ 9 7 2	**5.** ♠ 8 7 2
♡ 8 7 3 2	♡ 7	♡ J	♡ A J	♡ 6
◇ J 9 6 4	◇ 9 7 6 4	◇ 8 7 6 4	◇ K 8 6 2	◇ Q J 9 4 3
♣ 7 3	♣ 7 3 2	♣ J 9 8 5 4 2	♣ 9 7 5 2	♣ K 9 3 2

D. The bidding has been (1 ♠) : No : (2 ♠) : No, (No) to you. What action do you take with these hands?

1. ♠ 7	**2.** ♠ A 7 3 2	**3.** ♠ 2	**4.** ♠ 7 2	**5.** ♠ 7 2
♡ 7 6 4 3	♡ 8	♡ A J 5	♡ A J 9 2	♡ 6 2
◇ A Q 9 6	◇ Q 9 7 6	◇ Q 7 6 4 3	◇ Q 9 8 6 4 2	◇ Q J 9 4 3
♣ K J 7 3	♣ K 6 5 2	♣ J 8 5	♣ 7	♣ K Q 8 5

PARTNERSHIP BIDDING: How should these hands be bid? West is the dealer on each hand. All bids by North or South are natural, jump-overcalls are weak and there is no North-South bidding other than given.

SET 57 – WEST	SET 57 – EAST	SET 58 – WEST	SET 58 – EAST
1. North bids 2 ♣.	**1.** North bids 2 ♣.	**1.** South bids 1 ♠.	**1.** South bids 1 ♠.
♠ K 9 2	♠ Q 7 5 4 3	♠ 8 6	♠ A K 10 2
♡ A Q 8 7 4	♡ 2	♡ 9 8 6 4 3 2	♡ A 5
◇ K 8 6 3	◇ J 4 2	◇ J 8	◇ K 7 5
♣ 7	♣ Q 9 6 4	♣ 9 3 2	♣ K Q 8 6
2. South bids 2 ♡.	**2.** South bids 2 ♡.	**2.** North bids 1 ♠.	**2.** North bids 1 ♠.
♠ 5 2	♠ K Q 4 3	♠ A Q J	♠ 8 3 2
♡ A 6 3 2	♡ 8	♡ K Q 9	♡ 7 5
◇ 3	◇ A Q 8 7 5	◇ A K 4	◇ Q J 9 3 2
♣ J 10 7 5 3 2	♣ K 6 4	♣ 9 7 3 2	♣ A 6 5
3. North bids 2 ◇.	**3.** North bids 2 ◇.	**3.** South bids 2 ♡.	**3.** South bids 2 ♡.
♠ A Q 7 6 3	♠ 9	♠ 9 5	♠ A K 8 2
♡ K 5	♡ 9 8 4 2	♡ 8 7 4	♡ A 9
◇ K 9 8 4 2	◇ J 3	◇ Q 7	◇ A J 8 6 3 2
♣ 4	♣ Q 8 7 5 3 2	♣ Q 8 6 5 3 2	♣ 7
4. North opens 1 ♡.	**4.** North opens 1 ♡.	**4.** North opens 1 ♠.	**4.** North opens 1 ♠.
South raises to 2 ♡.	South raises to 2 ♡.	South raises to 2 ♠.	South raises to 2 ♠.
♠ A 4 2	♠ 8 6 5	♠ 9 4 3 2	♠ 6
♡ 9 7 4 3	♡ 2	♡ J 9 7 4 2	♡ Q 8 6 5
◇ A 8 7 2	◇ K 9 4 3	◇ K Q 3	◇ A 7 6 2
♣ Q 9	♣ K J 5 4 2	♣ Q	♣ K 10 3 2
5. North opens 1 ♠.	**5.** North opens 1 ♠.	**5.** North opens 1 ◇.	**5.** North opens 1 ◇.
South raises to 2 ♠.	South raises to 2 ♠.	South raises to 2 ◇.	South raises to 2 ◇.
♠ 8 7 5 2	♠ 4	♠ J 8 4	♠ A 6 3
♡ 6 4 2	♡ A J 9 3	♡ 3	♡ A J 10 7 4
◇ 3	◇ K Q 8 7 4	◇ A 7 5 2	◇ 8
♣ K 8 5 4 2	♣ A Q 6	♣ Q J 8 4 3	♣ K 6 5 2

PLAY HANDS ON RE-OPENING THE BIDDING

Hand 113: Coping with a bad trump break – Trump reduction – Management of entries

Dealer North : Love all

NORTH
♠ 4
♡ K Q 9 7 5
◇ 7 4 3 2
♣ A K Q

WEST
♠ A Q J 8 6 3
♡ 6
◇ K J 8
♣ J 6 2

EAST
♠ 10 9
♡ A J 4 3
◇ A Q 10
♣ 10 7 4 3

SOUTH
♠ K 7 5 2
♡ 10 8 2
◇ 9 6 5
♣ 9 8 5

WEST	NORTH	EAST	SOUTH
	1♡	No (1)	No (2)
2♠ (3)	No	3♠ (4)	No
4♠ (5)	No	No	No

Bidding: (1) Certainly not worth any action at this stage.
(2) Much too weak to respond.
(3) The jump-overcall in fourth seat shows a strong suit with a minimum opening hand.
(4) Enough to invite game. As West has shown six spades, prefer 3♠ to 2NT.
(5) Worth a shot at game since the spades are strong and the singleton is in their suit. Had West doubled initially, East would respond 2NT and again West would rebid 4♠.

Lead: ♣A. North naturally cashes the three club winners.

Correct play: After taking three clubs, North's natural continuation is the ♡K. The ace wins and, with no strong evidence to reject the spade finesse, the ♠10 is run and wins. Next comes the ♠9, also winning. When North shows out, it seems that South must win a trick with the ♠K. However, West can capture South's ♠K by *trump reduction technique.* Declarer's trumps must be reduced to the same length as South's and the lead must be in dummy at trick 11. So, ruff a heart, play a diamond to the ten, ruff another heart and lead a diamond to the queen. Lead dummy's 13th club (just in case South is now out of diamonds). If South ruffs, over-ruff and draw the last trump. If South discards, pitch your ◇K. There are only two cards left in each hand: lead either red card from dummy. South holds ♠K-7 and West has ♠A-Q and thus South's ♠K is trapped in this ending. (If North switches to a diamond at trick 4 or declines to cash three clubs and switches to a heart or a diamond, the same reduction technique is used after running the ♠10 and ♠9.)

Hand 114: Fourth seat bidding – Avoiding an over-ruff – Coping with a bad break – Trump reduction

Dealer East : North-South vulnerable

NORTH
♠ A K 6 2
♡ A K
◇ J 8 5 2
♣ A K 8

WEST
♠ 8 7 5 4 3
♡ 8
◇ 9 7
♣ 10 7 6 3 2

EAST
♠ Q J 10
♡ J 6 5 2
◇ A K Q 10
♣ Q 5

SOUTH
♠ 9
♡ Q 10 9 7 4 3
◇ 6 4 3
♣ J 9 4

WEST	NORTH	EAST	SOUTH
		1◇	No
No (1)	Dble (2)	No	1♡
No	2NT (3)	No	4♡ (4)
No	No	No	

Bidding: (1) It is unsound to bid when hopelessly weak, even though you are not keen on diamonds.
(2) Not quite strong enough to insist on game. Double is the best start. If partner bids spades, 4♠ would be a fair gamble.
(3) After 1♡, it is best to jump to 2NT to show around 21-22 points balanced, equivalent to a maximum 2NT opening.
(4) Exactly what you would bid over a 2NT opening and the double followed by a jump in no-trumps shows the values for a 2NT opening.

Lead: ◇9. Partner's suit and top from a doubleton.

Correct play: East wins as cheaply as possible and cashes two more diamonds. East continues with the fourth diamond, which would ensure defeat of 4♡ if West held the ♡10. South should ruff the fourth diamond with the ♡10 or ♡9. To ruff with the ♡Q and hope for the ♡J to fall has far less chance of success. When the heart ruff holds, South cashes the ♡A and ♡K. When West shows out, South must plan to trap East's ♡J-x via trump reduction: ♠A, ♠K (discard a club), ruff a spade, ♣A, ♣K and lead either black card from dummy at trick 12, when East has ♡J-6 and South has ♡Q-9 left.

Hand 115: Fourth-seat bidding – Card combination – Card-reading

Dealer South : North-South vulnerable

	WEST	NORTH	EAST	SOUTH
				1♡
NORTH	No	No (1)	Dble (2)	No
♠ 10 8 4	2◇	No	2♠ (3)	No
♡ A 5	3♣ (4)	No	4♠ (5)	All pass
◇ 9 7 5 4				
♣ 9 4 3 2				

WEST　　　　　　EAST
♠ 9 6 5　　　　♠ A Q J 7 3 2
♡ 9 7 2　　　　♡ 8 6 3
◇ A Q 10 3　　　◇ 6
♣ 8 6 5　　　　♣ A K Q

SOUTH
♠ K
♡ K Q J 10 4
◇ K J 8 2
♣ J 10 7

Bidding: (1) There is no shame in passing a weak hand.
(2) Too good for a jump to 2♠, which shows 6-7 losers.
(3) Double then new suit is still strong in the re-opening seat. 2♠ implies 5+ spades, 16+ points and 5-5½ losers.
(4) With 1½ quick tricks West is worth an invitation.
(5) With an extra spade and a shortage, East accepts the invitation, hoping West might hold shorter hearts.

Lead: ♡K. Obvious.

Correct play: North overtakes the ♡K with the ace and returns a heart. South wins and cashes the ♡Q.

South switches to a minor and declarer wins to start trumps. The normal play with this trump holding is to finesse the ♠Q, but here declarer should play the ♠A. When the ♠K falls, declarer's card reading is rewarded. Once North turned up with the ♡A, North could not hold the ♠K as well. That would give North 7 HCP and then North would not have passed 1♡. Once you place the ♠K with South, the spade finesse becomes futile. Play the ace and pray for the king to be singleton. If North lets the first heart go and wins ♡A at trick 2, declarer again has the information needed to reject the spade finesse. The best chance for declarer to go wrong is for South to lead ♡K and switch to a low diamond. If declarer takes the ◇A, declarer may misguess the spade position. However, declarer might finesse the ◇Q and discard a heart on the ◇A. Further, a canny declarer should ask why the defenders with hearts to cash, have been so eager to put declarer into dummy. A justifiably suspicious declarer would know the answer and cash the ♠A anyway.

Hand 116: Fourth-seat bidding – Strip and throw-in to avoid a finesse

Dealer West : Game all

	WEST	NORTH	EAST	SOUTH
	1♠	No	No (1)	Dble (2)
NORTH	No	2♡ (3)	No	4♡ (4)
♠ J 9 2	No	No	No	
♡ 10 9 4 3 2				
◇ 8 7 3				
♣ 7 2				

WEST　　　　　　EAST
♠ Q 10 8 6 5　　♠ 7 4 3
♡ A K　　　　　♡ 7
◇ K J 10　　　　◇ 6 5 4 2
♣ J 10 4　　　　♣ Q 9 8 6 3

SOUTH
♠ A K
♡ Q J 8 6 5
◇ A Q 9
♣ A K 5

Bidding: (1) Too weak to raise to 2♠. If East did bid 2♠, South would still double and raise 3♡ to 4♡.
(2) Best to start with a double and see what develops.
(3) You do not have to enjoy bidding – just do it.
(4) With five hearts and 23 HCP, a mere 3♡ would not do this justice.

Lead: 4♠. Partner's suit. Middle-up-down from three rags.

Correct play: Win with the ♠A and lead a trump. West wins the ♡K. If West cashes ♡A (best) and exits with a black suit, declarer cashes the top spades and clubs, ruffs a club in hand and ruffs a spade in dummy ('stripping').

With void opposite void in both black suits, declarer plays a low heart to the ten and a diamond, playing dummy's nine when East follows low. West wins and must return a diamond or concede a ruff and discard. The trap is to play a diamond to the queen. West wins and a diamond return gives declarer another diamond loser. (If West wins the ♡K and does not cash the ♡A, eliminate spades and clubs before leading the second heart. West is again endplayed.) If East hits on a diamond lead, declarer can still succeed: win ◇A; eliminate the black suits: ♠A, ♠K, ♣A, ♣K, club ruff, spade ruff, then lead a heart. West wins and must set up the ◇Q or give a ruff and discard.

CHAPTER 30

NEGATIVE DOUBLES (1)

In standard methods, when partner opens and the next player intervenes, responder's double is for penalties, unless the partnership is using negative doubles. A negative double is simply a takeout double *by responder*. The normal takeout double arises *after an opponent has opened*. The negative double is for takeout *after partner has opened*. If the partnership has decided to use negative doubles, then a double is for takeout if:

- Partner opened with a suit bid *and*

- Second player overcalled in a suit at the 1-level or 2-level.

For example:

WEST	NORTH	EAST	SOUTH
1♡	2♣	Double . . .	

If not using negative doubles, East's double is for penalties, asking West to *pass*.

If using negative doubles, East's double is for takeout, asking West to *bid*.

If West had opened 1NT, East's double is for penalties. Negative doubles apply only after a suit opening.

If North had overcalled 1NT or 2NT, East's double is for penalties. Negative doubles apply only after a suit overcall, not after a no-trump overcall.

If North overcalled 3♣, East's double is for penalties. Negative doubles apply only after intervention at the 1-level or 2-level unless the partnership has specifically agreed to extend negative doubles to higher levels.

Without negative doubles many hands become difficult and even impossible to bid sensibly after opposition interference. This is particularly so because of the strict requirements for a 2-level response (10+ points). Suppose you pick up ♠A 7 6 5 ♡K 6 4 2 ◇7 6 3 ♣8 7 and partner opens 1◇. You plan to respond 1♡, allowing the partnership to find any available major suit fit. However, when second player overcalls 2♣, you have a problem. You are too weak to respond at the 2-level and in standard methods you would have to pass. Obviously a good fit in either major could be lost.

Similarly, if you hold ♠7 6 2 ♡K 8 7 4 ◇A 7 3 2 ♣8 5 and the bidding begins 1♣ from partner, 1♠ on your right, a heart fit might be lost in standard methods, since there is no satisfactory response (too weak for 2◇ or 2♡, support too poor for 2♣ and the absence of a stopper in spades makes 1NT unattractive).

Negative doubles are popular, especially at duplicate, because:

- They cater for more hand types than penalty doubles do.

- They occur far more frequently than penalty double types.

- One can play negative doubles and still catch the opponents for penalties – see Chapter 32.

- They are a very effective competitive device.

- They solve many problems when the opponents intervene. Pairs playing 5-card majors should incorporate negative doubles in order to obtain the best results from the system they play. Pairs using 4-card majors will also do better if they use negative doubles, but for 5-card majorites, negative doubles are really essential.

WHAT DOES THE NEGATIVE DOUBLE PROMISE?

(1) 6+ points. The negative double promises enough strength to have made a 1-level response. There is no top limit. Just like a 1-level suit response, responder might have enough for game and if so, this will be revealed by a strong rebid later (see Chapter 31).

(2) Specific suit holdings. *The negative double denies support for a major suit opening.* There could be support if opener began with a minor. Responder guarantees certain suit holdings, depending on what has been bid so far. The negative double caters for unbid major suits and will promise 4 cards in any *unbid* major. The negative double promises both minors only when both majors have already been bid.

(a) *Minor – Minor:* Partner opens with a minor and they overcall in a minor, e.g., 1 ◇ : (2 ♣) or 1 ♣ : (1 ◇). **The double promises both majors, at least 4-4, but could be 5-4 or 6-4.** A response in a major suit at the 1-level, e.g., 1 ♣ : (1 ◇) : 1 ♡ or 1 ♠, can be a 4-card suit, but a response in a major suit at the 2-level, e.g., 1 ◇ : (2 ♣) : 2 ♡ or 2 ♠, shows a 5+ suit with 10+ points and is forcing (except by a passed hand).

(b) *Major – Minor or Minor – Major:* **The double promises the other major.** At least four cards are promised in the unbid major. If the overcall was 1 ♡, the double shows precisely four spades and 6+ points, while 1 ♠ over a 1 ♡ overcall promises 5+ spades and 6+ points. If their overcall was 1 ♠, a 2 ♡ response shows 5+ hearts and 10+ points. The double over the 1 ♠ overcall can contain either four hearts exactly and any strength from six points up (no upper limit) *or* 5+ hearts and 6-9 points. With 5+ hearts and 10+ points, bid 2 ♡ – do not use a negative double. It follows that if responder doubles the 1 ♠ overcall and later bids hearts to show 5+ hearts, responder's range must be 6-9 points because of the failure to bid 2 ♡ at once.

(c) *Major – Major:* Double shows both minors. Responder will hold at least four cards in each minor and 6+ points. If, instead of doubling, responder bids a new suit at the 2-level, this promises 10+ points.

OPENER'S REPLY TO THE NEGATIVE DOUBLE

1. Where fourth player passes the negative double: Opener is required to bid unless prepared to make a penalty pass (having trump length and trump winners in the suit overcalled). Where the negative double promised a specific major, opener replies as if responder had bid that major at the 1-level. For example, if the bidding began 1 ♣ : (1 ♠) : Double : (No), a 2 ♡ rebid by opener would be like 1 ♣ : 1 ♡, 2 ♡ without interference. Likewise, opener's 3 ♡ or 4 ♡ reply to the double is equivalent to 1 ♣ : 1 ♡, 3 ♡ or 1 ♣ : 1 ♡, 4 ♡ without interference. A rebid in no-trumps by opener denies support for any major shown by responder and would promise at least one stopper in the enemy suit. A jump-rebid by opener is encouraging, around 17-18 points and six losers, but is not forcing. With 12-16 points, the opener can afford to make a minimum rebid, because responder will bid again if holding 10+ points and so game will not be missed. Rebids by the negative doubler with 10+ points are covered in Chapter 31. If opener has 19+ points, that should be enough for game opposite the 6+ points promised by the negative double. Opener can bid the game at once or, if not sure of the best game, bid the enemy suit to force to game.

2. Where fourth player bids after the negative double: Opener is not obliged to bid, but may do so. If able to make a convenient bid at the 1-level or 2-level, opener should do so and this does not promise any extra strength. If fourth player changes suit, a double by either the opener or by the negative doubler is best played for penalties. If fourth player's action means opener would have to bid at the 3-level, opener should bid only with extra values. This situation usually arises when fourth player raises the overcalled suit. With a minimum opening, opener should pass. Responder will have another opportunity to compete and responder knows not to sell out at the 2-level when the opponents have a trump fit. With 16+ points or a 6-loser hand, opener should feel free to bid at the 3-level.

REBIDS BY THE NEGATIVE DOUBLER

Responder holds 6-9 HCP: Responder will normally pass any minimum action by opener, unless dissatisfied with opener's rebid as the final contract. If opener rebids with a jump, responder should pass with 6-7 points and accept the invitation to game with 8-9 points. Opener's jump will be 17-18 points. If the negative doubler rebids with a change of suit, this promises a 5+ suit and therefore only 6-9 points. With 10+ points *and* a long suit, responder should have bid the suit initially rather than use the negative double.

If fourth player bids over the double and this is passed back to the negative doubler, a double of a new suit or no-trumps is for penalties. The negative doubler is also permitted to pass fourth player's bid, but can take action with something worthwhile to show. However, *if fourth player raises the overcall to the 2-level, the negative doubler should take some action.* It is unsound strategy to pass out their 2-level contract if they have found a trump fit. The negative doubler can support opener's suit at the 3-level, bid a 5+ suit or double again. *The second double is still for takeout if fourth player raised the overcalled suit.* Any of these rebids can be made with just 6-9 points since the situation demands action.

WEST	NORTH	EAST	SOUTH	
				Even with 6-9 points, East should take action. The choices are
1 ◇	1 ♠	Double	2 ♠	3 ◇ with support, 3 ♣ or 3 ♡ with a 5+ suit, or double again,
No	No	?		still for takeout, if nothing better is available.

Responder holds 10-12 points or 13+ points: These ranges are covered in Chapter 31.

A. Partner opened 1♣ and RHO overcalled 1◊. What is your response on each of these hands?

1. ♠ K 7 5 2	2. ♠ K 7 5 2	3. ♠ A 8 5 3	4. ♠ K 7 2	5. ♠ 8 7 2
♡ A 8 7 3	♡ 7 3	♡ 8 6 5 3 2	♡ A J 4 2	♡ 6
◊ 9 6 4	◊ 9 6 4	◊ A 7	◊ 9 8 6 2	◊ A K 9 4 3 2
♣ 7 3	♣ A 8 7 3	♣ 5 4	♣ 6 3	♣ K 8 5

B. Partner opened 1◊ and RHO overcalled 1♠. What action do you take on each of these hands?

1. ♠ 9 7	2. ♠ A 7	3. ♠ A 7 2	4. ♠ 9 6 2	5. ♠ A 7 2
♡ Q 8 7 3	♡ Q J 9 6 4 2	♡ 9 5 3	♡ A J	♡ A J 9 7 4
◊ A 9 6 4	◊ 6 4	◊ 8 7	◊ 8 6	◊ K 9 4
♣ 6 3 2	♣ 7 6 2	♣ K J 8 5 4	♣ Q 9 7 5 4 2	♣ Q 2

C. You opened 1◊ and partner doubled LHO's 1♠ overcall. What is your rebid on each of these hands?

1. ♠ K 7	2. ♠ A 10 2	3. ♠ A 2	4. ♠ 7 2	5. ♠ 2
♡ Q 3 2	♡ 9 4	♡ 4 2	♡ A J 3 2	♡ A K 9 2
◊ A Q 9 6 4	◊ A Q 9 6 4	◊ A J 6 4 3	◊ A J 8 6 2	◊ A K 9 4 3
♣ K J 7	♣ A K 2	♣ K Q 7 5	♣ K 7	♣ K J 5

D. Partner opened 1♣, RHO overcalled 1♠ and you doubled. LHO raised to 2♠, back to you. Your action?

1. ♠ 9 7	2. ♠ 7 4	3. ♠ 5 4 2	4. ♠ 6 4	5. ♠ 4
♡ Q 8 7 3	♡ A Q 8 6 4 2	♡ K Q 5 2	♡ A J 7 2	♡ 7 6 4 3 2
◊ A Q 9 6	◊ J 10 2	◊ Q J 9 4 3	◊ 8 6 2	◊ A Q 4 3
♣ 8 6 2	♣ 3 2	♣ 8	♣ K 9 7 4	♣ Q J 2

PARTNERSHIP BIDDING: How should the following hands be bid? West is the dealer on all hands. The North-South bidding is natural, jump-overcalls are weak and there is no other North-South bidding.

SET 61 – WEST	**SET 61 – EAST**	**SET 62 – WEST**	**SET 62 – EAST**
1. South bids 1♠.	**1.** South bids 1♠.	**1.** North bids 1♠.	**1.** North bids 1♠.
North raises to 2♠.	North raises to 2♠.	South raises to 2♠.	South raises to 2♠.
♠ 9 2	♠ A 8	♠ A 8	♠ 9 7
♡ A J 7 3	♡ K 8 6 2	♡ K 8 4 3	♡ Q J 6 2
◊ J 10 9 3	◊ Q 4	◊ 6 3	◊ A 5 4 2
♣ J 6 5	♣ A Q 7 4 3	♣ A J 8 4 2	♣ Q 7 3
2. North bids 1♠.	**2.** North bids 1♠.	**2.** North bids 2♣.	**2.** North bids 2♣.
♠ A 8 4	♠ 3 2	♠ A K 8 3	♠ J 7 6 5
♡ 6 4	♡ Q J 10 8 5 3	♡ K 6 2	♡ A 9 4 3
◊ K Q J 6 3	◊ 8 4	◊ A K 4 3 2	◊ Q 7
♣ K Q 3	♣ A 6 4	♣ 9	♣ 7 4 2
3. South bids 2♡.	**3.** South bids 2♡.	**3.** North bids 2♡.	**3.** North bids 2♡.
♠ A 6 3 2	♠ K 8 7 4	♠ K 7 3	♠ A Q 8 5 4
♡ 6 5	♡ A J	♡ 9 5	♡ 3 2
◊ J 10 3 2	◊ 7 6	◊ K Q 7 5 3 2	◊ A 4
♣ K 8 7	♣ A J 4 3 2	♣ K J	♣ Q 9 8 6
4. North bids 2♡.	**4.** North bids 2♡.	**4.** North bids 1♠.	**4.** North bids 1♠.
♠ A 8 6 4 2	♠ 9	♠ A 7 6 4	♠ 3
♡ 8 6 3	♡ 10 5	♡ A J 7 2	♡ K 9 6 5
◊ A Q	◊ K 8 6 5 4	◊ 6	◊ 9 8 5 3 2
♣ K 7 2	♣ A 9 8 4 3	♣ K Q 9 3	♣ A J 6
5. North bids 1♡.	**5.** North bids 1♡.	**5.** North bids 1♠.	**5.** North bids 1♠.
South raises to 2♡.	South raises to 2♡.	South raises to 2♠.	South raises to 2♠.
♠ 8 7	♠ A 9 6 2	♠ A 7	♠ 9 4
♡ 8 4	♡ 6 2	♡ 8 6	♡ Q J 10 7 4 3
◊ A K 2	◊ Q 8 5 3	◊ A J 9 4 3	◊ K 8
♣ A J 9 8 4 3	♣ Q 7 2	♣ K 6 5 2	♣ Q 10 3

PLAY HANDS ON NEGATIVE DOUBLES (1)

Hand 117: Negative double – Coping with interference – Setting up a secondary suit

Dealer North : North-South vulnerable

NORTH
♠ 9 3
♡ A K 8 3
♢ 7 2
♣ A K 10 5 2

WEST
♠ K 6 4 2
♡ J 10 4
♢ K J 10 5
♣ J 6

EAST
♠ A Q J 8 7
♡ 9 7
♢ Q 6 4
♣ Q 8 3

SOUTH
♠ 10 5
♡ Q 6 5 2
♢ A 9 8 3
♣ 9 7 4

WEST	NORTH	EAST	SOUTH
	1♣	1♠	Dble (1)
2♠	3♡ (2)	No (3)	No (4)
No (5)			

Bidding: (1) Negative double on minimum values. Do not reject normal competitive moves because of the vulnerability.
(2) With only six losers, North is entitled to compete with 3♡ over 2♠. If minimum, opener should pass here and allow responder to compete to the 3-level. With this arrangement, the partnership can distinguish between minimum openings and those openings worth an invitation to game.
(3) With a minimum, do not bid again *in the direct seat*.
(4) With a minimum negative double, do not bid again if partner does not make a forcing bid.
(5) West should compete to 3♠. In a part-score competitive auction, bid on if your side has nine trumps as long as you do not push to the 4-level. On some days 3♠ will make. On others 3♠ will be a good sacrifice, one off when 3♡ is making. That is the case here. 3♡ is on and 3♠ has just five losers.

Lead: ♡7. A spade from A-Q does not appeal, even though partner supported, and Q-x-x is not attractive either. A trump lead is safe and when leading a trump it is standard to lead low-high from a doubleton.

Correct play: On a trump lead, draw trumps and then play ♣A and give up a club. Later you cash the clubs and lose two spades, one diamond and one club. The play is the same if the opponents cash two spades first.

Hand 118: Negative double to show the minors – Competitive Bidding – Crossruff

Dealer East : East-West vulnerable

NORTH
♠ Q J 10 8 6
♡ 10 5
♢ K 9 7 4
♣ 10 2

WEST
♠ 7
♡ 8 4 3
♢ A 10 6 5 3
♣ K 9 7 3

EAST
♠ A K 5 3 2
♡ J 6 2
♢ 8
♣ A Q J 5

SOUTH
♠ 9 4
♡ A K Q 9 7
♢ Q J 2
♣ 8 6 4

WEST	NORTH	EAST	SOUTH
		1♠	2♡ (1)
Dble (2)	No	3♣ (3)	No (4)
No (5)	No		

Bidding: (1) With a strong 5-card holding in the other major, it is much better to overcall in the major suit than to double.
(2) With both majors already bid, the negative double shows at least 4-4 in the minors and 6+ points. It would be timid of West to pass 2♡.
(3) East needs partner to hold about 12 points (or four cover cards) to make 5♣, so that there is no need to jump to 4♣. With enough for 5♣ to make, West will raise to 4♣ at least.
(4) Once the bidding has reached the 3-level, there is no urgency to compete unless you have significant extra values or a strong trump fit. There is no evidence of either here, so South should pass 3♣.

If South were to bid 3♡, this could be defeated by three tricks: ♠7 lead, ♠K wins; ♢8 to the ♢A; ♢3 returned for a ruff; ♣A; club to the king; diamond ruff; ♠A; three off.
(5) With a minimum double, do not bid again if opener makes a minimum rebid.

Lead: ♡A. It is natural for South to cash three hearts. The best switch then is to a trump as dummy is short in spades, and declarer must be short in diamonds. The best defence to a cross-ruff is repeated trump leads.

Correct play: Do not draw trumps. With dummy short in your long suit and you short in dummy's long suit, play a cross-ruff. Cash ♠A, ♠K, ♢A and ruff a diamond, ruff a spade, ruff a diamond, ruff a spade, etc. etc.

Hand 119: Replying to a negative double with a strong hand – Drawing trumps with care

Dealer South : Game all

NORTH
- ♠ 8 6 4 3
- ♡ A J 9 3
- ◊ J 7 6
- ♣ 9 2

WEST
- ♠ A K Q 10 5 2
- ♡ 5
- ◊ 5 4 3
- ♣ J 6 5

EAST
- ♠ J 9
- ♡ 10 8 7 4
- ◊ A K 10 8 2
- ♣ 10 4

SOUTH
- ♠ 7
- ♡ K Q 6 2
- ◊ Q 9
- ♣ A K Q 8 7 3

WEST	NORTH	EAST	SOUTH
			1♣
1♠ (1)	Dble (2)	No (3)	4♡ (4)
No	No	No	

Bidding: (1) This would be worth 2♠ if playing weak jump-overcalls (6-10 HCP and a good 6+ suit).

(2) Promises 4+ hearts and 6+ points.

(3) Opposite a 1♠ overcall, East is too weak for 2◊. Facing a weak 2♠ jump, East could increase the pressure with a raise to 3♠, but avoid an advance sacrifice of 4♠. North-South have not yet bid 4♡ and with East holding four hearts, there is nothing to say that they will bid it or make it. Do not sacrifice against a game that might fail.

(4) Worth around 20 points and therefore good enough for 4♡. South has only four losers and it is reasonable to expect partner to be able to cover one of those losers at least.

Lead: ♠A. East should signal with the ♠J. It is natural for West to try to cash another spade.

Correct play: South ruffs the second spade and must take care with the trump suit. With a strong outside suit, it is imperative to draw all the trumps. They are likely to break 3-2, but a 4-1 break is not improbable (a 28% chance). When cashing a suit or when drawing trumps, it is usually best to play the high cards first from the shorter holding. Therefore continue with ♡K and ♡Q (noting the 4-1 break), a heart to dummy and play dummy's last heart to draw the outstanding trump, discarding a diamond. Then run the clubs. The contract will fail if a low heart is led to dummy first or if the trumps are not all drawn.

Hand 120: Strong reply to the negative double – Do not put all your eggs in one basket – Timing

Dealer West : Love all

NORTH
- ♠ J 3
- ♡ A Q J 9 8 3
- ◊ 7
- ♣ A 10 6 4

WEST
- ♠ A K 10
- ♡ K 7 4 2
- ◊ A 5
- ♣ K Q 8 3

EAST
- ♠ Q 7 6 2
- ♡ 6 5
- ◊ K Q J 4 3
- ♣ 7 5

SOUTH
- ♠ 9 8 5 4
- ♡ 10
- ◊ 10 9 8 6 2
- ♣ J 9 2

WEST	NORTH	EAST	SOUTH
1♣ (1)	1♡ (2)	Dble (3)	No
3NT (4)	No	No	No

Bidding: (1) The standard way to show a balanced 19 points is to open with a suit and rebid with a jump in no-trumps.

(2) Too strong for a weak jump-overcall. If using intermediate jumps, this would be suitable for 2♡. If North did bid 2♡, East would still double and West would still jump to 3NT.

(3) Too weak for 2◊. The double promises exactly four spades and 6+ points. With five spades, East would respond 1♠.

(4) West knows that there is no 8-card spade fit and with enough for game, the practical shot is 3NT.

Lead: ♡Q. Prepared to concede a trick to the ♡K to set up the rest of the hearts. North hopes to come in with the ♣A before West can score nine tricks. Holding the ♣A, North could also lead the ♡A and continue with the ♡Q at trick 2.

Correct play: West wins the ♡K and must resist the instinctive play of ◊A and a diamond to dummy, planning to take five diamond tricks, three or four spades and the ♡K. When everything looks rosy, cater for bad breaks. If diamonds are 5-1, you have only four diamond tricks and you then need four spade tricks. Spades could be 3-3, but you can also take four spade tricks if the ♠J is singleton or doubleton. In that case, however, you need an entry to dummy to reach the ♠Q after cashing ♠A, ♠K and ♠10. If the diamonds behave, they will do so later, too. There is no rush for the diamonds. Correct is to cash the ♠A and ♠K first, then the ♠10 after the ♠J has dropped, then ◊A, diamond to dummy, cash the ♠Q and two more diamonds for your nine tricks.

CHAPTER 31

NEGATIVE DOUBLES (2)

RESPONDER'S APPROACH WITH 10-12 POINTS

With 10-12 points, responder is strong enough to change suit at the 2-level and thus could forego the use of a negative double. However, the negative double still has many benefits with strong hands. In general, if you hold 10+ points and a 5+ suit, bid your long suit first – do not double. With a 2-suiter you can bid your other suit on the next round if you wish. With 10+ points and no 5-card suit, it is better to use the negative double, as long as your hand has the correct suit content. On the next round, you can reveal the extra strength held.

Double and later raise opener to the 3-level shows 10-12 points and support for opener's suit. Double and later rebid 2NT shows 10-12 points, a balanced hand and a stopper in their suit.

With 10-12 points and a choice whether to rebid 2NT or support opener to the 3-level, responder should raise opener's suit if it is a major and should prefer 2NT if opener's suit is a minor. Responder cannot show 10-12 points by doubling and then changing suit. That shows only 6-9 points since the suit change shows at least a 5-card suit and if responder had a 5-card suit and 10+ points, the proper course of action would have been to bid the long suit initially, not double.

After responder has shown 10-12 points and support by raising opener to the 3-level, opener passes with a bare minimum opening and bids on to game with better than a minimum. If responder raised opener's major, opener passes or bids 4-Major. If responder raised opener's minor, opener may be interested in 3NT rather than 5-Minor. A new suit at the 3-level is stopper-showing (see Chapter 21), while a bid of the enemy suit asks for a stopper in that suit. If responder rebids 2NT, opener may pass or rebid a suit at the 3-level to sign off, or bid 3NT or some other game or a new suit at the 3-level as a forward-going move. If stuck for a bid, opener can always bid the enemy suit to force responder to bid again. Bidding the enemy suit asks for a stopper.

RESPONDER'S APPROACH WITH 13+ POINTS

Responder should have enough for game with 13+ points, but can still use a negative double. With 13+ points and a 5+ suit, responder bids the long suit initially and would not use a negative double. However, with 13+ points, balanced shape and four cards in an unbid major, the negative double is the best initial response. With support for opener's minor and a 4-card unbid major as well, responder should use the negative double initially. After opener's reply, responder may have enough information to bid the best game. If not, responder should bid the enemy suit as a force to game. Note the difference between these auctions:

A. WEST	NORTH	EAST	SOUTH		B. WEST	NORTH	EAST	SOUTH
1♦	1♠	2♠ ...			1♦	1♠	Double	No
					2♦	No	2♠ ...	

In A, East is showing the values for game with 2♠, but has denied four hearts because of the failure to double. In B, East's double of 1♠ promised four hearts, the unbid major. The subsequent 2♠ bid was a game-force. In other words, East B has a game-force with four hearts while East A has a game-force without four hearts. In each case, East figures to have a balanced hand and is asking opener for a stopper in spades.

♠ A 8 3 2   Suppose partner opened 1♦. You already know you have enough for game. If RHO bids
♡ 9 7 4 2   1♠, you double to show four hearts. If opener rebids 1NT, 2♣ or 2♦, your sensible rebid
♦ A K   is 3NT. If opener's rebid is 2♡, you should raise to 4♡. Now suppose RHO bid 1♡. You
♣ Q J 6   double, showing four spades. If partner bids spades, raise to 4♠; over 1NT, bid 3NT.

However, after 1♦ : (1♡) : Double : (No), 2♣ or 2♦ by opener, your best continuation is 2♡. If the values for game are present, but you cannot tell which game is best, bid the enemy suit as a game-force. Your 2♡ is forcing to game and asks for a stopper in hearts. Opener will bid no-trumps with a stopper or make some other descriptive rebid without a stopper. If opener has no stopper, clearly it is vital for you to avoid 3NT.

A. Partner opened 1 ◇ and RHO overcalled 1 ♠. What is your response with each of these hands?

1. ♠ 6 2	2. ♠ 6 2	3. ♠ 8 5 3	4. ♠ K 7 2	5. ♠ 8 6 3 2
♡ A 8 7 3	♡ A 8 7 3	♡ A Q 5 3 2	♡ A J 4 2	♡ A K J
◇ J 9	◇ A K J 7 3	◇ A 7	◇ Q 8	◇ A 3 2
♣ A K J 7 3	♣ J 9	♣ J 5 4	♣ K 9 6 2	♣ Q 8 5

B. You opened 1 ♡, LHO overcalled 2 ♣, doubled by partner (negatively), passed to you. What action do you take with each of these hands?

1. ♠ A 7	2. ♠ A 7	3. ♠ A Q	4. ♠ A Q 6 2	5. ♠ A 7
♡ Q 8 7 3 2	♡ A J 9 6 4	♡ A K 9 6 4	♡ A J 9 5 4	♡ A J 10 8 7 4
◇ A 9 6 4	◇ A Q J 3	◇ K Q J 2	◇ A 8 6	◇ K Q J
♣ K 2	♣ 6 2	♣ 5 4	♣ 2	♣ Q 2

C. Partner opened 1 ◇, RHO bid 1 ♠ and you doubled. Partner replied 2 ♣ to your double, passed to you. What is your rebid with each of these hands?

1. ♠ K 7 5	2. ♠ 10 7	3. ♠ 9 6 2	4. ♠ A J 2	5. ♠ 8 6 2
♡ J 7 3 2	♡ A 8 5 2	♡ K J 4 2	♡ A J 3 2	♡ A Q 9 2
◇ A 6 4	◇ J 4 3	◇ A J 6 3	◇ 9 8 6 2	◇ K J
♣ K 8 7	♣ A Q 8 2	♣ Q 9	♣ K 7	♣ A 8 5 3

D. What would your answers be on the hands in C. if partner's reply to your double had been:
(i) 1NT? (ii) 2 ◇ ? (iii) 2 ♡ ?

PARTNERSHIP BIDDING: How should the following hands be bid? West is the dealer on all hands. The North-South bidding is natural and there is no North-South bidding other than that given.

SET 63 – WEST	**SET 63 – EAST**	**SET 64 – WEST**	**SET 64 – EAST**
1. North bids 1 ♠.	**1.** North bids 1 ♠.	**1.** North bids 1 ♠.	**1.** North bids 1 ♠.
♠ A 7	♠ K 9 2	♠ 7 3	♠ A 10
♡ 7 2	♡ A 10 9 5	♡ A 8 6 5	♡ K J 7 3
◇ K Q 8 6 3	◇ J 5 2	◇ A J 7 3 2	◇ K Q 4
♣ A Q 9 2	♣ K 6 4	♣ A 5	♣ 7 4 3 2
2. South bids 1 ♠.	**2.** South bids 1 ♠.	**2.** North bids 1 ♠.	**2.** North bids 1 ♠.
♠ K 5 3	♠ 8 2	♠ 7 3	♠ A 10
♡ K Q 9 6	♡ A 3	♡ A 5	♡ K J 7 3
◇ K 8 4	◇ Q 7 2	◇ A 9 7 3 2	◇ K Q 4
♣ 7 4 2	♣ K Q J 9 6 5	♣ A J 6 5	♣ 7 4 3 2
3. North bids 1 ♠.	**3.** North bids 1 ♠.	**3.** South bids 1 ♠.	**3.** South bids 1 ♠.
♠ 8 4	♠ A 9	♠ Q J 4	♠ 7 6 5
♡ A 9 4 3 2	♡ K 5	♡ Q J 6 3	♡ A K 8
◇ K Q 2	◇ A 7 6 4 3	◇ K 6 4 2	◇ A Q 3
♣ A Q 2	♣ 10 9 8 3	♣ 3 2	♣ A Q 9 6
4. South bids 1 ♠.	**4.** South bids 1 ♠.	**4.** South bids 1 ♠.	**4.** South bids 1 ♠.
♠ 8 6 3	♠ A 2	♠ 8 4	♠ 7 6 5
♡ A K 9 2	♡ 8 7 4 3	♡ Q J 6 3 2	♡ A K 8
◇ J 8 7 3	◇ K Q	◇ K 6 4	◇ A Q 3
♣ K 9	♣ A J 7 6 2	♣ 8 3 2	♣ A Q 9 6
5. North bids 2 ♡.	**5.** North bids 2 ♡.	**5.** North bids 2 ◇.	**5.** North bids 2 ◇.
♠ A K J 9 7 3	♠ 8 6	♠ 7	♠ A K Q 2
♡ A 8 3	♡ 4 2	♡ A J 9 7 2	♡ 6 5
◇ K 10	◇ A Q J 5	◇ Q J 4	◇ 6 3 2
♣ J 10	♣ K 9 8 6 5	♣ K Q 8 3	♣ A J 9 6

PLAY HANDS ON NEGATIVE DOUBLES (2)

Hand 121: Setting up extra winners via ruffing finesse – Loser-on-loser – Keeping the danger hand off play

Dealer North : East-West vulnerable

NORTH
* ♠ K Q 10 8 4 3 2
* ♡ K 6 5
* ◇ 4 2
* ♣ A

WEST
* ♠ 9 7 5
* ♡ J 10 9
* ◇ K 8
* ♣ 7 6 4 3 2

EAST
* ♠ 6
* ♡ A Q 7
* ◇ Q J 10 9 7 5
* ♣ K 9 5

SOUTH
* ♠ A J
* ♡ 8 4 3 2
* ◇ A 6 3
* ♣ Q J 10 8

WEST	NORTH	EAST	SOUTH
	1♠ (1)	2◇ (2)	Dble (3)
No	3♠ (4)	No	4♠ (5)
No	No	No	

Bidding: (1) Too strong to pre-empt. To open 3♠ or 4♠ in first or second seat with such strength can result in missing a slam.
(2) With 12-15 HCP and a l-suiter, overcall rather than double.
(3) Better to show hearts first via the double than to reply 2NT.
(4) Despite holding only 12 HCP, this is worth a jump to 3♠ as it has just five losers. Even 4♠ would be acceptable. You may add three points when holding a good 7-card suit.
(5) South is worth only 4♠, but if South had a stronger hand and slam ambitions, a 4◇ cue-bid or 4NT could be used.

Lead: ◇ Q. Avoid abnormal leads.

Correct play: North can see nine winners. The tenth could come from the heart finesse, but East is almost sure to have the ♡A. East-West have 16 HCP. The ◇Q lead denies the ◇K and if West has ♡A and ◇K, East would have overcalled on an aceless 9-count, possible but very unlikely. Do not duck the first diamond: West can overtake with the ◇K and switch to a heart – disaster. The best chance is to use dummy's clubs. Take the ◇A; ♣8 to the ♣A; low spade to the jack; lead the ♣Q. If West covers, you ruff and lead a spade back to dummy to cash as many clubs as possible. When West plays low, do not ruff: discard your diamond loser (loser-on-loser and scissors coup), not a heart. (If you discard a heart. East can lead a diamond to West's king and a heart through defeats the contract.) East wins the ♣K, but now West has no entry. Ruff the diamond return, cross to the ♣A and discard two hearts on the club winners. Making eleven tricks.

Hand 122: Discarding a loser before touching trumps – Insuring against a bad break

Dealer East : Game all

NORTH
* ♠ 9 8 3
* ♡ J 10 7 5
* ◇ 10 8 7 6
* ♣ A 9

WEST
* ♠ A 5
* ♡ A K 9 4
* ◇ Q 5 4
* ♣ 8 7 5 4

EAST
* ♠ 7 6
* ♡ 8 6 3 2
* ◇ A K
* ♣ K Q J 6 2

SOUTH
* ♠ K Q J 10 4 2
* ♡ Q
* ◇ J 9 3 2
* ♣ 10 3

WEST	NORTH	EAST	SOUTH
		1♣	1♠ (1)
Dble (2)	No (3)	2♡ (4)	No
4♡ (5)	No	No	No

Bidding: (1) Worth 2♠ if playing weak jump-overcalls.
(2) Show the other major first via the double rather than reply in no-trumps first. West has enough for game and plans to play in 4♡ if a fit is found and in 3NT if no heart fit exists.
(3) Not enough for 2♠. A raise with three rags might cause partner to lead a broken suit with dire results. North passes for now, but plans to compete to 2♠ if East-West stop at the 2-level.
(4) No need to do more. With 10+ points, West will bid again.
(5) Clearcut. 3NT is easily defeated on a spade lead.

Lead: ♠K. How come you have such easy leads?

Correct play: Win the ♠A. Do not cash ♡A and ♡K yet. If you do, there is no entry to dummy to reach the ◇Q after cashing ◇A-K. You have to lose one club and one heart. If there are two heart losers, you cannot afford to lose a spade. Play off the ◇A-K first, cross to the ♡A and discard the spade loser on the ◇Q. Still do not cash the ♡K. If you do and trumps *are* 4-1, an opponent might take the ♣A and draw *your* trumps for down three or four. You have lost no tricks so far and can afford to lose a club and two hearts, so that a club ruff will not defeat you. If a bad trump split is a risk, set up the side suit first. Play clubs before cashing the other top heart. North wins the ♣A, but you win any return, cash the ♡K and then keep leading clubs.

Hand 123: Play from dummy at trick 1 – Keeping the danger hand off lead

Dealer South : Love all

```
           NORTH
           ♠ Q 5
           ♡ A 6 5 3
           ◊ 10 9 5 2
           ♣ A 6 2
WEST                    EAST
♠ A J 9 7 4 3          ♠ 10 8
♡ 9 2                  ♡ J 10 8 7 4
◊ K 6                  ◊ 8 3
♣ K 8 3               ♣ Q J 9 5
           SOUTH
           ♠ K 6 2
           ♡ K Q
           ◊ A Q J 7 4
           ♣ 10 7 4
```

WEST	NORTH	EAST	SOUTH
			1 ◊
1 ♠ (1)	Dble (2)	No	1NT (3)
No	3NT (4)	All pass	

Bidding: (1) This would be worth 2♠ if playing intermediate jump-overcalls (11-15 HCP and a good 6+ suit).
(2) Promises 4+ hearts and 6+ points.
(3) With a stopper in their suit and a 5-3-3-2 pattern, it is better to rebid 1NT than to repeat the 5-card suit.
(4) With 10-12 points and balanced shape, North is worth a raise to 3NT since opener's 1NT rebid indicated 15-16 points. Responder's raise to 2NT shows nine points. Opener's no-trump rebids in reply to a negative double are as though responder had bid at the 1-level (1NT 15-16, 2NT 17-18, 3NT 19).

Lead: ♠ 7. Fourth-highest of your long suit is normal.

Correct play: Play the *queen* from dummy, do not play low. With K-x-x opposite Q-x, or Q-x-x opposite K-x, play the honour from dummy's doubleton. If the honour wins, try to keep RHO, the danger hand, off lead. Here the ♠Q wins and you lead the ◊ 10, finessing. West wins, but your ♠K-6 is a stopper with West on lead. If West switches to a club, play the ace and take your nine tricks, unblocking ♡K, ♡Q early and using the ◊9 as an entry to dummy. If you duck the club switch, East wins and a spade shift takes you three off. If you fail to play the ♠Q from dummy at trick 1, 3NT will fail. East plays the ♠10 and if you take the king, West cashes five spades when in with the ◊K. If you duck East's ♠10, East leads another spade for the same outcome. If West leads a club initially, duck the first two clubs, win the third and finesse in diamonds. If East wins the first club and switches to a spade, duck it to dummy's queen and again finesse diamonds.

Hand 124: Hold-up play – Card combination – Keeping the danger hand off lead

Dealer West : North-South vulnerable

```
           NORTH
           ♠ Q J 5
           ♡ A 10 8 7 5
           ◊ J 8 3
           ♣ K 8
WEST                    EAST
♠ A 9 3                ♠ K 6 4 2
♡ K J 4                ♡ 9 3 2
◊ A K 6 2              ◊ Q 5
♣ 5 4 3               ♣ A Q 10 9
           SOUTH
           ♠ 10 8 7
           ♡ Q 6
           ◊ 10 9 7 4
           ♣ J 7 6 2
```

WEST	NORTH	EAST	SOUTH
1 ◊	1 ♡ (1)	Dble (2)	No
1NT (3)	No	3NT (4)	All pass

Bidding: (1) Only just worth an overcall. The strength is fine but the suit quality is minimal.
(2) Over 1 ♡, the negative double shows precisely *four spades*.
(3) Denies four spades. Shows 15-16 points and a heart stopper.
(4) With a balanced hand, East is happy to stick with no-trumps and 11 points is enough for 3NT.

Lead: ♡ 7. No reason to avoid the normal long suit lead.

Correct play: Let South's ♡Q win. It would be all right to win the ♡K if you could keep South off lead, since your ♡J-4 is a stopper against North. If you take the ♡Q with the king, and South gains the lead, a heart through your J-4 gives North four heart tricks for one off.

To score nine tricks, you need to tackle clubs, which involves two finesses. Unless North holds both the ♣K and ♣J, South will gain the lead. As you are unlikely to keep South off lead, it is better to duck the first heart. You still score a heart trick, but if North has the five hearts expected for the 1 ♡ overcall, South will be out of hearts after the next heart lead. South returns a heart, North wins and plays a third round. Now North has two heart winners and is the danger hand, but you can keep North off lead. Finesse the ♣9, not the ♣Q, win any return and another club sees you home when the ♣K appears. If the ♣K did not pop up, you would keep finessing in clubs.

CHAPTER 32

PENALTY DOUBLES & PENALTY PASSES

The principles for successful penalty doubles vary according to the level of the bidding. The most rewarding doubles are usually those of low-level contracts when an opponent overcalls and you sit over them with a strong trump holding. An overcall is a risky venture (although the risk must be taken), because there may be a worthless hand opposite or even if there are some values, they may be of little value for the suit overcalled. On the other hand, by the time the opponents have exchanged plenty of information and have reached a game or a slam, it is unlikely that you will be able to collect a huge penalty.

PARTNER OPENS WITH A SUIT BID, RHO MAKES A SUIT OVERCALL

In order to look for penalties, you should have:

- *A strong trump holding* – see the Rule of 6 and the Rule of 4 below.

- *8+ HCP* so that your side usually has at least 20 HCP and figures to take at least half the tricks.

- *A misfit with the suit opened.* A singleton holding is ideal and a void is excellent also. A doubleton is acceptable but with 3+ cards in partner's suit, you should be reluctant to seek penalties at the 1-level or at the 2-level. This misfit feature is important. If you are short in partner's suit, partner's winners in that suit will take tricks and you can ruff early if necessary. If you have length in partner's suit, partner's winners there are less likely to survive, as declarer or dummy could easily ruff and you will be unable to over-ruff.

How much length and strength is needed in their trump suit to seek penalties at the 1-, 2- or 3-level? If your hand conforms to both the Rule of 6 and the Rule of 4, your trump quality is adequate for penalties:

The Rule of 6: Add the number of trumps you hold to the level at which the opponent has overcalled. If the answer is six or more, you have enough trumps for penalties. If the answer is below six, you have insufficient trumps. For example, if the overcall was at the 1-level, you need at least five trumps ($1 + 5 = 6$). At the 2-level, you need at least four trumps ($2 + 4 = 6$) and at the 3-level at least three trumps ($3 + 3 = 6$).

The Rule of 4: Add the number of expected winners you hold *in their suit* to the level at which the opponent has overcalled. If the answer is four or more, you have enough trump winners to go for penalties. If the answer is below four, you do not have sufficient trump winners and should not play for penalties (yet). For example, if the overcall was at the 1-level, you need at least three trump winners ($1 + 3 = 4$). At the 2-level you need two trump winners ($2 + 2 = 4$), while at the 3-level you need at least one trump winner ($3 + 1 = 4$).

The Rule of 6 measures the trump *length* and the Rule of 4 measures the trump *strength* needed for penalties. On the above basis, if partner opens say 1♡ and RHO overcalls 2♣, you need four clubs including two club winners, plus the HCP and misfit requirements in order to try successfully for penalties.

HOW DO YOU COLLECT YOUR PENALTIES?

If your hand fits the above requirements, how can you collect the penalties bonanza? If you are not playing negative doubles, you have no difficulty: simply double. In standard methods, a double is for penalties if partner has already bid.

However, if you are playing negative doubles (see Chapters 30 and 31) – and it is very sensible to use negative doubles – you can still collect penalties. The principle is: *Pass For Penalties*. If partner opens with a suit bid and next player overcalls in a suit at the 1-level or 2-level and your hand fits the above requirements for penalties, *you pass*. If the bidding then goes No: (No) to opener, partner will keep the bidding alive. Partner's No. 1 choice when re-opening the bidding is a takeout double on all normal hands (see Chapter 29). If partner makes this re-opening takeout double, you *pass for penalties*. In other words, you convert partner's takeout double into penalties by passing. You are said to be making a 'penalty pass'. If opener does not re-open with a double, do not fret that you have missed out on penalties. This just means that if you would have made a penalty double, opener would have removed it anyway. The typical sequences for these penalty passes look like this:

WEST	NORTH	EAST	SOUTH		WEST	NORTH	EAST	SOUTH
1♣	1♠	No	No		1♠	2♦	No	No
Dble	No	No ...			Dble	No	No ...	

In each auction, East's second pass is a penalty pass and East is stacked in North's suit. If East has a poor hand and passed on the first round simply because of weakness, East will now reply to West's double, just as one normally replies to a takeout double. You pass the takeout double when you are strong in their suit and you take out the double on all other hand types, when you are not looking for penalties.

WHEN CAN THE OPENER DECLINE TO RE-OPEN WITH A DOUBLE?

When the bidding has been 1-suit : (Suit overcall) : No : (No) back to the opener, the opener will usually re-open with a double. Choose some other action with a freak hand (such as a 6-5) or with exceptional length in the suit opened (see Chapter 29). The opener should pass when holding length and strength in the overcalled suit, since responder then cannot have a penalty pass type. In this case, responder's pass indicates a weak hand without support for opener and unsuitable for a negative double. Opener is therefore better off defending with length and strength in their suit, so again *pass for penalties*. Opener is not obliged to re-open when LHO's action was a strong jump-overcall *or* when LHO's overcall was at the 3-level *or* when LHO's action was an intermediate jump-overcall and opener has Q-x-x or better in their suit. In addition, if fourth player bids, e.g., 1◊ : (1♡) : No : (2♡) or 1◊ : (1♡) : No : (1♠), there is no obligation on opener to bid. Indeed, if opener does bid over fourth player's bid, opener is showing better than a minimum opening.

PASSING OTHER TAKEOUT DOUBLES

1. Partner makes a takeout double of their 1-level suit opening: To pass this, your hand must satisfy the Rule of 6 and the Rule of 4. You need at least five trumps and three trump winners, and about 8+ points. You do not pass a takeout double out of weakness, but out of a deliberate desire to penalize their contract. To defeat their contract you need to win at least seven tricks. Thus you have to make 1-in-their-suit. To do this, you need excellent trumps, of course, as there is known to be a bad break against you. Where a 1-level takeout double has been passed out, if the doubler is on lead, the doubler should lead a trump. As partner's trumps should be better than declarer's, partner wants to draw declarer's trumps. A trump lead will help.

2. Partner makes a negative double at the 1-level or 2-level: Opener may pass partner's negative double with a strong holding in the suit overcalled (use the Rule of 6 and Rule of 4) and no fit for responder's suit(s). The bidding might start like this: 1♡ : (2♣) : Double : (No) ... With strong clubs and no spade fit, opener should pass. Opener also knows that responder has no fit with hearts, since the negative double denies support for opener's major. This kind of penalty can only be obtained by pairs using negative doubles.

SUBSEQUENT DOUBLES

After a penalty pass has been made, all subsequent doubles are for penalties. Thus, if they try to rescue themselves from one penalty, you should continue to double with a strong 4+ holding in any suit they try. Note that East's double in this auction is for penalties:

WEST	NORTH	EAST	SOUTH		West's re-opening double was for takeout. East's double
1◊	1♠	No	No		cannot be negative. If East has a negative double of 2♠,
Dble	2♠	Dble ...			East would have made a negative double of 1♠.

It is clear that East had a penalty pass of 1♠ doubled and North is about to regret bidding 2♠.

DOUBLES AFTER A 1NT OPENING

1. They open 1NT: The double of a 1NT opening is for penalties, not for takeout (see Chapter 28). You should double a weak 1NT with 15+ HCP and a strong 1NT when you hold the equivalent of the top of their range. You may double a 15-17 1NT with 17+ HCP, a 16-18 1NT with 18+ HCP, or slightly less if you have an excellent suit to lead. After a penalty double of 1NT, all subsequent doubles are also for penalties and you need only a strong 4-card holding in their suit and at least 20 HCP together with partner.

2. Your side opens 1NT, they overcall: All doubles after a 1NT opening are for penalties in standard methods. The requirements are the same as in the previous paragraph, a strong 4+ holding in their suit and 20+ HCP together with partner. All subsequent doubles are also for penalties.

DOUBLING THEIR 1NT OVERCALL

When partner has opened and RHO overcalls 1NT, double if your side has more points than they do. They are trying to win more than half the tricks with less than half the points and will generally fail. Accordingly, as partner's opening is usually based on 12+ HCP, double their 1NT overcall whenever you hold 9+ HCP. If unable to double, raise partner to the 2-level (5-8 points), bid your own suit at the 2-level (5-8 HCP and a 6+ suit), bid 2NT (a freak 2-suiter with game values) or jump to the 3-level (forcing, 6+ suit). After doubling their 1NT, if either opponent bids a suit, you or partner should double their escape attempt with a strong 4-card holding in the suit they bid. If unable to double their suit in second seat, pass it to partner who may be able to double. If their suit has been passed to you in fourth seat and you do not have a strong 4-card holding, you may support partner, bid a new suit or rebid 2NT. A new suit or a jump would be forcing, but supporting partner or 2NT can be passed.

PENALTY DOUBLES AFTER A STRENGTH-SHOWING REDOUBLE

If the bidding starts 1-Suit : (Double) : Redouble, responder is looking for penalties. All doubles after this redouble are for penalties. A strong 4+ holding in their suit is enough to double. Where the bidding has started 1NT : (Double) : Redouble, responder indicates enough strength to guarantee that the opening side has more HCP than the doubling side. If either opponent now bids a suit (as they probably will), all doubles are for penalties. Again, a strong 4-card holding in the suit bid is enough.

THE S.O.S REDOUBLE – REDOUBLING FOR RESCUE

Where your side has been doubled for penalties or where a takeout double of a suit bid by your side has been passed for penalties (a penalty pass has been made), redouble is used for takeout as a means of rescue. *The redouble of a takeout double shows strength, the redouble of a penalty double is S.O.S. for rescue.* In the following auctions, the final 'Rdble . . .' is for rescue (and PP indicates a penalty pass):

WEST	NORTH	EAST	SOUTH		WEST	NORTH	EAST	SOUTH
1♣	Dble	No	No (PP)		1♡	No	No	Dble
Rdble . . .					No	No (PP)	Rdble . . .	

WEST	NORTH	EAST	SOUTH		WEST	NORTH	EAST	SOUTH
1♡	1♠	No	No		1♠	Dble	Rdble	2♣
Dble	No	No (PP)	Rdble . . .		Dble	Rdble . . .		

WEST	NORTH	EAST	SOUTH		WEST	NORTH	EAST	SOUTH
1NT	Dble	2♣	Dble		1NT	Dble	Rdble	2◇
No	No	Rdble . . .			Dble	Rdble . . .		

This shows that you can make an S.O.S. redouble of your own suit as well as of partner's suit. A most useful situation for an S.O.S. redouble is after they have doubled partner's 1NT opening and you want to escape into a suit. Suppose you hold ♠9 7 4 3 ♡8 5 4 2 ◇J 5 3 2 ♣8 and it starts 1NT : (Double). You would be better off in a suit, but which suit? Bid 2♣. If this is doubled for penalties (as it almost certainly will be), redouble for rescue. Whichever other suit is chosen by partner will be better than 1NT doubled. If they do pass you out in 2♣, at least you are not doubled. After 1NT : (Double), what should you do with ♠9 7 5 3 2 ♡8 6 4 3 2 ◇9 ♣7 4? You belong in a major but which one? Since 2♣ over a double is clubs and not Stayman, you might feel that you have to take a guess. Not at all. Bid 2♣ anyway, pretending you have clubs. If this is doubled, redouble for rescue. If partner bids a major, you are in your best spot. If partner bids 2◇, bid 2♡, showing both majors. If 2◇ is doubled, redouble for rescue again, forcing partner to choose a major. The S.O.S. redouble can be fun!

In other situations where partner's suit has been doubled for penalties (or a penalty pass has been made), do not S.O.S. redouble with tolerance for partner's suit. You might be in a worse trump suit and at a higher level if you start rescue operations. With a void in partner's suit and the other three suits, or a singleton plus a 5-5 or freakier pattern, redouble for rescue. A better trump suit is likely to exist.

Note that the redouble of a takeout double or a negative double (which is a form of takeout double) is showing strength and is not S.O.S. If partner's 1NT has been doubled, the redouble is strength-showing and shows a desire to play in 1NT redoubled. It is not S.O.S. in standard methods, even though the double of 1NT was for penalties.

PENALTY DOUBLES AT THE 3-LEVEL

As doubles above 2 ◊ give them a game if they succeed, you need to be confident you will defeat them. At a lower level, you can occasionally try a speculative double. If it fails to come off, you have not lost much. If the double gives them a game, however, you should have a safety margin and the best approach is not to make a penalty double above 2 ◊ unless you expect to defeat the contract by at least two tricks. In that way, if one of your tricks fails to materialize because of an unexpected singleton or void with the opposition, you will at least still defeat the contract. If you follow the advice on page 162 of what you need for a penalty double or a penalty pass of a suit overcall (a trump stack, high card strength and a misfit), you should be able to defeat the opponents' contract normally by about three tricks. The safety margin is built into the requirements.

For a penalty double at the 3-level, you should expect to take 6+ tricks between you and partner, including at least one trump trick. It is risky to double at the 3-level without any trump winners. You can play partner to hold 1-2 tricks with 6-10 HCP and three tricks with 11-15 HCP. Add your winners to this expectancy.

If you are highly likely to make a game, do not settle for a small penalty. Prefer to bid on to your best game. If you can make a game, you need at least 500 points from the double as compensation for the game missed. On the other hand, if game chances are doubtful, take the penalty. Better to be a small plus from a penalty than to be minus because your game was not on.

PENALTY DOUBLES OF GAME CONTRACTS

The odds are stacked heavily against doubles of game contracts or higher, unless the opponents are taking a sacrifice or have been forced to guess at the contract because of a pre-emptive opening or pre-emptive overcall. By the time the opponents have reached a game or higher, they have usually been able to exchange enough information to have a good idea of their combined assets. In such circumstances, it is not common to collect a large penalty, because they rarely go more than one off. If, without any pre-emptive bid by your side, the opponents have bid a game, expecting it to make, and you feel that they are too high, take your profit and pass . . . do *not* double. If they make their doubled contract they score an extra 150 or 170. If you defeat them by one trick, you score an extra 50 or 100, depending on vulnerability. You have to be right more than two times out of three or three times out of four to show any profit. In addition, any doubled overtricks are hideously expensive (100 or 200 each, according to vulnerability) and if they redouble and make it, you have a real disaster. *Never double a freely bid game for just one off.* You need an expectation of at least two down to make the double worthwhile. Do not expect to defeat them just because you have a lot of points. If they have bid to the 4-level or 5-level and you hold 18+ HCP, what allows them to bid so high? Excellent shape . . . voids and singletons . . . and some of your hoped for tricks are likely to be ruffed.

Worst of all, an ill-judged double of a game contract can alert declarer to bad breaks and may indicate how the contract should be handled. Without warning, declarer might have gone down. What a calamity if your double tips declarer off and allows the contract to be made! If the opponents are in a contract you are happy to defend, because they are almost sure to fail, do not become greedy and double if they can run to some other contract, which might not be defeated. So do not double unless you can also double any other contract.

If declarer has offered a choice of suits and dummy has chosen one, do not be afraid to double if you have the values for a penalty double in the suit chosen even though you lack such values in the other suit. The fact that they have already made a choice means it is unlikely that they will run to the other suit (possibly at a higher level). Also, if you have their first choice sewn up, partner is bound to be stacked in their other possible trump suit if you are not. If their first choice is terrible for them, because *you* have a trump stack, their other choice will be at least as terrible since *partner* figures to have the trump stack there. Likewise, if they are bidding 3NT essentially on the basis of a long, running suit, double if you know their long suit is not breaking. Your profit could be huge.

If the opponents have had a strong auction to reach game, e.g., 1 ♠ : 2NT, 4 ♠, it is foolish to double them just because you know they are in for a bad trump break. They may have points to spare and you may make just your trump tricks. The best time to double their suit game is when they have struggled to reach the game and they are in for a bad break. Auctions like 1 ♠ : 2 ♠, 3 ♠ : 4 ♠ and 1 ♠ : 1NT, 2 ♡ : 2 ♠, 3 ♠ : 4 ♠ are ripe for a penalty double if their suits split badly. The auction shows that they have barely enough high card strength for game and if they are running into bad breaks as well, they are likely to go many down when the hand blows up. Double their limping auctions when the breaks are bad for them and you will collect big.

If your side has more high card strength than the opponents, who have bid above your game contract, make sure that you double them. Do not let them play in any sacrifice undoubled. You do not need trump tricks to double a sacrifice and you do not need to be sure where your tricks are coming from. The fact that you know you have more strength is sufficient. When they take a sacrifice and you have to decide whether to double or whether to bid on, the more balanced your hand, the more inclined you should be to defend. The more shapely your hand, the more inclined you are to bid on. The more strength you hold in their suit(s), especially kings and queens, the more you should double. Occasionally in such competitive situations, you double their sacrifice to warn partner not to bid on. If you are in second seat and short in their suit, pass the decision to partner if you are not sure what to do. As you are short in their suit, partner will probably have length in their suit. Partner will be in a better position to know whether to double or whether to bid on. The best lead after doubling a sacrifice is often a trump. If the enemy have less strength, they must be hoping to make tricks by ruffing. The more trump leads you can manage, the fewer ruffs they will obtain.

DOUBLING THEIR 3NT CONTRACT

When the opponents have bid to 3NT, double by the player not on lead calls for a specific lead:
* If the player on lead has bid a suit, the double asks for that suit.
* If the player doubling has bid a suit, the double asks for that suit.
* If both defenders have bid a suit, the double asks for the suit bid by the player on lead.
* If neither defender has bid a suit, the double asks for the first suit bid by dummy.
* If no suit has been bid at all, e.g., (1NT): (3NT), you can play that the double asks for a spade lead. Other methods exist, but they leave room for error in deciding which suit is requested. It is better to be certain of the suit partner will lead, so that the demand for a spade if no suit has been bid is sensible, practical and handy when it arises.

DOUBLING SLAMS FOR PENALTIES

The worst reason for doubling a slam is that you know you can defeat it! Suppose their bidding has been (1♡) : (3♣), (3♡) : (4NT), (5◇) : (6♡) and there you are, holding Q-J-10-9 of hearts! Do you double? There is no way that they can make 6♡, but it would dreadful to double! You are sure that you will defeat 6♡, but you cannot be sure that you will also defeat 6NT. If you double 6♡, they may suspect a bad trump break and run from the contract you can defeat to one which is unbeatable. Thus, for a measly extra 50 or 100 points, your greedy double has cost you over 1000 points. Be content to take their slams down undoubled and you will gradually acquire a reputation for being a kind and generous player, even though your motivation for not doubling is purely self-interest.

Similarly, if they have an auction like (1♠) : (3♠), (6♠) *or* (1♡) : (2◇), (4◇) : (6◇), and you have two aces, it is extremely naive to double. The opponents know about aces, too, and even the rawest novice has heard of Blackwood and how to ask for aces. Why do you think they did not ask for aces? You can be confident that the slam bidder has a void where you have an ace. Otherwise they *would* have asked for aces. If, in fact, you are able to cash both your aces and defeat their slam, what more do you want? With opponents like that, you do not want to double and *stop* them bidding such slams, do you? And again, by not doubling, you will prove to the world what a nice and magnanimous player you are. Little do they know . . .

DOUBLING THEIR SLAM FOR A PARTICULAR LEAD

Since we saw above that it is unsound to double their slam just because you feel you can defeat it (unless they are sacrificing), the double of their slam by the player not on lead demands a specific lead. This idea was devised by Theodore Lightner and is known as the Lightner Double. When partner doubles their slam and you are on lead, the double asks you to make an unusual lead. Do not lead a suit your side has bid (that is usual), do not lead an unbid suit (that is usual), do not lead a trump (that is not unusual). Lead the first suit bid by dummy – *that is unusual*. The doubler has either a void or a powerful holding in dummy's first bid suit and fears that you would never make that lead under normal circumstances. If dummy has not bid a suit, study the bidding and your cards and deduce the suit in which partner is likely to be void. The double alerts you to the fact that partner has a void and you should normally lead your longest suit. That is where partner's void figures to be. The double of an artificial bid while they are en route to slam, such as the double of the answer to an ask for aces or the double of a cue-bid, asks partner to lead the suit doubled. Use such doubles sparingly since they also tip off the opposition and it may help them more than your side.

A. Partner opened 1 ♡ and RHO overcalled 2 ♣. Which of these hands are suitable for penalties?

1. ♠ 6 2	**2.** ♠ 9 8 6 2	**3.** ♠ 8 6 5 3 2	**4.** ♠ 9 7 5 2	**5.** ♠ K 6 3
♡ A 8 7 3	♡ 3	♡ 2	♡ 2	♡ 8 7
◊ J 9 3	◊ A K J 7 3	◊ A 7	◊ 9 3	◊ K 6 3 2
♣ A K 7 6	♣ J 9 3	♣ A J 8 5 4	♣ Q J 7 6 4 3	♣ K J 10 5

B. You opened and LHO overcalled 2 ♡, passed back to you. What action do you take on each of these hands?

1. ♠ A Q 9 7 2	**2.** ♠ A J 8 3 2	**3.** ♠ A Q 5	**4.** ♠ A Q 8 6 2	**5.** ♠ 9 7
♡ 2	♡ K Q 9	♡ 4	♡ A J 9 5 4	♡ A J 10 4
◊ A 9 6 4	◊ A J 3	◊ K Q J 2	◊ J 8	◊ K Q J 7 5
♣ K 9 2	♣ 6 2	♣ K Q 9 3 2	♣ 2	♣ Q 2

C. Partner opened 1 ♡, RHO bid 2 ♣, passed back to opener who doubled. This is passed to you. Your action?

1. ♠ K 7 5	**2.** ♠ 10 8 7 6 4 2	**3.** ♠ 9 6 2	**4.** ♠ 9 6 2	**5.** ♠ 8 6 2
♡ J 7 3	♡ - - -	♡ 4 2	♡ 2	♡ 9 2
◊ 7 6 4	◊ J 4 3	◊ A J 6 3	◊ A 8 6 2	◊ Q 6 3
♣ 9 7 3 2	♣ J 6 5 2	♣ Q 7 6 2	♣ K J 5 4 2	♣ 9 8 5 3 2

PARTNERSHIP BIDDING: How should the following hands be bid? West is the dealer on all hands. The North-South bidding is natural and there is no North-South bidding other than that given.

SET 65 – WEST	**SET 65 – EAST**	**SET 66 – WEST**	**SET 66 – EAST**
1. North bids 2 ◊.	**1.** North bids 2 ◊.	**1.** North bids 1NT.	**1.** North bids 1NT.
♠ A Q 8 7 4	♠ 3	♠ A K 3	♠ 8 5
♡ K Q 9 3	♡ J 7 6	♡ K J 9 5 2	♡ Q 7 3
◊ 7 2	◊ A J 9 8 5	◊ J 10 3	◊ A K 8 2
♣ Q 4	♣ K 9 8 2	♣ 9 7	♣ J 8 6 5
2. North bids 1 ♡.	**2.** North bids 1 ♡.	**2.** South bids 2 ♠.	**2.** South bids 2 ♠.
♠ K Q 9 4	♠ 7 3	♠ K Q 8 3	♠ 9 5
♡ 3	♡ A Q 10 8 6 5	♡ A 7	♡ K J 9 4
◊ A Q 6	◊ K 7 4 2	◊ 7 6 4	◊ A K 5
♣ Q 9 8 3 2	♣ 6	♣ 8 6 5 2	♣ K 9 4 3
3. North bids 1 ♡.	**3.** North bids 1 ♡.	**3.** North bids 4 ♠.	**3.** North bids 4 ♠.
♠ A 6 5 3	♠ 10 8 4 2	♠ 7 6	♠ 2
♡ 8 2	♡ 7 6 4 3	♡ 10 9 5 4 2	♡ K Q J 8 3
◊ A Q 6	◊ K 4 3	◊ A K	◊ J 6 4
♣ A K Q 8	♣ 6 5	♣ K Q J 4	♣ A 8 5 2
4. South bids 2 ♣.	**4.** South bids 2 ♣.	**4.** South bids 2 ♣.	**4.** South bids 2 ♣.
♠ Q 9 8	♠ A 7	♠ 7 2	♠ A Q 9 8 3
♡ 7 5 3	♡ K Q 9 8 6	♡ K J 8 4	♡ 7 2
◊ 8 3 2	◊ K J 7 4	◊ 7 6 5 3 2	◊ K J
♣ J 7 4 3	♣ A 2	♣ 9 4	♣ K J 7 2
5. North doubles 1 ♠.	**5.** North doubles 1 ♠.	**5.** North bids 1 ♡.	**5.** North bids 1 ♡.
South bids 2 ♡.	South bids 2 ♡.	South bids 2 ♡.	South bids 2 ♡.
♠ A K 8 6 4 2	♠ 3	♠ A Q 3 2	♠ J 8 4
♡ 7	♡ A Q 10 4	♡ 7	♡ K J 10 6
◊ A J 3	◊ 10 9 5 2	◊ A K 8 4 3	◊ 7
♣ 9 4 2	♣ K Q 6 5	♣ A 9 6	♣ 8 7 5 4 3
6. South bids 2 ♣.	**6.** South bids 2 ♣.	**6.** North bids 2 ♠.	**6.** North bids 2 ♠.
♠ K 8 4 2	♠ J 10	♠ K Q 10 7	♠ 8 3
♡ 3 2	♡ A K 7 6 4	♡ A K 7 4 3	♡ 6 2
◊ A 9 8 6 4 2	◊ 7	◊ K 8 2	◊ A 9 7 5
♣ 3	♣ A J 10 8 5	♣ 9	♣ K Q 6 3 2

PLAY HANDS ON PENALTY DOUBLES & PENALTY PASSES

Hand 125: Penalty double of 1NT overcall – Leading partner's suit – Suit preference signals

Dealer North : Game all

NORTH
♠ 7 6 3 2
♡ 10 2
◊ 9 8 5 4
♣ 8 5 4

WEST
♠ J 10 8
♡ Q 6 3
◊ K 10 7 2
♣ A 10 6

EAST
♠ K Q 9
♡ A 9 7 5 4
◊ 6
♣ Q J 7 3

SOUTH
♠ A 5 4
♡ K J 8
◊ A Q J 3
♣ K 9 2

WEST	NORTH	EAST	SOUTH
	No	1 ♡	1NT (1)
Dble (2)	No (3)	No (4)	No (5)

Bidding: (1) 16-18 balanced with a heart stopper.
(2) Double the 1NT overcall when your side has more HCP.
(3) Do not try to rescue when balanced with no 5-card suit.
(4) You should remove a penalty double only on freak shapes, not just because the hand is unbalanced.
(5) 2 ◊ doubled fares just as badly as 1NT doubled.

Lead: ♡ 3. Unless you have a very strong suit, prefer to lead partner's suit. Lead the bottom card from Honour-x-x.

Correct play: East takes the ♡ A and returns the ♡ 5. With more than two cards left, lead top from a remaining sequence, but lead the original fourth-highest card if there is no sequence.

South should finesse the ♡ J and West wins the ♡ Q. On the third heart, East's hearts are 9-7-4 and it does not matter to East which one is played. East therefore chooses the *nine*, the highest, to tell partner to lead the highest suit, spades, to find East's entry. High card high suit, low card low suit. Note that if West later shifts to the ♣ A, that would give South a trick with the ♣ K. After winning the ♡ K, South plays ◊ A and ◊ Q: West wins and switches to ♠ J. When East gains the lead, East cashes the two heart winners and switches to the ♣ Q. This defence holds declarer to four tricks (one spade, one heart, two diamonds) for +800. Note that if West led the ♡ Q originally, this would give South an extra trick in hearts. Lead bottom from Q-x-x.

Hand 126: The penalty pass – Suit preference signal – Defensive technique

Dealer East : Love all

NORTH
♠ 3
♡ A 6 4
◊ A Q 9 6 3
♣ J 7 6 5

WEST
♠ J 8 2
♡ 8 7
◊ K J 10 8 5 4
♣ A K

EAST
♠ K 10 5 4
♡ J 10 5 2
◊ 2
♣ 10 9 8 2

SOUTH
♠ A Q 9 7 6
♡ K Q 9 3
◊ 7
♣ Q 4 3

WEST	NORTH	EAST	SOUTH
		No	1 ♠
2 ◊ (1)	No (2)	No (3)	Dble (4)
No (5)	No (6)	No (7)	

Bidding: (1) A *very* sound overcall and yet it comes to grief. Imagine the possible damage if you overcall on a weak suit.
(2) The North hand is ideal for penalties: misfit with opener, strong trumps and lots of HCP. If playing penalty doubles, North doubles and South passes. Using negative doubles, you pass for penalties and hope partner re-opens with a double.
(3) Do not bid opposite an overcall if weak. No heroics.
(4) Double is far superior to 2 ♡. If 2 ♡ is the right spot, North can bid it in reply to the double. North is unlikely to have hearts (no negative double) or spade support (no 2 ♠ raise).
(5) This would be a bad time to bid 3 ◊ to push the bidding up.
(6) The penalty pass closes the trap.
(7) The outside suits are too poor for an S.O.S. redouble.

Lead: ♣ 3. Partner should expect a spade shortage because you have made a low-level penalty pass.

Correct play: South wins and cashes the other top spade, North discarding the ♡ 6. South now leads the *nine* of spades for North to ruff, a high card asking for the high suit back. North ruffs, cashes the ♡ A and leads a heart to South. The defence has taken five tricks and North still has ◊ A-Q-9-6 left, sure to be three tricks, for +500. North exits each time with clubs and simply waits for the diamond tricks to come. On the spade lead, West should play low in dummy and drop the ♣ J from hand, trying to fool South that it is a singleton. South should not be misled. If the ♣ J is singleton, North would have three spades, inconsistent with a penalty pass.

Hand 127: Penalty pass – Suit-preference signal – Defensive technique

Dealer South : North-South vulnerable

	NORTH	
	♠ Q 10	
	♡ K Q 9 5 3	
	◇ J 8 7 6	
	♣ A K	

WEST		EAST
♠ A K J 8		♠ 9 6
♡ 7		♡ A J 10 8 6 2
◇ A Q 9 5 3		◇ 4
♣ 6 3 2		♣ Q J 9 8

	SOUTH	
	♠ 7 5 4 3 2	
	♡ 4	
	◇ K 10 2	
	♣ 10 7 5 4	

WEST	NORTH	EAST	SOUTH
			No
1 ◇	1 ♡ (1)	No (2)	No
Dble (3)	No	No (4)	No

Bidding: (1) Worth 1 ♡ even at adverse vulnerability. Double is inferior without tolerance for the black suits.

(2) Perfect for penalties: strong trumps, misfit with opener and enough HCP. If using penalty doubles, East doubles and West would pass. If sensibly using negative doubles, East passes for penalties and awaits a re-opening double.

(3) Double is superior to 1 ♠. If spades is the best contract, East will bid spades in reply to the double. East's failure to double or bid spades suggests East does not have spades. The double allows partner to bid or to pass, whichever is suitable.

(4) Things have gone exactly as East hoped.

(5) South might think of running but if South bids 1 ♠, West will double. After a penalty double or a penalty pass, all later doubles are for penalties. Both 1 ♠ doubled and 1NT doubled can be defeated by three tricks.

Lead: ◇ 4. Partner's suit is the normal lead.

Correct play: West wins and cashes a second diamond, East discarding a spade. West continues with the ◇ 9 (high card when giving a ruff = 'Play back the higher suit') and East ruffs. A spade allows West to cash a second spade before giving East another diamond ruff. E-W have six tricks so far and East still has ♡ A-J-10-8 over North's ♡ K-Q-9-5-3. As long as East does not lead trumps, but exits patiently with clubs, East takes three more tricks for three off, +800. (If South runs to 1 ♠, West doubles and leads a heart to East, who returns a diamond. After two diamond tricks, a defensive cross-ruff ensues: diamond ruff, heart ruff, etc., for three off.)

Hand 128: Negative double – Penalty pass – Suit preference signal – Defensive technique

Dealer West : East-West vulnerable

	NORTH	
	♠ J 10	
	♡ A K 7 6 5	
	◇ 7	
	♣ A J 10 8 5	

WEST		EAST
♠ Q 7 5 4 3		♠ A
♡ Q J 9		♡ 10 4 3
◇ Q 4 3 2		◇ K J 5
♣ 2		♣ K Q 9 7 6 4

	SOUTH	
	♠ K 9 8 6 2	
	♡ 8 2	
	◇ A 10 9 8 6	
	♣ 3	

WEST	NORTH	EAST	SOUTH
No	1 ♡	2 ♣ (1)	Dble (2)
No (3)	No (4)	No (5)	

Bidding: (1) An impeccable overcall, despite what happens.

(2) Negative double, promising 4+ spades and 6+ points. South is too weak to bid 2 ♠ or 2 ◇.

(3) There is no reason for West to panic. West is too weak to bid (since South's double showed spades, 2 ♠ would not be a bright move) and South's negative double is for takeout.

(4) What a delightful development! Only the negative doublers can score these penalties. If South bids 2 ◇ or 2 ♠, East would be off the hook and if South passed, North would pass out 2 ♣ (and collect undoubled penalties) since a double by North would be for takeout.

(5) East might have a fleeting thought that the opponents have muffed it and that 2 ♣ doubled might actually be making.

Lead: ♡ 8. Partner's suit and top from a doubleton.

Correct play: North wins the ♡ K and, knowing South will not have heart support because of the negative double, cashes the ♡ A. North continues with the ♡ 5 when giving South a heart ruff, lowest card for the low suit back (excluding trumps, of course). South ruffs and switches to ace and another diamond, giving North a ruff. With five tricks in, North's remaining ♣ A-J-10-6 will be good for three more tricks at least. After the ♡ K, North might consider switching to the ◇ 7 at once. That is not best (although it works here). If East had the ◇ A, East would win and draw South's trump. The defence would then miss the heart ruff.

REVISION TEST ON PART 4

   The answers to all these questions can be found in Chapters 25-32. Give yourself 1 mark for each correct answer. If you score less than 40, it will profit you to revise the relevant sections.

A. Partner opened 1 ♠, RHO bid 2 ◇. Using negative doubles, what action do you take with these hands?

1. ♠ A 9	2. ♠ 8 3	3. ♠ 6 3	4. ♠ K 8	5. ♠ 2
♡ K J 7 2	♡ K Q 9	♡ A K J 8	♡ A K 7	♡ A J
◇ K 3 2	◇ K 8 3 2	◇ 7 6	◇ 8 4 3 2	◇ K J 9 5 2
♣ 9 7 4 2	♣ K 7 6 2	♣ A Q 9 7 2	♣ A 9 4 2	♣ 9 8 5 3 2

B. RHO opened 1 ◇, you doubled and partner replied 1 ♠, pass on your right. What do you do now?

1. ♠ K 5 3	2. ♠ Q 5 2	3. ♠ A 2	4. ♠ A Q 9	5. ♠ A 3
♡ A Q J 9 3 2	♡ K Q 9	♡ A 2	♡ A K Q	♡ A K 2
◇ 8	◇ A K 2	◇ 9 4	◇ 8 3 2	◇ A 9 4
♣ A K Q	♣ A J 10 8	♣ A K Q 8 6 3 2	♣ A K Q 4	♣ A K Q 3 2

C. Partner opened 1 ♡ and RHO doubled. What should responder do with each of these hands?

1. ♠ 9 8 5 2	2. ♠ A 10 7	3. ♠ A J 5 3	4. ♠ Q J 8 2	5. ♠ A Q 7 5
♡ K 7 3 2	♡ 8 4 2	♡ 6	♡ Q 9 6 3	♡ - - -
◇ A 10 9 2	◇ A K 9	◇ A Q 9 6 2	◇ A Q 8	◇ A 9 7 4 3
♣ 2	♣ Q J 8 2	♣ 8 5 3	♣ 5 2	♣ K J 7 3

D. Partner opened 1NT, RHO bid 2 ♠. What should responder do with each of these hands?

1. ♠ K 9 4 2	2. ♠ 4 2	3. ♠ 7 2	4. ♠ 3 2	5. ♠ - - -
♡ 8 7 3	♡ K Q 3 2	♡ Q J 8 6 3	♡ A 2	♡ Q J 3 2
◇ A K 5 2	◇ Q J 2	◇ A K J	◇ K 9 6 2	◇ A J 7 6
♣ J 6	♣ A J 6 4	♣ K 4	♣ A Q 6 4 3	♣ A J 10 5 3

E. What are your answers for **D.** if RHO bid an artificial 2 ◇ over 1NT to show a 2-suiter including spades?

F. You opened 1 ◇, LHO overcalled 2 ♣, passed back to you. What action do you take with these hands?

1. ♠ K 7	2. ♠ K Q J	3. ♠ A 3	4. ♠ K	5. ♠ A J 7 2
♡ 7 3	♡ A Q J	♡ A K J 4	♡ A J	♡ 6
◇ A Q 9 6 4	◇ K Q 7 6 4	◇ Q J 8 7 4 2	◇ K Q J 8 5 4 2	◇ A K J 4 3
♣ K J 7 3	♣ 3 2	♣ 4	♣ 9 7 2	♣ 9 6 2

G. What would your answers be for **F.** if LHO's overcall had been 1 ♡ passed back to you?

H. You opened 1 ◇, LHO bid 2 ♡ (weak), negative double by partner, pass on your right. What now?

1. ♠ A K 6 2	2. ♠ Q 6	3. ♠ 8 3	4. ♠ 5 2	5. ♠ A 8 7 2
♡ 3	♡ 9 7 3	♡ 7 2	♡ K Q 10 8	♡ 6
◇ A Q 6 5	◇ A K Q 8 4	◇ A K Q J 8 7	◇ A 9 8 6 2	◇ A K 10 9 3
♣ Q 9 8 3	♣ A K J	♣ A K 5	♣ A K	♣ K Q J

I. Partner opened 1 ♠, RHO bid 2 ◇, you doubled (negative) and partner bid 3 ♣, passed to you. What now?

1. ♠ K 7	2. ♠ A 7	3. ♠ A	4. ♠ K 7 2	5. ♠ 2
♡ Q 9 7 3	♡ A Q 6 3	♡ A K J 2	♡ A J 10 9 3	♡ K 9 6 3
◇ 9 6 4	◇ 7 6 4	◇ Q 7 6 4	◇ 9 8 6 3 2	◇ 9 4 3
♣ K J 7 3	♣ K 7 6 2	♣ J 8 5 4	♣ - - -	♣ K Q J 9 2

J. Partner opened 1 ♡ and RHO overcalled 1NT. What should responder do with each of these hands?

	2. ♠ A 7	3. ♠ 8 7 5 4 2	4. ♠ A J 7 2	5. ♠ 9 2
♠ K 7				
♡ 7 3	♡ K 7 6 4	♡ K 9 5 4	♡ 7	♡ 6
◇ A Q 9 6	◇ Q J 8 6	◇ Q 7 6	◇ Q 9 7 3	◇ K Q J 10 8 3
♣ J 10 7 6 2	♣ 7 3 2	♣ 4	♣ 10 9 7 5	♣ 9 7 5 4

ANSWERS TO EXERCISES AND QUIZZES

(Note: No = no bid. In the Partnership Bidding sets, dealer's action is given first.)

Page	**Answers and Comments**
3	**Set 1:** 1. 1NT : 3NT, No 2. 1NT, 3NT : No 3. No : 1NT, 2NT : 3NT, No 4. 1NT : 3NT, No

5. No : 1♣, 1♦ : 1NT, 3NT : No ✗   **Set 2:** 1. 2NT : No   2. No : 2NT, 3NT : No ✗ 3. 2NT : 3NT, No
4. No : 2NT, 3NT : No   5. 2NT : 6NT, No

7   **A.** 1. 1♠   2. 1♥   3. 1♦   4. 1♦   5. 1♠   **B.** 1. 1♠ – show the major before supporting a minor
2. 1♥   3. 1♥   4. 1♥   5. 1♠ – 2♣ would show 10+ points
C. 1. 1♠   2. 2♥   3. 4♥   4. 2♥   5. 1♠   **D.** 1. 4♠   2. 2♠   3. 1NT – too weak for 2♦   4. 1NT   5. 2♠

10   **A.** 1. 1♠   2. 1♦   3. 1♠   4. 1♦   5. 1♥   **B.** 1. 2♥   2. 2♥   3. 1♠   4. 1♠ – too weak for 2♦   5. 4♥
C. 1. 1♥   2. 1♥   3. 1NT   4. 1♠   5. 3♣   **D.** 1. 2♥   2. 4♥ – 5 points for the void   3. 1NT   4. 1♠   5. 3♣
E. 1. 1♠   2. 1♠ – bid the major, not 1NT   3. 2♣   4. 3♦   5. 1NT   **F.** 1. 2♦   2. No   3. 2♣   4. 2♦   5. No
Set 3: 1. 1♣ : 2♣, No   2. No : 1♦, 2♦ : 3NT   3. 1♥ : 2♥, No   4. No : 1♠, 2♠ : 4♠
5. 1♠ : 4♠   6. No : 1♠, 2♠ : 3♠, No   **Set 4:** 1. 1♦ : 1NT, No   2. No : 1♥, 1NT : 3NT
3. 1♠ : 1NT, 2♥ : No   4. No : 1♥, 1NT : 3♦, 4♥   5. 1♠ : 1NT, 3♠ : No   6. No : 1♠, 1NT : 3♥, 4♥

11   **G.** 1. No   2. 4♠   3. 4♠   4. No   5. No   **H.** 1. No   2. 3♦   3. 3♠   4. 2♠   5. 2♠   **I.** 1. 2♠   2. 1NT
3. 2♣   4. 2♥   5. 1NT – prefer not to rebid a 5-card suit   **J.** 1-5: No – all too weak for further action
K. 1. No   2. 2♠   3. 2♥ – too weak for 2♦ or 2NT   4. No   5. 2♠   **L.** 1. No   2. 4♠   3. 4♠   4. 4♠   5. 4♠
Set 5: 1. 1♣ : 1♥, 1NT : 2♥, No   2. No : 1♣, 1♥ : 1♠, 1NT : No   3. 1♣ : 1♥, 2♣ : No
4. No : 1♦, 1♥ : 1♠, 2♠ : No   5. 1♦ : 1♠, 2♦ : 2♠, No   6. No : 1♦, 1♥ : 2♣, 2♦ : No
Set 6: 1. 1♣ : 1♠, 4♠   2. No : 1♦, 1♥ : 2NT, 3NT   3. 1♥ : 1♠, 3♦ : 3♠, 4♠
4. No : 1♣, 1♦ : 1♥, 2♥ : 4♥   5. 1♣ : 1♥, 1♠ : 2♥, 4♥   6. No : 1♥, 1♠ : 4♥, No

18   **A.** 1. 1♠   2. 1♥   3. 1♦ (or 1♠, intending to rebid 3NT if no spade fit is found)   4. 1♠   5. 1♦ – longest first
B. 1. 2♦   2. 2♣ – longest first   3. 2NT   4. 1♠   5. 3♦
C. 1. 2♥   2. 2♦   3. 2♣ – partner can bid 2♥ with 4 hearts   4. 2♠ – support spades on the next round
5. 3♠ – too strong for 2♠, even though the shape is poor
D. 1. 1♥ – bid 4-card suits up-the-line   2. 1♥ – 1NT would be a serious error   3. 3♦   4. 2♣   5. 3♣
Set 7: 1. 1♣ : 1♥, 1♠ : 3♠, 4♠   2. 1♠ : 1♥, 1NT : 3NT   3. 1♣ : 1♥, 2♥ : 3NT, 4♥
4. 1♣ : 1♥, 1♠ : 3♠, 4♠   5. 1♣ : 1♥, 2♣ : 3NT   6. 1♣ : 1♥, 3♠ : 3NT
Set 8: 1. 1♦ : 1♠, 1NT : 4♠   2. 1♦ : 1♥, 2♣ : 3♥, 3NT   3. 1♦ : 1♠, 2♦ : 2♥, 3♠ : 4♠
4. No : 1♦, 1♥ : 2♣, 3♣ : 3NT   5. 1♦ : 1♥, 3♣ : 3NT   6. 1♦ : 3♦, 3NT

19   **E.** 1. 2♠   2. 2♥ – too weak for 2♠, past the 2♥ barrier   3. 3♣   4. 4♣   5. 3♥ – too good for 2♥
F. 1. 2♥   2. 2♠ – too weak for 3♣, past the 2♠ barrier   3. 3♦   4. 3NT   5. 4♣ (or 3♠ and 4♠ next)
G. 1. 1♠   2. 3♣   3. 3♦   4. 2NT   5. 3NT   **H.** 1. 2♠   2. 4♥   3. 3♥   4. 3♣ – not forcing   5. 3♦
Set 9: 1. 1♠ : 2♦, 2♠ : 3NT   2. 1♠ : 2♦, 2♥ : 4♥   3. 1♠ : 2♣, 2♥ : 2NT, No
4. 1♠ : 3NT   5. 1♠ : 2♣, 2♥ : 4♠   6. 1♠ : 2♦, 2♠ : 4♠
Set 10: 1. 1♦ : 2♣, 2♦ : 2♥, 4♥   2. 1♦ : 2♣, 2♥ : 3♥, 4♥   3. 1♠ : 2♣, 2♠ : 3NT
4. 1♠ : 2♣, 3♠ : 3♠, 4♠   5. 1♦ : 2NT, 4♥   6. 1♦ : 2♣, 3♣ : 3NT

26   **A.** 1. 1NT   2. 4♠   3. 3♦   4. 2♦   5. 3♣   **B.** 1. No   2. 2♦   3. 3NT   4. 3♣   5. 3♦
C. 1. 2♥   2. 3♥   3. No   4. 2♥ – with equal length, prefer partner's first suit   5. 2♥ – false preference
D. 1. 3♠   2. 2NT   3. 2NT   4. 3♣ – no major suit support, no diamond stopper   5. 2♠ – delayed support

27   **E.** 1. 3♥   2. 4♥ (or 3♦, then 4♥ to show the club singleton)   3. 4♥   4. 2♠ – too weak for 3♦   5. 3♦
F. 1. 3♥   2. 3NT   3. 3♠ – no club stopper for 3NT   4. 4♦ – slam chances too good to bid 3NT   5. 4♥
G. 1. 1NT   2. 1♠   3. 2NT   4. 3♥   5. 4♥   **H.** 1. No   2. No – too weak for 2♠   3. 2♠   4. 3♣   5. 3♦
Set 11: 1. No : 1♠, 3♠ : 4♠   2. 1♠ : 1♠, 2♣ : 2♥, 3♠ : 4♠   3. 1♠ : 1♠, 2♣ : 2♥, 2NT : 3NT
4. 1♦ : 1♥, 1♠ : 2♦, No   5. 1♥ : 1♠, 2♣ : 2♦, 2♠ : 4♠   6. 1♦ : 1♥, 2♦ : 2♠, 3♥ : 4♥
Set 12: 1. 1♠ : 2♥, 3♥ : 4♥   2. 1♠ : 2♦, 2♠ : 3♦, 3♥ : 4♥   3. 1♠ : 2♦, 3♠ : 3♦, 4♥
4. 1♠ : 2♦, 2♠ : 3NT   5. 1♦ : 1♠, 2♣ : 2♦, No   6. 1♦ : 1♠, 2♣ : 2♦, 2♠ : 4♠

31   **Set 13:** 1. 1NT : 3♥, 4♥   2. 1NT : 3♠, 3NT   3. 1NT : 4♠
4. No : 1NT, 2♠ : No   5. 1NT : 4♥   6. 1NT : 2♥, No
Set 14: 1. No : 2NT, 4♠   2. 2NT : 4♥, No   3. No : 2NT, 3♠ : 4♠
4. 2NT : 3♥, 3NT   5. No : 2NT, 3♥ : 4♥   6. 2NT : 3NT (Do not show the minor)

35   **Set 15:** 1. 1NT : 2♣, 2♥ : 4♥   2. No : 1NT, 2♣ : 2♠, 3♠ : 4♠   3. 1NT : 2♣, 2♥ : 2NT, 3NT
4. No : 1NT, 2♣ : 2♦, 2NT : 3NT   5. 1NT : 2♣, 2♥ : 3NT, 4♠   6. No : 1NT, 2♣ : 2♥, 3♥ : 4♥
Set 16: 1. 2NT : 3♣, 3♥ : 4♥   2. 2NT : 3♣, 3♥ : 3NT, 4♠   3. No : 2NT, 3♠ : 3♦, 3NT
4. No : 2NT, 3♣ : 3♥, 4♥   5. No : 2NT, 3♣ : 3♦, 3♥ : 4♥   6. 2NT : 3♣, 3♥ : 4♥

Page   **Answers and Comments**
39   **Set 17:** 1. No : 1♦, 1♥ : 1NT, 2♦ : No   2. 1♦ : 1♥, 1NT : 4♥   3. 1♣ : 1♠, 1NT : 3♠, 4♠
4. 1♣ : 1♥, INT : 2♠, 3♥ : 4♥   5. 1♠ : 1♠, 1NT : 3♥, 3♠ : 4♠
           Set 18: 1. 1♦ : 1♠, 2NT : 3♥, 3♠ : 4♠   2. No : 1♣, 1♥ : 1♠, 2♠ : 3♠, 4♠ 3. 1♣ : 1♠, 2NT : 4♠
4. No : 1♦, 1♠ : 2NT, 3♣ : 3♠, 4♠ (3♠ over 2NT would not be forcing) 5. 1♣ : 1♠, 2NT : 4♥, 4♠

45   **A.** 1. 7   2. 7   3. 6   4. 8   5. 6   6. 4   7. 5   8. 7   9. 5   10. 4   11. 6   12. 4   13. 6   14. 7   15. 5
           B. (a) 1. 2♦   2. 2♦   3. 2♥   4. 2NT   5. 2♦   (b) 1. 2NT   2. 2NT   3. 2♥   4. 3♦   5. 3♦
           (c) 1. 2NT   2. 4♥   3. 3♥   4. 3NT   5. 2♠   (d) 1. 2NT   2. 4♠   3. 3♥   4. 3♠   5. 3♠
           C. 1. 2♥   2. 3♦   3. 2NT   4. 3♣   5. 2♥
           D. 1. 2NT – no support, no 5-card suit   2. 3♠ – stronger than 4♠   3. 3♥   4. 4♠ – see No. 2   5. 3♦
           Set 19: 1. No : 2♣, 2NT : 3NT, 6NT   2. No : 2♣, 2♦ : 2NT, 4♠   3. 2♣ : 2♦, 2NT : 3♠, 3♠ : 4♠
4. No : 2♣, 2♦ : 2NT, 3♣ : 3♥, 4♥   5. 2♣ : 3♠, 3NT : 4NT, 5♠ : 5NT, 6♣ : 7NT
6. 2♥ : 2♠, 3♥ : 4NT, 5♥ : 6♥   **Set 20:** 1. No : 2♣, 4♠ (two 2nd round controls, no 1st round control)
2. No : 2♣, 2♦ : 2♠, 3♠ : 4NT, 5♦ : 6♠   3. 2♣ : 2♦, 2♠ : 3♥, 4♥
4. 2♣ : 3♦, 4NT : 5♥, 5NT : 6♦, 7NT – you can count 13 winners in no-trumps
5. No : 2♣, 2♦ : 2♠, 3♥ : 4NT, 5♦ : 7♥   6. 2♦ : 2NT, 3NT (with 9 easy tricks, 3NT is a good chance)

48   **A.** 1. 1NT   2. 1NT   3. 2♣   4. 2♥   5. 4♠   6. 2♠   7. 1NT   8. 3♦   9. 3♣ (too good for 2♣)   10. 3♠
           B. 1. 1NT   2. 2♣   3. 4♥   4. 3♣   5. 4♠   6. 2♠   7. 2NT   8. 4NT   9. 2♥   10. 3NT
           C. 1. 2♣   2. 4♥   3. 2♣   4. No   5. 2♠   **D.** 1. 3♣   2. 3♥   3. 3♣   4. 3♣   5. 4♠
           E. 1. 3NT   2. 2NT   3. 6NT 4. 3♥   5. 3♠   **F.** 1. 7NT   2. 3♣   3. 7NT   4. 3♣   5. 3♣
           G. 1. 2♥   2. 3♥   3. 2♣   4. 3♠   5. 4♠   **H.** 1. 3♦   2. 3NT   3. 3♠   4. 3NT   5. 4♥

51   1. 1♥   2. No   3. 1♠   4. 2♣   5. No

52   **A.** 1. No   2. 1♠   3. 1NT   4. Dble   5. No   6. Dble   7. Dble   8. 1NT   9. Dble   10. Dble
           B. 1. No – suits too weak to overcall   2. 2♦ – strong suit   3. No   4. Dble – too strong for 1NT   5. No

53   **C.** 1. No   2. No – despite the good support   3. 2♥   4. No   5. 3♥   6. 1♠   7. 4♥   8. 1NT   9. 2NT
           10. 2♦   11. 3NT   12. 1NT – prefer not to raise with 4-3-3-3   13. 2♠   14. 3♦   15. 2♣ – artificial, forcing
           D. 1. No – diamonds too weak to bid   2. 2♠   3. 2NT – inviting 3NT if partner is maximum   4. 2♦ 5. No
           Set 21: 1. (1♣) : 1♠ : 4♠   2. (1♦) : 1♠ : 3♠, 4♠   3. (1♣) : 1♥ : 3♥, No   4. (1♥) : 2♠ : 2NT, 3NT
5. (1♣) : 1♠ : 2♠, No   **Set 22:** 1. (1♣) : 2♣ : 2♥, 4♥   2. (1♦) : 1♠ : 2♠, 4♠
3. (1♠) : 1NT : 3NT   4. (1♥) : 1NT : 3♠ (game force with 5 spades), 4♠   5. (1♦) : 1♠ : 4♠

57   **A.** 1. 1♠ – too strong for a weak jump   2. 1♥   3. 2♥   4. Double – too strong for any jump-overcall   5. 2♦
           B.(1) 1. 2♣   2. 1♥   3. 1♥   4. Double   5. 1♦   **B.(2)** 1. 1♠   2. 1♥   3. 1♥   4. Double   5. 1♦
           C. 1. 4♠   2. No – 3♠ will probably fail and you might defeat 3♦   3. No   4. 4♠   5. 4♥ – worth the risk
           Set 23: 1. (1♣) : 2♠ : No   2. (1♠) : 3♥ : 4♥   3. (1♥) : 3♠ : 3NT   4. (1♠) : 2♥ : 3♥, 4♥
5. (1♣) : 2♦ : No   6. (1♥) : 3♦ : 3NT   **Set 24:** 1. (1♦) : 2♣ : 3♠, No   2. (1♣) : 2♥ : 2♠, 4♠
3. (1♦) : 2♠ : No – give up early on a misfit   4. (1♥) : 3♣ : 3NT   5. (1♦) : 3♣ : No 6. (1♣) : 2♥ : 4♥

62   **A.** 1. 2♦   2. No   3. 2♦   4. 2NT   5. 2NT   6. Dble   7. 2NT   8. 2NT   9. 2♦   10. 2♣
           B. 1. No   2. Dble – looking for penalties in either minor   3. 4♥   4. 3♥   5. 4NT – slam in hearts likely
           C. 1. 3♦   2. 4♣   3. 3♣ – with equal length   4. 4NT – bid 6♦ opposite one ace and 5♦ opposite no aces
           5. 3♦   6. 5♣   7. No – very rare decision   8. 4♣   9. 3♠ – seeking support   10. 3NT – good chance
           D. 1. No   2. 5♠ (or 4♠)   3. No   4. 4NT   5. No   6. 4NT   7. Dble   8. 5♣   9. 3♠   10. Dble

67   **A. (a)** 1. 4♠   2. 4♥   3. 5♦   4. 4♠   5. 1♥   6. No   7. 3♣   8. No
           (b) 1. 3♠   2. 3♥   3. 5♦   4. 4♠   5. 1♥   6. No   7. No   8. No
           B. (a) 1. No   2. No   3. 4♥   4. No   5. 4♥   6. 3♠   7. 4NT   8. 4NT   9. 4♥   10. 4♥
           (b) 1. No   2. No   3. 4♥   4. 4♥   5. 4♥   6. 3♠   7. 4NT   8. 4NT   9. 4♥   10. 4♥
           Set 25: 1. 3♥ : 4NT, 5♦ : 7NT (can count 13 tricks)   2. 3♦ : 3NT   3. No : 4♠   4. 5♣ : 6♣, No
           Set 26: 1.3NT (Gambling) : No   2. No : 3NT, 4♣ : 4♦, No   3. 3NT : 5♣, No   4. 3NT : 6♦, No – note this

74   **A.** 1. Dble   2. Dble – 5-4 in majors   3. 1♥ – 5-3 in majors   4. No – not double   5. 1NT – not double
           B. 1. 1♠   2. 1♠   3. 1♠   4. 1♥   5. 2♣   6. 1♥   7. 1♠   8. 1♠   9. 2♣   10. 1NT – just OK
           C. 1. No   2. 3♠ – 4 losers   3. 3♥ – 4 losers   4. 2♠ – 5 losers   5. No – Do not rebid with a minimum
           Set 27: 1. (1♦) : Dble : 1♥, No   2. (1♣) : Dble : 1♠, No   3. (1♠) : Dble : 2♥, No
4. (1♥) : Dble : 1♠, 2♠ : No   5. (1♠) : No : (2♠) : Dble, 3♥ : No
           Set 28: 1. (1♦) : Dble : 1♥, 2♥ : No   2. (1♥) : Dble : 1♠, 3♠ : No
3. (1♦) : Dble : 1♥, 3♥ : 4♥   4. (1♣) : Dble : 1♠, 2♠ : No   5. (1♦) : No : (1♠) : Dble, 2♣ : 3♣, No

78   **A.** 1. 1♠   2. 1NT   3. 2♣   4. No   5. 1♠   **B.** 1. 2♥   2. 2♥   3. 2♥   4. 1NT   5. 2♦
           C. 1. 2♠   2. No   3. 3♦   4. 3♣ 5. 2♠   **D.** 1. No   2. 3NT   3. 2NT   4. 2♥   5. 3♠ – 4 losers

Page	Answers and Comments

78

Set 29: 1. (1♦) : Dble : 2♣, No   2. (1♣) : Dble : 1♥, 2♥ (5 losers) : 4♥   3. (1♠) : Dble : 2♥, No
4. (1♥) : Dble : 1♠, No   5. (1♦) : Dble : 1♠, (2♦) : No : 2♥, 2♠ : No
Set 30: 1. (1♠) : Dble : 1NT, No   2. (1♣) : Dble : 1♠, No   3. (1♣) : Dble : 1♠, No
4. (1♦) : Dble : 1NT, 2NT : 3NT   5. (1♠) : Dble : 2♦, (2♠) : No : 3♣, 3♦ : No

82

A. 1. 2♠   2. 2♥   3. 3♣   4. 2NT   5. 2♠   **B.** 1. 4♥   2. No   3. 2♠ – forcing   4. 3NT   5. 3♥
Set 31: 1. (1♦) : Dble : 2♠, 3♠ : 4♠   2. (1♦) : Dble : 2♥, 4♥   3. (1♥) : Dble : 2♠, No
4. (1♠) : Dble : 2♦, No   5. (1♠) : Dble : (2♠) : 4♥
Set 32: 1. (1♣) : Dble : 2NT : No   2. (1♠) : Dble : 2NT, 3NT   3. (1♦) : Dble : 3♣, 3♠ : 4♠
4. (1♣) : Dble : 2NT, 3♥ : 4♥   5. (1♥) : Dble : (2♥), 3♠ : 4♠

87

A. 1. No   2. Dble   3. 3♠   4. No   5. 3NT   6. 3NT   7. Dble   8. No   9. Dble   10. 4♦
B. 1. 3♠   2. 4♦   3. 4♠   4. 4♠   5. 3NT   **C.** 1. 3♠   2. No   3. 3NT   4. 3♥   5. 4♣ game force
Set 33: 1. (2♠) : Dble : 3♥, No   2. (2♠) : Dble : 4♥   3. (2♥) : 2NT, 3NT   4. (2♥) : 3♦, 3NT
5. (2♠) : Dble : 3♣ : 4♥ (4 losers)
Set 34: 1. (3♣) : Dble : 3♥, No   2. (3♠) : 3♥ (6 losers) : 4♥ (3 winners)   3. (3♦) : Dble : 4♥
4. (3♥) : No : Dble : No   5. (3♦) : Dble : 4♦ (game-force, pick a suit) : 4♠

90

A. 1. No   2. No   3. 4♥   4. Dble   5. Dble   **B.** 1. 2♥   2. 2NT   3. 2♦   4. Dble   5. 1NT
C. 1. 2NT   2. 2♥   3. 4♠   4. 3NT   5. 3♠   **D.** 1. 2♠   2. 2NT   3. 2♣   4. 2♠   5. 2♦
E. 1. No   2. Dble   3. Dble   4. 2NT   5. Dble   **F.** 1. No   2. 3♠   3. 2♠   4. 2NT   5. 2♠
G. 1. 2♣   2. 2♠   3. 1♠   4. 2NT   5. 1♠   **H.** 1. 2♣   2. 2♥   3. 3♥   4. 1NT   5. 3♣
I. 1. No   2. No   3. Dble   4. Dble   5. 3♣   **J.** 1. 4♦   2. 4♥   3. 3♠   4. 3NT   5. 3♠

94

A. 1. 2♠   2. 2NT   3. 3♣   4. 2♠ – looking for 3NT, too strong for 3♣   5. 2♠ – looking for heart support
6. 3♦   7. 2♠ – too strong for an invitational 3♦   8. 2♥   9. 3♥ – invitational   10. 2♠ – too strong for 3♥
B. 1. 3♦   2. 3NT   3. 3♥   4. 3♠   5. 4♣   6. 2NT   7. 3♦   8. 3♠   9. 3♥   10. 3♠ – too strong for 3♦
Set 35: 1. 1♣ : 1♦, 1♠ : 2♥, 2NT : 3NT   2. 1♣ : 1♦, 1♠ : 2♥, 3NT   3. 1♣ : 1♥, 1♠ : 2♦, 3NT
4. 1♣ : 1♥, 1♠ : 2♦, 3♦ : 4♥   5. 1♣ : 1♥, 1♠ : 2♦, 2♠ : 4♠   6. 1♦ : 1♠, 2♣ : 2♥, 3♦ : 3NT
Set 36: 1. 1♣ : 1♦, 1♠ : 2♥, 3♣ : 5♣   2. 1♠ : 2♣, 2♥ : 3♦, 3♠ : 4♠   3. 1♦ : 1♠, 2♣ ; 3♥, 4♥
4. 1♦ : 1♥, 1♠ : 3♥, 4♥   5. 1♣ : 1♦, 1♠ : 2♥, 3♣ : 4♠   6. 1♠ : 2♣, 2♥ : 3♦ (4ᵗʰ suit), 4♣
(delayed support; 5 spades, 4 hearts, 3 clubs = singleton diamond) : 4NT, 5♦ : 6♣

100

A. 1. 1NT – too weak for 2♥   2. 2♣   3. 2♦   4. 2NT   5. 2♥ – if worth 3♣, you are also worth 2♥
B. 1. 3♦   2. 3♥   3. 3♠   4. 2NT   5. 3NT   6. 2♠   7. 3♠ – 4ᵗʰ suit   8. 3♣   9. 4♦   10. 4NT
C. 1. 3♦   2. 3♥ – 4ᵗʰ suit   3. 4♦ – genuine support and strong hand   4. 3♠   5. 4♥ – freak 2-suiter
Set 37: 1. No : 1♦, 1♠ : 2♥, 3♦ : No   2. No : 1♦, 1♠ : 2♦, No   3. 1♦ : 1♠, 2♦ : 2♥, 4♥
4. 1♣ : 1♥, 2♦ : 2♥, No   5. 1♣ : 1♥, 2♦ : 3♥, 4♥ (not 3NT)   6. 1♥ : 2♣, 2♠ : 3♦ (4ᵗʰ suit), 3NT
Set 38: 1. No : 1♦, 1♠ : 2♥, 3NT   2. 1♠ : 1♠, 2♥ : 2NT, No   3. No : 1♣, 1♠ : 2♥, 2NT : 3♠, 3NT
4. 1♦ : 1♠, 2♥ : 3♣, 3NT   5. No : 1♣, 1♠ : 2♥, 3♦ : 3♠, 4♠   6. 1♦ : 1♠, 2♥ : 4♦, 4NT : 5♣,
5NT : 6♣, 6♦ : No

104

1. 1♦, 2♣, 3♣   2. 1♠, 2♦, 3♦   3. 1♠, 2♦, 3♦   4. 1♥, 2♦, 3♦   5. 1♦, 1♠, then rebid the spades
Set 39: 1. 1♠ : 2♣, 2♥ : 3♦ (4ᵗʰ suit), 3♥ : 4♥   2. 1♠ : 1♠, 2♣ : 2♥, 3♣ (no diamond stop) : 3♥, 4♥
3. 1♠ : 1♠, 2♣ : 2♥, 2NT (diamond stopper) : 3♥, 3NT   4. 1♦ : 1♠, 2♦ : 2♥, 3♠ : 4♠
5. 1♦ : 1♠, 2♣ : 2♠, No (you have spade tolerance)   6. 1♦ : 1♠, 2♣ : 2♠, 3♣ (no spade tolerance) : No
Set 40: 1. 1♦ : 1♥, 1♠ : 2♣ (4ᵗʰ suit), 2♠ : 4♠   2. 1♦ : 2♣, 2♥ : 2♠, 3♥ : 3♠ (shows the 6-5), 4♠
3. 1♥ : 2♦, 2♠ : 3♣, 3♠ (shows 6-5) : 4♥   4. 1♣ : 1♥, 2♦ : 2♠, 2NT : 3♠ (6-5 pattern), 4♥
5. 1♠ : 1♦, 2♣ : 2♠, 3♣ ; 3♠ (6-5 pattern), 4♦ : 5♦   6. 1♣ : 1♥, 1♠ : 1NT, 2♠ (shows weak 6-5) : No

108

A. 1. 2♣   2. 2♦ – clubs too weak to bother about   3. 2♦ – too weak to reverse   4. 2♥ – reverse 5. 4♠
6. 2♦ – too weak to reverse; too weak for 1NT   7. 1NT – weak long suits   8. 2♠   9. 2♣   10. 2♥ – reverse
Set 41: 1. 1♠ : 2♦, 2♥ : 2NT, 3♠ (shows 6-4) : 4♠   2. No : 1♦, 1♥ : 1♠, 1NT : 2♦ (weak 6-4), No
3. 1♣ : 1♠, 2♣ : 2♥, 2NT (diamond stopper) : 3♠, 4♠   4. No : 1♣, 1♥ : 1♠, 1NT : 3♣ (6-4), 3NT
5. 1♦ : 2♣, 2♦ (too weak to reverse) : 2♥, 3♥ : 4♥   6. 1♦ : 2♥, 2♠ : 3♦, 4♦ : 4♥ (6 hearts) : No
Set 42: 1. 1♦ : 1♠, 2♣ : 2♥ (4ᵗʰ suit), 3♠ (delayed support) : 4♠   2. No : 1♦, 1♥ : 2♣, 2NT : 3NT
3. No : 1♣, 1♦ : 1♥, 1NT : 2♠, 3♣ : No   4. 1♦ : 1♠, 2♠ : 4♠
5. No : 1♦, 1♥ : 1NT, No   6. 1♦ : 1♠, 2♣ : 2♥ (4ᵗʰ suit), 3♦ (no spade support, no heart stopper) : 3NT

112

A. 1. 3♦ – diamond stopper   2. 3♦   3. 3♠ – spade stopper   4. 4♥ – delayed support   5. 4NT – slam values
B. 1. 3NT – diamonds stopped   2. 4♣ – diamonds not stopped   3. 3♠ – excellent spades   4. 5♠   5. 3NT
Set 43 (a): 1. 1♠ : 2♣, 3♣ : 3♦, 3NT   2. 1♠ : 1♥, 3♣ : 3♠, 3NT   3. 1♠ : 1♥, 2♣ : 3♣, 3♦ : 3NT
4. 1♠ : 2♦, 3♦ : 4♠   5. 1♥ : 2♣, 3♣ : 3NT   6. 1♣ : 1♦, 3♦ : 3♥ (heart stopper), 3NT
Set 43 (b): 1. 1♠ : 2♣, 3♣ : 3♥, 3NT   2. 1♣ : 1♥, 3♣ ; 3♦, 3NT   3. 1♠ : 1♥, 2♣ : 3♣, 3♠ : 3NT
4. 1♠ : 2♦, 3♦ : 4♠   5. 1♥ : 2♣, 3♣ : 3NT   6. 1♣ : 1♦, 3♦ : 3♠ (stopper ask), 3NT

Page   **Answers and Comments**

112   **Set 44 (a):**   1. 1♥ : 2♣, 3♣ : 3♦, 4♣ : 5♣   2. 1♠ : 2♣, 3♣ : 3♦ (stopper), 3♠ (excellent spades) : 4♠
     3. 1♠ : 2♣, 3♣ : 3♥ (heart stopper), 5♣ (singleton diamond) : 6♣   4. 1♠ : 3♣, 3♠ (spade stop) : 5♠
     5. 1♥ : 2♣, 3♣ : 4♥   6. 1♣ : 1♦, 3♦ ; 3♥ (heart stopper), 4♦ (no spade stopper) : 5♦
  Set 44 (b):   1. 1♥ : 2♣, 3♣ : 3♠ (stopper ask), 4♣ : 5♣   2. 1♠ : 2♣, 3♣ : 3♦, 3♠ : 4♠, No
     3. 1♠ : 2♣, 3♣ : 3♦ (stopper ask), 5♣ (singleton diamond) : 6♣   4. 1♠ : 3♣, 3♦ : 3♥ 4♣ : 5♣
     5. 1♥ : 2♣, 3♣ : 4♥   6. 1♣ : 1♦, 3♦ : 3♠ (stopper ask), 4♦ (no spade stop, no spade singleton) : 5♦

116   **A.**   1. 2♥   2. 2♠   3. No   4. 3♣   5. No   **B.**   1. No   2. No   3. No   4. 3♣   5. 3♣ (length difference of 6)
  Set 45:   1. 1♠ : 1NT, 2♣ : 2♥, No   2. No : 1♠, 1NT : 2♣, 2♦ : No   3. 1♠ : 1NT, 2♦ : 2♥, No
     4. No : 1♠, 1NT : 2♠, No   5. No : 1♥, 1NT : 2NT, 3♣ : No (do *not* rebid 3NT) 6. 1NT : 2♠, 2♥ : 3♣, No
  Set 46:   1. No : 1♥, 1NT : 2♥, No   2. 1♥ : 1NT, 2♥ : 3♣, No   3. No : 1♠, 1NT : 2♣, 2♠ : No
     4. 1♠ : 1NT, 2♦ : 2♥, 4♠   5. 1♠ ; 1NT, 3♥ (jump shift) : 4♠, 5♣   6. No : 1NT, 2♣ (Stayman) : 2♥, No

121   **A.**   1. 3   2. 1   3. 1   4. 1   5. 1   6. 2   7. 2   8. 0   9. 0   10. 2   11. 2½   12. 3   13. 2   14. 2   15. 1
     16. 2   17. 1   18. 1   **B.**   1. 7; 4   2. 7½; 2   3. 4; 4   4. 7½; 4   5. 5; 5
  Set 47:   1. 1♠ : 4♠   2. No : 1♥, 2♥ : 4♥   3. No : 1♠, 3♠ : 6♠   4. 1NT : 4♠ 5. (1♣) : 1♠ : 4♠
  Set 48:   1. 1♣ : 1♠, 2♠ : 4♠   2. 1♠ : 1♠, 2♠ : No (note contrast 1 and 2)   3. 1♠ : 4NT, 5♠ : 7♠
     4. 1♦ : 1♥, 1♠ : 4NT, 5♠ : 7♠   5. (1♥) : Double : 2♠ (8 losers), No (8 losers)

125   **Set 49:**   1. No : 1♥, 2♥ : 3♣ (trial), 4♥   2. No : 1♥, 2♥ : 3♣, 3♥ : No   3. No : 1♥, 2♥ : 3♣, 3♥ : No
     4. 1♠ : 2♠, 3♣ : 4♠ (2 club losers but maximum)   5. 1♠ ; 2♠, 3♣ : 3♠, No   6. 1♠ ; 2♠, 3♣ ; 4♠
  Set 50:   1. 1♥ : 2♥, 3♦ ; 3♥, No   2. No : 1♠, 2♠ : 3♦, 4♠   3. 1♣ : 1♠, 2♠ : 3♦, 4♠
     4. 1♦ : 1♥, 2♥ : 3♣, 4♥ : 4NT, 5♥ : 6♥   5. 1♠ : 2♠, 3♦ : 4♠   6. 1♠ : 2♠ : 3♦ : 3♠, No

128   **A.**   1. 3NT   2. 3♥   3. 3♠   4. 4♣   5. 3NT   **B.**   1. 3♦   2. 2NT   3. 3♣   4. 3NT (maximum) 5. 4♦
  C.   1. 3♥   2. 3♠   3. 3NT   4. 3NT   5. 3♣   **D.**   1. No   2. 3♥ – stopper   3. 3♥   4. 3♠   5. 3NT
  E.   1. 3♣   2. 3NT (maximum)   3. 2NT   4. 2♥   5. 4♣   **F.**   1. 2♦   2. No   3. No   4. 2♦   5. 4♣
  G.   1. No   2. 3♦   3. 3♦   4. 2♠   5. 4♥   **H.**   1. No   2. No   3. 3♦   4. No   5. No – no safe move
  I.   1. 3♠   2. No   3. 4♠   4. 3♦   5. 4♣   **J.**   1. 4♠   2. 4♥   3. 3♠   4. 4♠   5. 4♠

131   **Set 51:**   1. (1♦) : 2♣ : 2♦, 2NT : 3NT   2. (1♥) : Dble : 3♣, 3♦ : 3♥, 3NT
     3. (3♣) : Dble : 4♣, 4♠   4. 1♠ : (2♦) : 2♥, 2♠ : 3♦, 3♥ : 4♥
     5. 1♠ : (2♥) : 3♣, 3♦ : 3♥, 3NT   6. 1♠ : 2♣ : (2♥), No : 3♥, 4♣ : 5♣
  Set 52:   1. 1♠ : (2♦) : 2♠, 3♣ : 3♦, 3NT   2. 1♣ : 1♦ : (2♠), 3♠ : 3NT
     3. 1♦ : 1♥ : (1♠), 2♠ : 3♥ : 4♥   4. 1♦ : 2♣ : (2♠), No : 3♥, 4♥
     5. (1♥) : 2♦ : 3♣, 3♠ : 3NT, 4♦ : 5♦   6. (1♠) : No : 2♠, 3♦ : 3♥, 4♣ : 4NT, 5♦ : 6♣

135   **A.**   1. 2♥   2. 4♠   3. 3NT   4. 2♥   5. 2♥   **B.**   1. 2♥ (or 2NT)   2. 2♠   3. 2♠   4. 2♠   5. 3♦
  Set 53:   1. (1♥) : Dble : 4♠ (excellent suit)   2. (a) (1♠) : Dble : 2♠, 3♦ : 3♥, 4♥
     (b) (1♣) : 1♦ : 1♥, 3♥ : 4♥   3. (1♦) : Dble : 2♦ (too strong for 3♣), 2♥ : 3♣, 3NT : No
     4. (1♠) : Dble : 2♣, 2♦ (up-the-line) : 2♥, 2♠ : 4♠
     5. (1♦) : Dble : 2♦ (3NT is premature), 2♥ : 2NT : 3NT   6. (1♣) : Dble : 2♣, 2♠ : 2NT, 3♥ : 4♠
  Set 54:   1. (1♠) : Dble : 1♥, 1NT : 2♥, No   2. (a) (1♣) : Dble ; 1♦, 1NT : 3NT
     (b) (1♦) : Dble : 1NT, 3NT   3. (1♦) : Dble : 1NT, 3♠ : 4♠   4. (1♣) : Dble : 1♦, 2♥ : 4♥
     5. (1♥) : Dble : 1♠, ♣ : No   6. (1♥) : Dble : 1♠, 3♦ : 3NT

140   **A.**   1. Rdble   2. 3♥   3. Rdble   4. 4♥   5. 2NT (Truscott) **B.**   1. 1♠   2. 2♣   3. 2♠   4. 1♠   5. 2♥
  C.   1. No   2. Dble (penalties) 3. No   4. 2♦   5. 2♥   **D.**   1. Dble   2. 3NT   3. 2NT   4. 3♥   5. 3♣
  Set 55:   1. 1♥ : (Dble) : 2NT (Truscott), 4♥   2. No : 1♠ : (Dble) : 3♣ : 4♠   3. 1♣ : (Dble) : 2NT, 3♣ : No
     4. 1♥ : (Dble) : Rdble : (2♣), No : Dble (penalties), No   5. 1♠ : (Dble) : Rdble : (2♦) : Double (penalties) : No
  Set 56:   1. 1♣ : (Dble) : 1♥, 1♠ : 3♥, 4♥   2. 1♦ : (Dble) 2NT, 4NT (or 4♦) : 5♥, 5NT : 6♣, 6♦
     3. No : 1♣ : (Dble) : 1♠ : 2♣, No   4. 1♠ : (Dble) : Rdble : (2♥), No : 3♣, 3♠ : 4♠
     5. 1♠ : (Dble) : Rdble : (2♣), 2♥ : 4♥

145   **A.**   1. Dble (penalties)   2. 3♥ (Stayman)   3. 2♠ (not forcing)   4. 3NT (no stopper needed) 5. 3♠ (forcing)
  B.   1. 3♣ (not forcing) 2. 2♠ (artificial, Stayman)   3. Dble (and double 2♠, too)
     4. 3NT (no stopper needed)   5. 4♥
  Set 57:   1. No : 1NT : (2♥), 2♠ (not forcing) : No   2. 1NT : (2♦) : 3♣ (not forcing), No – 3NT would be
     an error   3. 1NT : (2♠), 3NT (too strong for 3♦ ; no stopper needed for 3NT)
     4. No : 1NT : (2♠) Double (penalties), No
  Set 58:   1. 1NT : (2♥) : 3♥ – Stayman, 3♠ : 4♠   2. 1NT : (2♦) : 3♦ – Stayman, 3♠ : 3NT
     3. 1NT : (2♦) : 3♦ – Stayman, 3♥ : 3NT (not 3♠)   4. 1NT : (2♦) : 3♦ – Stayman, 3♥ : 3NT, 4♠   (the
     3♦ Stayman bid implies a major and as partner rejected hearts, there will be four spades opposite.)

Page   **Answers and Comments**

150
A.   1. Dble – perfect pattern   2. Dble   3. No – too much in hearts to bid again   4. 1NT – shows 17-19   5. 2♣

B.   1. Dble – better than 2♢   2. Dble – better than 2♡   3. No   4. Dble – rebid 2♡ over 2♢   5. No

C.   1. 2♡ – support and 0-5 points   2. 2♠ – 0-5 points because no negative double   3. 3♣   4. 2NT   5. No

D.   1. Dble   2. 2NT – delayed 2NT = minors   3. 3♢   4. Dble – and rebid 3♢ over 3♣   5. 2NT – minors

Set 59:   1. 1♡ : (2♣) : No, Double : 2♠, No   2. No : 1♢ : (2♡), No : Double, 3♣ : No

3. 1♠ : (2♢) : No, No   4. No : (1♡) : No : (2♡), No : (No) : 2NT – minors, 3♢ : No

5. No : (1♠) : Dble : (2♠), No : (No) : Dble, 3♣ : No

Set 60:   1. No : 1♣ : (1♠), No : 1NT, 2♡ : No   2. 1♣ : (1♠) : No, 1NT : 2NT, 3NT : No

3. No : 1♢ : (2♡), No : Dble, 3♣ : 3♢, No   4. No : (1♠) : No : (2♠), (No) : No : Double, 3♡ : No

5. No : (1♢) : 1♡ : (2♢), No : (No) : Double, 3♣ : No

155
A.   1. Dble   2. 1♠ – only 4 spades are promised over 1♢   3. Dble – shows both majors   4. 1♡   5. No

B.   1. Dble – show the hearts before supporting a minor   2. Dble – rebid 2♡ over 1NT, 2♢ or 2♣

3. 1NT   4. No   5. 2♡

C.   1. 1NT   2. 2NT – 17-18 + spade stopper   3. 2♣ – better than 1NT or 2♢   4. 2♡   5. 4♡

D.   1. Dble – for takeout.   2. 3♡ – do not sell out   3. 3♢ – do not sell out   4. 3♣   5. Dble

Set 61:   1. No : (No) : 1♣ (1♠), Dble : (2♠) : 3♡, No   2. 1♢ : (1♠) : Dble, 1NT : 2♡, No

3. No : 1♣ : (2♡), Dble : 2♠, No   4. 1♠ : (2♡) : Dble – minors, 3♣ – much better than 2♠ : No

5. 1♣ : (1♡) : Dble : (2♡), No : (No) : Dble, 3♣ : No

Set 62:   1. 1♣ : (1♠) : Dble : (2♠), No – too weak for 3♡ : (No) : Dble – do not sell out : (No), 3♡ : No

2. 1♢ : (2♣) : Dble – both majors, 4♠ – worth 20 points   3. 1♢ : (2♡) : 2♠ – not double, 3♠ : 4♠

4. 1♣ : (1♠) : Dble, 3♡ – too strong for just 2♡ : 4♡

5. 1♢ : (1♠) : Dble : (2♠), No : (No) : 3♡ – = 6-9 points, No

159
A.   1. 2♣   2. Dble – show the hearts, but 2♡ shows 5 hearts   3. 2♡ – not dble   4. Dble   5. 2♠ – not dble

B.   1. 2♢   2. 3♢ – too strong for 2♢ ; 3♢ = 16-18 points   3. 3♣ – game-force   4. 3♠   5. 3♢ = 16-18

C.   1. 2NT   2. 3♣   3. 3♢ – not just 2♢, which shows 6-9 points   4. 3NT   5. 2♠ – game force

D. (i)   1. 3NT   2. 3NT   3. 3NT   4. 3NT   5. 3NT   **(ii)**   1. 2NT   2. 3♢   3. 3♢   4. 3NT   5. 2♠

(iii)   1. 3♡   2. 3♡   3. 3♡   4. 4♡   5. 4♡ – when opener replies with a major, your rebid is routine

Set 63:   1. 1♢ : (1♠) : Dble, 2♣ : 2NT, 3NT : No   2. No : 1♣ : (1♠), Dble : 2♣, 2NT : 3♣, No – 3♣ is
a better choice than 2NT   3. 1♢ : (1♠) : Dble, 2♣ : 2NT, 3NT   4. No : 1♣ : (1♠), Dble : 2♡, 3♡ : 4♡

5. 1♠ : (2♡) : Dble – both minors, 3♠ – 16-18, 6+ spades : 4♠

Set 64:   1. 1♢ : (1♠), Dble : 2♡, 4♡   2. 1♢ : (1♠) : Dble, 2♣ : 3NT

3. No : 1♣ : (1♠), Dble : 2♠, 3NT   4. No : 1♣ : (1♠), Dble : 2♠, 3♡ : 4♡

5. 1♡ : (2♢) : Dble, 3♣ : 3♢ – game force and stopper ask, 3NT

167
A.   1. No – support hearts   2. No – clubs too weak – Double   3. Suitable   4. No – too weak   5. Suitable

B.   1. Dble   2. No – hearts strong, so partner's pass = weakness   3. Dble   4. No – strong hearts   5. No

C.   1. 2♡ – 0-5 points as you did not bid 2♡ earlier   2. 2♠   3. 2NT   4. No – penalty pass   5. 2♢

Set 65:   1. 1♠ : (2♢) : No, Dble : No   2. 1♠ : (1♡) : No, Dble : No   3. 1♣ : (1♡) : No, Dble : 1♠ : No

4. No : 1♡ : (2♣), No : Dble, 2♡ : No   5. 1♠ : (Dble) : Rdble : (2♡), No : Dble, No

6. No : 1♡ : (2♣), Dble : No

Set 66:   1. 1♡ : (1NT) : Dble, No   2. No : 1NT : (2♠), Dble – penalties : No   3. 1♢ : (4♠) : 5♡, No

4. No : 1♠ : (2♠), No : No   5. 1♢ : (1♡) : No (2♡) : No : Dble – extra values : No   6. 1♡ : (2♠) : Dble, No

170
A.   1. Dble   2. 2NT – 10-12 points, denies 4 hearts or support for spades   3. 3♣   4. 3♢   5. No (penalties)

B.   1. 3♡ – 4 losers, 5+ hearts   2. 1NT – shows 19-20 balanced   3. 3♣   4. 2♢ – forcing   5. 3NT

C.   1. 3♡   2. Rdble – aiming for 3NT   3. Rdble – aiming for penalties   4. 2NT – support, 10+ points   5. Redble

D.   1. Dble – for penalties   2. 3♣ – replacing Stayman   3. 3♡ – forcing   4. 3NT   5. 3♣ - Stayman

E.   1. Dble – for penalties   2. 2♠ – Stayman   3. 3♡   4. 3NT – no stopper needed   5. 2♠ – Stayman

F.   1. No – too strong in clubs   2. Dble – not quite enough for 3♣   3. Dble – but if partner bids 2♠,
remove this to 3♢   4. 2♢ – not suitable for low level penalties   5. Dble – but remove partner's 2♡ to 2♠

G.   1. Dble   2. 1NT – 17-19 balanced, worth 19 with the 5th diamond   3. No   4. 2♢   5. Dble

H.   1. 3♠ – too good for just 2♠   2. 3♡ – game force, stopper ask   3. 3♡ – as for 2.

4. No – penalty pass   5. 4♠

I.   1. No   2. 3♢ – 13+ points, stopper ask   3. 3NT   4. 4♠ – hearts cannot be better   5. 4♣

J.   1. Dble – penalties   2. Dble – penalties   3. 2♡   4. No – no reason to bid   5. 2♢ – not forcing

Congratulations if you have completed all the exercises and quizzes. Please do not spoil all this fine work and learning by incorrect behaviour at the table. You want to win and you will harm your chances if you bicker with partner and continually find fault. Partner is doing the best possible and if a mistake has occurred, it cannot be changed now. You will improve your chances of winning and be a popular partner if you maintain a pleasant disposition and display cheerfulness in the face of adversity. Always make sure it is happy bridging!

PLAY HANDS FOR NORTH

(After each hand, the dealer is given, followed by the vulnerability, e.g. S/Nil means Dealer South, love all.)

1	2	3	4	5	6	7	8
N/Nil	E/N-S	S/E-W	W/Both	N/N-S	E/E-W	S/Both	W/Nil
♠A6	♠KJ54	♠63	♠QJ973	♠107642	♠743	♠A5	♠Q76
♥843	♥1083	♥J4	♥J8	♥A10	♥8542	♥QJ10	♥K8765
◇1042	◇Q8	◇QJ10	◇J8765	◇1095	◇AKQ	◇7654	◇AQ
♣AKQ52	♣QJ105	♣J108643	♣3	♣A98	♣432	♣A1032	♣A64

9	10	11	12	13	14	15	16
N/E-W	E/Both	S/Nil	W/N-S	N/Both	E/Nil	S/N-S	W/E-W
♠A10543	♠A10642	♠3	♠KJ87	♠A96	♠KQ52	♠1053	♠KQ8643
♥AK76	♥Q109	♥9864	♥Q106	♥1043	♥Q10842	♥8	♥K2
◇Q6	◇943	◇AJ43	◇J1098	◇KJ875	◇5	◇KQ875	◇KQ
♣Q4	♣A10	♣AQ64	♣Q9	♣J8	♣AJ3	♣Q1054	♣764

17	18	19	20	21	22	23	24
N/Nil	E/N-S	S/E-W	W/Both	N/N-S	E/E-W	S/Both	W/Nil
♠K2	♠J10	♠KQJ1098	♠865	♠Q105	♠9542	♠32	♠A543
♥7654	♥98	♥964	♥Q95	♥AJ97	♥KQ106	♥1094	♥J2
◇A83	◇A97432	◇A	◇KQ109	◇K4	◇J84	◇Q962	◇872
♣AK94	♣KQ5	♣965	♣1075	♣KJ73	♣J10	♣KQ65	♣8762

25	26	27	28	29	30	31	32
N/E-W	E/Both	S/Nil	W/N-S	N/Both	E/Nil	S/N-S	W/E-W
♠KQ	♠975432	♠A93	♠KQJ10	♠AKJ42	♠Q1065	♠AKQ4	♠---
♥Q83	♥3	♥KQ3	♥94	♥J4	♥10984	♥KQJ9	♥J107
◇AQ964	◇A853	◇A83	◇A765	◇AK	◇76	◇AKQ	◇KQ86
♣Q107	♣94	♣KQ86	♣853	♣AKQ2	♣K87	♣A8	♣Q96543

33	34	35	36	37	38	39	40
N/Nil	E/N-S	S/E-W	W/Both	N/N-S	E/E-W	N/N-S	E/Nil
♠Q762	♠97	♠5	♠65432	♠AK4	♠A983	♠109	♠AK42
♥7	♥876	♥10865	♥AJ1095	♥KJ1094	♥AJ32	♥KJ1097	♥A5
◇A8432	◇98643	◇1092	◇9	◇J	◇54	◇105	◇Q3
♣Q97	♣1096	♣87653	♣A2	♣J1098	♣AQJ	♣AKQJ	♣87642

41	42	43	44	45	46	47	48
N/E-W	E/Both	S/Nil	W/N-S	N/Nil	E/Nil	S/E-W	W/N-S
♠J9	♠K10964	♠K654	♠8765	♠98	♠42	♠A83	♠AQ9
♥KQ6432	♥AJ	♥KQ5	♥---	♥653	♥KQ10	♥AJ10	♥63
◇AK103	◇65	◇763	◇Q984	◇A642	◇K1082	◇AQJ10	◇1098
♣7	♣7632	♣J73	♣A10432	♣AQ74	♣Q763	♣853	♣J9753

49	50	51	52	53	54	55	56
N/Nil	E/N-S	S/E-W	W/Both	N/N-S	E/Nil	S/Both	W/Nil
♠A742	♠J3	♠A95	♠A8	♠642	♠1086	♠1052	♠K3
♥AK6	♥KJ42	♥AKJ93	♥843	♥862	♥7532	♥109762	♥A8732
◇A10732	◇8653	◇K853	◇A10	◇K94	◇96	◇Q9	◇J6
♣6	♣1075	♣Q	♣KQ10832	♣KJ103	♣9743	♣1095	♣KQ42

57	58	59	60	61	62	63	64
N/E-W	E/Both	S/Nil	W/N-S	N/Nil	E/Nil	S/N-S	W/E-W
♠9	♠743	♠KQJ	♠AK95	♠AK1042	♠AQJ3	♠65	♠A942
♥AJ10	♥A932	♥10954	♥72	♥108	♥AJ762	♥A7	♥1074
◇Q1072	◇AQ84	◇KQJ108	◇KQ8	◇Q103	◇10	◇84	◇K10
♣AK987	♣J8	♣7	♣Q1074	♣J106	♣J82	♣KQ109873	♣10652

PLAY HANDS FOR NORTH

(After each hand, the dealer is given, followed by the vulnerability, e.g. S/Nil means Dealer South, love all.)

65 N/Nil	66 E/N-S	67 S/E-W	68 W/Both	69 N/N-S	70 E/E-W	71 S/Both	72 W/Nil
♠KQ72	♠865	♠AQ5	♠10	♠A96	♠AJ64	♠K10842	♠K2
♥KJ6	♥J105	♥932	♥J1096	♥10832	♥752	♥J9	♥AKQ3
♦K8	♦AK982	♦AJ1063	♦98432	♦Q103	♦J92	♦9765	♦KQJ93
♣K732	♣105	♣Q8	♣K106	♣QJ10	♣1083	♣98	♣75

73 N/E-W	74 E/Both	75 S/Nil	76 W/N-S	77 N/Both	78 E/Nil	79 S/N-S	80 W/E-W
♠93	♠92	♠AK754	♠J1087	♠J6	♠73	♠92	♠K9843
♥Q1065	♥K76	♥A86532	♥A92	♥K62	♥Q87	♥KJ1032	♥975
♦K764	♦A83	♦6	♦10	♦KQ865	♦KQ1087	♦96	♦Q1052
♣Q63	♣AQ743	♣5	♣Q9874	♣Q43	♣A108	♣A654	♣7

81 N/Nil	82 E/N-S	83 S/E-W	84 W/Both	85 N/N-S	86 E/E-W	87 S/Both	88 W/Nil
♠AJ1086	♠10	♠53	♠874	♠AJ3	♠AJ108	♠---	♠10982
♥K10	♥QJ1054	♥Q43	♥753	♥Q653	♥Q7	♥864	♥K42
♦96	♦10963	♦AK52	♦KQ8754	♦AQJ	♦75	♦AJ9532	♦A964
♣A843	♣1085	♣AK84	♣4	♣872	♣KJ952	♣Q743	♣A5

89 N/E-W	90 E/Both	91 S/Nil	92 W/N-S	93 N/Both	94 E/Nil	95 S/N-S	96 W/E-W
♠AKQ864	♠J98	♠K87653	♠J107	♠96	♠A954	♠9843	♠1097654
♥K8652	♥QJ8	♥4	♥J9	♥AQJ54	♥973	♥765	♥10
♦7	♦Q765	♦63	♦KQ7	♦A2	♦KQ4	♦J	♦K9
♣2	♣1063	♣A542	♣J10865	♣A932	♣Q108	♣KQ976	♣J985

97 N/Nil	98 E/N-S	99 S/E-W	100 W/Both	101 N/N-S	102 E/E-W	103 S/Both	104 W/Nil
♠107	♠QJ2	♠106432	♠10	♠Q9	♠K104	♠Q974	♠A53
♥AQ10965	♥953	♥952	♥AKQ864	♥QJ	♥A54	♥A	♥AKQJ108
♦K84	♦A9743	♦10753	♦9	♦AQJ107	♦A43	♦K983	♦AQ32
♣A10	♣54	♣J	♣AKQ76	♣Q985	♣Q743	♣A832	♣---

105 N/E-W	106 E/Both	107 S/Nil	108 W/E-W	109 N/Both	110 W/Nil	111 S/N-S	112 W/E-W
♠432	♠Q1052	♠KQ65	♠KJ643	♠AJ3	♠Q108	♠J942	♠AQ9653
♥42	♥A76	♥864	♥863	♥K986	♥AK9653	♥10	♥87
♦QJ1074	♦3	♦Q62	♦A104	♦A7	♦9	♦AQ4	♦KQ2
♣954	♣AK842	♣A93	♣A8	♣Q432	♣J102	♣AK863	♣J7

113 N/Nil	114 E/N-S	115 S/E-W	116 W/Both	117 N/N-S	118 E/E-W	119 S/Both	120 W/Nil
♠4	♠AK62	♠1084	♠J92	♠93	♠QJ1086	♠8643	♠J3
♥KQ975	♥AK	♥A5	♥109432	♥AK83	♥105	♥AJ93	♥AQJ983
♦7432	♦J852	♦9754	♦873	♦72	♦K974	♦J76	♦7
♣AKQ	♣AK8	♣9432	♣72	♣AK1052	♣102	♣92	♣A1064

121 N/E-W	122 E/Both	123 S/Nil	124 W/N-S	125 N/Both	126 E/Nil	127 S/N-S	128 W/E-W
♠KQ108432	♠983	♠Q5	♠QJ5	♠7632	♠3	♠Q10	♠J10
♥K65	♥J1075	♥A653	♥A10875	♥102	♥A64	♥KQ953	♥AK765
♦42	♦10876	♦10952	♦J83	♦9854	♦AQ963	♦J876	♦7
♣A	♣A9	♣A62	♣K8	♣854	♣J765	♣AK	♣AJ1085

PLAY HANDS FOR EAST

(After each hand, the dealer is given, followed by the vulnerability, e.g. S/Nil means Dealer South, love all.)

1 N/Nil	2 E/N-S	3 S/E-W	4 W/Both	5 N/N-S	6 E/E-W	7 S/Both	8 W/Nil
♠Q10985	♠A7	♠Q7542	♠AK	♠Q	♠86	♠98432	♠A1082
♥1076	♥AKQ	♥A1092	♥1062	♥KQ9862	♥7	♥K43	♥10
♦J965	♦A95	♦54	♦102	♦A74	♦987654	♦QJ8	♦K1053
♣4	♣A8642	♣95	♣A109876	♣Q106	♣A875	♣64	♣J1093

9 N/E-W	10 E/Both	11 S/Nil	12 W/N-S	13 N/Both	14 E/Nil	15 S/N-S	16 W/E-W
♠Q98	♠QJ3	♠Q98	♠3	♠Q73	♠107	♠Q	♠AJ9
♥Q10954	♥A8532	♥10	♥J53	♥A9	♥53	♥KJ9753	♥87
♦9	♦K86	♦Q1096	♦KQ42	♦64	♦K1097	♦A93	♦9652
♣J1096	♣Q3	♣KJ953	♣AJ752	♣AK7642	♣K10876	♣973	♣QJ95

17 N/Nil	18 E/N-S	19 S/E-W	20 W/Both	21 N/N-S	22 E/E-W	23 S/Both	24 W/Nil
♠109	♠865	♠3	♠KQJ4	♠AJ842	♠KQ	♠KQ864	♠J972
♥AQJ92	♥J1076543	♥QJ1032	♥AJ10	♥Q	♥AJ73	♥A873	♥A95
♦9762	♦---	♦KJ8	♦J42	♦J1086	♦Q103	♦J7	♦1053
♣J5	♣932	♣J843	♣AKQ	♣962	♣Q952	♣A2	♣J105

25 N/E-W	26 E/Both	27 S/Nil	28 W/N-S	29 N/Both	30 E/Nil	31 S/N-S	32 W/E-W
♠98532	♠AK	♠K876	♠A8742	♠Q93	♠K943	♠J10753	♠86543
♥107	♥AJ6	♥J8	♥8732	♥76	♥AKQ5	♥4	♥5
♦J	♦K94	♦10752	♦Q2	♦9865	♦AKQ	♦1098	♦A732
♣A9852	♣87632	♣AJ10	♣J2	♣10987	♣A6	♣Q643	♣J72

33 N/Nil	34 E/N-S	35 S/E-W	36 W/Both	37 N/N-S	38 E/E-W	39 N/N-S	40 E/Nil
♠A10	♠K5432	♠K973	♠7	♠J6	♠KQ2	♠AK8643	♠QJ9
♥KJ1094	♥J10	♥QJ43	♥K2	♥73	♥KQ7	♥6	♥74
♦KQJ	♦752	♦K3	♦QJ754	♦1083	♦Q3	♦762	♦AKJ94
♣1065	♣AQ3	♣KQ9	♣97643	♣AKQ764	♣K10543	♣1052	♣KJ5

41 N/E-W	42 E/Both	43 S/Nil	44 W/N-S	45 N/Nil	46 E/Nil	47 S/E-W	48 W/N-S
♠6	♠73	♠Q109	♠KQ1043	♠4	♠AQJ9765	♠K106542	♠87654
♥7	♥K98642	♥A987	♥109872	♥AKQ	♥7	♥K92	♥A2
♦QJ9642	♦AK10	♦54	♦7	♦J1095	♦763	♦8765	♦AKJ2
♣AQJ105	♣Q4	♣10842	♣97	♣108532	♣104	♣---	♣AK

49 N/Nil	50 E/N-S	51 S/E-W	52 W/Both	53 N/N-S	54 E/Nil	55 S/Both	56 W/Nil
♠Q108	♠8762	♠KQJ8	♠K	♠K975	♠J75	♠93	♠AQ98
♥QJ109	♥Q9	♥7	♥AQJ1092	♥A	♥J10	♥K54	♥9
♦65	♦KQ7	♦AQ72	♦KQJ7	♦QJ1086	♦KQJ108	♦A1053	♦AK753
♣AKQ9	♣AKJ6	♣A986	♣A7	♣Q85	♣J85	♣8732	♣J87

57 N/E-W	58 E/Both	59 S/Nil	60 W/N-S	61 N/Nil	62 E/Nil	63 S/N-S	64 W/E-W
♠AJ87	♠K862	♠A1093	♠Q	♠73	♠75	♠A1042	♠---
♥KQ54	♥KQJ107	♥KJ82	♥K854	♥6	♥5	♥KQ108	♥65
♦A964	♦10	♦A6	♦96543	♦AK98542	♦AK87432	♦AQ10	♦876542
♣4	♣A105	♣AJ2	♣932	♣532	♣Q94	♣42	♣KQJ73

PLAY HANDS FOR EAST

(After each hand, the dealer is given, followed by the vulnerability, e.g. S/Nil means Dealer South, love all.)

65 N/Nil	66 E/N-S	67 S/E-W	68 W/Both	69 N/N-S	70 E/E-W	71 S/Both	72 W/Nil
♠ 1096	♠ AJ94	♠ 9873	♠ 5432	♠ K8732	♠ K10952	♠ 73	♠ 9874
♡ AQ853	♡ 984	♡ A10765	♡ A87	♡ K4	♡ J9	♡ AQ8654	♡ J10542
◊ 1052	◊ 7	◊ K4	◊ KQJ107	◊ 754	◊ A643	◊ A3	◊ ---
♣ 54	♣ AK762	♣ 72	♣ 8	♣ 652	♣ 72	♣ 652	♣ QJ106

73 N/E-W	74 E/Both	75 S/Nil	76 W/N-S	77 N/Both	78 E/Nil	79 S/N-S	80 W/E-W
♠ J2	♠ A1085	♠ J	♠ A52	♠ 9	♠ 42	♠ AJ1065	♠ AQJ6
♡ 98	♡ 10	♡ Q104	♡ KJ1074	♡ J1097	♡ J106	♡ 76	♡ Q3
◊ AQ8	◊ J975	◊ QJ983	◊ 73	◊ J9	◊ A64	◊ A43	◊ 643
♣ AK9875	♣ K1096	♣ Q1092	♣ AJ6	♣ KJ8765	♣ KJ952	♣ Q97	♣ 9542

81 N/Nil	82 E/N-S	83 S/E-W	84 W/Both	85 N/N-S	86 E/E-W	87 S/Both	88 W/Nil
♠ K3	♠ A32	♠ K986	♠ AJ2	♠ Q985	♠ Q7652	♠ 953	♠ 3
♡ AJ743	♡ 92	♡ Q97	♡ A	♡ AJ942	♡ 9654	♡ KQ109	♡ AQ10865
◊ 82	◊ KQ	◊ 109874	◊ 9632	◊ 962	◊ K43	◊ Q108	◊ J5
♣ J1062	♣ AQJ643	♣ Q	♣ KQ1087	♣ J	♣ 8	♣ K109	♣ 9743

89 N/E-W	90 E/Both	91 S/Nil	92 W/N-S	93 N/Both	94 E/Nil	95 S/N-S	96 W/E-W
♠ 97	♠ A10743	♠ ---	♠ KQ985	♠ AK5	♠ KQ8	♠ K7	♠ A2
♡ Q109	♡ A642	♡ AK87	♡ AKQ862	♡ 1086	♡ J1084	♡ K932	♡ K9865
◊ KJ109	◊ A2	◊ Q1052	◊ 4	◊ J9863	◊ 985	◊ K10542	◊ 7
♣ A653	♣ 74	♣ J10876	♣ 3	♣ Q8	♣ K76	♣ J3	♣ AQ732

97 N/Nil	98 E/N-S	99 S/E-W	100 W/Both	101 N/N-S	102 E/E-W	103 S/Both	104 W/Nil
♠ KQJ3	♠ AK1097	♠ KJ87	♠ 764	♠ K865	♠ A82	♠ AK62	♠ J
♡ KJ	♡ K106	♡ J6	♡ 10972	♡ A742	♡ 97	♡ KQJ	♡ 9653
◊ AQJ765	◊ 10	◊ AKQ8	◊ K1043	◊ 95	◊ 95	◊ QJ4	◊ 98542
♣ 9	♣ 8763	♣ 875	♣ 103	♣ AJ10	♣ AKJ862	♣ K74	♣ 10854

105 N/E-W	106 E/Both	107 S/Nil	108 W/E-W	109 N/Both	110 W/Nil	111 S/N-S	112 W/E-W
♠ AQJ95	♠ AKJ	♠ 8	♠ ---	♠ Q76	♠ AK963	♠ Q1086	♠ 42
♡ K8	♡ J952	♡ J92	♡ KQJ2	♡ A42	♡ 72	♡ Q7	♡ AQ5
◊ 65	◊ AKQJ	◊ K873	◊ 9752	◊ KJ10964	◊ K862	◊ 10975	◊ A63
♣ KJ106	♣ 63	♣ 108642	♣ KQJ63	♣ 8	♣ K7	♣ J105	♣ K10643

113 N/Nil	114 E/N-S	115 S/E-W	116 W/Both	117 N/N-S	118 E/E-W	119 S/Both	120 W/Nil
♠ 109	♠ QJ10	♠ AQJ732	♠ 743	♠ AQJ87	♠ AK532	♠ J9	♠ Q762
♡ AJ43	♡ J652	♡ 863	♡ 7	♡ 97	♡ J62	♡ 10874	♡ 65
◊ AQ10	◊ AKQ10	◊ 6	◊ 6542	◊ Q64	◊ 8	◊ AK1082	◊ KQJ43
♣ 10743	♣ Q5	♣ AKQ	♣ Q9863	♣ Q83	♣ AQJ5	♣ 104	♣ 75

121 N/E-W	122 E/Both	123 S/Nil	124 W/N-S	125 N/Both	126 E/Nil	127 S/N-S	128 W/E-W
♠ 6	♠ 76	♠ 108	♠ K642	♠ KQ9	♠ K1054	♠ 96	♠ A
♡ AQ7	♡ 8632	♡ J10874	♡ 932	♡ A9754	♡ J1052	♡ AJ10862	♡ 1043
◊ QJ10975	◊ AK	◊ 83	◊ Q5	◊ 6	◊ 2	◊ 4	◊ KJ5
♣ K95	♣ KQJ62	♣ QJ95	♣ AQ109	♣ QJ73	♣ 10982	♣ QJ98	♣ KQ9764

PLAY HANDS FOR SOUTH

(After each hand, the dealer is given, followed by the vulnerability, e.g. S/Nil means Dealer South, love all.)

1 N/Nil	2 E/N-S	3 S/E-W	4 W/Both	5 N/N-S	6 E/E-W	7 S/Both	8 W/Nil
♠ J3	♠ Q10863	♠ AJ10	♠ 642	♠ J95	♠ A92	♠ 7	♠ 9
♥ AKQ	♥ 9765	♥ K853	♥ KQ94	♥ 743	♥ KQJ1063	♥ 8752	♥ QJ9432
♦ Q873	♦ J10	♦ A97	♦ KQ	♦ KQJ6	♦ 3	♦ A1093	♦ J72
♣ 9763	♣ K9	♣ AKQ	♣ J542	♣ KJ3	♣ KQJ	♣ J985	♣ K75

9 N/E-W	10 E/Both	11 S/Nil	12 W/N-S	13 N/Both	14 E/Nil	15 S/N-S	16 W/E-W
♠ K72	♠ K975	♠ AJ642	♠ A9542	♠ 108	♠ A43	♠ J974	♠ 2
♥ 32	♥ ---	♥ A7532	♥ 8	♥ J875	♥ K76	♥ A1042	♥ AQJ65
♦ AK852	♦ QJ107	♦ K7	♦ 53	♦ Q109	♦ AQ6432	♦ J102	♦ AJ843
♣ 873	♣ 97542	♣ 2	♣ K10643	♣ Q1095	♣ 4	♣ 86	♣ 32

17 N/Nil	18 E/N-S	19 S/E-W	20 W/Both	21 N/N-S	22 E/E-W	23 S/Both	24 W/Nil
♠ A76543	♠ Q942	♠ 542	♠ 10973	♠ 93	♠ A83	♠ AJ107	♠ Q1086
♥ 1083	♥ A2	♥ K85	♥ K3	♥ K542	♥ 985	♥ J6	♥ KQ106
♦ 1054	♦ 1085	♦ Q743	♦ A863	♦ AQ3	♦ A9652	♦ 854	♦ AKJ
♣ Q	♣ J1074	♣ AKQ	♣ J92	♣ AQ54	♣ 76	♣ J1093	♣ AQ

25 N/E-W	26 E/Both	27 S/Nil	28 W/N-S	29 N/Both	30 E/Nil	31 S/N-S	32 W/E-W
♠ J10764	♠ 108	♠ J10542	♠ 6	♠ 106	♠ 8	♠ 86	♠ J972
♥ A862	♥ Q975	♥ A952	♥ KJ5	♥ KQ532	♥ 73	♥ A532	♥ 93
♦ K32	♦ Q72	♦ K4	♦ J10984	♦ QJ43	♦ J10852	♦ J64	♦ J1095
♣ K	♣ KQJ10	♣ 72	♣ 10974	♣ J6	♣ 95432	♣ K752	♣ K108

33 N/Nil	34 E/N-S	35 S/E-W	36 W/Both	37 N/N-S	38 E/E-W	39 N/N-S	40 E/Nil
♠ K853	♠ 1086	♠ Q84	♠ J10	♠ 10972	♠ J6	♠ QJ5	♠ 753
♥ AQ8	♥ Q95432	♥ A9	♥ Q873	♥ 652	♥ 104	♥ 8542	♥ KQ10962
♦ 965	♦ AK	♦ AQ8654	♦ AK	♦ 976542	♦ AK8762	♦ 98	♦ 862
♣ AKJ	♣ KJ	♣ 102	♣ KQJ108	♣ ---	♣ 762	♣ 9743	♣ A

41 N/E-W	42 E/Both	43 S/Nil	44 W/N-S	45 N/Nil	46 E/Nil	47 S/E-W	48 W/N-S
♠ K10543	♠ 5	♠ AJ832	♠ ---	♠ AK106532	♠ 3	♠ Q7	♠ KJ103
♥ AJ109	♥ 7	♥ 6432	♥ AJ3	♥ 742	♥ 9652	♥ 86	♥ 105
♦ 87	♦ QJ9832	♦ AKJ	♦ K10532	♦ Q7	♦ QJ9	♦ 93	♦ Q73
♣ K3	♣ AJ1095	♣ A	♣ KQ865	♣ 9	♣ AK852	♣ KQJ10742	♣ Q1062

49 N/Nil	50 E/N-S	51 S/E-W	52 W/Both	53 N/N-S	54 E/Nil	55 S/Both	56 W/Nil
♠ KJ963	♠ AKQ5	♠ 643	♠ Q10976	♠ AQ3	♠ A42	♠ AJ8	♠ 65
♥ 72	♥ A753	♥ Q10	♥ 6	♥ KQJ	♥ K86	♥ J	♥ K654
♦ KJ9	♦ A4	♦ J104	♦ 98543	♦ A32	♦ A7542	♦ KJ964	♦ Q84
♣ 873	♣ 843	♣ J10752	♣ 94	♣ A742	♣ KQ	♣ QJ64	♣ 9653

57 N/E-W	58 E/Both	59 S/Nil	60 W/N-S	61 N/Nil	62 E/Nil	63 S/N-S	64 W/E-W
♠ Q106543	♠ AQJ10	♠ 7652	♠ 107432	♠ J986	♠ 86	♠ Q83	♠ 83
♥ 9	♥ 4	♥ 763	♥ 93	♥ AQ43	♥ 943	♥ 96543	♥ AKQJ98
♦ J85	♦ K952	♦ 75	♦ J2	♦ 76	♦ QJ96	♦ 6532	♦ A3
♣ 653	♣ KQ72	♣ Q963	♣ AKJ6	♣ AKQ	♣ AK103	♣ A	♣ A84

PLAY HANDS FOR SOUTH

(After each hand, the dealer is given, followed by the vulnerability, e.g. S/Nil means Dealer South, love all.)

65	66	67	68	69	70	71	72
N/Nil	E/N-S	S/E-W	W/Both	N/N-S	E/E-W	S/Both	W/Nil
♠ A5	♠ Q107	♠ KJ106	♠ QJ98	♠ QJ105	♠ 3	♠ Q965	♠ A653
♥ 92	♥ Q3	♥ 84	♥ 42	♥ J75	♥ AK43	♥ K102	♥ 96
♦ A9743	♦ 10653	♦ 72	♦ A5	♦ 92	♦ Q108	♦ J104	♦ A876
♣ AJ106	♣ QJ98	♣ AKJ65	♣ QJ973	♣ A987	♣ AK654	♣ KJ7	♣ AK4

73	74	75	76	77	78	79	80
N/E-W	E/Both	S/Nil	W/N-S	N/Both	E/Nil	S/N-S	W/E-W
♠ KQ108	♠ KQ763	♠ 863	♠ 6	♠ KQ8743	♠ KQ986	♠ K87	♠ 1075
♥ J4	♥ A9843	♥ 7	♥ Q653	♥ AQ43	♥ AK42	♥ 5	♥ 102
♦ 109532	♦ K2	♦ A75	♦ K985	♦ 74	♦ J	♦ 10875	♦ J987
♣ J10	♣ 2	♣ AKJ874	♣ K1052	♣ A	♣ Q43	♣ J10832	♣ AQJ10

81	82	83	84	85	86	87	88
N/Nil	E/N-S	S/E-W	W/Both	N/N-S	E/E-W	S/Both	W/Nil
♠ 74	♠ QJ76	♠ AJ742	♠ 10965	♠ K64	♠ 43	♠ KQ7642	♠ KJ6
♥ 962	♥ AK8	♥ AK	♥ QJ94	♥ 8	♥ J108	♥ A32	♥ J97
♦ AKJ	♦ 875	♦ Q3	♦ AJ	♦ 1053	♦ A986	♦ 64	♦ 1072
♣ KQ975	♣ 972	♣ 9653	♣ 653	♣ K109543	♣ AQ103	♣ A2	♣ QJ108

89	90	91	92	93	94	95	96
N/E-W	E/Both	S/Nil	W/N-S	N/Both	E/Nil	S/N-S	W/E-W
♠ 32	♠ 5	♠ AQ92	♠ 4	♠ 8732	♠ J10632	♠ QJ10652	♠ KQJ
♥ AJ743	♥ K9753	♥ J10	♥ 10543	♥ K732	♥ 5	♥ A8	♥ Q73
♦ A8	♦ J109	♦ AKJ74	♦ 10865	♦ 754	♦ AJ102	♦ A73	♦ Q10654
♣ J984	♣ 9852	♣ K9	♣ KQ97	♣ K5	♣ 953	♣ A2	♣ 106

97	98	99	100	101	102	103	104
N/Nil	E/N-S	S/E-W	W/Both	N/N-S	E/E-W	S/Both	W/Nil
♠ 86542	♠ 643	♠ 95	♠ J82	♠ J10732	♠ QJ972	♠ J105	♠ 7642
♥ 74	♥ AQ7	♥ AKQ1083	♥ ---	♥ 10985	♥ KQ63	♥ 76542	♥ 4
♦ 9	♦ KQ2	♦ J6	♦ A8652	♦ 82	♦ KJ6	♦ 1062	♦ J6
♣ J8652	♣ AKJ10	♣ K43	♣ J8542	♣ 64	♣ 9	♣ 96	♣ AJ7632

105	106	107	108	109	110	111	112
N/E-W	E/Both	S/Nil	W/E-W	N/Both	W/Nil	S/N-S	W/E-W
♠ 8	♠ 9764	♠ AJ7432	♠ A9752	♠ K92	♠ 7	♠ K53	♠ 87
♥ 10973	♥ 4	♥ AK3	♥ A54	♥ QJ107	♥ J104	♥ AJ4	♥ 10962
♦ AK82	♦ 9862	♦ J54	♦ KJ3	♦ 32	♦ QJ105	♦ KJ63	♦ J1094
♣ AQ83	♣ QJ97	♣ 5	♣ 92	♣ AK65	♣ 98653	♣ 742	♣ Q85

113	114	115	116	117	118	119	120
N/Nil	E/N-S	S/E-W	W/Both	N/N-S	E/E-W	S/Both	W/Nil
♠ K752	♠ 9	♠ K	♠ AK	♠ 105	♠ 94	♠ 7	♠ 9854
♥ 1082	♥ Q109743	♥ KQJ104	♥ QJ865	♥ Q652	♥ AKQ97	♥ KQ62	♥ 10
♦ 965	♦ 643	♦ KJ82	♦ AQ9	♦ A983	♦ QJ2	♦ Q9	♦ 109862
♣ 985	♣ J94	♣ J107	♣ AK5	♣ 974	♣ 864	♣ AKQ873	♣ J92

121	122	123	124	125	126	127	128
N/E-W	E/Both	S/Nil	W/N-S	N/Both	E/Nil	S/N-S	W/E-W
♠ AJ	♠ KQJ1042	♠ K62	♠ 1087	♠ A54	♠ AQ976	♠ 75432	♠ K9862
♥ 8432	♥ Q	♥ KQ	♥ Q6	♥ KJ8	♥ KQ93	♥ 4	♥ 82
♦ A63	♦ J932	♦ AQJ74	♦ 10974	♦ AQJ3	♦ 7	♦ K102	♦ A10986
♣ QJ108	♣ 103	♣ 1074	♣ J762	♣ K92	♣ Q43	♣ 10754	♣ 3

PLAY HANDS FOR WEST
(After each hand, the dealer is given, followed by the vulnerability, e.g. S/Nil means Dealer South, love all.)

1	2	3	4	5	6	7	8
N/Nil	E/N-S	S/E-W	W/Both	N/N-S	E/E-W	S/Both	W/Nil
♠ K742	♠ 92	♠ K98	♠ 1085	♠ AK83	♠ KQJ105	♠ KQJ106	♠ KJ543
♡ J952	♡ J42	♡ Q76	♡ A753	♡ J5	♡ A9	♡ A96	♡ A
◇ AK	◇ K76432	◇ K8632	◇ A943	◇ 832	◇ J102	◇ K2	◇ 9864
♣ J108	♣ 73	♣ 72	♣ KQ	♣ 7542	♣ 1096	♣ KQ7	♣ Q82

9	10	11	12	13	14	15	16
N/E-W	E/Both	S/Nil	W/N-S	N/Both	E/Nil	S/N-S	W/E-W
♠ J6	♠ 8	♠ K1075	♠ Q106	♠ KJ542	♠ J986	♠ AK862	♠ 1075
♡ J8	♡ KJ764	♡ KQJ	♡ AK9742	♡ KQ62	♡ AJ9	♡ Q6	♡ 10943
◇ J10743	◇ A52	◇ 852	◇ A76	◇ A32	◇ J8	◇ 64	◇ 107
♣ AK52	♣ KJ86	♣ 1087	♣ 8	♣ 3	♣ Q952	♣ AKJ2	♣ AK108

17	18	19	20	21	22	23	24
N/Nil	E/N-S	S/E-W	W/Both	N/N-S	E/E-W	S/Both	W/Nil
♠ QJ8	♠ AK73	♠ A76	♠ A2	♠ K76	♠ J1076	♠ 95	♠ K
♡ K	♡ KQ	♡ A7	♡ 87642	♡ 10863	♡ 42	♡ KQ52	♡ 8743
◇ KQJ	◇ KQJ6	◇ 109652	◇ 75	◇ 9752	◇ K7	◇ AK103	◇ Q964
♣ 1087632	♣ A86	♣ 1072	♣ 8643	♣ 108	♣ AK843	♣ 874	♣ K943

25	26	27	28	29	30	31	32
N/E-W	E/Both	S/Nil	W/N-S	N/Both	E/Nil	S/N-S	W/E-W
♠ A	♠ QJ6	♠ Q	♠ 953	♠ 875	♠ AJ72	♠ 92	♠ AKQ10
♡ KJ54	♡ K10842	♡ 10764	♡ AQ106	♡ A1098	♡ J62	♡ 10876	♡ AKQ8642
◇ 10875	◇ J106	◇ QJ96	◇ K3	◇ 1072	◇ 943	◇ 7532	◇ 4
♣ J643	♣ A5	♣ 9543	♣ AKQ6	♣ 543	♣ QJ10	♣ J109	♣ A

33	34	35	36	37	38	39	40
N/Nil	E/N-S	S/E-W	W/Both	N/N-S	E/E-W	N/N-S	E/Nil
♠ J94	♠ AQJ	♠ AJ1062	♠ AKQ98	♠ Q853	♠ 10754	♠ 72	♠ 1086
♡ 6532	♡ AK	♡ K72	♡ 64	♡ AQ8	♡ 9865	♡ AQ3	♡ J83
◇ 107	◇ QJ10	◇ J7	◇ 108632	◇ AKQ	◇ J109	◇ AKQJ43	◇ 1075
♣ 8432	♣ 87542	♣ AJ4	♣ 5	♣ 532	♣ 98	♣ 86	♣ Q1093

41	42	43	44	45	46	47	48
N/E-W	E/Both	S/Nil	W/N-S	N/Nil	E/Nil	S/E-W	W/N-S
♠ AQ872	♠ AQJ82	♠ 7	♠ AJ92	♠ QJ7	♠ K108	♠ J9	♠ 2
♡ 85	♡ Q1053	♡ J10	♡ KQ654	♡ J1098	♡ AJ843	♡ Q7543	♡ KQJ9874
◇ 5	◇ 74	◇ Q10982	◇ AJ6	◇ K83	◇ A54	◇ K42	◇ 654
♣ 98642	♣ K8	♣ KQ965	♣ J	♣ KJ6	♣ J9	♣ A96	♣ 84

49	50	51	52	53	54	55	56
N/Nil	E/N-S	S/E-W	W/Both	N/N-S	E/Nil	S/Both	W/Nil
♠ 5	♠ 1094	♠ 1072	♠ J5432	♠ J108	♠ KQ93	♠ KQ764	♠ J10742
♡ 8543	♡ 1086	♡ 86542	♡ K75	♡ 1097543	♡ AQ94	♡ AQ83	♡ QJ10
◇ Q84	◇ J1092	◇ 96	◇ 62	◇ 75	◇ 3	◇ 82	◇ 1092
♣ J10542	♣ Q92	♣ K43	♣ J65	♣ 96	♣ A1062	♣ AK	♣ A10

57	58	59	60	61	62	63	64
N/E-W	E/Both	S/Nil	W/N-S	N/Nil	E/Nil	S/N-S	W/E-W
♠ K2	♠ 95	♠ 84	♠ J86	♠ Q5	♠ K10942	♠ KJ97	♠ KQJ10765
♡ 87632	♡ 865	♡ AQ	♡ AQJ106	♡ KJ9752	♡ KQ108	♡ J2	♡ 32
◇ K3	◇ J763	◇ 9432	◇ A107	◇ J	◇ 5	◇ KJ97	◇ QJ9
♣ QJ102	♣ 9643	♣ K10854	♣ 85	♣ 9874	♣ 765	♣ J65	♣ 9

PLAY HANDS FOR WEST

(After each hand, the dealer is given, followed by the vulnerability, e.g. S/Nil means Dealer South, love all.)

65	66	67	68	69	70	71	72
N/Nil	E/N-S	S/E-W	W/Both	N/N-S	E/E-W	S/Both	W/Nil
♠ J843	♠ K32	♠ 42	♠ AK76	♠ 4	♠ Q87	♠ AJ	♠ QJ10
♡ 1074	♡ AK762	♡ KQJ	♡ KQ53	♡ AQ96	♡ Q1086	♡ 73	♡ 87
◇ QJ6	◇ QJ4	◇ Q985	◇ 6	◇ AKJ86	◇ K75	◇ KQ82	◇ 10542
♣ Q98	♣ 43	♣ 10943	♣ A542	♣ K43	♣ QJ9	♣ AQ1043	♣ 9832

73	74	75	76	77	78	79	80
N/E-W	E/Both	S/Nil	W/N-S	N/Both	E/Nil	S/N-S	W/E-W
♠ A7654	♠ J4	♠ Q1092	♠ KQ943	♠ A1052	♠ AJ105	♠ Q43	♠ 2
♡ AK732	♡ QJ52	♡ KJ9	♡ 8	♡ 85	♡ 953	♡ AQ984	♡ AKJ864
◇ J	◇ Q1064	◇ K1042	◇ AQJ642	◇ A1032	◇ 9532	◇ KQJ2	◇ AK
♣ 42	♣ J85	♣ 63	♣ 3	♣ 1092	♣ 76	♣ K	♣ K863

81	82	83	84	85	86	87	88
N/Nil	E/N-S	S/E-W	W/Both	N/N-S	E/E-W	S/Both	W/Nil
♠ Q952	♠ K9854	♠ Q10	♠ KQ3	♠ 1072	♠ K9	♠ AJ108	♠ AQ754
♡ Q85	♡ 763	♡ J10652	♡ K10862	♡ K107	♡ AK32	♡ J75	♡ 3
◇ Q107543	◇ AJ42	◇ J6	◇ 10	◇ K874	◇ QJ102	◇ K7	◇ KQ83
♣ ---	♣ K	♣ J1072	♣ AJ92	♣ AQ6	♣ 764	♣ J865	♣ K62

89	90	91	92	93	94	95	96
N/E-W	E/Both	S/Nil	W/N-S	N/Both	E/Nil	S/N-S	W/E-W
♠ J105	♠ KQ62	♠ J104	♠ A632	♠ QJ104	♠ 7	♠ A	♠ 83
♡ ---	♡ 10	♡ Q96532	♡ 7	♡ 9	♡ AKQ62	♡ QJ104	♡ AJ42
◇ Q6542	◇ K843	◇ 98	◇ AJ932	◇ KQ10	◇ 763	◇ Q986	◇ AJ832
♣ KQ107	♣ AKQJ	♣ Q3	♣ A42	♣ J10764	♣ AJ42	♣ 10854	♣ K4

97	98	99	100	101	102	103	104
N/Nil	E/N-S	S/E-W	W/Both	N/N-S	E/E-W	S/Both	W/Nil
♠ A9	♠ 85	♠ AQ	♠ AKQ953	♠ A4	♠ 65	♠ 83	♠ KQ1098
♡ 832	♡ J842	♡ 74	♡ J53	♡ K63	♡ J1082	♡ 10983	♡ 72
◇ 1032	◇ J865	◇ 942	◇ QJ7	◇ K643	◇ Q10872	◇ A75	◇ K107
♣ KQ743	♣ Q92	♣ AQ10962	♣ 9	♣ K732	♣ 105	♣ QJ105	♣ KQ9

105	106	107	108	109	110	111	112
N/E-W	E/Both	S/Nil	W/E-W	N/Both	W/Nil	S/N-S	W/E-W
♠ K1076	♠ 83	♠ 109	♠ Q108	♠ 10854	♠ J542	♠ A7	♠ KJ10
♡ AQJ65	♡ KQ1083	♡ Q1075	♡ 1097	♡ 53	♡ Q8	♡ K986532	♡ KJ43
◇ 93	◇ 10754	◇ A109	◇ Q86	◇ Q85	◇ A743	◇ 82	◇ 875
♣ 72	♣ 105	♣ KQJ7	♣ 10754	♣ J1097	♣ AQ4	♣ Q9	♣ A92

113	114	115	116	117	118	119	120
N/Nil	E/N-S	S/E-W	W/Both	N/N-S	E/E-W	S/Both	W/Nil
♠ AQJ863	♠ 87543	♠ 965	♠ Q10865	♠ K642	♠ 7	♠ AKQ1052	♠ AK10
♡ 6	♡ 8	♡ 972	♡ AK	♡ J104	♡ 843	♡ 5	♡ K742
◇ KJ8	◇ 97	◇ AQ103	◇ KJ10	◇ KJ105	◇ A10653	◇ 543	◇ A5
♣ J62	♣ 107632	♣ 865	♣ J104	♣ J6	♣ K973	♣ J65	♣ KQ83

121	122	123	124	125	126	127	128
N/E-W	E/Both	S/Nil	W/N-S	N/Both	E/Nil	S/N-S	W/E-W
♠ 975	♠ A5	♠ AJ9743	♠ A93	♠ J108	♠ J82	♠ AKJ8	♠ Q7543
♡ J109	♡ AK94	♡ 92	♡ KJ4	♡ Q63	♡ 87	♡ 7	♡ QJ9
◇ K8	◇ Q54	◇ K6	◇ AK62	◇ K1072	◇ KJ10854	◇ AQ953	◇ Q432
♣ 76432	♣ 8754	♣ K83	♣ 543	♣ A106	♣ AK	♣ 632	♣ 2

INDEX